Cosmology, Ontology, and Human Efficacy

Cosmology, Ontology, and Human Efficacy

ESSAYS IN CHINESE THOUGHT

Edited by

Richard J. Smith and D. W. Y. Kwok

 UNIVERSITY OF HAWAII PRESS / HONOLULU

Library of Congress Cataloging-in-Publication Data
Cosmology, ontology, and human efficacy : essays in Chinese thought /
edited by Richard J. Smith and D. W. Y. Kwok.
p.   cm.
Includes index.
ISBN 0–8248–1443–6 (alk. paper)
1. China—Intellectual life—1644–1912.   2. Cosmology, Chinese.
3. Ontology.   I. Smith, Richard J. (Richard Joseph), 1944–
II. Kwok, D. W. Y. (Daniel Wynn Ye), 1932–
DS754.14.C68   1993
951'.03—dc20   92–31229
                                                          CIP

Designed by Paula Newcomb

Contents

Introduction

RICHARD J. SMITH

Most studies of the thought and culture of late imperial China lean to one side: they stress continuity *or* change, theory *or* practice, unity *or* diversity, orthodoxy *or* heterodoxy, elite *or* popular attitudes, individual thinkers *or* general patterns of thought. In contrast, this volume attempts to give attention to both sides of these dichotomies and to place special emphasis on the evaluation of certain philosophical concepts that had particular significance in the intellectual debates surrounding the dramatic Ming-Ch'ing transition. A number of the essays were originally delivered as papers for a two-part panel titled "Ontology and Human Efficacy in Chinese Thought of the Ch'ing Period," organized by Professor Kwang-Ching Liu for the 1986 meeting of the Pacific Coast Branch of the American Historical Association. Since that time, the contents of this volume have been enriched by additional scholarly contributions that not only extend the historical perspective and broaden the conceptual framework but also underscore the conflicts and contradictions of Chinese intellectual life across space, time, and social class.

As the title indicates, the essays we have collected are concerned both with metaphysical issues and concrete human actions and with the relationship between the two. From the standpoint of cosmology and ontology, vigorous and substantial debate existed among Ch'ing scholars throughout the dynasty regarding the status of *li* (principle) and *ch'i* (material force), and their various manifestations in the realm of earthly affairs. At the same time, however, virtually all these individuals accepted the idea of a spiritual resonance or oneness uniting heaven and man and agreed on the existence of certain cosmic variables, such as *yin* and *yang* and the five agents or phases *(wu-hsing),* that influenced human actions in various ways. Moreover, all accepted the moral imperatives of self-cultivation and service to society, as well as the *I-ching*'s injunction to avail oneself of the incipient opportunities *(chi)* provided by changing times. But although every good Confucian (and Buddhist or Taoist) knew what to do, one's understanding of cosmology and ontology invariably affected the way it was done, not least by providing a sense of the possibilities inherent in any given situation.

To put the matter somewhat differently, Chinese intellectuals of all social backgrounds, personality types, political persuasions and professional affiliations found themselves engaged in a complex, ongoing process by which they negotiated (and renegotiated) the boundaries of the metaphysical and the concrete. They did so primarily because they shared a morally grounded worldview in which their understanding of the nature of the universe conditioned their sense of the place and role of human beings within the natural order. Their task, then, was to determine what was given about the cosmos (i.e., what was fated or mandated [*ming*]) and what was constructed by the minds and actions of individuals—including, of course, themselves. Under these circumstances, spiritual and mental self-cultivation could no more be detached from cosmology and ontology than knowledge could be separated from moral responsibility and active engagement in social and political affairs.

The negotiation and renegotiation of philosophical boundaries assumed special significance in the Ch'ing dynasty—in large measure because the decline and fall of the Ming was so closely and explicitly identified not only with Lu-Wang neo-Confucianism but also with late Ming syncretic thought generally. Making matters worse, or at least more complex, alien Manchu rule brought with it a powerful reassertion of Ch'eng-Chu orthodoxy and a special sensitivity to political criticism. Meanwhile, as is well known, a series of important social and economic changes had been taking place in China: urbanization of the lower Yangtze valley, the growth of regional trade, the emergence of a national market in bulk commodities, increased geographical mobility, the explosion of popular literacy, an increase in both the size of the gentry class and the power of lineage groups, the professionalization of local managerial activities, and so forth. These changes, together with the dramatic political events of the Ming-Ch'ing transition, led to transformations in the style of local Chinese politics, in patterns of personal and intellectual affiliation, and, ultimately, in modes of thought. They conduced, among other things, to the rise of new iconoclastic schools, such as that of evidential research *(k'ao-cheng hsueh),* and contributed to an evolving redefinition of the relation between elite and popular culture.

Most of the essays in this volume bear directly on issues related to one or both of these two important developments. Among the questions they address (and often provide different answers for) are: How objective were the scientific *k'ao-cheng* scholars of the Ch'ing dynasty? How unified was their world of discourse, and how broad was their base of support? In what particular ways was *k'ao-cheng* scholarship subversive of the existing neo-Confucian intellectual order and a tool for the radical restructuring of Chinese thought? On the other hand, to what extent did it serve to reinforce certain long-standing patterns of political and social behavior? How pervasive was the *k'ao-cheng* assault on the inherited cosmology, and what effect did it have on time-honored practices such as divination, which had been practiced at all levels of Chinese society for literally thousands of years? On the whole, did the efforts of *k'ao-cheng* scholars serve to reduce or widen the gap between elite and popular culture in late imperial China?

Although our book focuses primarily on the Ch'ing period, it begins with two broad-ranging interpretive studies that examine both the potentialities and the limitations of China's complex Confucian intellectual heritage. The first, by D. W. Y. Kwok, titled "*Ho* and *T'ung* in Chinese Intellectual History," examines a pair of deceptively simple-sounding and often overlooked evaluative terms in the classical Chinese tradition: harmonizing *(ho)* and identifying *(t'ung)*. These concepts, which are fundamental to an understanding of the way that Confucian ethics and cosmology were interpreted and transmitted over time, had far-reaching implications. Professor Kwok shows how the intellectual predominance of *ho*, implying "the capacity of containing and accommodating all manner of logicalities," over *t'ung*, which suggests the tendency to identify, classify, equalize, and unify, shaped the Chinese world view and may have profoundly influenced China's scientific and economic development.

Chang Hao's essay, "The Confucian Cosmological Myth and the Neo-Confucian Tradition," also deals with the themes of harmonization and particularity. His analysis draws on a wide range of Sung and post-Sung philosophical writings, from those of Chang Tsai, Chu Hsi, and Chen Te-hsiu, to those of Wang Yang-ming, Li Chih, and Lu Shih-i. His particular interest is in conceptions of self-cultivation and transcendence and their relation to the "ontological awareness" of a link between man and heaven in classical Confucian thought. By exploring such fundamental ideas as mind *(hsin)*, nature *(hsing)*, and principle *(li)* within the sociopolitical framework of Tung Chung-shu's famous "Three Bonds" *(san-kang)*, he underscores various tensions within the neo-Confucian intellectual tradition and suggests the different ways these tensions were resolved in late imperial times.

The essays by On-cho Ng, Benjamin Elman, and Richard Shek emphasize conceptual change in the early and mid-Ch'ing period. Professor Ng's study, "Toward an Interpretation of Ch'ing Ontology," identifies the concept of *ch'i* (material force) as the ontological point of departure for a wide variety of thinkers in the Ch'ing period, including Wang Fu-chih, Ku Yen-wu, Huang Tsung-hsi, Lu Shih-i, Li Yung, Hui Tung, Tai Chen, Chiao Hsun, and Juan Yuan. This vitalist strain in Ch'ing thought turned orthodox neo-Confucian metaphysics inside out, by denying or at least minimizing the long-standing ontological and epistemological tension between *li* (principle) and *ch'i* that was so central to the thought of Chu Hsi. The result was a particularly pronounced tendency to replace metaphysical speculation with a view of reality centered on life experience, in which particular manifestations and circumstances overshadowed ultimate universal truths.

Professor Elman's essay, "The Revaluation of Benevolence *(Jen)* in Ch'ing Dynasty Evidential Research" uses the central Confucian ethical principle of *jen* (benevolence) as its point of departure. Focusing on philological issues raised and discussed by Tai Chen, Yen Yuan, Juan Yuan, and Chiao Hsun, Professor Elman examines the debate between exponents of evidential research *(k'ao-cheng hsueh)* and Sung learning *(tao-hsueh)* during the eighteenth and nineteenth centuries. Like several other essays in this volume, his analysis touches directly on issues of mind, nature, and human desires *(yü)*, underscoring the intellectual break with neo-Confucian orthodoxy that occurred in the realms of Confucian ethics and metaphysics during the Ch'ing period, as well as the subversive conceptual trends that, in his view, laid the foundations for the "ultimate rejection of the Confucian imperium by Chinese intellectuals in the late nineteenth and early twentieth centuries."

Richard Shek takes a somewhat different tack. Inspired by the writings of Yü Ying-shih, Professor Shek argues that despite the predominance of "solid" and "real" scholarship in eighteenth-century China, the long tradition of philosophy, ethics, and a "religious quest for meaning" persisted. To illustrate his point, he examines the career of P'eng Shao-sheng, a well-known but rather poorly understood Confucian scholar and lay Buddhist who provided living testimony to the resiliency of Wang Yang-ming's learning of the mind *(hsin-hsueh)* as well as to the tenacity of metaphysical inquiry generally in China. Metaphysical speculation, although no longer fashionable in the eighteenth century, was still inescapable. Moreover, Buddhism provided special solace to individuals in trying times. For this reason, presumably, it experienced a strong revival in the late Ch'ing period, as Liang Ch'i-ch'ao reminds us.

San-pao Li's essay, "Ch'ing Cosmology and Popular Precepts," dislodges discourse on ethics and cosmology from the elite world of high culture. He

analyzes Chinese popular literature of the Ch'ing period to show how proverbs and morality tales instilled basic Confucian ethical values and at least a
rudimentary metaphysics in all levels of Chinese society. These values and
concepts remained, in Professor Li's words, "an overwhelmingly strong
intellectual and moral force" whose influence could perhaps only be ignored
by "the most defiant or the most desperate" members of Chinese society.

Similarly, Richard J. Smith's study, "Divination in Ch'ing Dynasty
China," identifies certain cosmological and ethical common denominators
surrounding the notion of fate *(ming* or *ming-yun)* that were expressed not
only in state calendars and imperially sanctioned versions of these official
works but also in popular almanacs of all kinds and virtually all Chinese
fortune-telling practices. These publications and practices were not only
pervasive in their social and geographical spread but also persistent in their
appeal over time. Professor Smith argues that, despite the new epistemology
and cosmological critiques generated by *k'ao-cheng* scholarship in the seventeenth and eighteenth centuries, the traditional Chinese worldview had
remarkable staying power.

Furthermore, even among those members of the Ch'ing intellectual elite
who rejected the orthodox metaphysical dualisms of neo-Confucian
thought, and who derived their principles of interpretation from the sort of
monistic and materialistic ontology that Professor Ng describes, a practical
concern with ritual *(li)* remained central to their daily lives. In fact, their
reformulated ontology provided philosophical justification for their practical quotidian preoccupations.

To be sure, as the studies of both Professor Elman and Professor Kai-
wing Chow illustrate, the philological investigations of *k'ao-cheng* scholars
might lead them to view the Confucian admonition to "conquer the self and
return to the rites" *(k'o-chi fu-li)* in a very different light from that of Chu
Hsi and his adherents. But as Professor Chow demonstrates convincingly in
"Purist Hermeneutics and Ritualist Ethics in Mid-Ch'ing Thought," the
long-standing emphasis on ritual as a means of moral cultivation received
powerful reinforcement from *k'ao-cheng* scholars such as Tai Chen, Ling
T'ing-k'an, and Juan Yuan. Thus, although evidential scholarship had an
undeniably subversive potential in controverting Ch'eng-Chu orthodoxy, it
could also be an effective purifying weapon in the defense of certain authoritarian values. "Paradoxically," as Professor Chow notes, "the 'intellectualism' that characterized . . . [*k'ao-cheng*] methodology yielded an ethical
position that underscored the elite's importance in rendering comprehensible the teaching of ancient sages." In their effort to reverse the populist ten-

dencies of late Ming Confucianism, these evidential scholars encouraged submission to external authority.

The essays by Erh-min Wang and Don C. Price explore questions of continuity and change in Chinese thought of the late Ch'ing period. Professor Wang's "The 'Turn of Fortune' (Yun-hui): Inherited Concepts and China's Response to the West" shows, for example, how inherited ideas about predestination and the cosmic resonance between heaven and man affected Chinese perceptions of, and responses to, the unprecedented nineteenth-century Western challenge. Although the persistence of traditional cosmology did impede scientific advancement under some circumstances, Professor Wang shows us how a number of progressive Chinese thinkers in the late Ch'ing period, including Yen Fu and T'ang Ts'ai-ch'ang, used the ancient concept of yun-hui to argue for modernizing change. He also reminds us that the sages of the late Ch'ing period, like the sages of old, faced the problem of reconciling their belief in heaven-ordained fate with the Confucian imperative of self-exertion.

Finally, Professor Price's "Escape from Disillusionment: Personality and Value Change in the Case of Sung Chiao-jen" shows the ambiguous legacy of Ch'ing thought to the modern era. On the one hand, Sung, like many scholars of his time, brought with him into the twentieth century an eclectic intellectual background encompassing most of the traditional concerns discussed in this volume, including a preoccupation with moral cultivation, training in neo-Confucian orthodoxy, and a solid grounding in k'ao-cheng scholarship. Moreover, he was deeply imbued with the popular concept of the righteous hero (ying-hsiung). On the other hand, the attractiveness of a new Western cosmology, answering needs generated by his own personal growth, confronted Sung with a situation that "called less for the leadership of a hero, than the guidance of a statesman." His response to the late Ch'ing crisis, although atypical, exemplifies the problem of conflicting roles and moral imperatives in a substantially altered political, social, and cultural environment.

This volume is dedicated to Professor Kwang-Ching Liu, whose contributions to the study of Ch'ing history span nearly forty years and cover an extraordinarily wide range of intellectual terrain. His numerous writings on Chinese social ethics, issues of orthodoxy and heterodoxy, statecraft scholarship (ching-shih chih hsueh), late Ch'ing politics and reformist thought, and various aspects of the complex nineteenth-century Sino-Western economic and cultural interaction, as well as his pioneering bibliographical and archival research, have provided invaluable guidance and inspiration for two generations of scholars. The contributors to this volume represent both those generations. Many have studied directly under Professor Liu, and all have learned from him. As a scholar who has kept abreast of modern methodological currents while remaining fully conversant with the vast classical Chinese tradition, Professor Liu meets the highest Confucian pedagogical and scholarly standards as one who constantly "reviews the old and knows the new" *(wen-ku erh chih-hsin)*. May his ever-broadening intellectual search continue for many years to come.

1

Ho and *T'ung* in Chinese Intellectual History

D. W. Y. KWOK

This essay is offered as a note to the already voluminous and erudite literature on two varying, but related, themes in the interpretation of Confucian thought and Chinese civilization. The first theme concerns the place of scientific thought (and, by extension, analytic philosophy and modern thought in general) in China. It has had such able critics as Fung Yu-lan in the 1920s, Chin Yueh-lin in the 1940s, and Ch'ien Wen-yuan in the 1980s.[1] Opposed to them is Joseph Needham's monumental work, now well beyond the five volumes originally planned, which propounds the idea that China not only had science but actually surpassed Europe in this field until the early eighteenth century. Agreeing with Needham are many scholars who take pride in the imperfect (for China) present.[2] But then Needham also accepts the fact that, in spite of all the advances in Chinese science, the revolution in natural science did not take place in China. I point out later that for all the labor Needham has expended in extolling and documenting Chinese scientific achievements, his volumes do not yet convey an accurate sense of the cultural milieu in which these achievements are to be viewed.

The other theme is that Confucian values and thought are compatible with the modern capitalist temper and that they are not only compatible, but they may contain that kernel, or impetus, which brought about capitalism. The occasion for this new appreciation of Confucianism is the series of economic miracles performed during the past thirty years by the four tigers (five if Japan is included) of South Korea, Taiwan, Hong Kong, and Singapore. All came under the Confucian persuasion at one time or another in their historical development. The people of all four are noted for hard work and inner-directed dedication to education, family, and society. The Confucian ethic, as portrayed in such writings as those of Herman Kahn, Chin Yao-chi, Tu Wei-ming, William T. de Bary, and Yü Ying-shih, seems strikingly similar to Max Weber's Protestant ethic, which Weber found to be the motivating factor in the rise of capitalism over mere merchant activities.[3] The irony here is that, although this attribution of a religious nature and core to the "starting mechanism" for capitalism is taken from Weber, the borrowers all think that Weber is wrong about China's failure to develop capitalism because of a lack of this starting mechanism.

The relation between the rise of modern science and capitalism is far too complex to be handled beyond mere acknowledgment here. But it is worthy of note that two major Western scholars, dealing with two major areas of modern civilization, should (in the case of Needham) find science present and (in the case of Weber) find capitalism absent. Those scholars who agree with Needham have unearthed tantalizing feats of technological virtuosity but show no corresponding relation of this virtuosity to society and culture. Detractors of Weber have also formulated new interpretations of Confucian ethics and personality, and even the vocabulary of merchant culture.[4] Both groups, as those who do not share their views would agree, argue in the face of a historical record that does not seem to show traditional China to be adept at either, much less endowed with the capacity to originate both.

It is in the interstices between the arguments over these positions on Confucian thought and Chinese civilization that I wish to offer the following observation: from a historical point of view, neither science nor capitalism had an essential and habit-changing role to play in forming traditional Chinese civilization. Let us begin with a look at Confucian culture, using the *Analects (Lun-yü)* of Confucius as our point of departure.

In reacquainting myself with the *Lun-yü,* as indeed all must in considering the imprint of Confucian thought and values on subsequent Chinese intellectual development, I came across the rather bland and familiar phrase in the "Tzu-lu" chapter (13:23): "The sovereign man[5] harmonizes but does not identify; the petty man identifies but does not harmonize [*Chün-tzu ho erh pu-t'ung; hsiao-jen t'ung erh pu-ho*]." Taken in its familiar configuration, this *ho-t'ung* correlation belongs to the realm of social and ethical values. It also belongs to that range of qualities of superior and inferior persons in whom Confucius had vested such contrasts as magnanimity opposed to parsimony, composure opposed to fretfulness, principle opposed to speciousness, frankness opposed to deviousness. Thus the harmonious *(ho) chün-tzu* and the identity-seeking *(t'ung) hsiao-jen* describe preferences in Chinese social ethics and reinforce the general view of Confucianism as essentially a social creed, which is not given to metaphysical pursuits of meaning or philosophical abstractions. Most students of Chinese thought have come to generalize that such a preoccupation with social action and theory accounts for China's not having developed modern science, a scientific philosophy or even a pre-Sung metaphysics.

My rereading of this *ho-t'ung* correlation, however, has produced more than an awareness of the social and ethical message. Considered fully in relation to other formulations of thought in the *Lun-yü* (which is not noted for its systematic argumentation) the *ho-t'ung* correlation has important cosmological connotations, enough to explain the subsequent direction of Chinese thought. In other words, if the Chinese scientific tradition is to be explained as the product of ethical preoccupations, it can just as well be understood from the standpoint of a cosmology that predisposed the Chinese to this or that kind of ethical action. Approached in this way, the *ho-t'ung* contrastive correlation suggests that Joseph Needham's *Science and Civilization in China* might more aptly be titled *Science or Civilization in China*. Similarly, the Weberian dictum explaining the lack of capitalism in China should be recast in terms of a deliberate intellectual preference rather than passive incapacity.

Although *ho* and *t'ung* are contrastive, they are not necessarily antithetical. For example, in common usage, *ho* and *t'ung* may belong to the same general class of good and desirable qualities; and under certain circumstances, *t'ung* may even share with *ho* the same sense of harmonious community. Consider, for instance, the expressions *t'ung-jen* (fellowship, commonalty), *t'ung-hsin t'ung-te* (one heart, one virtue), *t'ung-tao* (common way, companion), *t'ung-ch'ing* (sympathy), and *t'ung-kan kung-k'u* (sharing both pleasure and pain).

The similarity of meaning in *ho* and *t'ung* can also be seen in the philosophical commentaries of the Later Han. For instance, in commenting on the phrase *ta-t'ung* in the well-known sentence from the "Li-yün" chapter of the *Li-chi* (Book of rites) that states, "When thievery and brigandage do not arise and the front doors can be left open, it is called the great unity [*ta-t'ung*]," Cheng Hsuan (127–200) noted that *ho* and *t'ung* both mean unity. And Kao Yu, when commenting on the sentence in the "Chün-shou" chapter of the *Lu-shih Ch'un-ch'iu* (Lu's *Spring and autumn annals*), which reads, "Leaving society and departing from human association mean the same thing," indicated that *t'ung* and *ho* both refer to sameness.

But when *ho* and *t'ung* are contrasted, one perceives a fundamental difference between the two. Taken this way, they possess at least two related levels of meaning: one of social discourse and one of cosmological inference. Both levels invite comparisons with other major polarities found in early Confucian writings: for example, *i-li* (righteousness-utility), *wen-*

chih, (refinement-native substance), *tao-ch'i* (way-instrument), and *pen-mo* (ends-means). Confucian writings are replete with assertions that harmony *(ho)* arises from righteousness, and utility or profit arises from identification *(t'ung),* that the superior person measures himself against righteousness, and the petty person against utility *(Lun-yü,* "Li-jen" chapter, 4:12, 16, etc.). The priority of *ho* over *t'ung* is unmistakable.

In other classical literature this contrastive usage of *ho* and *t'ung* is also manifest. For instance, the *Tso-chuan* (Tso's commentary to the spring and autumn annals) records a celebrated conversation between Yen-tzu and Duke Ching of Ch'i, in which Yen-tzu remarks: "Chü is actually *t'ung* . . . ; how then can it be *ho* at the same time?" Duke Ching asks, in turn: "What then are the differences between *ho* and *t'ung?*" Yen-tzu responds: "*Ho* is like preparing broth, in which water, firing power, and the tasting ingredients are well mixed to blend fish and meat. The chef harmonizes [*ho*] them all, blending taste by supplementing inadequacies and reducing excesses. . . . The same applies to relations between ruler and minister. When the ruler wants to do something and he should not, the minister ought to point out the 'should-not' in order to enhance what the ruler actually does. When the ruler does not do what he ought to do, the minister ought to point it out so that the rulers will not err." Again, the "Cheng Yü" of the *Kuo-yü* (Discourses of the states) records a conversation in which Duke Huan asks, "Must Chou be in decline?" Shih-po answers, "That the Chou is close to its end is because it chose *t'ung* and abandoned *ho.* In actuality, *ho* nurtures the myriad things, and *t'ung* discontinues them. When two entities are in balance, it is called *ho;* in this way, all things flourish and the country is together. But, when one *t'ung* is compared with another *t'ung,* all are lost and dispersed. Therefore the Former Kings saw the myriad things as composed of a balance between the five elements [*wu-hsing*], and found their palates pleased when the five flavors were harmonized."

On the level of social discourse, this form of ethical juxtaposition reached full expression in the *Chung-yung* (Doctrine of the mean), a work written much later than the *Lun-yü.* On *ho,* the *Chung-yung* tells us: "The state before human sentiments are expressed is called the Mean [*chung*]; when they are expressed and all are in the moderate mode, it is called Harmony [*ho*]. *Chung* is the real nature of the universe and *ho* is when the universal way prevails. When *chung* and *ho* are both reached, heaven and earth are in place, and the myriad things are nurtured" (chap. 1). With *t'ung* taking a subordinate, though still nonpejorative, role, the *Chung-yung* states, "In today's world, carts share [*t'ung*] the same axles, books the same writing, and behavior the same ethics. But even if someone has the position of king, if he does not possess virtue, he should not tamper with rites and music. And even if someone has the virtue, if he is also not a king, he should not deal with rites and music" (chap. 27). Thus, a country may be unified *(t'ung)* in one sense, but only a sage-king can be entrusted with matters as important as rites and music. Rites and music, in turn, have everything to do with *ho*, harmony, and hence true civilization.[6]

It is in comparison with the *wen-chih* correlation that the social content of *ho* and *t'ung* reveals cosmological shadings. Here *ho* shares with *wen* (pattern, refinement, literature) the meaning of wholeness; *t'ung* (identity) and *chih* (native substance) that of specificity and particularity. Confucius said, "When native substance exceeds refinement, crudeness results; when refinement is excessive, facile pedantry results. When *wen* and *chih* are in balance, gentlemanliness prevails" (*Lun-yü*, "Yung-yeh" chap. 6:16). In spite of the demand for balance, it is clear than *wen* has a slight priority over *chih*, refinement over rusticity, pattern over discrete parts. *Wen*, from its root meaning of pattern—as in the ripples on water and plumage of birds— by the time of the *Lun-yü* already possessed its present connotations of literature (from pattern to markings to symbols to writing to language to literature), as well as art (from pattern to adornment to refinement to art).

The word *wen* has come to be used in any conjunction denoting culture and civilization. This usage contrasts markedly with the Western word *civis*, connoting city or citizenship. The compatibility of *ho* and *wen* lies in their preference for the general to the particular, the whole to the part, the harmonized to the jaggedly individual. When discussing harmony and decorum with Confucius, Yu Jou said, "Of all the assertions of decorum, the most valuable is harmony. The ways of the Former Kings all show this to be the most attractive, and great and small deeds follow the example. But then this should not always be so, for it will not work for someone to practice harmony, without being tempered by decorum, simply because harmony is all that he knows" (*Lun-yü*, "Hsueh-erh" chap. 1:12) We may note once again that there is no implied or explicit "either . . . or" here, nor is there the attribution of absoluteness to *ho*. It simply is to be preferred and always in relation to something.

The transsocial properties of *ho* are also seen in its exquisite relation to music. The "Shih-yueh" chapter of the *Erh-ya* notes that the small *sheng* is called *ho*. The *Li-chi* refers to "sounds that become soft because they are *ho*" ("Yueh-chi"). By the third century A.D., Juan Chi (210–263) could say in his *Yueh-lun* (On music): "Music . . . is the ultimacy of the universe, as well as the nature of the myriad things. When the ultimacy is not dispersed and the nature is availing, then harmony ensues. Separation from the ultimacy and loss of that nature will produce discordance."[7] *Ho*, then, implies the capacity of containing and accommodating all manner of logicalities, whatever their temporal or spatial definitions.

The world of logicalities, on the other hand, is the world of *t'ung*, of identifications and identifiables. The term contains also implications of equalizing, unifying, and classifying. All such tendencies, as scientific philosophy and the philosophy of science demonstrate, are essential to the scientific method.[8] Clearly traditional China did not lack this notion of *t'ung*; Joseph Needham has abundantly demonstrated the many Chinese achievements in technology that required *t'ung* thinking. But *t'ung* was neither valued absolutely by itself nor valued above all else. In short, it could not produce habit-changing ruptures in Chinese society.[9]

Similarly, *li* (utility or profit) remained clearly subordinate to its correlate, *i* (righteousness). The value Mencius attached to the latter is legendary; like *t'ung*, *li* was a quality fit only for the petty person. It is true that *li* acquired a measure of respect over time, as the thought of Chang Tsai (1020–1076) indicates. Chang said, "Profit intended for the people is acceptable profit. Profit for the self, or even for the country, is not proper profit. When speaking of proper utility, one should liken it to real beauty. It is not easy to speak of profit, and one must not be categorical about it."[10] By the late Ming period, Ku Yen-wu could speak in his celebrated political treatise about *li* as being valuable against the problems facing China. And, as Professor Yü Ying-shih's work has shown, by Ming-Qing times the world of *li* produced a great appreciation for wealth, merchant status, and even merchant culture.[11] But *li*, like *t'ung*, never occupied a position of prestige, much less absolute value. As subordinate concepts, *li* and *t'ung* did not possess sufficient power to serve as the intellectual prerequisites for the development of either capitalism or modern science in China.

The polarities cited above are of varying degrees of evenness and unevenness, but they correlate with each other, allowing for and adjusting to each other's presence in the social, political, and philosophical continuum of traditional China. That the Chinese historical experience shows a singular success in integrating the social, political, philosophical, and natural worlds is by now textbook knowledge and does not require discussion here. What should be said is that behind this integration was an early settlement on an organismic, correlative cosmology.

The Chinese worldview from the start entertained a balanced coexistence of all substances in the universe, quite unlike the Western conception of a celestial lawgiver.[12] Although these substances existed, they were not created by an authority external to nature. They obeyed their own natures and formed patterns—whether cosmic, organic, or social. Substances were not reducible, nor were they meant to be reduced, for it was the universe as pattern *(wen)* that ultimately mattered. Associated with this view of the universe was the idea of heaven *(t'ien)* as cosmic function. The whole of humanity, from self to family to state to world, was part of a harmonious cosmic order, overseen by *t'ien*. Heaven represented by its mandate *(ming)* the orderly process that humans should emulate, and, when humans strayed from this model, the moral mind of heaven expressed its displeasure by means of portents. Although Confucius mentions the mandate of heaven *(t'ien-ming)* only twice in the *Lun-yü*, it is clear that he viewed heaven and humans as bound together in a single cosmological pattern *(t'ien-jen ho-i)*. Only at age fifty, he tells us, did he fully understand [*chih*] heaven's mandate" (*Lun-yü*, "Wei-cheng" chap. 2:4).

This cosmology also predisposed the Chinese to view the world as without sin, at least in the Judeo-Christian sense and hence without its consequences. What this means is that in China a cosmic dynamism of the sort outlined above precluded a sin-centered dynamism of the religious psyche, as in the West. In a correlated cosmos such as China's, there was no place for wrongful or undesirable parts. Disturbances and malfunctions of the order or of the parts within it might indeed occur, but they would be only temporary, and could be rectified. Also, because evil had neither a positive role nor any sort of permanence, not to speak of personification, human errors were human in origin, social in character, and retributable in human and social terms. Aligning the moral order with the cosmic order was the therapy for evil—itself viewed as a temporary malfunction of the natural process and not the wronging of a personal god. The Chinese approach to ethics emphasized self-education and self-correction, in addition to external demands for orderly or refined *(wen)* behavior.

The pervasive influence of cosmology on Chinese culture is nowhere more impressively evident than in the very notion of culture and civilization. That *wen* and its associated idea of *ho* have come to denote civilization, as we have seen, is our best evidence of the relation of cosmology (how the universe works) and social precepts (how the human component ought to work). Subsequent Chinese accomplishments in the arts of civilization can be traced ultimately to this cosmological interest in the workings of the universe, to this approach to cosmic functions with its rational expectations of order, pattern *(wen),* and harmony *(ho)* in the processes of life. A reversal of the *ho-t'ung, wen-chih,* and *i-li* polarities would have meant a different cosmology and therefore a different Chinese civilization.

Notes

1. See Feng Yu-lan, "Why China Has No Science—An Interpretation of the History and Consequences of Chinese Philosophy," *International Journal of Ethics* 32 (1922): 237–263. Also Chin Yueh-lin's "Chung-kuo che-hsueh" (Chinese philosophy), which appeared first in mimeograph in 1943 in Kunming, was subsequently published in the first issue of the English edition of the *Social Sciences in China* (1980) and then appeared in Chinese translation in the *Che-hsueh yen-chiu* 9 (1985): 38–44. Consult also Wen-yuan Qian, *The Great Inertia: Scientific Stagnation in Traditional China* (London, 1985).

2. A representative collection would be *Ancient China's Technology and Science,* edited by the Institute of the History of Natural Sciences, Chinese Academy of Sciences (Beijing, 1983).

3. Only certain representative works of the authors are cited for illustrative purposes. All are prolific writers, and they often disagree with one another over premises and conclusions, but all point to the inner vitality of the Confucian ethic. See Herman Kahn, *World Economic Development* (Boulder, Colo., 1979); Chin Yao-chi, *Ts'ung ch'uan-t'ung tao hsien-tai* (From tradition to modernity) (Taipei, 1983); Wei-ming Tu, *Humanity and Self-Cultivation: Essays in Confucian Thought* (Berkeley, 1979); Wm. Theodore de Bary, *Self and Society in Ming Thought* (New York, 1970)—especially his own essay on individualism; Yü Ying-shih, "Ju-chia ssu-hsiang yü ching-chi fa-chan: Chung-kuo chin-shih tsung-chiao lun-li yü shang-jen ching-shen" (Confucian thought and economic development: Modern Chinese religious ethic and the merchant ethos), *Chih-shih fen-tzu* (The Chinese intellectual) 2, no. 2 (winter 1986): 3–45. For a wider sampling of the discussion on the phenomenon, consult especially the last-mentioned periodical, 1, no. 2 (winter 1985); 2, no. 4 (summer 1986); and 3, no. 2 (winter 1987). The first two issues of the *Chiu-chou hsueh-k'an* (Chinese culture quarterly), fall and winter 1986, carry excellent articles on the Confucian ethic, especially those of Tu and Yü and the latter's queries of the former. Recent issues of the *Che-hsueh yen-chiu* (Philosophical research) have also entered into the discussion.

4. Yü Ying-shih, cited above.

5. My own translation of the *chün-tzu* as a morally sovereign man, one who is in total grasp of his moral faculties.

6. A recent article which treats China's philosophy of harmony and moderation in a positive light is by Teng Hung-lei, "Lun Chung-kuo ch'uan-t'ung ho-hsieh li-lun ti ch'uang-tsao-hsing chuan-che" (On the creative permutation of traditional Chi-

nese theories of harmony), *Che-hsueh yen-chiu* 1 (January 1987): 60–65. Teng centers the discussion on the idea of mean *(chung-yung)*.

7. Quoted in Mou Tsung-san, *Ts'ai-hsing yü hsuan-li* (Talent and metaphysics) (Hong Kong, 1963), p. 309.

8. The materials on this subject are overwhelming. For brief statements, see Wen-yuan Qian, cited above; and D. W. Y. Kwok, *Scientism in Chinese Thought, 1900–1950* (New Haven, 1965), pp. 20–30. Ch'ien's work is especially good on the indispensability of reductionism in science. Mere organismic patterning is insufficient to "change" matter.

9. On the idea of continuity and rupture, see Chang Kuang-chih, "Lien-hsu yü p'o-huai: I-ko wen-ming ch'i-yuan hsin-shuo ti ts'ao-kao" (Continuity and rupture: A draft of a new theory of the origin of civilization), *Chiu-chou hsueh-k'an* (Chinese culture quarterly) 1, no. 1, (September 1986): 1–8.

10. Chang-tzu, *Ch'üan-shu* (Complete works of Master Chang), vol. 14, "Hsing-li shih-i," quoted by Yü Ying-shih, p. 23.

11. Ibid.

12. Worldview and cosmology are used interchangeably here. Good treatments of Chinese cosmology are by John B. Henderson, *The Development and Decline of Chinese Cosmology* (New York, 1984); Frederick Mote, *Intellectual Foundations of China* (New York, 1971); and Benjamin I. Schwartz, *The World of Thought in Ancient China* (Cambridge, Mass., 1985). See especially Schwartz's chapter on correlative cosmology. I attempt only a summary outline here.

2

Confucian Cosmological Myth and Neo-Confucian Transcendence

HAO CHANG

Whatever one may say about Confucianism in late imperial China, there is no question that the doctrine of the Three Bonds *(san-kang)* occupied a central place in it. Yet from the beginning, developments existed in Confucian worldviews and values that, if not running directly counter to the doctrine, certainly existed in tension with it. This essay aims, by exploring such tensions as they obtained in the neo-Confucian tradition, to shed some light on the place of the doctrine in the tradition. Let me start with some preliminary observations about developments that led up to the formation of the doctrine in the Confucian tradition.

Although a fully articulated doctrine of the Three Bonds crystallized only in Han Confucianism, some of its basic elements can be traced back to the cosmological myth that lay at the heart of the archaic civilization when the latter first arose in the second millenium B.C. By cosmological myth I mean the belief that the social order is embedded in the cosmic order, or to borrow Eric Voegelin's words, it is the "mythical expression of the participation, experienced as real, of the order of society in the divine being that also orders the cosmos."[1] Toward the end of the second millenium B.C., this archaic cosmological myth began to undergo some rationalization that attended the rise of the new religious belief in heaven *(t'ien)*. The rationalization resulted in some basic differentiation in the archaic consciousness between the institution of kingship and the human occupant of the institution. Although the institution was still believed to be inherent in the cosmic order, the human occupant was seen as changeable by human effort.[2] The compact, substantial unity of the existing order on earth with the divine-cosmic order was thus somewhat broken. However, the archaic cosmological myth in its essential form remained intact.

Seen against this background, the rise of Confucianism in the so-called axial age is very significant. True, all the Confucian classics assumed as given the two institutions—kinship and kingship—that lie at core of the cosmological myth. Thus, classical Confucianism may be said to have involved no fundamental break with the archaic cosmological myth. On the other hand, however, in these classics were also found values and worldviews that reflected moral-spiritual experiences of an order different from that of the cosmological myth. Two such values and worldviews need to be mentioned in passing here: One was the "ethics of spiritual aspirations," centered on some unprecedented moral-spiritual consciousness. In the first instance there was an "awareness of the horizon" that envisaged all the people on earth as one universal community, as embodied in the ideal of "all-under-heaven in one family."[3] Concomitant with this awareness was a tendency to define an individual person not in terms of his or her class background, ethnic origin, or what gods he or she worshipped, but in terms of some attainable moral-spiritual qualities.[4] In classical Confucianism this "ethics of spiritual aspirations" was bound up with ontological awareness of an inner linkage of man with heaven, an awareness that produced a sense of inward transcendence. The self was believed to have an inner core, a sort of vital center, which partakes of the encompassing whole. In this way there is an inner unity not only between each human being and the sacred beyond but also between all the people on earth.[5] Consequently, the ethics of spiritual aspirations and the ontological awareness of inner unity came to be fused into one worldview that involves a drive on the part of the self to go beyond any concern with the partial and the particular and to reach out toward the whole—in short, an impulse toward inward transcendence, which exists in tension with the archaic cosmological myth.

When the doctrine of Three Bonds was formulated in Han Confucianism, it signified the presence of a cosmological myth of a more complex type in the Confucian tradition. It assumed a symbolic form that differs significantly from that of the archaic cosmological myth inasmuch as it envisages the central components of the institutional order—kingship and kinship—rather than the whole order, as inherent in the cosmos. Meanwhile, the ethics of spiritual aspirations and its ontological awareness of inward transcendence were also partly incorporated into the new symbolic structure on the basis of the doctrines of *yin* and *yang* and the five elements *(wu-hsing)*. A moral-spiritual meaning was thus injected into the center of the institutional order. The center was not just a fixed linkage with the cosmic order; it was also the indispensable channel through which a moral order could be made to prevail on earth. On the other hand, however, the sense of transcendence and critical impulses that were carried in the classical Confucianism, now being contained and circumscribed by the view of kingship and family as sacred and unalterable institutions, were significantly weakened.[6] We may call the whole complex of beliefs, as epitomized in the doctrine of Three Bonds, the Confucian cosmological myth as distinguished from its archaic predecessor.

Specifically the Confucian cosmological myth was built around two beliefs: First was the belief that three out of the Confucian five relationships, namely, ruler and subject, father and son, and husband and wife, must be governed by the principle of superordination and subordination. Second, there was the belief that homologized the principle of superordination and subordination with the cosmological symbolism centered on the ideas of *yin* and *yang* and *wu-hsing,* resulting as it did in the absolutization of the Three Bonds as something given in the cosmic order. In this way the two central institutions of society—monarchy and family—became cosmic fixtures.[7]

Finally these beliefs were articulated within, and fortified by, a ritual order that looked on the two institutions as the foci of its cult complex—the ancestral cult, representing family, and the cult of heaven, representing the monarchy. Although an ordinary person could achieve some communication and attunement with the cosmic order through ancestral worship (or other cults), he or she had no access to the controlling power of the cosmos, heaven, except through the medium of the emperor, who performed the state sacrifices on behalf of all his subjects. In other words, the attunement of all people on earth with the cosmic order could be effected only through the institution of kingship.[8] This complex of myth and rituals remained by and large intact even at the height of Buddhist and Taoist influence in medieval China.[9]

The Neo-Confucian Reappropriation of the Classical Heritage

What was the role of this cosmological myth in the neo-Confucian tradition? It must be remembered that during its formative stage neo-Confucianism was a movement to meet the challenges of Buddhism and Taoism by recapturing the moral faith of classical Confucianism. Because this moral faith was articulated primarily in its ethics of spiritual aspirations rooted in an ontological awareness of the inner unity between all human beings and the sacred beyond, the reappropriation of this ontological awareness naturally became the focal point of fresh developments in the neo-Confucian tradition.[10] On the basis of this reappropriation a number of ontological worldviews developed over the centuries. What was the relation of these worldviews to the Confucian cosmological myth? As is shown below, each of these worldviews carried some critical impulses in tension with the latter. These critical impulses failed in the end to dislodge the cosmological myth from a crucial place in neo-Confucianism, but the tensions they generated were an essential part of the tradition. Although it is beyond the scope of this paper to treat fully the critical impulses carried by these worldviews, I explore some key figures and signal developments to illustrate the complex relation between these neo-Confucian worldviews and the cosmological myth.

Chang Tsai (1020–1077) may be regarded as a representative figure of the early phase of neo-Confucianism. The thrust of Chang Tsai's thought is a vision of reality that reaffirms the Confucian moral faith and by the same token refutes the nihilistic worldviews of Buddhism and Taoism. Seen in this vision the cosmos is an encompassing whole constituted by a single substance—material force *(ch'i)*. All things are made up of this basic substance. Consequently, a fundamental kinship links all existence and makes for a primordial unity of the whole. Human beings, however, have a unique place among the "ten thousand things" inasmuch as they alone are capable of becoming aware of this kinship and unity.[11]

This primordial sense of kinship and unity is usually blocked in the actual human world, however, because all human beings, after birth, inevitably go through individuation and thereby take on different bodily forms and physical identities that separate and isolate them from each other. On the other hand, each human being is capable of dissolving this blockage and transcending the individualized bodily self in which each person is felt to be imprisoned. The basic reason is that each has a mind-heart *(hsin)* capable of two kinds of knowledge: knowledge of sense perception *(wen-chien chih chih)* and moral-spiritual intuitive knowledge *(te-hsing liang-chih)*.[12] Through the latter an individual person is able to enlarge his mind *(ta ch'i hsin)* and thereby shed his attachment to the self-ego. In this way one can achieve a sort of self-transcendence and merge back into the all-encompassing whole. Thus Chang Tsai's vision of reality is that of a selfless whole and mystic oneness—a vision that he obviously derived from an ontological awareness of the unity of heaven with man and that later became an enduring strain of neo-Confucianism.[13] This vision of mystic oneness and a selfless whole was a predominant theme in the *Cheng-meng* (Correct discipline for beginners), Chang Tsai's major philosophical writing. It was this vision that prompted some later scholars in the neo-Confucian tradition to see in Chang Tsai's thought the Mohist ideal of undifferentiated love *(chien-ai),* an ideal that threatened to undermine the ideals of hierarchical harmony and differentiated love underlying the Confucian social order.[14] However, side by side with this predominant theme were many passages in the book where Chang Tsai attempted to spell out his vision of mystic oneness in terms of an ideal social order. These passages, vaguely formulated as many of them were, added up to a clear commitment to the so-called feudal utopia of the Confucian tradition. The ritual and institutional order of the feudal utopia were by no means identical with the latter-day dynastic order for Chang Tsai. In fact he, like many other neo-Confucian scholars, tended to see a yawning gap between feudal utopia and the existing dynastic order. Nonetheless, to the extent that Chang Tsai's feudal utopia was still organized around the institutions of kingship and extended patrilineage, there was a certain basic institutional affinity between his feudal utopia and the dynastic order.[15]

These twin themes of mystic oneness and feudal utopia came together in a key, synoptic section of his *Cheng-meng,* well known as the "Western Inscription" *(Hsi-ming),* where he portrayed an ideal order of social harmony. Significantly, the social harmony was depicted in terms saturated with images of patriarchal kinship and cosmological kingship. The principle of superordination and subordination that informed these two institutions was simply assumed as inherent in the cosmic order. Consequently, the Western Inscription projected a utopia that was not so much a transcendence of the central institutions of the existing order as their extension.[16]

Thus the vision of mystic oneness that emerged from the Western Inscription was not the same mysticism that stemmed from Mahayana Buddhism and philosophical Taoism. Buddhist and Taoist mysticism involved clear transcendence; Chang Tsai's transcendence was somewhat truncated, because his vision of reality still featured some basic continuity with the Confucian cosmological myth.

Chu Hsi and Truncated Transcendence

After the thirteenth century, neo-Confucianism gradually split into two distinct schools: the Ch'eng-Chu school and the Lu-Wang school. In the case of the Ch'eng-Chu school, Chu Hsi (1130–1200) was, of course, the key figure. Because Chu considered the *Ta-hsueh* (Great learning) to be the gate-way to the heart of Confucian teachings, I shall use his commentaries on the text to get at some of the implications of the neo-Confucian ethics of spiritual aspirations and its underlying ontological worldview. In the foreground of the *Ta-hsueh* is what we may call a paradigm of Confucian education. Significantly, the paradigm envisages an ideal of moral perfection—a kind of Confucian summum bonum *(chih-shan)* as the goal of education. The attainment of this goal, according to the paradigm, involves the pursuit of two interdependent concerns: the individual concern with self-realization and the social concern with building up a moral society.[17]

For Chu Hsi this paradigm had some important implications that he emphasized and developed in his commentaries on the *Great Learning*. First of all it contains a summons to participation and service to the state and in society. Such sociopolitical activism, however, must be preceded and governed by a concern with self-cultivation. In consequence, neo-Confucian moral education characteristically takes the form of a process capped by sociopolitical activism but beginning with self-cultivation as an essential first step.[18]

For Chu Hsi, self-cultivation is not just a matter of character discipline or moral conduct in the mundane sense. It is also a religious concern, insofar as self-cultivation is seen as a moral-spiritual quest for communication and attunement with the ultimate reality—heaven. This "religious" character of Confucian self-cultivation is evident when one takes a close look at Chu Hsi's concept of self-cultivation and its underlying worldview.

Seen in the context of his commentaries on the *Great Learning*, self-cultivation is an endeavor made up of four phases of effort: investigation of things *(ko-wu)*, extension of knowledge *(chih-chih)*, rectification of mind *(cheng-hsin)*, and sincerity of intentions *(ch'eng-i)*. These four phases constitute a process of cultivation of the human mind-heart *(hsin)* that is understood not so much in the psychological as in the ontological sense.[19] The ontological nature of *hsin* must be underscored, because Chu Hsi's conception in this regard is predicated on the neo-Confucian worldview of the unity of heaven and man. Within that framework, *hsin* is believed to partake of the ultimate reality—heaven—insofar as it contains an inner essential nature *(hsing)* believed to be an endowment from heaven. In short, *hsin* serves as an essential linkage between heaven and the individual person, a sort of sensorium of transcendence in the individual self.[20]

Girded up by the worldview of a fundamental unity between heaven and man, Chu Hsi's conceptions of mind-heart and self-cultivation promise to make possible in the neo-Confucian tradition what Eric Voegelin calls "an order of soul," as opposed to the given sociopolitical order.[21] For the human mind, once believed to be a sensorium of transcendence as well as the authoritative source of moral-social action in the external world, cannot but have high potential for critical consciousness vis-à-vis the outside social order. Yet in Chu Hsi's writings as a whole, the potential never materializes to its fullest extent.

The reason can be seen in a number of key concepts in his ontological worldview. First of all, as mentioned above, Chu Hsi saw a heaven-bestowed moral-spiritual capacity *(hsing)* built into the human mind-heart. The mind-heart was not, however, considered by Chu a self-sufficient agency for moral actualization. For in addition to its inherent moral-spiritual capacity, the mind-heart also comprised a material force *(ch'i)* that, although not necessarily evil by itself, was nonetheless prone to becoming "turbid and congealed," thereby preventing the inherent moral-spiritual potential from developing into a guiding force for the human personality. Consequently, guidance and help had to be sought from outside to purify the material force and make the moral-spiritual capacity manifest. This is why intellectual knowledge in general—and especially knowledge of the Confucian scriptural heritage—occupied an essential place in Chu Hsi's approach to self-cultivation.[22] The cultural tradition and the Confucian scriptural heritage were thus indispensable sources of moral and spiritual enlightenment, capable of keeping the human mind-heart from evolving into an independent center of meaning and value that might challenge the social order and its philosophical foundations.

Chu Hsi's view of the inner nature *(hsing)* of human beings was even more responsible for keeping a true sense of transcendence from evolving. Although he considered the inner nature of the human individual to be a manifestation of heavenly principle *(li)*, he also followed a tendency already evident in the writings of the Ch'eng brothers and other early neo-Confucian philosophers to identify cosmic principles with the Confucian code of ritual and behavioral propriety *(li)*. For example, Chu Hsi once said: "The code of *li* refers to the institutional expression of heavenly principles. But since the principles which represent what ought to be in the world are intangible, the code of *li* is created to depict the heavenly principle for people to see and for education to rely on as the standard; *li* is the regulation and refinement of the heavenly principle."[23]

To be sure, Chu Hsi did not necessarily identify the code of *li* with the ritual and social order of his own time. In fact, he often stressed the gap between the two to express his dissatisfaction with the status quo.[24] But despite his effort to maintain distinctions of this sort, there were significant entanglements between Chu Hsi's notions of heavenly principle and the central values and institutions of the existing order. For instance, we can see in Chu Hsi's notions of higher reality the influence of the doctrine of the Three Bonds. Lacking a clear differentiation between his conceptions of *hsin, hsing,* and heavenly principle on the one hand and his notion of the order of society on the other, transcendence was bound to be constricted. In other words, Chu Hsi's ontological awareness was different, but not entirely disentangled, from the Confucian cosmological myth.

A truncated transcendence was also reflected in Chu Hsi's influential philosophy of history. Chu adhered to the dualistic tendency in the Confucian tradition that views the world in terms of the distinction between essence and existence or between a higher and lower reality. Such a dualism was already discernible in the classical Confucian ontological awareness but became even more pronounced in neo-Confucianism, where the ontological worldview of the unity of heaven and man and the related notions of *hsin* and *hsing* clearly entailed a conception of inner essence differentiated from actual existence and rooted in the ultimate reality.[25] Inherent in this dualistic worldview is what Paul Tillich characterized as "a triadic movement" that carries strong critical potential. The triadic movement begins with the distinction between essence and existence, which is accompanied by a tendency to temporalize the distinction by way of identifying the essence with the primordial beginning in the past and existence with the later historical developments that led up to the present. Inevitably this temporalization of the dualistic worldview entails viewing the existing sociopolitical order that grows out of historical development as a degeneration, as a sort of fall from the pure primordial state of the world.[26]

Chu Hsi's view of history grew out of this dynamics of the triadic movement inherent in his belief in the unity of heaven and man. According to Chu Hsi, at the inception of Chinese, or rather human, history, there was a paradigmatic era, the so-called Three Ages *(san-tai)* when heavenly principles prevailed *(t'ien-li liu-hsing).* The triumph of heavenly principles was reflected in a blissful fusion of spirit and politics, or of virtue and power, symbolized by the presence of sage-kings. Human history after that era, especially after imperial history began with the Ch'in dynasty, was a fall, when spirit disappeared from politics and power was no longer redeemed by the infusion of virtue. In this view, periods that were generally regarded as the glorious ages of collective achievements, the Han and T'ang dynasties, became epochs of darkness. Chu Hsi's critical view of history thus seems to have resulted in an almost total negation of the latter-day dynastic order.[27]

But a closer look at Chu Hsi's thought in this regard reveals a historical consciousness not as radical as it appears on the surface. As pointed out above, the source of Chu Hsi's critical view is his idealization of a paradigmatic era in antiquity as the embodiment of heavenly principles on earth. But as also indicated above, Chu Hsi's notion of heavenly principles was not clearly differentiated from the central values and institutions of dynastic order. In fact, the latter were often seen as part and parcel of spirit and virtue—indeed, of the *tao* (way) that Chu Hsi considered the saving force in human history. Thus, the sanctity of the Three Bonds was written into Chu Hsi's very definition of the paradigmatic era. The sense of transcendence that emerges in his view of history turns out to be as much truncated as that in his ontological worldview.

The Critical Impulse and Its Variants

Because Chu Hsi was the dominant figure of the Ch'eng-Chu school, the truncated transcendence reflected in both his ontological worldview and his historical outlook may be taken as representative of at least the mainstream of the school. But in order to shed further light on the limits and extent of critical consciousness in the Ch'eng-Chu tradition, two later developments need to be taken into account.

One was started by Chen Te-hsiu (1178–1235), a leading scholar of the Chu Hsi school in the Southern Sung, who wrote a collection of commentaries and treatises on the *Great Learning* titled *Ta-hsueh yen-i* (The developed meaning of the *Great Learning*), intended as a further development of Chu Hsi's basic commentaries on the text.[28] Enhanced by a supplement compiled by an early Ming scholar, Ch'iu Chün (1420–1495), Chen Te-hsiu's collection became very influential reading among scholar-officials of the Ming and Ch'ing periods.[29] The *Ta-hsueh yen-i* and its supplement, built solidly on the foundation of Chu Hsi's commentaries on the *Great Learning*, naturally inherited the truncated sense of transcendence that existed in Chu Hsi's ontological worldview and historical consciousness. But there was another aspect to Chen Te-hsiu's texts that further dampened critical impulses. As we have seen, the *Great Learning* was originally meant to be a text of moral education that contained a summons to political participation for anyone who set his goal on moral fulfillment. But in the *Ta-hsueh yen-i,* a special interpretation of the Confucian scripture was advanced, designed specifically to address the issue of the moral cultivation of the emperor. A general moral-spiritual text was thus turned into a moral handbook for the ruler. Some critical spirit was certainly retained inasmuch as the moral expectation that runs through the *Great Learning* was now applied to the person of the monarch, but meanwhile the institution of emperorship was assumed to be beyond the reach of moral critique. The *Ta-hsueh yen-i* and its supplement thus bespoke a major development within the Ch'eng-Chu school by which Chu Hsi's commentaries on the *Great Learning* were interpreted to accommodate explicitly central values and institutions of the dynastic order at the cost of the critical intent of Chu Hsi's moral idealism.

But although Chen Te-hsiu's *Ta-hsueh yen-i* represented an erosion of the critical spirit in Chu Hsi's school, other more radical exponents of Chu Hsi's thought in the seventeenth century pushed the critical spirit further than was possible in the Ch'eng-Chu mainstream. We may look at Lu Shih-i (1611–1672) as a leading figure of this radical persuasion.[30] Part of Lu's critical impulses stemmed from the dualistic historical consciousness he had inherited from Chu Hsi. Looking back at the Three Ages as the paradigmatic era of feudal utopia, he condemned the latter-day bureaucratic rule *(li-chih)* as a sort of fall.[31] Yet Lu's political radicalism went beyond a mere condemnation of bureaucratic rule. In fact, some impulses of Lu's thought went so far as to challenge the very foundation of the dynastic order—the imperial institution.

To see these radical impulses clearly, we have to examine Lu's magnum opus, *Ssu-pien lu* (Notes of reflective thinking), which, true to the spirit of Chu Hsi's school, was organized around the paradigm of moral education offered by the *Great Learning*. Thus, on the one hand, it placed a premium on sociopolitical activism; on the other, it insisted on self-cultivation as the precondition for this activism.[32] In propounding his notion of self-cultivation, Lu attached the highest importance to the concept of reverence *(ching)*. To be sure, reverence already had an essential place in the thought of Ch'eng I and Chu Hsi. But in their thought it is only one of the two requisites for moral fulfillment, the other being intellectual inquiry. Lu, however, according reverence a higher priority, viewed it as the prerequisite for both moral practice and intellectual inquiry.[33]

By *ching* Lu referred primarily to a piety held by the human mind toward heaven. The primacy of this piety reflected the centrality of the human mind-heart *(hsin)* in Lu's approach to self-cultivation. He believed that through the cultivation of reverence, *hsin* could be turned into a repository of heavenly principles and thereby a sensorium of transcendence. *Hsin* was thus the self-sufficient source of moral-spiritual fulfillment, the vehicle through which the *tao* could be made manifest on earth.[34]

To Lu, the core of neo-Confucian teaching was the study of how to bring about this manifestation, a study that he called the learning of the *tao (tao-hsueh)*.[35] The transmission of such a sacred learning depended on the teacher as its human agent and formal education as its institutional agency. This explains why he considered the role of the teacher on a par with those of both ruler and father. In fact, he sometimes went so far as to claim for the teacher a higher status than for the ruler, on the ground that the teacher represents the *tao*—the ultimate reality.[36] By emphasizing the role of the teacher and the importance of formal education, Lu obviously was attempting to establish a center of meaning and value independent of the traditional centers of social order—kingship and kinship.

But these radical impulses, significant though they were, never completely dominated Lu's thought. For in his vision of the external order, rituals in the traditional sense still had an essential place. At the heart of the sociopolitical order were still the twin pillars of imperial sacrifices to heaven and of the ancestral cult. His acceptance of traditional rituals and cults implied that he still saw family and monarchy as two indispensable linkages with the unseen sacred order.[37] Thus, in his writings on the learning of the *tao,* the notion of the Three Bonds is sometimes discussed not as something to be transcended but as something taken for granted in the nature of things. Clearly some impulse toward transcendence existed in Lu's thought, but this impulse never completely severed certain basic linkages with the existing order.[38]

Wang Yang-ming: The Abortive Breakthrough

In the development of the neo-Confucian tradition, critical consciousness came closest to a radical break with the Confucian cosmological myth with the Lu-Wang school. The most important figure in this strain of neo-Confucianism was, of course, Wang Yang-ming (1472–1529), whose intellectual divergence with Chu Hsi can be best understood in the framework of the paradigm of moral education found in the *Great Learning*. Wang was as committed as Chu Hsi to the paradigm and to its moral goals for individual and society. He disagreed, however, with Chu Hsi over the sources for and the proper approach to self-cultivation. Whereas Chu Hsi considered the human mind-heart to be insufficient as the source of moral cultivation and hence in need of external sources for guidance, Wang believed that the mind-heart was of itself quite sufficient for moral fulfillment.[39]

Wang Yang-ming's conception of mind-heart was basically derived from Mencius' notion of the moral mind. For Mencius the human mind is in possession of innate moral knowledge *(liang-chih)* that, when cultivated and developed, will lead to fulfillment. This mind is also a means of reaching for transcendence, because through cultivation of the mind the individual self can live in attunement with heaven.[40] Wang Yang-ming, although accepting the Mencian notion of mind, evolved it further on the basis of the neo-Confucian ontological belief in the unity of heaven and man. Taking sharp exception to Chu Hsi's notion that mind is a fusion of heavenly principles and material force, Wang regarded *hsin* as made up solely of principle, in which case material force presented no impediment to moral perfection.[41]

Having identified the principles of heaven with the mind-heart, Wang injected a heightened sense of inward transcendence into it. He often spoke of the "substance of mind-heart" *(hsin-t'i)*, or the "original substance of intuitive knowledge" *(liang-chih pen-t'i)*, as the deep inner reality—the core of the "true self," which can master the physical self. There was, moreover, a remarkable tendency in Wang's thought to characterize this inner higher reality as beyond the distinction between good and evil.[42] This tendency bespoke a greater sense of transcendence than any that obtained in the Confucian tradition up to that point, because Wang considered the mundane moral dichotomy of good and evil to be an inadequate characterization of the transcendent reality that lies deep within each of us. With such a notion of transcendence it is quite understandable that Wang sometimes compared his idea of the substance of mind-heart to the Buddhist notion of emptiness and the Taoist notion of void. For Wang the Confucian concept of inner reality was just as transmoral as its Buddhist or Taoist counterparts.[43]

From its pre-imperial beginnings the Confucian notion of inner transcendence, combined with the impulse for social activism, had been rich in critical potential. The critical impulses were already discernible in Mencius' thought, especially in his dualistic conception of the human personality, with its emphasis on the primacy of the inner true self *(ta-t'i* or *kuei-t'i)* over the outer physical self *(hsiao-t'i* or *chien-t'i)*. The human mind was endowed by heaven with dignity and authority—what Mencius called heavenly honor and rank *(t'ien-chüeh),* that could rival or outmatch any human honors and rank *(jen-chüeh)* conferred by the government.[44] The critical note in Mencius' thought found a resounding echo in Lu Hsiang-shan's (1139–1193) dichotomy of *hsin* or *li* (mind or principle) versus *shih* (authority and power), which upheld human conscience as a source of moral authority against the existing sociopolitical order.[45] This critical thrust of the Mencian tradition was given a sharper edge by Wang Yang-ming's notion of inner transcendence, as reflected in his famous declaration: "The point of learning is to learn through the judgment of mind-heart. If words are examined by the mind-heart and found to be wrong, I dare not accept them as correct, even if they have come from the mouth of Confucius."[46]

However, Wang Yang-ming never carried this critical impulse far enough to question the institutionalized Confucian values. In fact, Wang's thought all along rested on an unstated assumption that a preestablished, natural accord existed between the moral promptings of the human mind and Confucian social values. This is why he tended to take for granted the institutional foundations of the traditional sociopolitical order instead of questioning them throughout his writings. His conservatism in this regard is nowhere seen more clearly than in some of his commentaries on the Confucian Five Classics where he explicitly affirmed the sanctity of cosmological kingship and the doctrine of the Three Bonds.[47]

Late Ming Radicalism

More critical impulses came to the surface, however, among Wang Yang-ming's disciples and intellectual descendents. Of the latter, the so-called left wing of the Wang Yang-ming school was notable for its far-out, nonconformist views. A principal leader was, of course, Wang Ken (1483–1541), who founded the T'ai-chou group among the left wing's members. Central to Wang Ken's thought was his famous interpretation of the Confucian idea of the investigation of things (ko-wu), which meant to him setting up the self as the measure of things and implied that the individual mind was the source of norms and standards for ordering human relationships and society as a whole. This radical affirmation of self is predicated on his view that the self can embody the tao to the extent that the two become identical.[48] What did he mean by the tao?

Wang Ken's conception of the tao was shaped by two decisive experiences in his life: One was the mystic experience of spiritual enlightenment that he went through at the age of twenty-nine—an experience that he characterized as an elevating and euphoric feeling of becoming one with the universe. The other was the beginning of his contact with Wang Yang-ming at thirty-nine and the ensuing, gradual conversion to the latter's teachings about the intuitive knowledge of the mind-heart. Wang's teachings not only fortified and validated his mystic experience of selfless oneness, they also had the effect of awakening him to the identity of the self's vital center *(chung)* with the principles of heaven—hence the convergence of one's inner nature with the dictates of the cosmic order.[49]

At the heart of Wang Ken's conception of *tao* lay two visions of reality, which reflected two different ways of conceptualizing a worldview predicated on the unity of heaven and man: one that involved merging oneself into the encompassing whole, and one that entailed linking up with heaven at the vital center of self. Both visions have implications that could generate tensions with the existing sociopolitical order. For instance, the feeling of an undifferentiated oneness with all the rest of the universe, which attends the vision of a selfless whole, generated an impulse for equality that went counter to the hierarchical structure of Chinese society. The other vision, that of one's vital center partaking of principles of heaven, also had radical implications: For one, the idea that to follow the natural promptings of one's mind is to fulfill the dictates of heaven led to a cult of spontaneity in tension with the normative order of society. Moreover, the belief that one's self embodies the *tao* and that one's mind is attuned to heaven tended to generate a heightened sense of dignity and confidence vis-à-vis the political authority that the mere self, standing alone, would not dare defy.

Wang Ken and many of his T'ai-chou followers lived out this radical vision. The writings of the T'ai-chou school from the beginning were marked by a degree of egalitarianism, nonconformism, and anti-establishmentarianism unprecedented in the Confucian tradition.[50] Among T'ai-chou scholars, it was Ho Hsin-yin who pushed the radical implications of their worldviews to the brink of a break with the cosmological myth. In the direction of expressing his egalitarianism he took the radical step of singling out friendship from the Confucian Five Relationships for special emphasis. Ho sometimes viewed friendship as more exalted than the other relationships, and at other times he matched it with the ruler-subject relationship as the two linchpins of society.[51] Further, Ho, following Wang Ken, emphasized a particular social bond outside the Confucian Five Relationships, namely the teacher-disciple relationship. For him the teacher imbodied the *tao* and hence deserved the highest respect in human society.[52]

With these unconventional views regarding friendship and the authority of teachers, Ho began to envisage, however inchoately, an organized scholarly community outside the two pillars of traditional social organization, family and bureaucracy. To be sure, Ho's thought was not always consistent; the new departures in his thinking were sometimes counterbalanced by more conventional ideas in his writings, notions that reflected a conception of family and monarchy related as cosmic imperatives.[53] Furthermore, neither of these strains alone might have produced a completely new departure. Nevertheless, taken together they did point to a tendency to move away from a worldview dominated by the doctrine of the Three Bonds.

Another major figure in the left wing of the Wang Yang-ming school, Li Chih (1527–1602), shared Ho Hsin-yin's notion that friendship was no less important than the other four Confucian social relationships to the structure of Chinese society.[54] And he seems to have departed from the doctrine of Three Bonds by upholding the complementary and equal relationship between husband and wife as the most basic relationship from which all others were derived and on which they should all be modeled.[55] But Li went further than the T'ai-chou group in challenging the intellectual establishment of the Confucian tradition—primarily because he accepted Wang Yang-ming's idea of inward transcendence without affirming the sanctity of cosmological kingship and the conventional hierarchy of the Three Bonds.

Among the first generation of Wang's disciples it was Wang Chi (1498–1583) who was largely responsible for developing the idea of the substance of mind-heart being beyond good and evil. Wang Chi, in return, influenced other followers of Wang Yang-ming, including Li Chih.[56] In Wang Chi's interpretation of *hsin,* the substance of mind is an ineffable, transmoral reality identical with that which underlies the Taoist and Buddhist spiritual enlightenment. Consequently, the idea of radical transcendence was present in Wang Chi's belief in the "identical nature of the Three Teachings," which carried an impulse to break through and go beyond any moral consciousness that was confined by norms of the existing order. Wang Chi nevertheless did not draw any practical political implications from this notion of radical transcendence.[57]

Li Chih, however, did. Pursuing the belief in the identical nature of the Three Teachings, he went so far as to equate the transcendental *prajna-paramita* of Mahayana Buddhism with the illustrious virtue *(ming-te)* of the *Great Learning.*[58] As a corollary, he arrived at the view that truth, inasmuch as it results from the inward transcendence of the individual mind-heart, needs no imprimatur of Confucius' authority. Carrying a step further Wang Yang-ming's exhortation to form one's own judgment independent of Confucius' authority, Li Chih observed: "It is because people all accepted Confucius' judgment as their own that they never had their own sense of right and wrong."[59]

Li Chih's iconoclasm led him to attack the officially honored neo-Confucianism of the Ch'eng-Chu school. He was skeptical regarding the authority of the Confucian classics, and he repudiated the Ch'eng-Chu theory of the orthodox transmission of the Confucian *tao*.[60] Yet such radical thrusts were still not necessarily directed against Confucian values themselves. Through the influence of the Wang Yang-ming school Li still had a basic sympathy with much of Confucian moral-spiritual thought.[61] What he really opposed was the idea that truth is determined by authority outside the individual mind-heart. The intent of his iconoclasm was vividly expressed by an analogy he drew between underground water and the *tao*. The *tao* is present in every one of us, he said, just as underground water exists everywhere. To get at the truth we must dig into our own mind-heart to tap the *tao* that lies within, rather than seek it outside, in some arbitrarily authoritative source.[62] Li Chih meant to set the internal "order of soul" against any external authority, whether of tradition or of his own society.

Huang Tsung-hsi's Critique of Cosmological Kingship

Li Chih and other left-wing members of the Wang Yang-ming school found themselves experiencing two kinds of tensions: one with some of the dominant values and institutions of the existing society, the other with traditional intellectual authority. Skepticism regarding intellectual authority was by and large confined to Wang Yang-ming's left-wing followers, but the critique of Chinese social values and institutions found expression among individuals outside the left wing, notably the Ming loyalist, Huang Tsung-hsi (1610–1695).

Huang Tsung-hsi's philosophical position was shaped by his teacher, Liu Tsung-chou (1578–1645), the late Ming philosopher who tried to reformulate Wang Yang-ming's idea of moral inwardness without abandoning the latter's basic philosophical framework. Following Liu, Huang accepted the premises of Wang Yang-ming's teachings, including the primacy and autonomy of mind-heart and the emphasis on independent judgment.[63] However, although Wang Yang-ming and his late Ming followers such as Li Chih directed the animus of their nonconformism against the traditional intellectual establishment of Confucianism, Huang aimed his attack primarily on the political establishment, including the institution of the emperorship. Using almost the same phraseology with which Wang Yang-ming and Li Chih asserted their intellectual independence vis-à-vis Confucius' authority, Huang expressed his view on political authority in this way: "What the Son of Heaven considers as true is not necessarily true; what he considers as false is not necessarily false."[64] Underlying this fierce nonconformism was a political radicalism virtually unrivaled in the Confucian tradition.

Huang's political radicalism harked back to Mencius, whose teachings were central to Wang Yang-ming's school. This heritage led Huang to view Wang Yang-ming's thought as basically a recovery of the Mencian belief in the moral-spiritual autonomy of the self.[65] In early life, Huang had written a comprehensive commentary on the *Mencius* to accompany Liu Tsung-chou's commentaries on the other three texts of the Four Books—the *Analects,* the *Great Learning,* and the *Doctrine of the Mean.*[66] A principal theme of Huang's commentary was his explication of the Mencian idea of the original goodness of human nature in terms of the conceptions of moral inwardness and inward transcendence developed by Liu Tsung-chou and other late Ming neo-Confucian thinkers.

Significantly, Huang did not hesitate to draw on the writings of the T'ai-chou group, even though Huang and Liu were known to have had sharp disagreements with the group over some basic philosophical issues.[67] For example, Huang fully endorsed Wang Ken's doctrine of *ko-wu,* in which one's own mind-heart was regarded as the standard for evaluating and setting things right in the world.[68] Clearly implied in Huang's endorsement was the belief that the self is an agent of the *tao* and a custodian of truth, having priority over both the order of society and the authority of tradition. This position derived logically from the Mencian conception of the individual's moral inwardness and autonomy. It is not surprising that elsewhere in his writing Huang states that Wang Yang-ming's teachings had made possible a rekindling of faith in the Mencian ideal that everyone can become a Yao or Shun.[69]

Although some of the radical implications of this expansive conception of self were already manifest in Huang's commentaries on Mencius, his political radicalism was not fully evolved until late in life, when he wrote the now-famous *Ming-i tai-fang lu* (A plan for the future prince.)[70] In this treatise, literati are viewed as agents of the *tao* and custodians of truth before whose authority not only officialdom but also the emperor must show deference. Further, these literati should be given a forum in schools and academies where truths are sought independent of the emperor's authority. In this way Confucian literati could have an independent center of meaning and value, which rivaled the imperial center itself. Schools and academies would thus become institutional counterweights to the emperorship.[71]

Moreover, Huang Tsung-hsi's radicalism directly challenged cosmological kingship as an integral part of the doctrine of the Three Bonds. Huang defined kingship solely in secular and functional terms. In the beginning, he asserted, every human individual was selfish, and hence people were unable either to cope with the problems they faced in common or to promote the interests they all shared. Hence, government was set up and rulership was instituted as a matter of practical necessity.[72] Absent is the notion of kingship as a cosmological linchpin. Because the ruler-minister relationship or the ruler-subject relationship was conceived completely as a functional one, Huang saw it as different from the primary, natural relationship between father and son. Although the latter was unchangeable, Huang argued, the former could be altered, depending on the part one played.[73] If one serves in the government, one's role is that of teacher or friend to the ruler, in a sense enjoying an equal status to the latter. If one remains outside of government, one would be a mere stranger to the ruler. Huang did not completely deny that government consisted of a hierarchy of ranks or offices with the ruler at the top. But he maintained that the status differentiation between the ruler and the officials was no different from that between different grades of officials. There was still differentiation, to be sure, but only in degree, not in kind. In short, in Huang's view there was nothing extraordinary about kingship that warranted special respect, no unbridgeable gap between the emperor and the rest of the official hierarchy.[74]

If monarchy is justified entirely in terms of the moral functions it performs, naturally the emperorship would lose legitimacy if these functions were not fulfilled. This is exactly how Huang came to downgrade kingship. According to Huang, the moral functions of rulership were fulfilled only during the ancient Three Ages. After that blissful era, the institution of kingship had come to be corrupted by the selfishness of individual rulers. Consequently he wondered whether China would have been better off without the monarchy, because in that case people would at least have been able to pursue their own individual interests. By implication, anarchy would be preferable to the existing system of kingship.[75] Huang thus challenged an integral part of the doctrine of Three Bonds—namely, the ruler-subject relationship—although he apparently never questioned the sanctity of the other two bonds.

Conclusions

This brief overview of the tensions in the neo-Confucian tradition leads me to the following tentative observations. First, the ethics of spiritual aspiration and its underlying ontological awareness of the unity of heaven and man were the major source of tensions with the myth. In the initial phases of neo-Confucianism as well as in its mainstream—the Ch'eng-Chu school—critical consciousness was generated and sometimes developed quite far, as evidenced in some of its developments in the seventeenth century. But even at its most radical, the critical consciousness in the Ch'eng-Chu school fell short of achieving a clear break with the myth. Only in the Lu-Wang school did the tension sometimes grow to an extent no longer containable by the myth. We have seen that some of its radical strains in the sixteenth and seventeenth centuries threatened to break with the cosmological myth, at least in part, if not in toto.

Second, after the seventeenth century the intellectual landscape in the Confucian tradition witnessed a drastic change with the growing vogue of the empirical scholarship *(k'ao-cheng hsueh)*. The Lu-Wang school was now barely discernible on the scene. Meanwhile, in the Ch'eng-Chu school, the predominant trend was toward an intellectualistic orientation, accompanied by a turn toward moral praxis. The moral-spiritual thrust of Chu Hsi's ontological views and the sense of inward transcendence they carried were clearly on the wane. So also were the critical impulses and radical tensions in the Confucian tradition as a whole. In view of these developments, it can be argued that the Confucian cosmological myth had a firmer place in the Confucian tradition during the last two centuries of imperial China.

Notes

1. For a general elucidation of the concept of the cosmological myth, see Eric Voegelin, *Order and History: Israel and Revelation* (Baton Rouge, 1969), pp. 1–11. Voegelin's concept emerges largely from his analysis of ancient Near Eastern cultures. But, in my view, it can also be applied to Shang culture. For one thing, as Paul Wheatley observed, "the ruling monarch was a member of a lineage which coexisted ontologically on earth and in the heavens above." What Wheatley says here about the royal lineage can be said about the aristocratic lineages in general. Further, oracle bone inscriptions show clearly that the royal house, as well as the aristocratic families in general, consulted their ancestors for almost every major action they took on earth. All this points to a self-understanding on the part of the Shang people, which saw the sociopolitical order on earth as part and parcel of the larger cosmic order. On this aspect of Shang culture see Paul Wheatley, *The Pivot of the Four Quarters* (Chicago, 1971), pp. 55–56, 411–451. See also Ch'en Meng-chia, *Yin-hsu p'u-tz'u tsung shu* (A general account of the oracle bone inscriptions of the Yin rites) (Peking, 1956), pp. 561–603; David N. Keightley, "The Religious Commitment:

Shang Theology and the Genesis of Chinese Political Culture," *History of Religions* 17 (1978): 211–225.

2. I am referring here to the doctrine of the mandate of heaven as spelled out in the *Book of Documents* and the *Book of Poetry*.

3. Awareness of the horizon is a concept that I borrowed from Ernst Nolte, *Three Faces of Fascism* (New York, 1969), pp. 452, 553.

4. Hsu Fu-kuan, *Chung-kuo jen-hsing lun-shih, hsien-Ch'in pien* (A history of Chinese views of human nature: The pre-Ch'in part) (Taichung, 1963), pp. 63–312.

5. Ibid.

6. See Tung Chung-shu, *Ch'un-ch'iu fan-lu* (Luxuriant dew of the *Spring and Autumn Annals*) 12:68–69; 8:47–50. See also *Po Hu T'ung* (Comprehensive discussions in the White Tiger Hall) (n.d.), 7:58–59.

7. *Po Hu T'ung,* pp. 58–59.

8. *Ch'un-ch'iu fan-lu,* 15:78–82. *Po Hu T'ung,* pp. 14–15.

9. For a discussion of the Taoist challenges to the Confucian cosmological myth during the Age of Disunity, see Tang Hsi-yu, *Hsuan-hsueh, wen-hua, fo-chiao* (Metaphysics, culture, and Buddhism) (Taipei, 1980), particularly the chapters dealing with the so-called debate on language and meaning, and the general development of Taoist metaphysics during this period, pp. 23–44, 45–58, 121–132. For a discussion of the Buddhist challenges to the Confucian cosmological myth, see Kenneth K. S. Ch'en, *The Chinese Transformation of Buddhism* (Princeton, N.J., 1973), pp. 65–81.

10. These themes are discussed by several contributors to this volume.

11. See Wang Fu-chih, *Chang-tzu cheng-meng chu* (Commentaries on Chang Tsai's correct discipline for beginners) (Beijing, 1959), especially the following chapters: "T'ai-ho p'ien," "T'ien-tao p'ien," "Shen-hua p'ien," "Cheng-ming p'ien," and "Ta-hsin p'ien."

12. *Chang tzu cheng-meng chu,* "Cheng-min p'ien," pp. 69–101, "Ta-hsin p'ien," pp. 103–113.

13. Ibid.

14. See Wing-tsit Chan, *A Sourcebook in Chinese Philosophy* (Princeton, N.J., 1963), pp. 500–517; Chien Mu, "Cheng-meng ta-i fa-wei" (An interpretation of the general meaning of the correct discipline for beginners), in *Chung-kuo hsueh-shu ssu-hsiang shih lun-tsung* (A collection of essays on the history of Chinese scholarship and thought) (Taipei, 1978), pp. 85–112.

15. See *Chang-tzu cheng-meng chu,* especially the following chapters: "Yu-ssu p'ien," "Yueh-chi p'ien," and "Wang t'i p'ien."

16. Ibid., "Ch'ien ch'eng p'ien," pp. 265–270.

17. *Chu-tzu yü-lei* (Classified conversations of Chu Hsi) (reprint; Taipei, 1970) 14:397–435.

18. Ibid.

19. Ibid., 14:402; 15:501; 16:515–558; and 18:625–687.

20. Ibid., 14:415–426; and 15:501. See also Chien Mu, *Chu-tzu hsin hsueh-an* (A new study of Chu Hsi's scholarship) (Taipei, 1971), 2:1–24.

21. See Eric Voegelin, *The New Science of Politics* (Chicago, 1952), pp. 52–75.

22. *Chu-tzu hsin hsueh-an* 2:1–24, 504–550.

23. Ibid., 4:158.

24. Ibid., 4:133, 140, and 145.

25. This dualistic view of human existence was certainly implied in a pivotal neo-Confucian concept—that of recovering the lost nature *(fu-hsing)*. It suggests the conception of an ideal existence that embodies nature as distinguished from an actual existence that loses its nature.

26. See Paul Tillich, "The Political Meaning of Utopia," in *Political Expectation* (New York, 1971), pp. 133–134.

27. *Chu-tzu hsin hsueh-an* 1:413–419; 5:64–65.

28. Wing-tsit Chan, *Sourcebook*, p. 567. See also Chen Te-hsiu, *Chen-wen-chung-kung ch'üan-chi* (The collected writings of Chen Te-hsiu, Taipei) (reprinted in *Ssu-pu ts'ung-k'an* [Shanghai, 1920–1922], "Hsu" (preface), pp. 2b–3a.

29. Ch'iu Chün, "Ta-hsueh yen-i pu yuan-hsu (The original preface to *Ta-hsueh yen-i pu*), in Ch'en Hung-mou, *Ta-hsueh yen-i pu chi-yao* (The essential selections from the supplement to the developed meaning of the *Great Learning*) (1842), pp. 1a–4b.

30. "Fu-t'ing hsueh-an" (A study of Lu Shih-i's scholarship) in *Ch'ing-ju hsueh-an* (Studies of the scholarship of the Ch'ing Confucianists), ed. Hsu Shih-ch'ang (reprint; Taipei, 1966) 3; 1:1–36; 2:1–29.

31. "Fu-t'ing hsueh-an," 1:27–28; 2:19.

32. Ibid., 1:1. See also Lu Shih-i, *Ssu-pien lu chi-yao* (The essentials of Lu Shih-i's notes on reflection) (1887) in *Cheng-i-t'ang ch'üan-shu* 4:3b–6a, 11b.

33. Lu Shih-i, 2:8a–14a.

34. Ibid., 2:8a–16a.

35. Chiang Wei-chiao, *Chung-kuo chin san-pai-nien che-hsueh shih* (A history of Chinese philosophy in the last three hundred years) (Taipei, 1972), pp. 11–12.

36. Lu Shih-i, 20:5a–5b, 5b–6a, 6a–6b, 7b–8a; 21:6a.

37. Ibid., 21:1a–23b.

38. Ibid., 3:1b. The truncated transcendence was also reflected in the strong endorsement Lu Shih-i gave to Chen Te-hsiu's *Ta-hsueh yen-i,* as well as in his enthusiastic acceptance of traditional rituals regarding state and family. See Lu Shih-i, 21:1a–23b.

39. Julia Ching, *To Acquire Wisdom: The Way of Wang Yang-ming* (New York, 1976), pp. 52–74.

40. Ibid., pp. 104–124.

41. Ibid., pp. 52–124.

42. See Wang Yang-ming, *Wang Wen-ch'ien-kung ch'üan-shu* (Complete works of Wang Yang-ming) (1572 ed.).

43. Ibid., pp. 125–165.

44. *Ssu-shu tu-pen* (A reader of the Four Books) (Taipei, 1967), pp. 453–456.

45. *Lu Hsiang-shan ch'üan-chi* (The complete works of Lu Hsiang-shan) (Taipei, 1966), p. 108.

46. *Yang-ming chuan-hsi lu* (Taipei, 1966), 2:50.

47. In fact Wang Yang-ming basically accepted the Confucian conception of the Three Bonds. *Wang Wen-ch'ien-kung ch'uan-shu,* 26:742–743; 31:885–888.

48. *Wang Hsin-chai ch'üan-chi* (The collected writings of Wang Ken); (Taipei, date unknown), 2:8a; 3:1b–4a; 4:3a, 4a–5b, 6b–9a.

49. "Nien-pu" (Chronological biography), in *Wang Hsin-chai ch'üan-chi* 1:2b–3a, 4b–6a.

50. William Theodore de Bary, "Individualism and Humanitarianism in Late Ming Thought," in *Self and Society in Ming Thought,* ed. William T. de Bary, (New York, 1970), pp. 145–247.

51. Yung Chao-chu, ed., *Ho Hsin-yin chi* (A collection of Ho Hsin-yin's writings) (Beijing, 1960), vol. 2, "Lun yu" (On friendship), p. 28; vol. 3, "Yü Ai Lun-hsi shu" (A letter to Ai Lun-hsi), pp. 65–66. See also Donald G. Dimberg, *The Sage and Society: The Life and Thought of Ho Hsin-yin* (Honolulu, 1974), p. 86; Hou Wai-lu, *Chung-kuo ssu-hsiang t'ung-shih* (A general history of Chinese thought) (Beijing, 1960), 4:2, pp. 1024–1025.

52. *Ho Hsing-yin chi,* vol. 2, "Shih shuo" (On teachership), pp. 27–28.

53. Ibid. 3:51–52.

54. Li Chih, *Hsu Fen-shu* (Shanghai, 1959), vol. 1, "Yü Wu Te-chang shu" (A letter to Wu Te-chang), p. 17. See also Li Chih on "teacher and friend," in *Chu t'an chi,* vols. 11–20.

55. Li Chih *Fen-shu* (Shanghai, 1936), vol. 3, "Fu-fu" (Husband and wife), pp. 101–102. Li Chih's emphasis on the primacy of the husband-wife relationship is seen clearly in the fact that he starts his *Chu t'an chi* with sections on husband-wife relations and ends with sections on ruler-minister relations. His preface indicates that he made this arrangement deliberately, on the ground that he considered the husband-wife relationship to be the source of the other four. See *Chu t'an-chi* (Shanghai, 1974), *ts'e* 1, "Fu-fu pien tsung-lun" (A general disquisition on the husband-wife relationship), pp. 1–2.

56. T'ang Chün-i, "The Development of the Concept of Moral Mind from Wang Yang-ming to Wang Chi," in *Self and Society in Ming Thought,* pp. 93–117.

57. E.g., Wang Chi did not draw any practical implications from his conception of radical transcendence when he discussed the Confucian Five Relationships. See *Lung-hsi hsien-sheng ch'üan-chi* (The collected writings of Wang Chi) (Taipei, n.d.), 2:12a–b.

58. *Hsu Fen-shu,* 1:3–4; 2:75–76, 77–78.

59. Li Chih, *Ts'ang shu* (A book to be hidden away) (Beijing, 1962), "Ts'ang-shu shih-chi lieh-chuan tsung-mu ch'ien-lun," p. 7.

60. *Fen-shu* 3:110–112.

61. Wu Tse, *Ju-chiao p'an-t'u Li Cho-wu* (An infidel of Confucianism—Li Chih) (Shanghai, 1949), pp. 77–83.

62. Li Chih, *Ts'ang-shu,* vol. 32, "Te-yeh ju-ch'en ch'ien-lun" (Preface to Confucian officials of moral achievements), p. 517.

63. See Huang Tsung-hsi, "Tzu Liu-tzu hsing-chuang" (A biographical sketch of Liu Tsung-chou), and "Hsien-shih chi-shan hsien-sheng wen-chi hsu" (A preface to a collection of essays by my teacher, Liu Tsung-chou), in *Huang Li-chou wen-chi* (A collection of Huang Tsung-hsi's essays) (Shanghai, 1959), pp. 36–45, 318–319. See also Huang Tsung-hsi, *Meng-tzu shih-shuo* (My teacher's view of the book, *Mencius*), in *Ssu-k'u ch'üan-shu* 1:13b–15b.

64. Huang Tsung-hsi, *Ming-i tai-fang lu* (A plan for the future prince) (Shanghai, 1957), p. 10.

65. Huang Tsung-hsi, "Yü-yao hsien chung hsiu ju-hsueh chi" (Comments on the reestablishment of a Confucian academy in Yü-yao county), in *Huang Li-chou wen-chi,* pp. 396–397.

66. Huang Tsung-hsi, *Meng-tzu shih-shuo,* "Yuan-hsu," pp. 1a–1b.

67. *Meng-tzu shih-shuo* 1:21b–22a, 28a–b.

68. Ibid. 1:2, 5b–6a.

69. "Yü-yao hsien chung hsiu ju-hsueh chi," pp. 396–397.

70. See Ch'ien Mu, *Chung-kuo chin-san-pai nien hsueh-shu shih* (A history of Chinese scholarship in the last three hundred years) (Taipei, 1964), 1:33–34.

71. *Ming-i tai-fang lu,* "Hsueh-hsiao" (School), pp. 9–13.

72. Ibid., "Yuan ch'en" (On the origin of the institution of minister), p. 5.

74. Ibid., "Tse hsiang" (On setting up premiership), pp. 7–8.

75. Ibid., "Yuan chün" (On the origin of the rulership), p. 2.

3

Toward an Interpretation of Ch'ing Ontology

ON-CHO NG

In the seventeenth century, Chinese thought and learning underwent a process of notable change. Although historians argue over the precise genesis, logic, nature, and significance of the new developments, there can be little doubt that Chinese thought entered a new phase in the late Ming and early Ch'ing periods when it pried out old ideas, impugned antecedent concepts, and inaugurated new approaches.[1] Most palpably, we discern the dismantling of neo-Confucianism *(tao-hsueh)* as the context of validation, as the hegemonic paradigm of intellection.

In the Sung and Ming dynasties, neo-Confucianism had functioned as the principal arbiter and authority that governed the formulation and application of philosophical concepts. Neo-Confucian categories, such as the cognitive theory of *ko-wu* (investigation of things), or the metaphysical entities of *li* (principle) and *ch'i* (material force) became mediating categories by which concepts and ideas were formulated, critiqued, and subsumed. In the process, the workings of society, family, government, and the world at large acquired intelligibility. This is to say that perceptions toward these putative objects attained their interpretive value primarily through the identification with and mediation of these neo-Confucian verbal and conceptual propositions.

However, with the onset of philosophical skepticism in the late Ming, neo-Confucian categories were laid bare and subjected to critical reevaluation. Clearly, in the domain of neo-Confucian metaphysics, there was the redefinition of the nature and relative importance of the two metaphysical entities, *li* and *ch'i*. In other words, a reformulated ontology arose, ontology here defined as the inquiry concerning the universal nature of being and the meaning of reality of that which transcends all things.

Moreover, as neo-Confucianism went through the process of reformulation, the previously accepted metaphysical principles, although remaining components of Ch'ing thought, gradually lost their status as the principal philosophical underpinning. In time, the revised ontology was to transmute into what can be called a vitalist ontology premised on materiality and concreteness. Indeed, down to the eighteenth century, the metaphysics of *ch'i* and the attendant ontological constructs appeared to have ceased to inspire intellectual imaginations. They had by then been taken for granted and were no longer problematic. The metaphysically ontological was eventually subsumed under, and in turn absorbed by, the historically concrete, conceptualized in this paper as vitalism.

William T. de Bary has employed the term "vitalism" to describe the neo-Confucian perception of the *tao* (Way), the essence of which was vitality or creativity *(sheng-sheng)*. According to de Bary, this vitalistic view had already been developed by Wang Yang-ming and especially his followers in the late Ming who saw the mind *(hsin)*

> as a spiritual faculty embodied in physical force, a manifestation of the dynamic life force, or ether *(ch'i)*. Often . . . mind *(hsin)* and ether *(ch'i)* were spoken of in the same terms, as "alive," "living," "life-giving," or "life-renewing" *(sheng or sheng sheng),* and as such were identified as the basis of man's nature *(hsing)*. This follows Wang's efforts to conceive of man's nature not as abstract principle or norms, but as active principle in a dynamic mind. Frequently, the essential reality was described in the assertion that "Throughout Heaven-and-earth, all is mind *(hsin),*" where *hsin* and *ch'i* were used interchangeably to represent the vital force in man and the universe. . . . [T]he significance of this development in the late Ming is manifold, but a major element lies in its stress on the actualities of life and human nature.

This vitalism, with its emphasis on *ch'i,* gave rise to the monistic philosophy of *ch'i* in the seventeenth century.[2]

We should bear in mind that de Bary has borrowed the term "vitalism" with its classical philosophical meanings largely intact. The kernel of the vitalist tenet consists in the enthusiastic championing of life, but to classical vitalists, such as Henri Bergson, "the defense of life took the form of the metaphysical postulation of an *élan vital* or vital impetus at the heart of being."[3] Thus, the term "vitalism," as applied to late Ming and early Ch'ing intellectual life, might suggest that it, too, was predicated on metaphysical speculation, "its stress on the actualities of life and human nature" notwithstanding. Yet vitalism came to be defined in a way that undermined the importance of metaphysical and symbolic constructs in China.

Accordingly, as it is used in this essay, vitalism refers to a philosophy of life that restricted attention in large part to the evidence provided by life grasped from within the body, the self, or external thing. This evidence gave no support for the hypothesis of an unchanging, eternal, and transcendental creative power, such as the absolute and constant *tao* of neo-Confucianism. Rather, Chinese thinkers conceived of embodied experience as composed of concrete tendencies that were not readily dissolved by metaphysical speculation. This life grasped from within the actualities of the self and the external world was finite. Thus vitalism was opposed to the mysticism of the overarching *tao* and the immutable *li,* which pointed to the limitless and infinite.

Ch'ing vitalism objected to these symbolic metaphysical constructs that aspired to reveal the essence of being. Instead, it stressed the vivid, immediate, and ultimate completion of a concrete and dynamic life expressed in terms of *ch'i* (material force) and *ch'i* (concrete things and implements). Vitalism was a dynamic monism: it was dynamic in that it rejected the existence of an immutable *tao* bearing unchanging and infinite truths in favor of a relativized *tao* embodying transient and finite truths; it was monistic in that it repudiated the neo-Confucian dichotomy of the superior *li* (belonging to the metaphysical and spiritual realm), and the inferior *ch'i* (belonging to the perceptual and experiential realm), in favor of a monistic reduction of all reality to *ch'i.* Life, within this vitalistic framework, was ineluctably dependent on circumstances. It was particularized, relatively indifferent to ultimate universal truth. It was also individualized by, and expressed in, the external signs of the self's contingency, frailty, and finitude. Life was the synthesis of the functions that related it to its circumstances, including sensory perceptions, feelings, desires, emotions, and so forth.[4]

In general, scholars of Chinese thought, including de Bary, have pointed to the growing preponderance of the philosophy of *ch'i* since the late Ming era. Some, such as Yamanoi Yū and Irene Bloom, have maintained that it eventually became one of the dominant intellectual trends in the entire Ch'ing period. Yamanoi Yū has identified no less than twelve thinkers in the Ming period, beginning with Lo Ch'in-shun (1465–1547), who advocated this philosophy of *ch'i.*[5] Early Ch'ing savants such as Huang Tsung-hsi (1610–1695) and Wang Fu-chih (1619–1692) further developed this philosophy, which reached maturity in the thought of Tai Chen (1723–1777). After Tai came other illustrious exponents of a *ch'i*-based worldview, including Chiao Hsun (1763–1820) and Juan Yuan (1764–1848).

In the Ch'ing period, the philosophy of *ch'i* provided a new sense of coherence in Chinese intellectual life. Irene Bloom remarks, for example, "[I]t was primarily by virtue of an emphasis on *ch'i* that an otherwise disparate group of Ch'ing thinkers was united; Huang Tsung-hsi, Ku Yen-wu, Wang Fu-chih, Yen Yuan, Li Kung and Tai Chen, for example, whatever philosophical differences they had among themselves, were at one in denying the reality of *li,* or principle, as independent of *ch'i.*"[6] But it would be misleading to characterize Ch'ing thought as grounded in some sort of formalized, *ch'i*-oriented metaphysics. Indeed, there is a general consensus among scholars that, in spite of the intimate connection between neo-Confucianism and Ch'ing thought, the latter was demonstrably more practical and classical, less metaphysical, in orientation than Sung learning.[7]

It could be argued that this change in orientation was in part a consequence of the championing of a monism of *ch'i* in viewing the world and cosmos, which proffered a whole and autonomous reality to concrete things and affairs.[8] However, formal philosophical lucubration in terms of the neo-Confucian categories of *li* and *ch'i* had ceased to capture the imagination of most Chinese thinkers by Ch'ing times. Therefore, although it is quite correct to assert that the philosophy of *ch'i* was a predominant development in the late Ming and early Ch'ing intellectual world, Chinese thinkers of the period did not dwell on metaphysical and ontological speculation and polemics. If *ch'i* (the experiential and material realm of life) did indeed gain ascendancy in intellectual articulations and discourses, it was not as a coherent and formal philosophy. Quite the contrary, it molded an intellectual posture distinctly averse to metaphysical pondering. Out of the philosophy of *ch'i* grew the *ch'i* of thought—that is, a philosophy of concreteness engendered concern with the concreteness of thought. Thus, the term "vitalism," with *ch'i* as its predicate, refers to a general and pervasive attitude toward concrete reality in the Ch'ing period that neither required nor in fact generated a well-shaped formal philosophy.

By the Ming-Ch'ing transition of the early seventeenth century, many Chinese thinkers had come to share an ontological view that stressed the primacy of *ch'i*—the visible, the concrete, the tangible, the material, and so forth. This was an inversion of the traditional neo-Confucian metaphysical approach, which reduced man and material beings to an attribute (manifestation, appearance) of *li,* or the *tao.* Yet the sanction for a *ch'i*-based ontology could be found in Sung scholarship. When Kao P'an-lung (1562–1626), the well-known Tung-lin leader and one of the Seven Worthies of the Ming, declared his alliance with a monistic philosophy of *ch'i,* he called on the authority of a prominent Sung neo-Confucian, Chang Tsai (1020–1077). "Within the universe," Kao wrote, "there is nothing but one mass of *ch'i*. This is what Master Chang meant when he said 'The void is *ch'i*.' This *ch'i* is perfectly empty and perfectly spiritual; in man it becomes mind [*hsin*]. Being possessed of order and principles, in man it becomes nature [*hsing*]."[9] Elsewhere, he remarked: "*Ch'i* is the mind, it is nature. [They are] one. . . . Nature is that which is above the realm of corporeal forms [*hsing erh shang*]; mind and *ch'i* are in the realm of corporeal forms [*hsing erh hsia*]."[10]

Kao thus followed Chang Tsai's metaphysical view that *ch'i* was the primal and original stuff of the universe, out of which tangible things (*ch'i* in its concrete manifestations) were made. He also adopted Chang Tsai's theory on human nature. To Chang, everything in heaven and earth was wrought with *ch'i*, the condensed form of the basic shapeless *ch'i* of the Great Void (*t'ai-hsu*)—the dynamic universe in its original, pristine form. Accordingly, there were two natures in man—the heaven nature (lit., heaven-earth nature; *t'ien-ti chih hsing*), composed of primordial *ch'i*, and the physical nature (*ch'i-chih chih hsing*), consisting of condensed *ch'i*. The former was good and universally the same; the latter varied with individuals. As the source of human desires, the physical nature remained the source of evil. The responsibility and goal of a person were to overcome this physical nature in order to fulfill the heaven nature. Despite the monism of *ch'i*, there lurked in Chang Tsai's thought an obvious dualism.[11]

In some of his writings, Kao appeared to have accepted Chang's starkly bifurcated conception of human nature. He remarked, for example: "[Heaven-] nature is the source of learning. Only after knowing that [heaven-] nature is good can learning be discussed. . . . Master Chang said, 'Only after there are forms can there be physical nature. In heaven-and-earth, there are myriad different [physical] natures of the forms.' . . . Heaven-nature cannot be restored without learning. Therefore it is said that learning is mainly to change and transform the physical constitution [*ch'i-chih*]." But Kao hastened to add that the two natures cannot be neatly dichotomized as two different entities. He used the metaphor of water placed in two receptacles, one dirty, one clean. In both cases, water is nevertheless water.[12] In another revealing passage, Kao pinpointed the oneness and inseparability of heaven-nature and physical nature: "As for the physical nature, which comes into being after there is form [*hsing*], it is after man has received his form that heaven-nature becomes physical nature. It is not that apart from heaven-nature, there is also physical nature. On the contrary, physical nature is the same as heaven-nature. . . . [Thus] it is wrong to separate the two."[13]

Liu Tsung-chou (1578–1645), like Kao, an important late Ming thinker associated with the Tung-lin party, affirmed the priority and primacy of *ch'i* more plainly: "Replete in heaven-and-earth is but one *ch'i*. Only when there is *ch'i* is there destiny [*shu*]; only when there is destiny are there images [*hsiang*]; only when there are images are there names [*ming*]; only when there are names are there things [*wu*]; only when there are things is there the nature [*hsing*]; only when there is the nature is there the Way. Therefore, the Way arises later [than *ch'i*]."[14] Liu also went further than Kao in undermining the dualistic implications of Chang Tsai's monistic metaphysics on the question of moral nature versus physical nature: "*Li* is the *li* of *ch'i*, which is definitely not prior to or outside of *ch'i*. Knowing this, then we know that the mind of the Way is the original mind of the human mind. Moral nature [*i-li chih hsing*] is the original physical nature [*ch'i-chih chih hsing*]."[15] In another essay he wrote: "What is above the realm of corporeal forms is known as the Way; what is amidst the realm of corporeal forms is known as a concrete thing. When concrete things are present, the Way is present. Without concrete things, the Way could not be visible. . . . Replete in heaven-and-earth is only the physical nature [*ch'i-chih chih hsing*]. There is, moreover, no moral nature [*i-li chih hsing*]."[16]

To Liu, the affinity between, and in fact the oneness of, moral nature and physical nature, meant that principle could be discovered only in concrete feelings. He maintained, therefore, that one should "discuss the heaven-conferred nature *(hsing)* in terms of feelings, rather than see the heaven-conferred nature as something preserved in feelings." In other words, Liu's *ch'i*-oriented view of the universe moved him away from Chang Tsai's ideas of *ch'i* in relation to the nature of things and humanity. Physical nature, concrete feelings, and concrete things now became the loci where a veridical reality could be established—small wonder that Liu rejected the notion that "imminent issuance *(i-fa)* is the feelings." His philosophical monism demanded the dissolution of any artificial distinction between externalized experience and concrete things on the one hand, and heaven-conferred nature on the other.[17]

One of the central ideas in Liu's *ch'i*-oriented philosophy was the idea of the moral will or intention *(i)*. In fact it was this "willingness to realize the good and to be good" that constituted the mind's nature. Liu overtly emphasized the primacy and priority of the affective (considered by many neo-Confucians as belonging to the inferior realm of *ch'i*) in one's consciousness.

Moral cultivation was the cultivation of creative will, which was alive with feelings. In his book *Jen-p'u* (A genealogy of man), Liu prescribed ways to establish man as the ultimate *(jen-chi)*. He advocated studying men in history whose will *(i)* was invariably oriented toward actual social and cultural circumstances in each historical age. This meant that the internal *ch'i* of the affective and emotive will was irrevocably tied up with the external *ch'i* of the sociocultural world, both also subject to the changes of time.[18] In this manner, Liu invested his ontology with a pragmatic and activist impulse.

Without question, the most systematic and elaborate ontology of the early Ch'ing period was propounded by Wang Fu-chih (1619–1692), who explicitly championed Chang Tsai's *ch'i*-based metaphysics.[19] Consider the following three statements by Wang: "*Ch'i* is what *li* follows."[20] "In actuality, *li* exists within *ch'i*. *Ch'i* is nothing but *li*. When [*ch'i*] agglomerates and produces men and things, then forms *(hsing)* appear. When [*ch'i*] disperses itself in the supreme void, it is then formless."[21] "To say that man is born without the nourishment of *ch'i*, that *li* could be sought outside of *ch'i*, that forms are illusions, and that the nature [*hsing*] is real, is to degenerate into heterodoxy."[22] These utterances clearly establish the primacy of *ch'i* as the basic stuff of the primeval Supreme Void. They also point to the oneness of *li* and *ch'i*. In his view, the former was but the agglomeration and dispersion of the latter.

Although Wang adhered to Chang Tsai's *ch'i*-based metaphysical premise, in viewing human nature he tended to downplay the dualistic implications inherent in Chang's demarcation of heaven-nature and physical nature, which indeed found philosophical expression in the Ch'eng-Chu dichotomy of *li* (principle as identified with heaven-nature) and *ch'i* (material force as identified with physical nature). Wang opined:

> When one speaks of the physical nature this is like saying that the nature lies within the matter of *ch'i* (*ch'i-chih*). This matter *(chih)* is man's material form *(jen chih hsing-chih)*, within the confines of which the principles of life *(sheng chih li)* are manifest. Since they (the principles of life) lie within this matter, *ch'i* permeates them, and as what fills the universe both inside and outside the human body is nothing but *ch'i*, so too is it nothing but principle. Principle operates within *ch'i*, where it controls and apportions *ch'i*. Thus the matter [of individual things] envelopes the *ch'i* and *ch'i* envelopes principle. It is because this matter envelopes *ch'i* that a given individual possesses a nature. For this reason, before his envelopment has taken place there can only be the principles and *ch'i* of the universe, but not the individual man. Once, however, there is the matter incorporating *ch'i*, this *ch'i* inevitably possesses principle. As far as man

is concerned . . . this nature as found in the matter of the *ch'i* [i.e., physical nature] is still the original nature.[23]

Here, Wang indicates that, because *ch'i* is the all-pervading productive force in the universe, the physical nature of man, wrought of *ch'i,* must be considered the original nature. He does not, however, refer to the aggressiveness and acquisitiveness of humans that, in Chang Tsai's opinion, stemmed from the inferior *ch'i* of physical nature.[24] Wang's more generous perception of physical nature brought with it the concomitant reevaluation of human desires—the affective and the emotive—which, for Wang, had a principle-conferring ability. He asserted that physical nature was one of the principles of life and claimed that "principles and desires *(yü)* are all natural *(tzu-jan)* and not of man's making."[25]

Even propriety *(li)* could not be properly manifested in the absence of human desires: "Although propriety is purely the external adornment of the principles of heaven, it must reside in human desires for it to be seen. That being the case, in the final analysis, there cannot be a heaven separate from man, or principle separate from desires. . . . Hence in sounds, colors, smells and flavors one can clearly see the common desires *(kung-yü)* of all beings, and their common principles *(kung-li)*. . . . Mencius followed Confucius' teachings and saw that where human desires were manifested, heavenly principles were also manifested."[26] In fact, the ideal path of kingly virtue *(wang-tao)* was itself one with human feelings *(jen-ch'ing)*. Wang put the matter this way: "The kingly way is based on human sentiments. Human sentiments are the same sentiments shared by both the superior man and the mean person. . . . Mencius, understanding thoroughly the origin of the oneness of heaven's principles *(t'ien-li)* and human sentiments, recognized the possibility of the kingly way. After seeing the beginning, it could then be extended and expanded. . . . Heaven's principles reside in private desires *(ssu-yü)*."[27]

Wang concatenated the inner world of values (principles of nature reified as propriety) and the outer world of experience (sensual, perceptual, and emotive) by virtually translating the physical aspects of man into spiritual values (from *kung-yü* to *kung-li*). He also pointed to the interpenetrability of the public *(wang-tao)* and private *(jen-ch'ing)* domains, whereby the universal *(t'ien-li)* achieved a union with the particular *(ssu-yü)*. In such a view of reality, the body and its affectations, perceptions, and emotions, became a locus of ethical experience (principle). Desires rightfully formed one of the matrices of a person's rights and of his or her ethical will in the world and also represented the physical limit of freedom. Desires constituted the external form of the person's freedom and the choice of signifying one's intentions. The ultimate of these intentions was to serve the world, to realize the kingly way. No act, then, with respect to physical nature, was devoid of significance. There was ineluctably a meaning conferred on actions defined as functions of the perspective from which they were seen and of the moral and other presuppositions that the actors and things brought to bear.

It is no wonder that Wang, in explicating the idea of exhaustively realizing the nature *(chin-hsing),* claimed that "everything in the world is of the same origin as myself, and depends on me for response and completion."[28] The individual was the fulcrum on which the world moved, and this mandated an activist role; the holism of human nature could be sustained and fully developed only by activism of the human being. Practice *(hsi),* then, was the key to exhaustively realizing one's nature: "As for changing from evil to goodness, it is a matter of nurturing one's *ch'i* well. In time, one's matter [*chih*] is accordingly altered. . . . This is man's ability, which is precisely practice. Thus, *ch'i* changes with practice and nature is realized with practice. Matter is the residence of nature, nature is the regulating of material force, and *ch'i* is the filling of matter. [*Ch'i*] is what practice can control."[29] Thus, the basic stuff of the universe, *ch'i,* ultimately must be considered and understood in human terms. Metaphysics must seek fulfillment in human actions.

In short, Wang's ontology not only collapsed the Ch'eng-Chu dualism premised on the dyadic scheme of *li* and *ch'i;* it also shunned the potential drift toward dualism in Chang Tsai's conception of human nature. His ontology, centering on *ch'i* with its variegated manifestations, imbued overt and externalized human experience and concrete things with a legitimacy that was denied in Chang Tsai's maintenance of the inferior realm of physical nature. Now, affirming the mulifarious *ch'i* as a monistic totality, Wang was able to bestow authenticity on life as grasped from within the actualities of the self and of the external world, thereby also to grant activism in this world an ontological foundation and justification.[30]

Ku Yen-wu (1613–1682), unlike Wang Fu-chih, did not attempt to formulate a systematic ontology. He did, however, give attention to the issue of *ch'i* and its relation to the generative forces of nature.[31] He wrote: "Replete in heaven-and-earth is *ch'i.* When *ch'i* prospers, it becomes *shen* [spirit]. *Shen* is the *ch'i* of heaven-and-earth and the mind of man."[32] And again: "Coalescing to form a body is called *wu* [things, affairs]; dispersing in a shapeless manner is called *pien* [change]. . . . Coalescing is the coalescing of *ch'i;* dispersing is the dispersing of *ch'i.*"³³ In the first statement, Ku asserted outright the self-sufficiency and pervasiveness of *ch'i*. In this regard, *ch'i* need not be literally things, objects, or events, for their formal aspects are derived from the interpretive activity of the perceptual apparatus and understanding. Hence, the causal and implied cognitive relation between the abstractions of *ch'i,* spirit, and mind. However, in the second statement, Ku explicitly identified *ch'i* with objects, things, or affairs. Because *ch'i* was self-sufficient, immanent, and pervasive, the objects, things, and affairs identified with it were also self-sufficient, immanent, and pervasive. They in fact became the sources of clarity, hypostatizing the abstract *tao:* "What is above the realm of corporeal forms is called the *tao;* what is amidst the realm of corporeal forms is called a concrete thing. Without concrete things, the *tao* has nowhere to reside."³⁴

This conception of *ch'i* in concrete things also concretized Ku's idea of the mind as the "*ch'i* of heaven and earth." Ku explained: "[B]enevolence, propriety and things are the mind. To work earnestly on benevolence is to work earnestly on the mind; to improve propriety is to improve the mind; to put things in practice is to put the mind in practice."³⁵ The mind was not, then, quietistic and empty but something that, in Ku's words, "embodies the multitude of principles and responds to the myriad of things." He went on to say: "A person who seeks to rectify his mind also desires to exercise it in ruling the country and bringing harmony to the world." "Principles are embodied in the mind of the self and verified in affairs and things."³⁶

In brief, Ku monistically reduced the common neo-Confucian categories —the Way, principle, mind, concrete things, and *ch'i*—into a homogeneous *ch'i*-based ontology, in which nature was readily knowable and definable. By this means, the world—the sum of its *ch'i,* phenomena, and appearances —could be apprehended and categorized by the human mind and could thereby become clear, distinct, regular, and consistently thinkable. In such a way Ku Yen-wu made sense of Confucius' statement that "the ten thousand things are all replete in me."³⁷

Ku's holistic ontological view, built on the advocacy of *ch'i,* did demonstrate some clear biases in its definition of *wu* (things, objects, affairs) in relation to the neo-Confucian cognitive theory of "investigating things and broadening knowledge to the utmost" *(ko-wu chih-chih)*. He wrote:

To broaden knowledge to the utmost is to know the ends. What is knowing the ends? The end of being a son is filial piety. The end of being a father is kindness.

The end of communicating with people in the country is trust. These are called ends. The intercourse between rulers, officials, fathers, sons and fellow-countrymen, and the three hundred rites and the three thousand august ceremonies, are all called *wu*. . . . It is indeed insignificant if the 'investigation of things' is taken as knowing broadly the names of birds, beasts, grass and trees. A knowledgeable person knows everything, [but he will] attend to matters of immediate importance."[38]

The world monistically expressed in terms of *ch'i* and concretized by *wu* was conceived primarily as a world of human affairs with its moral and social concerns. *Wu* was used in the sense of *shih* (affairs, events). It referred not so much to physical objects as to social relations, institutions, rulership, history, and so forth.

Another great thinker of the Ming-Ch'ing transition, Huang Tsung-hsi (1610–1695), also conflated *li* and *ch'i,* following his teacher, Liu Tsung-chou. In Huang's straightforward formulation, "*Li* is the *li* of *ch'i*. If there is no *ch'i,* then there is no *li*."[39] The differences between *li* and *ch'i* were to Huang merely lexical and semantic in nature: "The terms *li* and *ch'i* are made up by man. Speaking of the phenomena of floating, submerging, rising and falling, there is *ch'i*. Speaking of the unmistakable laws of floating, submerging, rising and falling, there is *li*. In the end, they are the two names for one entity, not two entities in one being."[40]

Elsewhere, Huang explained more clearly the substantive interrelation and mutual identification that existed between *li* and *ch'i*: "[W]ithin heaven-and-earth, there is only one *ch'i*. Its rise and fall, coming and going, are the *li*. Acquired by a person, . . . [*li*] becomes the mind, which is also *ch'i*. If *ch'i* is not self-governed, why is it that after spring, there inevitably comes summer, autumn and winter? What controls the blossoming and withering of plants, the congeniality and severity of the topography, the good and the bad flow of astrological portents, and the birth and growth of men and things? All are self-governed by *ch'i*. Since it is self-governed, it is called *li*."[41] Huang thus dissolved the *li-ch'i* duality by consigning inclusiveness and conclusiveness to *ch'i*. *Ch'i,* in his view, referred to all the concrete things and phenomena and their changes in the world. *Li* meant the intrinsic organization of these actualities and the pattern of their transformation. In Huang's view, *li* in itself did not have any actual existential status. It was merely an abstraction inductively derived from the observation of the experiential and the material.

How did this monistic metaphysics bring itself to bear on Huang's conception of the human being? He remarked: "What is *ch'i* in heaven is the mind [*hsin*] in man. What is *li* in heaven is the nature in man. Just as *li* and *ch'i* are [the same], so too are the mind and nature. They are definitely not different [from each other]." Huang issued this statement as a critique of Chu Hsi's tendency to separate nature from the mind, which embodied the feelings or sentiments *(ch'ing)* of "pleasure, anger, sorrow, and joy"—the mind's emotive and affective elements. Huang continued: "Therefore, pleasure, anger, sorrow and joy, regardless of whether they are already issued [*i-fa*] or not yet issued [*wei-fa*], are all sentiments. Their inner equilibrium and harmony is nature. . . . It is not true that there is first the nature of benevolence, righteousness, propriety and wisdom, which are then in turn issued as the mind's sympathy, shame, humility and the sense of right and wrong. . . . Therefore . . . to seek the nature outside of this cognitively natural and self-regulating mind is like abandoning the flexible and [constantly] changing *ch'i* in order to seek a separate *li*."[42]

By attributing ultimate value to *ch'i*, Huang invested human sentiments with a steadfast solidity that withstood dissolution in the putative realm of existence lying above the experiential: "Replete in heaven-and-earth is *ch'i*. The movement of this one *ch'i* in the human mind . . . naturally separates itself into pleasure, anger, sorrow and joy. Accordingly, the names of benevolence, righteousness, propriety and wisdom arise. Separated from *ch'i* there is no *li;* separated from the mind, there is no nature."[43]

Given this ontological view, it is easy to see that Huang's definition of *ko-wu* (investigation of things) was based on a scheme that suggested an intimate interrelatedness of some crucial elements in man's consciousness: "The mind has the will as its substance. The will has knowing as its substance. Knowing has things as its substance." To "investigate things" was thus to probe the workings of these "four *ch'i*"—mind, will, knowing, and things.[44] By reifying *ch'i* as the essence of the world and the cosmos, Huang forged a union between being and substance on the one hand and experience and phenomena on the other. Human actions became, then, existentially requisite and significant.

Even among scholars of Sung learning *(Sung-hsueh)* in the early Ch'ing, who by and large submitted to the dualism of the Ch'eng-Chu school, there were some who acknowledged the monistic implications of the neo-Confucian *li-ch'i* scheme. Lu Lung-ch'i (1630–1693), for instance, criticized Lo Ch'in-shun's failure to distinguish between *li, tao-hsin* (the mind of the tao) and *pen-jan chih hsing* (the originally natural nature) on the one hand and *ch'i, jen-hsin* (the mind of man) and *ch'i-chih chih hsing* (physical nature) on the other; he argued that "*li* is not separate from *ch'i,* but it is also not mixed up with *ch'i.*" To Lu, this statement clearly indicated the duality within the oneness of *li-ch'i.*[45] But Lu also stressed the importance of Chu Hsi's contention that "*ch'i* is not separate from *li,* and *li* is not separate from *ch'i.*" He explained: "What is replete inside my body [*shen*] is all *ch'i,* and what pervades and moves inside *ch'i* is *li.*" Further, he wrote: "the mind is the assemblage of the essence of *ch'i,* the source of the myriad *li.*"[46] On another occasion, Lu underscored even more plainly the importance of *ch'i:* "In the universe, there is but one *ch'i.* The *ch'i* in the universe is but one *li.* *Ch'i* cannot be separated from *li,* and *li* cannot be separated from *ch'i.*"[47] Lu, in all, accepted as a truism Chu Hsi's conception of the fundamental holism of the *li-ch'i* schema: "In the universe there has never been any *ch'i* without *li,* or *li* without *ch'i.*"[48] Ultimately, it was the idea of *i-pen* (the one fundamental source) that Lu attempted to expound. *Li* and *ch'i* achieved essential unity and union in this one fundamental source.[49]

Lu Shih-i (1611–1672), regarded as a staunch follower of the Ch'eng-Chu tradition, also moved in the direction of making inferences about the intrinsic oneness in the *li-ch'i* binary scheme. To be sure, Lu in general accepted the priority and supremacy of *li,* claiming that in "all-under-heaven, there is not one affair or thing which is not *li.*"[50] However, he also affirmed Chang Tsai's emphasis on the central importance of *ch'i:* "[Chang's] 'Western Inscription' must not be unread. Without reading the 'Western Inscription,' it will not be known that the ten thousand things are the one body of the *ch'i* image *(ch'i-hsiang).*"[51] More significantly, Lu repudiated a mechanistic distinction between the physical constitution *(ch'i-chih)* and heaven-conferred moral principle *(i-li).* Rather, he acknowledged his debt to the Tung-lin scholars with respect to the idea that "the innately good nature *(hsing-shan)* belonged to physical constitution." If one's physical constitution or nature *(hsing)* was in fact innately good, he argued, it would be incorrect "to refer to evil and attribute it to *ch'i-chih,* and refer to goodness and attribute it to *i-li.*" Man, Lu affirmed, possessed the Four Beginnings *(ssu-tuan)*—a feeling of sympathy and compassion, a sense of shame and dislike, the idea of humility and reverence, and a recognition of right and wrong. "With reference to these Four Beginnings," he wrote, "it is known that [moral principle] possesses the permanent and regular Five Constant Virtues [*wu-ch'ang,* i.e., benevolence, righteousness, propriety, knowledge, and sincerity]. With reference to the permanent and regular Five Constant Virtues, it is known that the permanent and regular Five Constant Virtues are in fact based on the virtues of *yin-yang* and the five elements [*wu-hsing*, i.e., metal, wood, water, fire, and earth]. These are not called heaven-conferred moral principle. It is not a separate thing outside of *yin-yang* and material form [*hsing-ch'i*]." In other words, within one's physical nature resided heaven-conferred moral principle, which embodied the heaven-endowed cardinal virtues. The innate goodness of human nature (*jen-hsing*) could be found precisely in physical nature.

Lu could not ignore the neo-Confucian argument that man's physical nature was potentially and probably evil. Whereas the will of heaven (*t'ien-ming*), which conferred physical nature, was universally uniform and good, physical nature, in its concrete manifestation, varied from individual to individual. Sagely people, for instance, possessed all the Five Constant Virtues in their physical nature; the ordinary could claim no such complete possession. According to Lu, it was only in such a way that one could identify physical nature with evil.[52] But by maintaining the innate and original goodness of physical nature, Lu alleviated the grudging sense of stark contrast evident in Chang Tsai's dichotomy of heaven-nature and physical nature. In the process, the realm of material endowment acquired a philosophical importance hitherto largely downplayed. In restating neo-Confucian metaphysics, Lu moved closer to an ontology of material and physical concreteness.

Li Yung (1627–1705), who attempted a syncretization of the Ch'eng-Chu and Lu-Wang approaches, also downplayed the dichotomy of *li* and *ch'i*, the inner and outer, the abstract or contemplative and the experiential. Like Lu Shih-i, Li affirmed the original goodness of physical nature. He argued that one simply could not, with alacrity, assert that nature (*hsing*) itself was good and that physical nature was bad: "If we talk about the heaven-conferred nature (*hsing*) and disregard physical nature [*ch'i-chih*], where then does this so-called heaven-conferred nature reside? Where can the so-called innately good heaven-conferred nature [*hsing-shan*] be seen? Just like the vision of the eyes, it is *ch'i*. The clarity of vision is the goodness of the heaven-conferred nature. . . . All the myriad empathies and feelings [*ying-kan*] are *ch'i*. The *tao* is fully realized with empathies and feelings. . . . If there were no such *ch'i*, even if the heaven-conferred nature was innately good, how could its goodness be seen?"[53]

The *tao* was thus perceived by Li not as an abstract entity, but as "daily utility and quotidian practicality" (*jih-yung ch'ang-hsing*). Contrary to conventional Taoist wisdom, as expounded in the first line of the *Tao-te ching* (The Way and its power), the *tao* that counted in Li's estimation was "the *tao* that can be verbally articulated" (*k'o-tao chih tao*). This *tao* manifested itself in the five social relationships, prescribing "the constants of heaven-and-earth" *(t'ien-ti ch'ang-ching)* and "the order of human relationships" *(jen-sheng lun-chi)*. One must ceaselessly examine one's mind and one's physical constitution, he believed, so as to make certain that there were no thoughts and deeds that ran counter to benevolence, righteousness, propriety, humane intelligence, and sincerity. By so cultivating oneself in action *(hsiu-hsing)*, the principle of heaven *(t'ien-li)* could be realized.[54]

It seems safe to say that in the early Ch'ing, the philosophy of *ch'i* had attained a certain universal validity, as evidenced in the thoughts of the eponymous scholars. The denial of the ontological and epistemological tension between *li* and *ch'i* became virtually a token of the authenticity of early Ch'ing thought. The *problematik* of this dualism found its dissolution in the dynamic monism of *ch'i*. However, in spite of its universality, as I have indicated, the philosophy of *ch'i* was seldom coherently presented in the realm of formal metaphysical speculation. (Wang Fu-chih was, perhaps, the primary exception.) In fact, this sort of thinking became expendable, for pure contemplation on corporeality and concreteness was nonetheless pure contemplation. Therefore, *ch'i* did not become an abstract term confined to the domain of formal thought. Rather, it served as the ontological point of departure from which Ch'ing thinkers launched their manifold intellectual undertakings. Ku Yen-wu, Huang Tsung-hsi and Wang Fu-chih delved into a host of subjects, such as historical scholarship, institutional studies, and research on the classics.[55] The Ch'ing conception of *ch'i* gave rise to a particular ontology that, as we have suggested, was vitalist in nature, appealing not so much to symbolic metaphysical constructs as to the actualities grasped in everyday life.

This vitalist sensibility found full expression in the eighteenth century with a strong affirmation of the primacy of materiality and the nominally natural. Hui Tung (1697–1758), a classical exegete, commented on *li* and *tao,* for example: "*Li* is the pattern of how things [*wu*] are formed. The *tao* is that which is formed by the ten thousand things. Therefore it is said, 'The tao is *li*.' " Hui objected to seeing *li* solely as the rational, true, innately virtuous and universally valid aspect of human nature, and believed that desires *(yü)* were equally a part of both nature *(hsing)* and heaven's decree *(t'ien-ming)*. Principle and the Way were derived from things, which included human desires and feelings.[56]

Tai Chen (1723–1777) systematically developed a philosophy based on the fundamental presupposition that all existents were things. He said:"*Tao* is the name which refers to actual bodies and actual affairs. . . . Speaking of the *tao* in terms of heaven-and-earth, it can be readily seen with reference to its actual bodies and actual affairs. . . . Speaking of the *tao* in terms of man, it is the concrete affairs of quotidian practicality in human relations which pervade the *tao*. . . . None that arises from the body is not the *tao*. . . . The *tao* is living, drinking, eating, talking and moving. One's self and what immediately surround oneself are all appropriately [regarded as the *tao*]." In other words, the *tao* was nothing but the concrete ordinary experience in life, the quotidian practicality in human relations. Of course, this *tao* still embodied the inalienable moral and ethical criteria of benevolence, righteousness, and propriety so that, as Tai put it, "in the realization of quotidian practicality in human relaions, there is no flaw."[57]

Tai Chen criticized the Sung neo-Confucians for artificially separating those moral criteria from everyday social relations and activities. These scholars called the assemblage of benevolence, righteousness, and propriety *li* (principle), which they considered above the realm of corporeal forms *(hsing erh shang)*—"empty, boundless and subtle." In contrast, they regarded the quotidian practicality in human relations as amidst the realm of corporeal forms *(hsing erh hsia)* with its "multivalent and multifarious manifestations." Tai imputed this conceptualization to the Taoist and Buddhist abandonment of human relations and daily utility in favor of a separate noble way *(kuei-tao)*. On this conceptualization was premised the Sung Confucians' discourse on *li*. Tai concluded: "[The Sung Confucians claimed that] with respect to heaven-and-earth, *yin-yang* cannot be called the *tao;* with respect to man, the physical endowment *(ch'i-ping)* cannot be called nature; affairs and things relating to the quotidian practicality in human relations cannot be called the *tao*. There is nothing in the words of the Six Classics, Confucius and Mencius that agrees with them."[58]

Principle to Tai was not abstract and transcendent. As he stated, "With regard to heaven-and-earth, men and things, and affairs and deeds, [I] have not heard of *li* which could not be verbally articulated."[59] Yü Ying-shih has shown how Tai set out to demolish the *li-ch'i* dichotomy by defining *li* as the inner texture of things *(t'iao-li)*. *Li* (and thus the *tao* and the so-called original substance or *pen-t'i*) did not exist in the mind as an independent metaphysical entity but was found in all things in the world. In brief, *li* became nothing more than the organizational pattern and textural configuration of *ch'i*. In terms of man, *li* could therefore not be divorced from desires *(yü)* and feelings *(ch'ing)*, that is, *ch'i*. It simply manifested and fulfilled *ch'i*.

Tai further elaborated on the meaning of the *li-yü* nexus by differentiating between what was natural *(tzu-jan)* and what was necessitarian *(pi-jan)*:

"The desires of nature are the signs of the natural. The virtue of nature is conducive to the attainment of necessity. What is conducive to the attainment of necessity conforms to and perfects what is natural about Heaven and Earth. This is called the utmost attainment of the natural."[60] The natural was thus *yü* and the daily activities of men; the necessitarian was the internal texture of the natural, that is, *li*. The natural was the foundation on which the necessitarian principle rested. Tai further opined: "The ears, the eyes, and all the other bodily organs desire those things on which our physical nature [*ch'i-chih chih hsing*] depends for nourishment. The so-called desires of human nature originate from the process of the formation and transformation of Heaven and Earth [*t'ien-tao*]; in the case of man, they are rooted in human nature and find expression in his daily affairs; in this sense, they form the Way of man [*jen-tao*]."[61]

If desires, integrally a part of physical nature, constituted both the way of heaven and the way of man, it would obviously be incorrect to treat human nature as truncated and to pit physical nature against heaven-nature, as Ch'eng and Chu had done. After all, the term "physical nature" was merely their invention. According to Tai, human nature *(hsing)* as a wholesome totality comprised blood and breath *(hsueh-ch'i)* and mind and knowing *(hsin-chih)*. The former was the psychophysiological, or, for short, physical, nature; the latter was the cognitive-spiritual nature. Both, as a whole, were derived from the "*yin* and *yang* and the five elements," and "originated from the process of the production and transformation of heaven-and-earth" *(yuan yü t'ien-ti chih hua)*.

Tai explicated the various manifestations of these two natures in specifically social human terms:

> What blood and breath depend on for nourishment are sounds, colors, smells and tastes. With mind . . . we know that there are [the relationships of] father and son, elder and younger brother, husband and wife. [Such knowledge] does not extend only to the confines of family relations. We also know that there are ruler and minister, and that there are friends. These five relationships establish among themselves affinity and order. Following feelings and stimuli come the appropriate responses of pleasure, anger, sorrow and joy. Combining the desires for sound, color, smell and taste with the feelings of pleasure, anger, sorrow and joy, there is the complete way of man. Desires are rooted in blood and breath, and so they are called nature.

Nature was ineluctably one, notwithstanding its embodiment of both the psychophysiological and cognitive-spiritual natures. The Sung neo-Confucians were wrong, Tai thought, in failing to regard physical nature as the original nature derived from heaven. In narrowly singling out only innate moral principles *(i-li)* as originating from heaven and hence as the heaven-conferred nature, they had, in Tai's judgment, erroneously interpreted the Mencian view of human nature, which referred to "the nature of blood and breath, of mind and knowing." The following rhetorical question neatly sums up Tai Chen's view on the nature of man: "As for the fact that a man is a man, if physical endowment [*ch'i-ping*] and physical constitution [*ch'i-chih*] are discarded, in what way can a man be described as a man?"[62]

Tai's arguments struck at the heart of the central neo-Confucian notion that *li, t'ien-tao,* and *i-li chih hsing* were prior and fundamentally substantive. To Tai, the stuff out of which the universe was wrought came from the realm of the natural and corporeal, defined in neo-Confucian metaphysics as the realm of *ch'i.* Tai's philosophy was in essence integrative *(li* in *ch'i)* as opposed to dualistic *(li* vis-à-vis *ch'i);* it stressed, in short, the materiality and concreteness of being. Following in the footsteps of Tai Chen, though by no means as systematically, thinkers such as Chiao Hsun (1763–1820) and Juan Yuan (1764–1849) also expressed a monistic *ch'i*-oriented view of human nature.

Both Chiao and Juan rejected the artificial and tension-ridden distinction between *hsing* (heaven-conferred nature) and feelings and desires. Chiao remarked: "The heaven-conferred nature is a *yang* of the *tao;* feelings are a *yin* of the *tao.* . . . Nature is inert when it is born with man. When it communicates with other men, it becomes feelings and desires. . . . As [the *Li-chi* (Record of rites)] states, '[A man] acts when [he] is affected by things. It is due to the desires of his nature.' . . . When blood and breath, and mind and knowing become, the feelings of pleasure, anger, sorrow and joy, desires arise. Desires originate from nature." Chiao asserted that "to talk about goodness while ignoring feelings, to seek benevolence while ignoring desires, and to illuminate the *tao* while ignoring capability" was to misconstrue the meanings of the sages' teachings.[63]

As with Tai Chen, Chiao sought to restore the holism intrinsic to the Mencian conception of human nature, which had been torn asunder by the Sung neo-Confucians. To Chiao, what Mencius regarded as nature included physical nature—the mouth as regards tastes, the eyes as regards colors, the ears as regards sounds, the nose as regards smells, and the limbs as regards rest. What were known as benevolence, righteousness, propriety, and wisdom were in actuality names reifying blood and breath, mind and knowing. They were the virtues that "originated in the process of the production and transformation of heaven-and-earth." Thus the way of heaven could be realized if "all under heaven" appropriately followed the desires of their mouths, noses, ears, and eyes and accommodated "the constant workings of benevolence, righteousness, propriety and wisdom."[64] Chiao thus proposed an ontology that examined man's being as it was lived from within itself, courageously coming to grips with its feelings and desires.

Echoing Chiao Hsun and Tai Chen, Juan Yuan sought to allay the neo-Confucian tension between nature and desires, the physical and the innately moral. *Hsing* (nature) must comprise both blood and breath and mind and knowing, he averred.[65] Nature and feelings were consequently not at odds with each other: "Feelings stem from nature. . . . Tasting, seeing, hearing, smelling, pleasure, anger, sorrow and joy are all based on nature and manifested as feelings. Feelings are included within nature. They are not autonomous entities on their own, separated from and counterposing nature."[66] And again: "Desires are born within feelings and are inside nature. It cannot be said that within nature there is no desire. Desire is not the evil [referred to] in the goodness-evil [polarity]."[67]

Juan rejected the neo-Confucian notion of the mind as the internal, original substance *(pen-t'i)*, empty of any consciously specific concepts and sensations. Instead, he interpreted the mind as that which was "delicate, minute and sharp," inexorably exposed to and in contact with its surroundings. Elucidating the etymology of the word *hsin,* Juan pointed out that it could mean the sharp, small thorns of the jujube tree and not the heart wrapped inside the bark. He cited the *Book of Odes* in which there was the line: "[The wind] blows at the heart of jujube until it looks tender and beautiful." He then asked, "If the heart was really inside, how could it be that the wind could blow at it?" In so defining the heart, by metaphorical extension, Juan redefined the mind as an entity that obtained knowledge through perception and analysis of the phenomenal world. Just as the "heart" of the jujube tree became tender and beautiful with the blowing wind, so, too, the human mind became enlightened and achieved knowledge through contact and interplay with the experiential world.[68]

In all, a vitalist impulse animated the thinking of Ch'ing scholars. It made *ch'i* and its attendant manifestations an ultimate principle of reality. But strictly speaking, such thinking could not be labeled as materialism or naturalism in the Western sense of these words. For instance, material human desires alone were never considered principle in themselves, even though they were inseparably an authentic part of the heaven-conferred nature, which had to be nurtured and properly cultivated. The concrete reality of

Ch'ing vitalism was in many ways, as Thomas Metzger puts it, "teleologically infused with divine meaning." Putative notions of *li* and *tao* continued to loom large; dynamism was often still explained pseudoscientifically in terms of the workings of *yin* and *yang*. The important point is, however, that in the Ch'ing, all these metaphysical categories were largely apprehended with reference to the sphere of materiality.[69]

Equivocation, ambivalence, and ambiguities notwithstanding, the Ch'ing vitalist sensibility, with the predicate of *ch'i,* had significantly altered the traditional neo-Confucian perception and conception of the universe. It established, as it were, a commonsensical state of affairs in two moves: First, it discredited the notion that *li* and *tao* could be grasped noetically as actualities obtained from heaven and embodied in the mind. Second, it acknowledged man and other beings as independent and dynamic particulars —as alternative bases of ultimate reality. It seems unquestionable that already by the seventeenth century, *ch'i* had been invested with a new content and significance, so much so that it became the supreme substance in the ontological realm. From it stemmed the mature vitalism of the eighteenth century—mature because by then, the primacy of *ch'i* was taken for granted and ceased to be problematic. Formalistic metaphysical discussion on *li* and *ch'i* had ceased to be central in Ch'ing intellectual discourse. For this reason, Tai Chen's systematic and detailed philosophical and metaphysical studies were deemed empty and not taken seriously by many scholars.[70] In light of the mid-Ch'ing climate of thought, these studies assumed merely a centrist, as opposed to a central, position.

In short, vitalism, though *ch'i*-based, could by no means be properly understood as a formal philosophy in the vein of neo-Confucian metaphysics. Rather, it was a fundamental attitude or disposition assigning centrality to concrete things and their changes. It was an ontology that found life's meaning, possibilities, and motives in the actualities of a corporeal world, mitigating the role of symbolic completions and harmonies. The "ten thousand things," and especially man with his experiential life, became worthy (perhaps the only truly worthy) subjects of intellectual investigation. Knowledge acquired through the intercourse of the senses with the external world *(wen-chien chih chih)* now claimed clear priority over moral knowledge acquired through spontaneous knowing *(te-hsing chih chih).*[71]

This development was paradoxical, for the decline of the formal philosophy of *ch'i* owed much to its triumph in transposing itself into an extreme nominalist attitude toward life and learning—a commonsense realism, so to speak. Ironically, an ontology that metaphysically established the veridicality of the experiential and corporeal tolled the death knell of ontology itself. Metaphysics, dissolved in the ametaphysical temper of the age, was translated into other modes of intellectual reflection that would do justice to the multiplicity and dynamism of concrete things and phenomena—classical, historical, scientific, and cosmological studies. Thus, the proper matrix for the study of mid-Ch'ing self-consciousness must not be the victory of the philosophy of *ch'i* qua philosophy. Rather, it should be the success of solid learning yielded by a reformulated neo-Confucian ontology of vitalism. With the decline of the metaphysical criteria of intelligibility, any discussion of ontology that sought to reveal the essence of being was, almost inexorably, emotionally flaccid, although at times intellectually necessary. Despite its ontological roots, Ch'ing vitalism represented the attenuation of ontology in Ch'ing thought. A full-fledged metaphysical ontology gave way to a watered-down vitalist ontology.

Notes

This chapter is a revised version of a paper of the same title presented in August 1986 at the annual meeting of the Pacific Coast Branch of the American Historical Association. The author gratefully acknowledges the comments of Professors D. W. Y. Kwok, Kwang-Ching Liu, Benjamin Elman, and Kai-wing Chow.

1. The "Ch'ing" in this paper refers to the period from the Ming-Ch'ing transition to the high Ch'ing, from approximately the early seventeenth to the early nineteenth century.

2. William T. de Bary, "Neo-Confucian Cultivation and the Seventeenth-Century 'Enlightenment,' " in *The Unfolding of Neo-Confucianism,* ed. William T. de Bary (New York, 1975), pp. 194–195.

3. Michael A. Weinstein, *Structure of Human Life: A Vitalist Ontology* (New York and London, 1976), p. ix.

4. Ibid., pp. ix–xi, 1–23. I have paraphrased some of Weinstein's remarks.

5. Yamanoi Yū, *Minshin shisōshi kenkyū* (Studies on Ming-Ch'ing intellectual history) (Tokyo, 1980), p. 162. For Yamanoi's often insightful discussion on the rise and the development of the philosophy of *ch'i* since the Late Ming, see pp. 149–198.

6. Irene Bloom, "On the 'Abstraction' of Ming Thought: Some Concrete Evidence from the Philosophy of Lo Ch'in-shun," in *Principle and Practicality,* ed. W. T. de Bary and Irene Bloom (New York, 1979), p. 76. Bloom criticizes Liang Ch'i-ch'ao for failing to discuss the importance of *ch'i* in his well-known book on intellectual trends in the Ch'ing dynasty.

7. See, e.g., de Bary, "Neo-Confucian Cultivation," p. 203.

8. Bloom, "On the 'Abstraction' of Ming Thought," pp. 76, 98–106.

9. Quoted in Ian McMorran, "Wang Fu-chih and the Neo-Confucian Tradition," in de Bary, *Unfolding,* p. 431.

10. Kao P'an-lung, *Kao-tzu i-shu* (Surviving writings of Master Kao) (1876 ed.) 3:32a–b.

11. For a systematic discussion of Chang Tsai's thought, see Ira E. Kasoff, *The Thought of Chang Tsai (1020–1077)* (Cambridge, 1984). See in particular, pp. 36–53, 66–81 for Chang's ideas on *ch'i* and human nature.

12. Kao, *Kao-tzu i-shu* 3:34a–35b.

13. Ibid. 1:21a.

14. Huang Tsung-hsi, *Ming-ju hsueh-an* (Scholarly records of the Ming Confucians) (Beijing, 1985), p. 1520.

15. Ibid., p. 1521.

16. Quoted in Ch'ien Mu, *Chung-kuo chin-san-pai-nien hsueh-shu-shih* (A history of Chinese learning and scholarship during the last three hundred years) (Taipei, 1964) 1:23–24.

17. Ibid. See also Thomas A. Metzger, *Escape from Predicament: Neo-Confucianism and China's Evolving Political Culture* (New York, 1977), p. 163.

18. This aspect of Liu Tsung-chou's thought has been well discussed in T'ang Chün-i, "Liu Tsung-chou's Doctrine of Moral Mind and Practice and His Critique of Wang Yang-ming," in de Bary, *Unfolding,* pp. 305–331.

19. Wang's thought in this regard has been admirably examined elsewhere by able scholars. See, e.g., McMorran (see n. 9, above), and also Chung-ying Cheng, "Reason, Substance, and Human Desires in Seventeenth-Century Neo-Confucianism," in de Bary, *Unfolding,* pp. 469–509.

20. Wang Fu-chih, *Ssu-wen lu nei-pien* (Inner chapters of the records of reflections and inquiries), collected in *Ch'uan-shan i-shu* (Surviving writings of [Wang] Ch'uan-shan) (hereafter abbreviated as CSIS), (Shanghai: 1935), 12b.

21. *Chang-tzu Cheng-meng chu* (Annotations to Master Chang's correct disciplines for beginners) collected in CSIS 1:5b.

22. Ibid. 1:6b.

23. Quoted in McMorran, p. 443. Note that McMorran seizes on the fundamental similarity between Wang and Chang on this issue and neglects the nuanced differences.

24. Kasoff, *The Thought of Chang Tsai,* pp. 73–74.

25. Quoted in McMorran, "Neo-Confucian Tradition," pp. 443–444.

26. *Tu Ssu-shu ta-ch'uan shuo* (Discourse on readings of the Four Books), collected in CSIS 8:10b–11a.

27. *Ssu-shu hsun-i* (Admonishing meanings of the Four Books), collected in CSIS 26:2a–3a.

28. Quoted in McMorran, "Neo-Confucian Tradition," p. 448.

29. *Tu Ssu-shu ta-ch'uan shuo* 7:11a–b.

30. McMorran has also noted that, because Wang conceived of the universe as a

dynamic whole of ever-changing *ch'i*, he developed a sense of history characterized by the stress on making appropriate changes in particular time and space, spurning symbolic constructs that presumed universality and eternality. See McMorran, "Neo-Confucian Tradition," pp. 453–457.

31. Yamanoi, *Minshin shisōshi kenkyū*, p. 166.

32. Ku Yen-wu, *Jih chih lu* (Records of daily knowledge) (Shanghai, 1934) 1:20.

33. Ibid.

34. Ibid.

35. Ibid. 6:110.

36. Quoted in Hou Wai-lu, *Chung-kuo ssu-hsiang t'ung-shih* (A comprehensive history of Chinese thought) (Beijing, 1980) 5:211–213.

37. Ibid., p. 214.

38. *Jih chih lu* 3:19–20.

39. *Ming-ju hsueh-an,* p. 140.

40. Ibid., p. 1064.

41. Ibid., p. 46.

42. Ibid., pp. 1109–1110.

43. Ibid., p. 1512.

44. Huang Tsung-hsi, *Nan-lei wen-ting ch'ien-chi* (Former chapters of the *Established writings of [Huang] Nan-lei*), collected in *Ming-Ch'ing shih-liao hui-pien* (A Compilation of Ming-Ch'ing historical sources), ed. Shen Yun-lung (Taipei, 1969) 5:456–457.

45. Lu Lung-ch'i, *Wen-hsueh lu* (Record of inquiry and learning) (Shanghai, 1936), p. 18.

46. Lu Lung-ch'i, *San-yü-t'ang wen-chi* (Writings from the Three Fish Studio) (1701 ed.) 1:3b–6a.

47. Ibid., *wai-chi* 1:6a.

48. Wing-tsit Chan, *A Source Book in Chinese Philosophy* (Princeton, N.J.: 1963), p. 634.

49. *San-yu-t'ang wen-chi* 1:3b–5a.

50. Lu Shih-i, *Ssu-pien-lu chi-yao* (Interpretive abridgment of *Reflection on Things at Hand*) (Shanghai, 1936), p. 25.

51. Ibid., p. 6.

52. Lu Shih-i, *Hsing-shan t'u-shuo* (Diagrammatic discourse on the innate goodness of nature), collected in *Lu Fu-t'ing hsien-sheng i-shu* (Surviving writings of Mr. Lu Fu-t'ing) (1899 ed.), 1a–9b.

53. Li Yung, *Li Erh-ch'u hsien-sheng ch'üan-chi* (Complete collected works of Mr. Li Erh-ch'u) (1930 ed.) 4:1b–2a.

54. Ibid. 10:2a.

55. On the emphasis on practicality in seventeenth-century neo-Confucianism, see Wing-tsit Chan, "The *Hsing-li ching-i* and the Ch'eng-Chu School of the Seventeenth Century," in de Bary, *Unfolding,* pp. 543–579.

58   ON-CHO NG

56. Cited in Yang Hsiang-k'uei, *Chung-kuo ku-tai she-hui yü ku-tai ssu-hsiang yen-chiu* (Studies on ancient Chinese society and thought) (Shanghai, 1964) 2:910–911.

57. Tai Chen, *Meng-tzu tzu-i shu-cheng* (Evidential textual investigation of the meanings of the words of Mencius) (Beijing, 1956), pp. 69–72.

58. Ibid., pp. 71–72.

59. Ibid., p. 38.

60. Yü Ying-shih, "Tai Chen and the Chu Hsi Tradition," in *Essays in Commemoration of the Golden Jubilee of the Fung Ping Shan Library,* ed. Chan Ping-leung, et al. (Hong Kong, 1982), pp. 386–389. See also Chung-ying Cheng, *Tai Chen's Inquiry into Goodness* (Honolulu, 1971), pp. 14–53.

61. Translated in Chung-ying Cheng, *Tai Chen,* pp. 76–77.

62. See the essay titled *"Hsing,"* in *Meng-tzu tzu-i shu-cheng,* pp. 51–64.

63. Quoted in Hou Wai-lu 5:559–560.

64. Chiao Hsun, *Meng-tzu cheng-i* (Correct Meanings of *Mencius*) (Taipei, 1965) 8:80.

65. Juan Yuan, *Yen-ching-shih chi* (Collected writings from the Studio of Classical Studies) (Taipei, 1967), p. 169.

66. Ibid., p. 199.

67. Ibid., p. 206.

68. Ibid., p. 4.

69. Metzger, pp. 162–163, 173–174.

70. Benjamin A. Elman, *From Philosophy to Philology: Intellectual and Social Aspects of Change in Late Imperial China* (Cambridge, 1984), pp. 19–20.

71. Yü Ying-shih, "Ch'ing-tai hsueh-shu ssu-hsiang-shih chung-yao kuan-nien t'ung-shih" (Elucidation of important concepts in the history of Ch'ing learning and thought," *Shih-hsueh p'ing-lun* 5 (January 1983): 45–55.

4

The Revaluation of Benevolence *(Jen)* in Ch'ing Dynasty Evidential Research

BENJAMIN A. ELMAN

Michel Foucault has noted that periodically a society suddenly stops thinking the way it did and its leading voices strike out in new and different directions: "Thus, in place of the continuous chronology of reason, which was invariably traced back to some inaccessible origin, there have appeared scales that are sometimes very brief, distinct from one another, irreducible to a single law, scales that bear a type of history peculiar to each one, and which cannot be reduced to the general model of consciousness that acquires, progresses, and remembers."[1]

In European intellectual history, such discontinuities in discourse reveal how the formation of concepts and their modes of connection and coexistence can change dramatically from one epoch to another. More often than not, what we frequently refer to as a zeitgeist (spirit of an age) is a shorthand method for discerning the modes of thinking peculiar to a particular historical epoch. Such a "map of the mental universe" of an age presents us with its predominant concerns and new directions. In Foucault's terms, an archaeological analysis of knowledge reveals that at any given moment there are discernable prerequisites that define epistemologically the conditions for acceptable knowledge and inference, whether expressed in theory or "silently invested" in practice.[2]

The seventeenth century in Europe marked such a discontinuity in the history of Western philosophy. The "great grid of empirical knowledge" that emerged three centuries ago represented a fundamental shift among elites in the common codes of knowledge through which the world was perceived. The mental vocabulary of educated Europeans during the eighteenth-century Enlightenment in turn reinforced this shift from Christian rationalism to skeptical and secular empiricism.[3]

After the British empiricists John Locke (1632–1704), George Berkeley (1685–1753), and David Hume (1711–1776) set up the principle that prior to all other philosophic considerations one must determine how far human reason extends, epistemology, the theory of knowledge, was raised to the highest level of philosophic priority. Until then, with exceptions, the outlook or program that stressed the power of a priori reason to grasp substantial truths about the world—that is, rationalism, had dominated Scholastic and Renaissance thought.[4] By making experience rather than reason the source of acceptable knowledge, empiricists contended that the legitimate reach of human ideas should be evaluated by the manner in which such ideas arise. This program was possible only by exact delineation of the sources from which knowledge was derived and of the course of development that brought it about. An epistemological position that stressed that valid knowledge must be corroborated by external facts and impartial observations in turn added impetus to study of the natural world and the concomitant emergence of the scientific revolution.

I have argued at length elsewhere that a similar epistemological revolution occurred among elites in seventeenth-century China.[5] For reasons quite different from the European case, there occurred in Confucian discourse a remarkable turn from neo-Confucian rationalism typified by the philosophy of Chu Hsi (1130–1200), to a commitment to empirically based philological inquiry. In sharp contrast to their neo-Confucian predecessors, Ch'ing scholars of evidential research (*k'ao-cheng*, lit., search for evidence) stressed exacting research, rigorous analysis, and the collection of impartial evidence drawn from ancient artifacts and historical documents and texts. Abstract ideas and a priori rational argumentation gave way as the primary objects of discussion among leading Confucians to concrete facts, verifiable institutions, and historical events.[6]

Although their epistemological position was not as clearly articulated as by their European contemporaries, Ch'ing evidential scholars also made verification a central concern for the emerging empirical theory of knowledge they advocated.[7] This program involved the placing of *cheng* (proof) and *cheng* (verification) at the center of the organization and analysis of the classical tradition. A full-blown scientific revolution did not ensue, but it is interesting and significant that *k'ao-cheng* scholars made astronomy, mathematics, and geography high priorities in their research programs.[8]

Animated by a concern to restore native traditions in the precise sciences to their proper place of eminence, after receiving ridicule and little attention during the Ming dynasty, evidential scholars such as Tai Chen (1724–

1777), Ch'ien Ta-hsin (1728–1804), and Juan Yuan (1764–1849) successfully incorporated technical aspects of Western astronomy and mathematics into the Confucian framework. Ch'ien Ta-hsin, in particular, acknowledged this broadening of the Confucian tradition, which he saw as the reversal of centuries of focus on moral and philosophic problems: "In ancient times, no one could be a Confucian who did not know mathematics. . . . Chinese methods [now] lag behind Europe's because Confucians do not know mathematics."[9]

In contrast to their neo-Confucian predecessors, Ch'ing evidential research scholars inhabited a climate of criticism stimulated by their discovery of precise empirical methods to verify and evaluate knowledge drawn from a wide variety of sources. In general, they took Sung and Ming neo-Confucian discourse to be an obstacle to verifiable truth because it seemed to discourage further inquiry along empirical lines. During this time, scholars and critics had begun to apply historical analysis to the Confucian classics. Classical commentary by now had yielded to textual criticism.

As Foucault has perceptively noted, "Commentary halts before the precipice of the original text, and assumes the impossible and endless task of repeating its own birth within itself: it sacralizes language."[10] Criticism, on the other hand, can analyze a text, however sacred, only in light of truth, accuracy, or expressive value. It desacralizes or, in more recent parlance, deconstructs language so that the textual monuments of classical traditions are reduced to their vocabularies, their syntaxes, or the sounds of their languages.

In the late seventeenth century, Yen Jo-chü (1636–1704) dramatically demonstrated that the Old Text chapters of the *Shang-shu* (Documents classic) were a later forgery and not the original chapters discovered in the second century B.C. Hu Wei (1633–1714), Yen's friend and colleague, exposed the heterodox origins of neo-Confucian cosmograms. Such studies brought in their wake corrosive implications that would not end in the seventeenth and eighteenth centuries. A form of criticism emerged in elite circles that would one day exceed the Confucian boundaries Ch'ing scholars attempted to impose.[11]

Language itself became an object of investigation. So much so, that the foundations of contemporary Chinese linguistics and phonology were laid during this period. Tai Chen described such investigation as follows: "The Classics provide the route to the *tao*. What illuminates the *tao* is the words [of the Classics]. How words are formed can be grasped only through [a knowledge of] philology and paleography. From [the study of] primary and derived characters we can master the language. Through the language we can penetrate the mind and will of the ancient sages and worthies."[12] The distinguished classicist and historian Wang Ming-sheng (1722–1798) echoed Tai's words: "The Classics are employed to understand the *tao*. But those who seek the *tao* should not cling vacuously to 'meanings and principles' [*i-li*] in order to find it. If only they will correct primary and derived characters, discern their pronunciation, read the explanations and glosses, and master the commentaries and notes, the 'meanings and principles' will appear on their own, and the *tao* within them."[13]

Their program was taken quite literally by thousands of Confucians trained in *k'ao-cheng* methods during the eighteenth and nineteenth centuries. In this way, students of evidential research were determined to pierce what they considered the thick veil of Sung and Ming metaphysical and cosmological systems of thought—known popularly as *tao-hsueh* (studies of the *tao*), that is, neo-Confucianism. They hoped thereby to recapture the pristine meaning formulated by the sage-kings of antiquity in the Confucian classics. They were in effect calling into question the dominant imperial ideology, the Ch'eng-Chu tradition, which the Manchu rulers had enshrined as the proper norm in imperial examinations and official ideology. Toward the end of the eighteenth century, the prestige of the classics, though outwardly unchanged, had actually diminished appreciably among scholars. Using the phrase "the Six Classics are all Histories," Chang Hsueh-ch'eng (1738–1801) placed the timeless classics within the framework of the endless flux of history, and Chang was not unique in his appraisal, even in the eighteenth century.[14]

Philosophic concepts were not immune to this sort of empirical analysis either. Though most *k'ao-cheng* scholars preferred the comfortable confines of an empirical program for research that left little room for theoretical discussion, a few, led by Tai Chen, saw in linguistic analysis (*hsun-ku*, glossing of terms) the key to a new and more precise etymological approach to traditional philosophical questions. Important Confucian concepts and ideals, as a result of Tai Chen's influence, were subjected to philological study. A methodology that had proven fruitful in textual criticism gave promise of being equally productive in moral philosophy.

The Revaluation of Benevolence

One of the most telling classical passages, associated with Confucius himself, was the master's response to his disciple Yen Yuan's query concerning benevolence *(jen).*[15] According to D. C. Lau's translation, Confucius re-marked: "*To return to the observance of the rites through overcoming the self constitutes benevolence. If for a single day a person could return to the observance of the rites through overcoming himself, then the whole Empire would consider benevolence to be his. However, the practice of benevolence depends on oneself alone, and not on others.*"[16] The keys to this passage in the *Analects* are the two phrases *k'o-chi fu-li wei-jen* and *wei-jen yu-chi,* italicized in the translation above.

In his commentary to this passage, Chu Hsi, whose views on the matter were regarded as orthodox in the imperial examination system from 1313 until 1905, gave the following glosses for the phrase *k'o-chi:* "*K'o* means to conquer [*sheng*]. *Chi* refers to the selfish desires of the self [*shen chih ssu-yü*]. According to Chu Hsi, this passage meant that "to practice *jen* [*wei-jen*], one must conquer the selfish desires of the self and return to the observance of the rites." In this manner, the perfect virtue of the original mind *(pen-hsin chih ch'üan-te),* which Chu equated with heavenly principle *(t'ien-li),* could be attained.[17]

It was precisely Chu Hsi's gloss, "to conquer the selfish desires of the self," for *k'o-chi* to which many Ch'ing critics objected. Tai Chen saw in this gloss confirmation of Chu Hsi's bifurcation of human desires from heavenly principle. Chu was in effect reading into this passage from the *Analects* his own bifurcation between *li* [moral principles] and *ch'i*—variously rendered as "material force," "ether," and "stuff."[18]

Tai's critique of Chu Hsi's latent dualism drew on his philological train-ing. He contended that, if Chu Hsi's gloss of *chi* as "selfish desires of the self" were correct, then it made the following phrase in the text *wei-jen yu-chi* incomprehensible. How could the practice of jen *(wei-jen)* proceed from the selfish desires of the self *(yu-chi)?* This is what logically followed if Chu's gloss were used for *chi* in both *k'o-chi* and *yu-chi.* Chu Hsi's interpre-tation, Tai argued, was thus contradictory.[19] Chu's definition of human desires *(yü)* was the key issue for Tai Chen. In his discussion of the *k'o-chi* passage Tai noted: "Lao-tzu, Chuang-tzu, and the Buddha [all spoke of] 'having no desires' [*wu-yü*], not of 'having no selfishness' [*wu-ssu*]. The way of the sages and worthies was 'to have no selfishness' and not 'to have no desires.' To equate [the self] with selfish desires is therefore a notion the sages totally lacked."[20]

The theoretical debate was drawn over the affirmation or negation of human desires. For Tai Chen, the Chu Hsi line of inquiry had scorned the essential characteristics of humanity in favor of attention to heavenly principles: "The sages ordered the world by giving an outlet to people's feelings [ch'ing] and by making it possible for them to realize their desires [yü]. In this way, the tao of the sages was brought to completion. . . . With regard to the Sung Confucians, however, [the people] believe in them, thinking that they are the equivalent of the sages. Everyone can talk about the distinction between moral principles [li] and human desires. Therefore, those who control the people today pay no attention to the sages giving an outlet to people's feelings and making it possible for them to realize their desires."[21] Tai's political criticism of the way in which classical values had been used to stifle the interests of the common people was a direct result of his revaluation of the Chu Hsi interpretation of classical terms such as jen.

We should recognize that Tai Chen's critique was not altogether unique. Although it is hard to demonstrate any direct link to Tai between Yen Yuan (1633–1704) and Li Kung (1659–1733), both had already taken Chu Hsi to task for his interpretation of the k'o-chi fu-li wei-jen passage.[22] Yen, for example, had earlier linked Chu Hsi's mistaken interpretation to his tendency to view human desires in light of the bifurcation between li and ch'i. In an essay titled "To refute that the nature of material form is evil," Yen said: "If one claims that ch'i is evil, then li is too. If one claims that li is good, then so is ch'i. In all likelihood, ch'i is the ch'i of li, and li is the li of ch'i. How can one argue that li alone is good and that material form on the other extreme is evil?"[23]

In addition, Yen Yuan accused Chu Hsi of bringing in Hsun-tzu's theory that human nature was evil through the back door, and thus of compromising Mencius' correct view that human nature was good.[24] Tai Chen, several decades later, did much the same. Affirming that material form (ch'i-chih) was inherent in the nature of man, Tai wrote: "Sung Confucians in establishing their theories appear the same as Mencius, but in reality they differ. They appear different from Hsun-tzu, but in reality they are the same."[25] Then Tai added: "Today we see that Mencius was the same as Confucius and that Ch'eng [I] and Chu [Hsi] were the same as Hsun-[tzu] and Yang [Chu]. . . . What the latter called nature [hsing] was not what Confucius and Mencius had called nature. What [Ch'eng I and Chu Hsi] called the nature of material form [ch'i-chih chih hsing], isn't this what Hsun-[tzu] and Yang [Chu] called nature?"[26]

From a discussion of the meaning of jen, the debate with Chu Hsi had carried over into the nature of man and the problem of human desires. It did not end there, however. Tai and his followers were reevaluating and continuing, in historical terms, a major philosophic debate that had animated late

Ming Confucianism as well. In the process, *k'ao-cheng* scholars like Tai, Juan Yuan, and Chiao Hsun (1763–1820) were throwing their weight behind a rejection of what they perceived as the pernicious influence of Ch'eng-Chu dualism in favor of a more practical and down-to-earth interpretation of classical values and ideals.[27]

From Tai Chen to Juan Yuan

The emergence of *k'ao-cheng* philosophy took a while before it was accepted by more empirically minded scholars. In addition, more orthodox contemporaries of Tai Chen, such as Chang Hsueh-ch'eng, were troubled by attacks on Chu Hsi. Chang thought it permissible "to correct the flagrant errors of Sung Confucians," but Tai was going too far in his dismissal of Sung moral teachings. Chang accused Tai of "forgetting where his ideas ultimately came from."[28]

The popularity of moral philosophy and practical statecraft in the nineteenth century has usually been explained as a revival of Sung and Ming neo-Confucianism. By opposing the earlier turn to philology, some scholars argue, nineteenth-century Confucians initiated a reaffirmation of neo-Confucian forms of moral cultivation. The reappearance of philosophical concerns among Ch'ing literati, however, was also the result in part of an important turn in the evidential research movement in the late eighteenth century.

Initially, the *k'ao-cheng* program for research was sharply biased by its powerful methodology. Its ostensible goal of philosophic reconstruction based on meticulous philological analysis was ignored. With Tai Chen, however, a viewpoint began to emerge from the philological results that had accumulated. In a discussion of Hui Tung (1697–1758), the Soochow founder of the Han learning school there, Tai stated the credo for a philosophy based on the *k'ao-cheng* theory of knowledge: "Thus, if ancient glosses are clear, the ancient Classics will be clear. If the ancient Classics are clear, the meanings and principles [*i-li*] of the worthies and sages will be clear. Moreover, what unites my mind [with these meanings and principles] will accordingly also be clear. Meanings and principles of the worthies and sages refer to nothing else but the fact that they reside in the statutes and institutions [set up by the worthies and sages]."[29] For Tai Chen, the role of philological analysis was only preliminary. If it did not serve as a first step to philosophical reconstruction, then its agenda was bankrupt: "If ancient glosses are not used to illuminate meanings and principles, what function do they serve?"[30] Philological rebellion added impetus to a philosophic rebellion against the Ch'eng-Chu orthodoxy.

In his philosophic works, Tai was writing for a limited audience in the late eighteenth century. Attacked for their views by orthodox Sung learning scholars on the one hand, evidential research scholars who took an interest in philosophic problems were criticized by their colleagues for dealing with unverifiable issues usually associated with *tao-hsueh*. Chu Yun (1729–1781), an influential patron of Han learning, ridiculed Tai Chen's excursion into theoretical issues: "[Tai] need not have written this sort of thing. What he will be known for has nothing to do with such writing."[31]

In the nineteenth century, however, the academic climate changed. Scholars were increasingly receptive to philosophic issues, and once again they stressed the theoretical aspects of Confucian discourse. Nor could the *k'ao-cheng* agenda remain untouched by the political and social tremors that began to affect the society at large. The revival of Sung learning and New Text studies was paralleled and in part provoked by an intense moral concern for the state of the country and involvement with administrative problems growing out of the social and political pressures of the late eighteenth and early nineteenth centuries.[32]

Juan Yuan, a distinguished Han learning scholar from Yangchow, composed three major essays on Confucian philosophy between 1801 and 1823.[33] Modeled after Tai Chen's etymological approach to philosophic terms, Juan's best known treatises included philological examination of the graph *jen* in the *Analects* and *Mencius*. In his examination of the meaning of *jen* in the *Analects*, Juan reconstructed Han dynasty glosses of its meaning at the same time that he removed the later overlay of what he considered mistaken interpretations that had begun after the fall of the Han dynasty in the third century A.D. According to Juan, later scholars had read into the meaning of *jen* metaphysical notions that were theoretically so disembodied from practical reality that they misrepresented the concrete social aspects of Confucius' use of *jen*.[34]

Juan based his reconstruction on the gloss for *jen* first given by the later Han dynasty classicist Cheng Hsuan (127–200), who had defined it as people mutually concerned for each other (*hsiang-jen ou*, lit., "people living together"). Juan noted: "In all cases, *jen* must first be exhibited in personal actions before it can be observed. In addition there must be two people involved before *jen* can be seen. If a person shuts his door and lives peacefully alone, closes his eyes and sits still with a peaceful attitude, although his mind contains virtue and principles, in the end this cannot be counted for what the sagely gate called *jen*."[35]

To buttress this rejection of quietism and private meditation, which he associated with Sung learning, Juan Yuan cited the explanation of the graph *jen* given in the *Shuo-wen chieh-tzu* (Analysis of characters as an explanation of writing) dictionary, compiled in the Later Han by Hsu Shen (58–147). This work, a primary source for the paleographical reconstruction of over nine thousand different graphs arranged according to 530 radicals, noted that the graph *jen* consisted of two parts, *jen* (person) and *erh* (two), a combination meaning "two people" that literally represented the social dimensions of *jen*. [36]

Like Tai Chen, Juan focused on the *k'o-chi fu-li wei-jen* passage. Taking the opposite tack from Chu Hsi, Juan argued that what Confucius had meant by *jen* was the fulfillment of human desires, not their denial: "If for a single day one controls the self and returns to the observance of the rituals, then the whole empire would consider *jen* his. This is the way whereby maintaining one's personal desires one maintains others, whereby developing one's personal desires one develops others." [37] For his gloss of *k'o-chi,* Juan cited the definition *yueh-shen* [to control the self] given by Ma Jung (79–166), who along with Cheng Hsuan and Hsu Shen, was one of the most important Later Han classical scholars.

After discussing the occurrence of the *k'o-chi fu-li* passage in the *Tso-chuan* (Tso's commentary to the *Spring and Autumn Annals*), which he compared to its meaning in the *Analects,* Juan Yuan then turned to a direct attack on the Ch'eng-Chu reading of *chi* (self) as *ssu* (selfishness), which was the accepted gloss for the imperial examination system. To do this, Juan cited Mao Ch'i-ling (1623–1716), an earlier critic of the Ch'eng-Chu school, who had written: "As a result of [Ch'eng I's and Chu Hsi's glosses], all writings after the Sung annotated *chi* as *ssu*. They then cited the *k'o-chi fu-li* passage in the *Analects* as proof [for this gloss]. This is an error of extreme magnitude. It goes without saying that the meaning of the graph [*chi*] never had this [meaning of *ssu*]. Based on the original text, [we note] that the graph *chi* also appears in the expression *wei-jen yu chi*. If one uses *shen* [self] to gloss the latter [use of *chi*] and *ssu* to gloss the former, how can this make any sense?" [38]

By reiterating Yen Yuan's and Tai Chen's earlier analysis of this issue, Juan in his citation demonstrated how a questionable gloss had become the orthodox interpretation. If this veil of interpretation could be lifted, then more accurate definitions given by Han dynasty classicists could be revived. The unveiling process revealed the pernicious influence of Ch'an Buddhism on Sung and Ming Confucians. The latter had coopted the *wu-yü* (having no desires) doctrine from the former and read it into the teachings of Confucius. The process of reconstruction demonstrated that Cheng Hsuan had been right in his down-to-earth gloss of *jen* as *hsiang-jen ou* (people mutually concerned for each other). The key to this virtue was not its metaphysical status but the manner in which one man governed his relations with another.[39]

In his discussion of the meaning of *jen* in the *Mencius,* Juan turned to the relation of the mind *(hsin)* and *jen.* Mencius had given two significant glosses for *jen:* In one he had said, "*Jen* is [the distinguishing characteristic of] man" *(jen yeh che jen yeh).* In the second he claimed, "*Jen* is the human mind" *(jen jen-hsin yeh).*[40] In Sung commentaries to these passages, commentators saw in Mencius' linkage of *jen* and mind justification for the metaphysical claim that identified *jen* with a human nature *(hsing)* endowed by heaven. Chu Hsi had noted: "*Jen* is the virtue of the mind. Ch'eng I had been correct when he said the mind is like the seed for grain and *jen* is the nature of its growth. If one only spoke of *jen,* however, people would not know that it is in close contact with the self [*ch'ieh yü chi*]. To contrast [*jen* from *chi*], one therefore calls *jen* 'the human mind.' Accordingly, one can see that the mind is the ruler of the self's [*shen*] social relations and myriad transformations."[41]

Wang Yang-ming (1472–1529) and his Ming dynasty followers had stressed the link between *jen* and the mind because this gloss confirmed them in their claim that the mind was the key to Confucius' teachings. Taking the Sung Confucians' metaphysical interpretation to its logical end, Wang Yang-ming, when discussing the *k'o-chi fu-li wei-jen* passage with Ch'en Chiu-ch'uan (1495–1562), said: "The man of *jen* regards all things as one body. If one fails to achieve this unity, it is because his selfishness has not been eliminated. If the true nature of *jen* is preserved, then all under heaven will come under this *jen,* or 'the whole universe is inside my room.'"[42]

Juan Yuan objected to such metaphysical interpretations. Instead he appealed to a more concrete and limited understanding of the relation between *jen* and the human mind: "*Jen* is complete in the mind, but what is complete in the mind is [only] the beginning of *jen.* It must be enlarged and filled so that it will be manifested in actions and human affairs, before it can be called *jen.* . . . Mencius spoke of innate moral potential [*liang-neng*] and innate moral knowledge [*liang-chih*], but these are only the beginnings of *jen.* Innate moral potential refers to practical human affairs. To put aside practical affairs and speak only of the mind is not Mencius' original lesson."[43]

The phrase "*jen* is [the distinguishing characteristic of] man" *(jen yeh che jen yeh)* also appeared in the *Doctrine of the Mean.* Juan Yuan noted that Cheng Hsuan's Han dynasty gloss for this passage again defined *jen* as *hsiang-jen ou* (people mutually concerned for each other). As before, Juan appealed to a more down-to-earth reading, one more in line with Han dynasty commentators who were closer to the time of Confucius and Mencius and thus more likely to have transmitted the ancient meanings of classical texts intact.[44] Juan then dismissed the doctrine of innate moral knowledge, which Wang Yang-ming and his school had made a central tenet in their studies of the mind *(hsin-hsueh),* as an unimportant term that appeared very few times in the *Mencius* text. Because it was not a very important term in the *Mencius,* it was odd that Wang Yang-ming would single out *liang-chih* as the "secret for the sages' and worthies' transmission of the mind." Juan concluded that Wang Yang-ming, although he was not the first, was guilty of reading Buddhist doctrine into this term and turning it into a key moral and metaphysical doctrine. After the fall of the Han dynasty, native traditions of mysterious teachings *(hsuan-hsueh)* had been mixed together with Buddhism. Later Confucians had fallen under the spell of such otherworldly teachings and mistakenly incorporated them into Confucianism.[45]

Juan Yuan's best known treatise, titled "Hsing-ming ku-hsun" (Ancient glosses on "nature" and "external necessity"), made use of etymology and phonology to analyze the key concepts of *hsing* (nature, human and otherwise) and *ming* (external necessity, predetermined forces, etc.). Going through what he considered the earliest references to these terms, Juan discovered that *hsing* unlike *ming* did not become an important concept until relatively late in the classical period. When it did appear with its meaning of "nature," it was invariably coupled with *ming* as complementary and mutually related concepts.[46] Nature was what heaven imparted to all living and inanimate things in the world. The *Doctrine of the Mean* had made this clear when it stated, "What is called nature is the external necessity imposed by heaven" *(t'ien-ming chih wei-hsing).* According to Juan Yuan, this meant that "external necessity is that by which nature is formed, and nature is that by which external necessity is formed."[47]

Chu Hsi, when commenting on this passage in the *Doctrine of the Mean,* placed particular stress on *hsing* and mentioned *ming* only in passing. The gloss Chu Hsi gave for *hsing* was his famous *hsing chi li* (nature equals principle) equation, which raised the formulation for *hsing* to equal status with Chu's definition for *li.* The problem of nature then became an important element in Chu's bifurcation of *li* from *ch'i.* Chu Hsi went on to assimilate this gloss into his discussion of human nature: "[T]he reason for making a distinction between the human and moral mind is that some [perceptions] arise from personal concerns, which derive from material form; others have their origin in the correct ways of nature [*hsing*] and predetermined forces [*ming*]. The way perceptions are formed is thus different."[48]

Tai Chen, as we have seen, took Chu Hsi to task for this dualistic reading of human nature. Chu had distinguished between *ch'i-chih chih hsing* (nature of material form) and innately good nature *(li-i chih hsing)* drawn from heavenly principle *(t'ien-li)*. Evil derived from the former via selfish emotions *(ch'ing)* and human desires *(jen-yü)*, according to Chu Hsi. Tai rejected Chu's reading as untrue to the teachings of Confucius and Mencius. Instead, he replaced Chu Hsi's gloss with the formulation "nature is formed by [the action of] *yin* and *yang* and the five phases *(wu-hsing)*. Principles and meanings derive from nature." This reading meant that *ch'i* had priority over *li* and that the latter was subordinate to the workings of *ch'i* via *yin* and *yang* and the five phases. Human desires and emotions were endowed by heaven and thus were the most important constituents of human nature. To label them as evil was contrary to sagely teachings.[49]

Although he agreed on all counts with Tai Chen's analysis, it is interesting that Juan Yuan used Li Ao (d. ca. 844), not Chu Hsi, as the foil for his critique of post-Han interpretations of *hsing* and *ming:* "When people of the Chin and T'ang dynasties mentioned *hsing* and *ming*, they wanted to infer from these [terms] the most metaphysical aspects of the self [*shen*] and the mind [*hsin*]. People of the Shang and Chou dynasties, when they spoke of *hsing* and *ming*, saw their scope limited to features closest at hand."[50] In Juan's opinion, Li Ao's doctrine of recovering nature *(fu-hsing)* had overturned the concrete teachings of Confucius and Mencius. In the process, Taoist and Buddhist speculations had been incorporated into the heritage of the sages and worthies.

Li Ao had explicitly blamed human feelings *(ch'ing)* for betraying man's innately good nature. Only through quiescence and purification of the mind, he believed, could evil feelings be overcome. Li wrote in his famous tract titled "Fu-hsing shu" (Treatise on the recovery of nature): "Man's feelings are the evil aspect of his nature. If one realizes that they are evil, then this evil will not exist in the first place. If the mind is in a state of absolute quiet and inactivity, depraved thoughts will cease of themselves."[51] Juan Yuan used Li Ao's formulations to lash out at the Buddhist penetration of Confucian teachings: "Heaven gave birth to humans, endowing them with flesh and blood, and mind and knowledge. Thus it is impossible to have no desires [*wu-yü*]. Only Buddhist teachings first spoke of "cutting off desires" [*chueh-yü*]. If all persons in the Empire were to cut off their desires like the Buddha, then in all the world there would be no births of humans. Birds and animals [alone] would proliferate."[52] In contrast to the ancients who only spoke of concrete affairs, Li Ao and those who followed had reached the point where, according to Juan, it was no longer possible to distinguish any difference between Confucianism and Buddhism.[53]

For Juan, this overlay had to be removed in order to realize the practical teachings from which the Confucian meanings for *hsing* and *ming* derived. Taoists and Buddhists had been so adept at citing passages in the *Book of Changes* and *Doctrine of the Mean* to justify their heterodox doctrines that Confucians had been swindled of their birthright. Li Ao had been the first in a long line of Confucians who had "preached Buddhism under the guise that it was Confucianism" *(yin-Shih yang-Ju).*[54]

From Juan Yuan to Chiao Hsun

Juan Yuan's fellow townsman from Yangchow, Chiao Hsun, added very little new to the theoretical debate in his discussion of the *Analects* and *Mencius*. He did, however, make it clear that Tai Chen had opened a new path to understanding classical teachings, which went beyond the limits that philologically minded Han learning scholars had imposed. Refuting the claim that Tai Chen was simply continuing the neo-Confucian tradition of learning—the so-called studies of meanings and principles *(i-li chih hsueh)*—Chiao held that Tai had struck out in new directions:

> Of the works that Tai Tung-yuan [Tai Chen] wrote during his lifetime, his *Meng-tzu tzu-i shu-cheng* [Evidential analysis of meanings of terms in the *Mencius*] in three chapters and his *Yuan-shan* [Inquiry into goodness], [also] in three chapters, were the most outstanding. Seeing that he had especially investigated these issues, then his achievements [in this area] were bound to be profound. Thus, just before he died, [these issues] were always on his mind. Hence, what Tai called "studies of meanings and principles" were a means to cultivate the mind. The meanings and principles that Tai managed to grasp on his own, accordingly, were not the meanings and principles of the "Western Inscription" or the "Supreme Ultimate" of discursive [*chiang-hsueh*] scholars [such as Chang Tsai (1020–1077)].[55]

Chiao was creating distance between Tai Chen and Sung neo-Confucians —even those like Chang Tsai, who had advocated a monistic philosophy based on the priority of *ch'i* over *li*. Tai's philosophy, according to Chiao, was based on precise classical scholarship, which drew its methodology from such tools as the six rules for graph formation *(liu-shu)*, investigation of institutions, and analysis of ancient texts and artifacts *(wen-wu)*. Sung and Ming neo-Confucians, he maintained, had merely argued discursively, giving little or no justification based on concrete evidence for their theoretical positions. For Chiao, Tai was a *k'ao-cheng* philosopher, not a *tao-hsueh* scholar.[56]

On the other hand, Chiao Hsun was equally dissatisfied with the lack of philosophical discussion among scholars of Han learning. The latter, he opined, "preserved the sayings of the ancients intact but missed the thought-world [*hsin*] of the ancients." Members of the Han learning camp, Chiao believed, had lost sight of what their program for research was supposed to achieve: "When I say that I learn from Confucius, how shall I say I do it? 'By means of Han learning' [is the reply]. Unfortunately, the Han is many years after Confucius. Moreover, the Han is many years before today. Scholars learn from Confucius. Those scholars who study Han [Confucians] use the latter to discuss Confucius. Then they shunt Confucius aside and discuss [only] Han Confucians. Are the teachings of Han Confucians in fact equivalent to those of Confucius?"[57] Clearly the answer was no. Chiao Hsun was unhappy with both sides in the Han-learning-versus-Sung-learning debate. Both sides were more concerned with loyalties to their respective schools than with the fundamental issues themselves. On this level, Tai Chen had surpassed both sides in his efforts to work out the theoretical implications of *k'ao-cheng* inquiry.[58]

In addition to carrying on Tai Chen's interest in mathematics and astronomy, Chiao Hsun compiled a detailed commentary to the *Mencius,* which he titled *Meng-tzu cheng-i* (Orthodox meanings in the *Mencius*). This philological analysis of the text represented the culmination of years of painstaking research based on the fruits of Han dynasty sources and Ch'ing dynasty evidential research. On technical matters, Chiao relied heavily on Juan Yuan's famous *Shih-san-ching chiao-k'an-chi* (Collation notes to the Thirteen Classics), which was based on Juan's private Sung dynasty edition of the *Shih-san-ching chu-shu* (Notes and annotations to the Thirteen Classics). For geographical terms, Chiao frequently cited Yen Jo-chü's definitive *Ssu-shu shih-ti* (Explanations of geography in the Four Books). Other scholars cited included Tuan Yü-ts'ai (1735–1815), Tai Chen's disciple, and Wang Nien-sun (1744–1832), whom he quoted as experts in the fields of paleography and etymology, respectively.[59] On questions of theory, however, it was Tai Chen who provided the evidence for the "orthodox meanings" in the *Mencius*. Over and over again, Chiao provided long quotations from Tai's *Meng-tzu tzu-i shu-cheng* in an effort to overturn heterodox Sung interpretations of the text. With regard to definitions of *jen,* the nature of man *(hsing),* and the role of human desires *(jen-yü)* Sung interpretations were rejected in favor of Tai Chen's formulations.[60]

Using Tai Chen as a weapon to refute Sung and Ming interpretations, Chiao himself rarely cited any neo-Confucian sources in his voluminous notes. He let Tai do the talking for him. He was, however, more meticulous in his use of Han dynasty sources than Tai Chen had been. For an example, we might note that he agreed with Cheng Hsuan's definition of *jen* as "people mutually concerned for each other," which Juan Yuan had cited as the correct gloss for the passage *jen yeh che jen yeh* (see above).[61]

When he turned to the *Analects,* Chiao gave his fullest statement regarding the affirmation of desires in human life. In the *Analects,* Confucius discusses shame *(ch'ih)* in response to a remark by one of his disciples, who says: "If a man refrain from ambition, boasting, resentment, and desire, it may, I suppose, be counted to him for *jen?*" The master replies: "It may be counted as difficult, but whether for *jen* I do not know."[62] To elucidate this response, Chiao quoted from the *Mencius* and then concluded with a remarkably strident affirmation of human desires:[63] "Mencius said of King Liu that he loved wealth, and of King T'ai that he loved feminine beauty, and that yet by allowing the common people also to gratify these feelings, they were able to maintain their ricks and granaries, while there were no dissatisfied women or unmarried men.[64] In his learning, Mencius succeeded in fully comprehending the doctrine of Confucius, and his idea in this statement is: 'Developing oneself one develops others, and maintaining oneself one maintains others.' "[65]

Chiao goes on to say:

To insist on having no desires oneself, and at the same time to be indifferent to the desires of others, is to be nothing more than a "dried-up gourd."[66] Therefore, men who refrain from ambition, boasting, resentment, and desire are ascetics whom Confucius did not like. Such men are not equal to those who through their own desires come to know the desires of others, and who through their own dislikes come to know the dislikes of others. To make analogies [in this way] is not difficult, and yet *jen* already consists in this. But if one cuts off one's own desires, he will be unable to comprehend the hopes of others, and such is not to be considered *jen*."

In Chiao's view, desires were the bedrock of human nature. He noted: "[N]ature is nothing but eating and passion, and that is all. Drinking and eating, male and female, [in these matters] people and things are all the same."[67] The sages had brought order to these innate conditions in man. Through their wisdom (chih), human values (jen-lun, lit., human relations) had been realized, and correct rituals (li) established: "At the time of our human predecessors, they knew they had a mother but did not know they had a father. Hence, there was no distinction between male and female. They ate birds and beasts uncooked. They did not know of the efficacy of fire. Thus, there was no etiquette for drinking and eating. Sages appeared and demonstrated [to the people] the ritual of marriage. Accordingly, people realized there were [indeed] human values."[68]

Rituals were contrasted sharply with the moral principles of Sung learning. In a genealogical examination of the origins and evolution of these two different terms that shared the same sound (li), Chiao sharpened the edge of his powerful historicist analysis. The sage-kings, he said, had used rituals to bring order to the empire by basing rituals on human feelings (yin jen-ch'ing). Later ages abandoned rituals, and people spoke only of moral principles.[69]

According to Chiao Hsun, the logicians (ming-chia) of the late classical period had emerged from earlier court officials in charge of ritual (li-kuan). Legalists (fa-chia), on the other hand, had been court officials in charge of criminal law (li-kuan). Thus in its origins, li had been associated with hsing (criminal law or punishments) and contrasted sharply with ritual, which was used to give expression to human desires.[70] Over the centuries, legal punishments had taken precedence over ritual in dealing with the people. The triumph of li (read "law") over li (i.e., ritual), Chiao contended, had been disguised in the association of li with moral principle by later Confucians. But if one saw through the disguise, then it was clear that the antisensualistic metaphysics of the Sung neo-Confucians was in part derived from earlier legal institutions that had maintained a tradition of criminal punishments to control the people and keep them in line.[71]

As conceptual events among members of the elite, much is at stake in these critiques. Philology had led to decisive conceptual change in the eighteenth and nineteenth centuries. From the point of view of the neo-Confucian humanist tradition, the Ch'ing dynasty evidential research movement represented a decisive intellectual break with the ethical ideals of the state orthodoxy based on the Ch'eng-Chu tradition. From another perspective, however, this apparent betrayal of the neo-Confucian philosophical tradition by *k'ao-cheng* scholars can be seen in a more positive light. Philology and the conceptual reorientation that ensued, spilled over into the political arena as well. Textual criticism of the Ch'eng-Chu school presupposed some political criticism of its role in the examination system and official Confucian rhetoric.

The debilitating aspects of the imperial orthodoxy, which by the late empire had become a powerful formalism dedicated to enhancing the prestige and power of autocratic rulers, was vividly described by Tai Chen. Using the *Mencius* as a foil to criticize the creeping autocracy since Sung times, Tai contended that in the final analysis the fundamental problem lay within the ideological nature of the neo-Confucian orthodoxy and its support for an autocratic state that dominated Chinese political culture:

> The high and mighty use *li* [moral principles] to blame the lowly. The old use *li* to blame the young. The exalted use *li* to blame the downtrodden. Even if they are mistaken, [the ruling groups] call [what they have done] proper. If the lowly, the young, and the downtrodden use *li* to struggle, even if they are right they are labelled rebellious. As a result, the people on the bottom cannot make their shared emotions and desires [in all persons] in the world understood by those on top. Those on top use *li* to blame them for their lowly position. For these uncountable throngs of people, their only crime is their lowly position. When a person dies under the law, there are those who pity him. Who pities those who die under [the aegis] of *li*?"[72]

Chiao Hsun's later analysis in particular echoed ominously Tai Chen's picture of an imperial orthodoxy that had betrayed its roots in the humanism of Confucius and Mencius. *K'ao-cheng* philosophers were not simply attacking neo-Confucian philosophy. They were taking on a powerful imperial ideology that even in their own day continued to dominate Chinese political culture. We can readily see how the preliminary contributions of Ch'ing scholars, building on late Ming currents of criticism, contributed to the ultimate rejection of the Confucian imperium by Chinese intellectuals in the late nineteenth and early twentieth centuries.[73]

Notes

1. Michel Foucault, *The Archaeology of Knowledge* (New York, 1972), p. 8. See also Foucault, *The Order of Things: An Archaeology of the Human Sciences* (New York, 1973), p. 50.

2. Foucault, *The Order of Things*, p. 168. See also Patrick Hutton, "The His-

tory of Mentalities: The New Map of Cultural History," *History and Theory* 20, no. 3 (1981): 237–259.

3. Foucault, *The Order of Things,* pp. 76–77.

4. Wilhelm Windelbandt, *A History of Philosophy* (New York, 1901) 2:447ff. See also Peter Gay, *The Enlightenment: An Interpretation: The Rise of Modern Paganism* (New York, 1977), p. 408; and Basil Willey, *The Seventeenth Century Background* (New York, 1953), pp. 11–30.

5. See my *From Philosophy to Philology: Social and Intellectual Aspects of Change in Late Imperial China* (Cambridge, Mass., 1984), passim. For a discussion of social and political factors, see pp. 88–169.

6. For more detail, see my "The Unravelling of Neo-Confucianism," *Tsing Hua Journal of Chinese Studies,* n.s. 15 (1983): 67–89.

7. By "empirical" I mean an epistemological position that stresses that valid knowledge must be corroborated by external (textual and otherwise) facts and impartial observations. Ch'ing evidential scholars were not "empiricists" in the strict philosophic sense, although they were in favor of knowledge based on experience.

8. Kondo Mitsuo, "Shinchō keishi ni okeru kagaku ishiki" (The scientific consciousness of Ch'ing classicists), *Nihon Chūgoku gakkai hō* 4 (1952): 97–110. See also Nathan Sivin, "Wang Hsi-shan," in *Dictionary of Scientific Biography* (New York, 1970–1978) 14:159–168, and my "Geographical Research in the Ming-Ch'ing Period," *Monumenta Serica* 35 (1981–1983): 1–21.

9. Ch'ien Ta-hsin, *Ch'ien-yen t' ang wen-chi* (Collected essays of the Hall of Subtle Research) (Taipei, 1968) 3:94–95.

10. Foucault, *The Order of Things,* pp. 80–81.

11. Joseph Levenson, *Confucian China and Its Modern Fate: A Trilogy* (Berkeley, 1968) 1:94.

12. See my "From Value to Fact: The Emergence of Phonology as a Precise Discipline in Late Imperial China," *Journal of the American Oriental Society* 102, no. 3 (July-October 1982): 493–500. See also *Tai Chen wen-chi* (Tai Chen's essays) (Hong Kong, 1974), p. 146.

13. Wang Ming-sheng, "Hsu," in *Shih-ch'i-shih shang-ch'ueh* (Critical study of the seventeen dynastic histories) (reprint, Taipei, 1960), p. 2a.

14. Tu Wei-yun, *Ch'ing Ch'ien-Chia shih-tai chih shih-hsueh yü shih-chia* (Historians and historical studies in the Ch'ien-lung and Chia-ch'ing eras) (Taipei, 1962), passim.

15. See *Lun-yü yin-te* (Concordance to the *Analects)* (Taipei, 1966), 22/12/1. Translations for *jen* are many. In addition to "benevolence" (D. C. Lau), other translations include "perfect virtue" (James Legge), "goodness" (Arthur Waley), "humanity" (Wing-tsit Chan), and "human-heartedness" (Derk Bodde). For a discussion, see Wing-tsit Chan, "The Evolution of the Confucian Concept *Jen,*" *Philosophy East and West* 4 (1954–1955): 295–319; also Wei-ming Tu, "The Creative Tension between *Jen* and *Li,*" *Philosophy East and West* 18, nos. 1–2 (January-April

1968): 29–39; and Lin Yü-sheng, "The Evolution of the Pre-Confucian Meaning of *Jen* and the Confucian Concept of Moral Autonomy," *Monumenta Serica* 3 (1974–1975): 172–198. For a discussion of the Confucian concept of man and *jen*, consult Donald Munro, *The Concept of Man in Early China* (Stanford, 1969), pp. 70–73.

16. Translation by D. C. Lau, *Confucius: The Analects* (New York, 1979), p. 112.

17. See Chu Hsi, *Lun-yü chi-chu* (Collected commentaries on the Four Books) (Taipei reprint of Ming edition, 1980) 6:10b–11a.

18. Mizoguchi Yūzō, "*Mōshi jigi soshō* no rekishi teki kōsatsu" (The refraction and development of Chinese early modern thought), *Tōyō bunka kenkyūjo kiyō* 48 (1969): 144–145, 163–165. See also Yamanoi Yū, "*Mōshi jigi soshō* no seikaku" (The nature of Tai Chen's *Meng-tzu tzu-i shu-cheng*), *Nihon Chugoku gakkai ho* 12 (1960): 108–126. We should note that James Legge took Chu Hsi's gloss as "an acknowledgement of the fact—the morally abnormal condition of human nature—which underlies the Christian doctrine of original sin." See Legge, *The Four Books* (New York, 1966), p. 156, for the note on *k'o-chi*. In order to encompass all the various meanings of *ch'i*, I simply use the Chinese term in this paper.

19. Tai Chen, *Meng-tzu tzu-i shu-cheng* (Evidential analysis of the meanings of terms in the *Mencius*) (Beijing, 1961), p. 56.

20. Ibid.

21. Ibid., pp. 9–10.

22. Yen Yuan, *Ssu-shu cheng-wu* (Corrections of errors on the Four Books) 4:5a, in *Yen-Li ts'ung-shu* (Collectanea of Yen Yuan and Li Kung) (reprint, Taipei, 1965) 1:70. For discussion, see Mizoguchi Yūzō, "*Mōshi jigi soshō* no rekishi teki kōsatsu," pp. 145–148. Hu Shih and others have claimed a direct link from Yen Yuan to Tai Chen, but Ch'ien Mu in his *Chung-kuo chin san-pai-nien hsueh-shu shih* (Intellectual history of China in the past three hundred years) (Taipei, 1972), pp. 355ff., dismisses this contention. Mizoguchi, "*Mōshi jigi soshō*," p. 158, sees only a historical connection.

23. Li Kung, *Lun-yü chuan-chu wen*, p. 21b, in *Yen-Li ts'ung-shu* 3:904; and Yen Yuan, *Ts'un-hsing p'ien* (Honoring the nature), "Po ch'i-chih-hsing o," 1:1a, in *Yen-Li ts'ung-shu* 1:156. See also Wei-ming Tu, "Yen Yuan: From Inner Experience to Lived Concreteness," p. 532; and Chung-ying Cheng, "Reason, Substance, and Human Desires in Seventeenth-Century Neo-Confucianism," pp. 490–496, both in W. T. de Bary, ed., *The Unfolding of Neo-Confucianism* (New York, 1975).

24. Yen Yuan, *Ts'un-hsing p'ien* 1:11a, in *Yen-Li ts'ung-shu* 1:161.

25. Tai Chen, *Meng-tu tzu-i shu-cheng*, p. 34.

26. Ibid., p. 37.

27. Mizoguchi Yūzō, pp. 171–176, 181–207. See also Yamanoi Yū, "Min-Shin jidai ni okeru 'ki' no tetsugaku (The philosophy of *Ch'i* in the Ming-Ch'ing period)," *Tetsugaku zasshi* 56, no. 711 (1951): 82–103.

28. Chang Hsueh-ch'eng, *Chang-shih i-shu* (Bequeathed writings of Chang

Hsueh-ch'eng) (reprint, Shanghai, 1936) 8:25. See also Ying-shih Yü, "Tai Chen and the Chu Hsi Tradition," in *Essays in Commemoration of the Golden Jubilee of the Fung Ping Shan Library,* ed. Chan Ping-leung, et al. (Hong Kong, 1982), pp. 376–377.

29. *Tai Chen chi* (Shanghai, 1980), p. 214. See also Yang Hsiang-k'uei, *Chung-kuo ku-tai she-hui yü ku-tai ssu-hsiang yen-chiu* (Study of ancient Chinese society and thought) (Shanghai, 1964) 2:920–961.

30. *Tai Chen chi* (Tai Chen's collected writings) (Ssu-pu pei-yao ed.; Shanghai, 1927–1935), p. 214. Yü Ying-shih in his *Tai Chen yü Chang Hsueh-ch'eng* (Hong Kong, 1976), pp. 82–123, has thoughtfully discussed this aspect of Tai Chen's thought. See also Chung-ying Cheng, Introduction to *Tai Chen's Inquiry into Goodness* (Honolulu, 1971), pp. 3–53.

31. For Chu Yun's remarks, see Chiang Fan, *Kuo-ch'ao Han-hsueh shih-ch'eng chi* (Record of Han-learning masters of the Ch'ing dynasty) (Shanghai, 1927–35) 6:6a.

32. See my "The Ch'ang-chou New Text School: Preliminary Reflections," in *Chin-shih Chung-kuo ching-shih ssu-hsiang yen-t'ao-hui lun-wen chi* (Collected essays from the conference on modern Chinese statecraft thought) (Taipei, 1984), pp. 253–271.

33. Tai Chen lived and taught in Yangchow from 1756 to 1762. The city became one of the leading centers of evidential research in the Ch'ing period. See my "Ch'ing Dynasty 'Schools' of Scholarship," *Ch'ing-shih wen-t'i* 4, no. 6 (December 1981): 12–14.

34. Juan Yuan, "*Lun-yü* lun jen lun," in *Yen-ching-shih chi* (Collection from the studio for the investigation of the classics) (Taipei, 1964) 1:160. Cf. Wing-tsit Chan, "The Evolution of the Confucian Concept *Jen,*" pp. 305–307, on Sung treatment of *jen* as a metaphysical reality. On Chu Hsi's treatment of *jen,* see Chan's "Lun Chu-tzu chih jen shuo," *Che-hsueh yü wen-hua* 8, no. 6 (June 1981): 383–396. For a discussion of Juan Yuan's philosophy, consult Yang Hsiang-k'uei, *Chung-kuo ku-tai she-hui yü ku-tai ssu-hsiang yen-chiu,* 2:1007–1030.

35. Juan, "*Lun-yü* lun jen lun," p. 157.

36. Ibid., p. 159. See also Chan, "The Evolution," p. 311.

37. Juan, "*Lun-yü* lun jen lun," p. 161, paraphrasing the *Analects.* See *Lun-yü yin-te,* 11/6/30.

38. Juan, "*Lun-yü* lun jen lun," p. 162. For the occurrence of the *k'o-chi fu-li* passage in the *Tso chuan,* see *Ch'un-ch'iu ching-chuan yin-te* (Concordance to the *Spring and Autumn Annals* classic and its commentaries) (Taipei, 1966), 379/Chao 19/9 *Tso,* where Confucius refers to the earlier origins of this maxim. For a discussion of Juan's decision to use "control" to gloss *k'o,* see Wing-tsit Chan, *A Source Book in Chinese Philosophy* (Princeton, 1963), p. 38 n. 128. See also the analysis of this issue by Wei-ming Tu, "The Creative Tension," p. 30, especially n. 3. Tu notes that the typical meaning of *k'o* in the *Tso-chuan* is "conquer."

39. Juan Yuan, "*Lun-yü* lun jen lun," p. 173.

40. *Meng-tzu yin-te* (Concordance to the *Mencius*) (Beijing, 1941), 56/7B/16 and 45/6A/11.

41. Chu Hsi, *Meng-tzu chi-chu* 11:12b.

42. *Wang Yang-ming ch'üan-chi* (The complete works of Wang Yang-ming) (Taipei, 1972), p. 85, translated by Wing-tsit Chan in *Instructions for Practical Living and Other Neo-Confucian Writings by Wang Yang-ming* (New York, 1963), pp. 284–285. See also Chan, "The Evolution," pp. 305–309.

43. Juan Yuan, "*Meng-tzu* lun jen lun," in *Yen-ching-shih chi* 1:175–176.

44. Ibid., pp. 180–181. Cf. Wei-ming Tu, *Centrality and Commonality: An Essay on Chung Yung* (Honolulu, 1976), pp. 71–73. See also *Shih-san-ching chu-shu* (Notes and commentaries to the Thirteen Classics) (1816; reprint, Taipei, 1972) 52:18b.

45. Juan Yuan, *Meng-tzu*, pp. 182–184. We might note that Chu Hsi had also stressed Mencius' use of *liang-hsin*. See his *Meng-tzu chi-chu* 11:9a.

46. Juan Yuan, "Hsing-ming ku-hsun," in *Yen-ching-shih chi* 1:193–195. For a survey of the evolution of *hsing*, see Fu Yun-lung, *Chung-kuo che-hsüeh-shih-shang te jen-hsing wen-t'i* (On the question of human nature in Chinese philosophy) (Beijing, 1982), passim. For a continuation and critique of Juan's essay, consult Fu Ssu-nien, *Hsing-ming ku-hsun pien-cheng*, in *Fu Ssu-nien ch'üan-chi* (The complete works of Fu Ssu-nien) (Taipei, 1980), 2: especially 165–171. See also Lin Yü-sheng, "The Evolution of the Pre-Confucian Meaning of *Jen*," p. 174 n. 4.

47. Juan, p. 204. See Wei-ming Tu's discussion in *Centrality and Commonality*, pp. 39–40; and *Shih-san-ching chu-shu* 52:1a.

48. Chu Hsi, *Chung-yung chang-chü* (Parsing of phrases in the *Doctrine of the Mean*) (Taipei reprint of Ming ed., 1980), p. 1a; and Chu Hsi, "Hsu," in *Chung-yung chang-chü*, pp. 1a–1b. For discussion, see my "Philosophy versus Philology: The *Jen-hsin Tao-hsin* Debate," *T'oung Pao* 69, nos. 4–5 (1983): 179–181.

49. Tai Chen, *Meng-tzu tzu-i shu-cheng*, pp. 25–26.

50. Juan, p. 197.

51. Li Ao, *Li Hsi-chih hsien-sheng wen-chi* (The collected works of Mr. Li Ao) (Shanghai, 1920) 1:4b, translated by Wing-tsit Chan in *A Source Book*, p. 457.

52. Juan, p. 206.

53. Ibid., pp. 194, 205, 211.

54. Ibid., pp. 213–214.

55. Chiao Hsun, *Tiao-ku chi* (Collected writings from the [Studio of] Engraved Bamboo) (Shanghai, 1935–1937) 2:95. Chang Hsueh-ch'eng, as we have seen above, linked Tai Chen to Chu Hsi, a position that Yü Ying-shih uncritically accepts. See n. 28, above.

56. Chiao, *Tiao-ku chi* 2:95.

57. Ibid., 2:104–109.

58. Sakade Yoshinobu, "Shō Jun no *Rongo tsushaku* ni tsuite," in *Chūgoku te-*

tsugaku kenkyū ronshū, compiled by the Committee in Commemoration of Araki Kengo (Tokyo, 1981), pp. 636–641.

59. Chiao Hsun, *Meng-tzu cheng-i* (Correct interpretation of the *Mencius*) (Taipei, 1979), passim, especially 30:6a–6b.

60. Ibid., 7:8b; 15:1a–1b; 15:4a–4b; 22:5a–6a; 22:11a–12a; 22:13a–13b; 22:15a–15b; 22:19b–23b; 23:12a–12b; 26:2a; 28:21b–22a, provides a sample of citations from Tai's *Meng-tzu tzu-i shu-cheng.*

61. Ibid., 28:14a.

62. *Lun-yü yin-te,* 27/14/1, following the translation by Derk Bodde in Fung Yu-lan, *A History of Chinese Philosophy* (Princeton, 1952) 1:70.

63. Chiao Hsun, *Lun-yü pu-shu,* in the *Huang-Ch'ing ching-chieh* (Ch'ing dynasty exegesis of the classics) (1860; reprint, Taipei), 1165:9b–10a, translated by Bodde in Fung Yu-lan, *A History* 1:70.

64. *Meng-tzu yin-te,* 7/1B/5.

65. *Lun-yü yin-te,* 11/6/30.

66. Ibid., 35/17/6.

67. Chiao, *Tiao-ku chi* 3:127.

68. Ibid. One can see a good deal of Hsun-tzu, who was then being revived by Ch'ing Confucians, as well as Han Fei, in these words. For a discussion, see Sakade Yoshinobu, pp. 646–647.

69. Chiao Hsun, *Tiao-ku chi* 3:151.

70. Ibid. Chiao's analysis is not so farfetched. We might note that the institution known as *Ta-li ssu,* whose function was the general supervision of criminal law administration, had existed by tradition since the Three Dynasties (Hsia, Shang, and Chou), and remained part of the imperial bureaucratic structure through the late empire. See *Li-tai chih-kuan piao* (Historical chart of official positions) (Hong Kong, n.d.), p. 107; and H. S. Brunnert and V. V. Hagelstrom, *Present Day Political Organization of China* (reprint, Taipei, 1971), pp. 79–80. Whether Chiao's analysis is actually correct, however, is another matter.

71. Chiao Hsun 3:151.

72. Tai Chen, *Meng-tzu tzu-i shu-cheng,* p. 10.

73. For discussion of neo-Confucian types of orthodoxy, see William T. de Bary, Introduction to *Principle and Practicality: Essays in Neo-Confucianism and Practical Learning,* ed. William T. de Bary and Irene Bloom (New York, 1979), pp. 15–22.

5

Testimony to the Resilience of the Mind: The Life and Thought of P'eng Shao-sheng (1740–1796)

RICHARD SHEK

Recent works by John Henderson and Benjamin Elman, along with those written by Yü Ying-shih earlier, provide much depth and texture to our understanding of eighteenth-century Chinese thought.[1] Despite the difference in perspective and emphasis, all three scholars confirm the perception, made popular by Liang Ch'i-ch'ao and Ch'ien Mu decades earlier, that the intellectual milieu of High Ch'ing was characterized by a revulsion against the empty, metaphysical speculation of the Sung-Ming period and a distinct preference for concrete scholarship and textual analysis.[2] Yü's study of Tai Chen (1724–1777) and Chang Hsueh-ch'eng (1738–1801), however, gives this shift a subtle and ingenious explanation. Yü argues, quite convincingly, that the two intellectual giants of the eighteenth century, though distinguished for their concrete scholarship and solid learning, were in fact ultimately concerned with philosophical purpose and metaphysical meaning. The shift "from philosophy to philology," as Elman has so cleverly put it, was by no means so complete. If I understand Yü's thesis correctly, the change in intellectual discourse in Ch'ing China involved a shift in emphasis from *tsun te-hsing* (honoring moral nature) to *tao wen-hsueh* (following inquiry and study) without affecting the ultimate end of personal cultivation itself.

What I am proposing to do in this essay is to give further testimony to Yü's argument that, despite the predominance of "solid" and "real" scholarship, the tradition of philosophy, ethics, and religious quest for meaning persisted in the eighteenth century. I focus my study on the life and thought of P'eng Shao-sheng (1740–1796), a Confucian scholar and lay Buddhist whose life coincided rather neatly with the reign of Emperor Ch'ien-lung

(1736–1796).[3] Through a detailed examination of P'eng's struggle with and synthesis of classics, religion, and morality, I hope to contribute to the further understanding of thought in the High Ch'ing.

P'eng Shao-sheng: A Brief Biography

A native of Ch'ang-chou in Kiangsu, P'eng Shao-sheng came from an academically distinguished and officially illustrious family. Ch'ang-chou (present-day Soochow county), as Elman has shown, was one of the most important areas in the lower Yangtze valley in the eighteenth century from which a substantial number of evidential literati and officials emerged.[4] Originally, the P'eng family came from Ch'ing-chiang county in Kiangsi. During the Yuan-Ming transition in the fourteenth century, a certain P'eng Hsueh-i, who was the head of a local militia in Kiangsi, moved his family to Ch'ang-chou and enlisted in the Soochow garrison. P'eng Hsueh-i died without an heir, so his elder sister's son was designated by the authorities to inherit his military register.[5]

The fortunes of the P'eng family improved dramatically by the turn of the sixteenth century, as it produced the first holder of the *chin-shih* degree. Thereafter, practically every generation of the P'eng family produced a *chin-shih* scholar during the rest of the Ming dynasty. The succeeding Ch'ing dynasty saw the P'engs reach new heights in prestige and wealth. P'eng Shao-sheng's great-great-grandfather, P'eng Lung (1613–1689), received his *chin-shih* degree in 1659. He served as county magistrate in Kwangtung. Shao-sheng's great-grandfather P'eng Ting-ch'iu (1645–1719) was a *chin-shih* in 1676 and came first in the palace examination given later that year. He was eventually appointed expositor of the Hanlin Academy. He also served as court diarist and tutor at the Imperial Academy.[6] Shao-sheng's own father, Ch'i-feng (1701–1784), passed first in the metropolitan examination in 1727 and third in the palace examination. The Yung-cheng emperor, however, gave special consideration to his illustrious background and personally raised him to first place.[7] At the height of Ch'i-feng's career, he was president of the Board of War. Reviewing the success of his family, P'eng Shao-sheng could thus observe with pride: "Since the middle of the Ming dynasty, the P'eng family has prospered as Confucian scholars for a hundred and some odd years. It became even more important with the inauguration of the present dynasty. Thus the P'eng family has often been respected as the representative of eminence in the region east of the river [Yangtze]."[8]

P'eng Shao-sheng was born in 1740, the fourth of the six sons of P'eng Ch'i-feng. His eldest brother Shao-ch'ien was a *chü-jen* and served as a sub-prefect at Ts'ao-chou. Second elder brother Shao-kuan was a *chin-shih* and was reader at the Hanlin Academy. Immediate elder brother Shao-hsien, a senior licentiate who, like eldest brother Shao-ch'ien, died young. Shao-sheng had two younger brothers, Shao-chieh and Shao-chi, both of whom either died prematurely or warranted no further mention in the family biography.[9]

Shao-sheng's mother was Lady Sung, who was eulogized by him as an obedient daughter-in-law, an exemplary wife, and a stern mother. Obviously a literate woman, she taught Shao-sheng the *Shih-ching* (Book of poetry) and *Hsiao-ching* (Classic of filial piety), as well as Chu Hsi's (1130–1200) *Hsiao-hsueh* (Primary instruction). Because Shao-sheng was her youngest son, she was particularly close to him. Shao-sheng later fondly recalled that she often admonished him to become an upright scholar with integrity.[10]

When Shao-sheng was eight *sui,* he stumbled over a door sill and blinded one eye. This apparently did not affect his studies for the examination, for he easily passed the various levels of the test and, before he was twenty, he already attained the coveted *chin-shih* degree. A year before that, he was married to a Miss Fei, a native of nearby Soochow and daughter of an affluent family there. She was two years his senior. They had two daughters.[11] By Shao-sheng's own admission, his real learning began when he was twenty-four *sui.*[12] It is noteworthy that well after he had established his reputation as a successful examination candidate, P'eng for the first time seriously made a commitment to study. His search for the Way *(tao)* took him to a reexamination of the classics as well as the writings of the Sung-Ming philosophers. Unlike his contemporaries, he did not show any interest in Han learning, nor did he engage in any textual scholarship. His only interest in the Han period was the political figure Chia I (200–168 B.C.), whose character and accomplishments he admired.[13] At one point during this period of intellectual quest, Shao-sheng was fired by the zeal to make his contribution to the world through active political involvement and official duties. He wanted to present proposals for reform and to distinguish himself with official performance.

This zeal for political activism, however, did not last long. It gave way to more sedate and spiritual interests, in part encouraged by his fast friends Hsueh Chia-san (1734–1774), Lo Yu-kao (1734–1779), and Wang Chin (1725–1792).[14] Hsueh Chia-san was a family friend who was orphaned very young. He was brought up by his maternal uncle who was a Buddhist monk. Chia-san learned from him that Confucianism and Buddhism shared an identical emphasis on the realization of nature *(chien-hsing)*. Chia-san never swerved from his conviction that the two religions were compatible, a conviction that obviously left its mark on Shao-sheng himself. He recalled that Chia-san had talked to him often about Buddhism as they studied together. Yet his frequent response was to brush such talks aside, to dismiss it laughingly by saying, "You and I are both operating in [*nei*] this world, so why should we honor the Buddha?" But once Chia-san retorted, "It is you who excludes and alienates [*wai*] yourself from the Buddha. You do not know that the Buddha excludes nothing. After all, what can you claim to be inside anyway?" Startled by this rebuke, P'eng thus began his serious look at Buddhism.[15]

Lo Yu-kao was a native of Jui-chin who was fascinated with knight-errantry while young. He dabbled in boxing and swordsmanship and studied military strategy. It was when Lo was a student at the Imperial Academy in Peking that he first met Shao-sheng, who was at the time living with his father, then president of the Board of War, at the capital. The two became attracted to each other and studied together. Lo was deeply immersed in the teaching of such Sung-Ming philsophers as Ch'eng Hao (1032–1085), Lu Hsiang-shan (1139–1193), and Wang Yang-ming (1472–1529). He was also steeped in the *Surangama Sutra* and other Mahayana texts.

Wang Chin was a native of Soochow. Senior to Shao-sheng in age by fifteen years, Wang acted as the avuncular mentor who not only confirmed for him the validity of his interest in Sung-Ming philosophy but also was instrumental in leading P'eng to examine Pure Land Buddhism and its compatibility with Confucian teaching. Wang's influence on the impressionable young Shao-sheng can be seen clearly in one of the latter's essays: "My friend Wang Ta-shen [Chin]," Peng wrote, "is a Confucian scholar who roams in the ocean of Buddhism. He enjoys discoursing on Buddhism with Buddhist friends. I originally followed the Confucian teaching. Later I set my mind on Pure Land Buddhism. Mr. Wang enjoys talking to me about Pure Land, in particular using Confucian terms to illustrate its subtle meaning. He says, 'Those who cultivate the Pure Land should model themselves after Yen Hui (Confucius' favorite disciple), namely, unless it is the Pure Land, one must not look, hear, speak, or act. When the whole world returns to benevolence *(jen)*, it will be the realm of the Amitabha Buddha."[16]

By now it is quite obvious that P'eng Shao-sheng and his group of close friends did not belong to the mainstream of eighteenth-century scholarship. They did not share that common epistemological perspective of their contemporaries who, as Elman has observed, formed a community of professionals bent on reconstructing the past through textual analysis and evidential study (k'ao-cheng).[17] Rather than downgrading Sung-Ming intuitionism, Shao-sheng and his friends continued to derive meaning and inspiration from the neo-Confucian scholars, irrespective of their internal differences. Moreover, their belief in the efficacy of the mind also allowed them to explore the Buddhist tradition without prejudice and to come to the conclusion that it was compatible with Confucian teaching.

Actually, P'eng Shao-sheng's sympathy for Sung-Ming neo-Confucianism and his open-mindedness to non-Confucian traditions did not come entirely from his friends. His own family tradition was also partly responsible for his eclecticism. His great-grandfather P'eng Ting-ch'iu had already set the tone for Shao-sheng's intellectual outlook. Shao-sheng had this recollection of his great-grandfather: "My great-grandfather Nan-yun [Ting-ch'iu] was an ardent admirer of Kao P'an-lung (1562–1626). Through Kao he went back through Wang Yang-ming and Chu Hsi to reach Confucius. He thus obtained the true essence and the logical ultimate of the Confucian teaching. He was distressed that the conventional literati used Chu Hsi's thought to attack Wang Yang-ming. . . . He thus authored the Yang-ming shih-hui lu [Debunking the slanders against Wang Yang-ming] . . . thereby illuminating further Chu Hsi's thought and arresting the further decline of Wang Yang-ming's teaching."[18]

P'eng Ting-ch'iu was convinced that Yang-ming's ideas were correct. In his Yang-ming shih-hui lu, part of which was quoted by Shao-sheng, he argued: "The collapse of the Ming dynasty cannot be blamed on factionalism or roving banditry. It can directly be attributable to scholarship. If indeed the officials in late Ming had used the teaching of extending innate knowledge [chih liang-chih] to remind and motivate one another, then such malfeasance as sycophancy and corruption, persecution of the upright and the loyal, as well as allowing the bandits to harm the people would not have occurred. Enlightened ones only lament the failure of Yang-ming's teaching being implemented. To have the slanderers distort the facts and confuse black with white like this is intolerable."[19]

P'eng Ting-ch'iu also departed from the Confucian purists by organizing a vegetarian society that was modeled after the Tou-fu hui (Assembly of beancurd eaters) founded by Kao P'an-lung.[20] At the same time, he initiated the practice of purchasing fish to be released in ponds, a practice that was made popular by the Late Ming monk Chu-hung (1535–1615) among lay Buddhists. The P'eng family maintained this practice for decades.[21] P'eng Ting-ch'iu was also directed by his father P'eng Lung to study the *T'ai-shang kan-ying p'ien* (Book of moral retribution by the supreme lord on high), the paragon of Taoist morality books, popular since the Southern Sung. Ting-ch'iu was an ardent worshipper of the Taoist-Confucian deity Lord Wen-ch'ang, the god of literature who was the patron saint of the examination candidates. More significantly, P'eng Ting-ch'iu was the compiler of *Tao-tsang chi-yao* (Essential excerpts from the Taoist canon), the single most important Ch'ing dynasty publication on Taoism. All these indicate that Ting-ch'iu was not a narrow partisan of the Confucian tradition. Rather, he was a broad-minded eclectic who excluded nothing in his search for meaning and purpose in life.

Shao-sheng's father P'eng Ch'i-feng was equally open-minded about Buddhism and Taoism. In 1753 he constructed a pond in the back garden of the family compound for the release of fish. Realizing the fleeting nature of fame and fortune in life, Ch'i-feng studied the *Diamond Sutra* with earnest devotion.[22] Like his grandfather Ting-ch'iu, he observed the worship of Lord Wen-ch'ang with dedication. Thus Shao-sheng grew up in a family atmosphere that was nondogmatic and ecumenical with respect to the Three Teachings.

While he was seriously reexamining the Confucian classics and the works of the Sung-Ming philosophers in his early twenties, Shao-sheng also experimented with Taoist techniques of immortality at the urging of a friend named Chao Ken-fei. He attempted to master skills that supposedly would enable him to ascend to heaven in broad daylight *(fei-sheng)* and to release through the corpse *(shih-chieh)*, both of which had been traditionally practiced by religious Taoists in search of longevity and immortality.[23] To that end he learned esoteric formulas and secret chants, in addition to reading spiritual texts and conducting séances. He became a regular visitor to the Jade Altar (Yü-t'an), a place where, according to Shao-sheng, the "scholars of Soochow congregated to honor Taoism and to cultivate the art of perfection."[24] He also undertook his Taoist practices at the Wen-hsing ko (Pavilion of the Literary Star), a P'eng family building reserved for religious activities and solitary study. This period of Taoist cultivation lasted three years when, realizing that the pursuit was futile, he abandoned it.

However, some of the séance sessions with the Taoist immortals did lead him to Buddhism, when he was directed by one of them to examine Buddhism as an alternative. He began by reading the works of the Late Ming monk Chen-k'o (1543–1603). Later he was drawn to the writings of Chu-hung, Te-ch'ing (1546–1623), and Chih-hsu (1599–1655). He was deeply impressed with the devotion of these four eminent monks, which resulted in his writing of a lengthy biographical work on them.[25] He attributed to them his final liberation from mundane concerns. Thenceforth he was increasingly attracted by the promise of the Amitabha Buddha to deliver all the suffering souls to his Pure Land, and he longed to return to that blissful realm. He thus called himself the "master who knows to return" (Chih-kuei tzu).[26]

He became a disciple to a famous monk named Shih-ting (1712–1778), from whom he received the dharmic name Chi-ch'ing (encountering purity) and with whom he took the formal *upasaka* vow to become a Buddhist layman and to abide by the Three Refuges and the Five Abstinences.[27] Shao-sheng had, since age nineteen, started to observe a vegetarian diet intermittently. By age twenty-nine he abandoned meat eating permanently. In the following year he began a life of celibacy that continued until his death. He composed two stanzas to commemorate his steadfast adherence to vegetarianism and celibacy. To the animals he wrote,

> My body is your body; your flesh is my flesh
> The greatest virtue is life itself; I nurture that with you.

To his wife he declared:

> From ignorance is born love; it passes through ten thousand births and deaths.
> Once it is severed cleanly, heaven and earth return to tranquility.[28]

It was at this juncture that Shao-sheng was offered an official appointment as a county magistrate somewhere, but he declined. He clarified his state of mind with the following verse:

> Green grass in the yard, pleasant breeze in the woods
> I enjoy my peace, for there is no winter or summer.[29]

His energies were instead devoted to a major project, which was the compilation of the *Chü-shih chuan* (Biographies of literati Buddhist laymen). A work that began in the summer of 1770, the *Chü-shih chuan* contains the biographies of close to three hundred Buddhist literati laymen in fifty-six *chüan,* beginning with Mou-tzu in the Eastern Han and ending with P'eng Shao-sheng himself.[30] These biographies stressed the common devotion of each individual and ignored their sectarian differences. With the help of Wang Chin and the encouragement of Lo Yu-kao, Shao-sheng completed the project in fall 1775. This single work alone established his permanent fame in the history of Chinese Buddhism, for no one before or after him did anything comparable to bring attention to the phenomenon of lay devotionalism in Chinese Buddhist history.

Despite P'eng Shao-sheng's lack of official status, he enjoyed considerable prestige in the lower Yangtze region because of his family background, his *chin-shih* degree, his erudition, and his charitable works. Shao-sheng conducted himself very much like a prominent member of the gentry. Though the P'eng clan as a whole was quite affluent (it owned five thousand *mu* of land and had about one hundred adult males), there were still members who were impoverished and needy.[31] He helped these less fortunate clan members by donating and collecting money to purchase land for distribution among them. Continuing an effort begun by his father, he also maintained some three hundred *mu* of communal land whose income was used for the benefit of needy clansmen so that the landless would receive free grain, the poor would be given cash for weddings and funerals, and the aged, the sick, the orphaned, and the childless would be taken care of.[32] At times of natural disasters, such as after a flood, Shao-sheng would purchase grain for resale to his fellow villagers at prices well below the inflated market. Concerned that the physically weak would be no match for their strong and aggressive neighbors, he would issue everyone coupons according to the geographical location of their residences so that all the needy would have equitable access to the bargain-price grain.[33]

It was true that Shao-sheng made a conscious choice to stay away from the circles of textual analysts and was serenely detached from the monumental *Ssu-k'u ch'üan-shu* project that began in the 1770s. Yet he was still embroiled in a major controversy with the recognized authority of *k'ao-cheng* scholarship of the time, Tai Chen (1724–1777). In a way, this controversy represents the last-ditch battle between Sung-Ming neo-Confucianism and the new empirical style of philological studies. We shall return to the debate later.[34]

Meanwhile, life as a lay Buddhist devotee was leisurely and tranquilizing. In a letter to his friend Lo Yu-kao, Shao-sheng described the following daily routine:

I recite the Buddha's name about forty to fifty thousand times a day. . . . After morning service, I retire to the garden. With a few strikes on the wooden fish and a stick of incense, with the prayer beads slowly running through my fingers and all being quiet, I wonder if life at the Lotus Society at Tung-lin [organized by the monk Hui-yuan and the layman Liu I-min in Eastern Chin] or the bamboo window on Mt. Yun-ch'i [where Chu-hung founded his temple in the Late Ming] will be any different? . . . I get up at the fourth watch. During the day I usually stay at the Han-ch'ing ko [Pavilion Cherishing Purity]. In the evening I enter the inner chamber and occasionally explain the Buddha's teaching to the women folks. I also listen to Huan and Ying (my two daughters) recite aloud several pages from the Lotus Sutra. I then drink a cup of Dragon-well tea. After performing more invocations outside, I turn in at the second watch.[35]

This idyllic life was interrupted in 1784, when his father died at age of eighty-three. In the following year Shao-sheng retired to the Wen-hsing ko, where he cloistered himself until the end of his life. He renamed his dwelling place the I-hsing chü (Residence of the Single Act) and led a solitary Buddhist life there.[36] His wife, who also had taken the Buddhist vow and adopted a vegetarian diet shortly after Shao-sheng did, died in 1790 at the age of fifty-three. Six years later P'eng himself also died an uneventful death, just as the White Lotus Rebellion began to rage in western China, marking the end of the High Ch'ing.

Shao-sheng's literati Buddhism exerted much influence on later scholars such as Kung Tzu-chen (1792–1841) and Wei Yuan (1794–1856).[37] In the middle of the nineteenth century, Yang Wen-hui (1837–1911) revived this tradition of literati Buddhism and founded a publishing house in Nanking to print Buddhist texts in an attempt to popularize the lay Buddhist movement again. Late Ch'ing reformers such as K'ang Yu-wei (1858–1927) and T'an Ssu-t'ung (1865–1898) were all inspired by this movement.

In addition to his magnum opus, the *Chü-shih chuan*, Shao-sheng published the *Erh-lin-chü chi* (Collected essays of the Erh-lin residence) as a collection of his more Confucian writings. *Erh-lin* refers to the two Tung-lin sites headed by his two heroes, Liu I-min (d. 410) in Eastern Chin and Kao P'an-lung in the Late Ming. His primarily Buddhist writings were collected in the *I-hsing-chü chi*, published posthumously in 1825. In addition, he compiled two *chüan* on devout Buddhist laywomen, which he titled *Shan nü-jen chuan*.[38] He also authored the *I-ch'eng chueh-i lun* (Resolving doubts with the single vehicle) to refute many Confucian charges leveled against Buddhism, and the *Hua-yen nien-fo san-mei lun* (On the teaching of

Samadhi and Buddha recitation in Hua-yen Buddhism) to resolve the differences between Ch'an and Pure Land.[39]

P'eng Shao-sheng's Thought

The following account, related by Shao-sheng himself, is most telling about his spiritual inclinations and his philosophical identity:

> I once dreamt that I was a teacher, discoursing on the loyal feats of Kao T'ao and Pi Kan, as well as on the teachings of Fu Hsi, King Wen, Duke of Chou, and Confucius. There were hundreds and thousands of students surrounding me, listening intently to my instruction. All of them were enlightened and satisfied. I was happy. Then I dreamt that I was a monk, sitting alone on a quiet mountain. A nearby brook made occasional murmurs. With the prayer beads running through my fingers slowly, my six senses were all in tranquility and my five *skandha* [body, feelings, perceptions, state of mind, awareness] were all quiet and undisturbed. Again I was happy.[40]

What this dream reveals is P'eng's dual identity as a Confucian scholar and as a devout Buddhist.

At a time when most of his contemporaries were virulently anti-Buddhist, why did Shao-sheng adopt a contrary stand? What gave him the intellectual strength and the self-assurance to feel that, although he knew he was running counter to the scholarly current of his time, he was nevertheless ultimately correct? In order to answer these questions, we must first try to determine P'eng's understanding of the Confucian vision. In other words, we must first try to know how P'eng understood the central message of the Confucian tradition and how he interpreted the ultimate aim of Confucian scholarship.

In his reading notes on the *Ta-hsueh* (Great learning), Shao-sheng provides an important clue to his concept of Confucianism. "The Great Learning," he maintains, "is a study whereby the ancient sages transmit the Mind. This transmission of the Mind is exhaustively revealed in the phrase 'illuminating the brilliant virtue' [*ming ming-te*]. 'To love the people' [*ch'in-min*] is the natural application of this brilliant virtue."[41] Another reading note on the *Commentaries on the Analects* makes things even clearer: "Learning means to be awakened [*chueh*] and to grow [*tzu*]. To be awakened is to attain self-illumination. To grow is to renew ourselves daily. Human nature is originally good, but in awakening there is quick and slow. Therefore learning is nothing more than restoring my original illumination and return-ing to my original good."[42] What these two statements suggest is Shao-sheng's understanding of the Confucian vision, which is essentially an affir-mation of the basic goodness of humanity and an insistence on the nurturing and the returning to this goodness. P'eng was unswerving in this under-standing and explicated it in his correspondence with his friends. To one Sung Tao-yuan he wrote that "the learning of the sages is nothing more than the recovery of our nature [fu-hsing]. The effort of recovering our nature lies in illuminating our brilliant virtue."[43]

Shao-sheng's confidence in the validity of this view was gained through his serious and detailed reading of the classics and the writings of the Sung-Ming scholars. He was particularly attracted to the ideas of Ch'eng Hao, Lu Hsiang-shan, and Wang Yang-ming, in the same way that his friend Lo Yu-kao had been. These three thinkers were obviously closer to his intellectual proclivity than Chu Hsi was.[44] He credited Ch'eng Hao with the correct transmission of the Confucian teaching after it had been obscured since the time of Mencius. He praised Lu Hsiang-shan for the latter's advocacy of honoring moral nature (tsun te-hsing), which could be achieved through self-examination and the correction of mistakes. He declared unequivocally that Lu's teaching was the teaching of the sages.[45] He also admired Wang Yang-ming for his teaching of innate knowledge (liang-chih) and its exten-sion (chih liang-chih).[46] All three philosophers confirmed and reinforced P'eng's conviction that the Confucian goal of scholarship and cultivation was identifiable and attainable.

Yet Shao-sheng was not narrowly partisan. Although it is clear that his intellectual predilection was for the Lu-Wang school, he noted with respect the contribution made by Chu Hsi and his followers to the clarification of such Confucian subjects as ching (seriousness, reverence) and i (righteous-ness). Without hesitation, P'eng declared that Chu had received the direct transmission from Confucius and Mencius.[47] Moreover, he reserved special praise for Kao P'an-lung, the Tung-lin leader in Late Ming who was an ardent follower of Chu Hsi and a harsh critic of Wang Yang-ming and his followers. He wrote: "Learning aims at the exhaustive study of human nature. In this undertaking nothing takes precedence over illuminating goodness [ming-shan]. When Master Kao discoursed on ko-wu [investiga-tion of things], he used the goodness of nature as his basis. When he com-mented on chu-ching [treating reverence as a primary], he held as funda-mental the total elimination of thought in one's mind. He was truly skillful in explicating the hidden meaning of the ideas of Ch'eng I and Chu Hsi, and matching them with the transmitted teaching of Tzu-ssu and Mencius."[48] That he saw a kindred spirit in Kao can be directly attributable to the fact that Kao, despite his avowed hostility toward Wang Yang-ming's teaching, had grasped the true essence of the Confucian message.[49]

It is apparent that P'eng Shao-sheng was rather eclectic in his espousal of Confucian doctrines. To him, the Ch'eng-Chu and Lu-Wang schools both shared the transmission of the teaching of the sages. Neither had any monopoly on the truth, and each had its own deviants who, failing to grasp the essence of the respective schools, walked down a path that led them astray from the Way. Yet their mistakes and excesses in no way vitiated the basic validity of, nor caused Shao-sheng to deny, his Confucian heritage. He remained until his death a Confucian scholar.

P'eng Shao-sheng's loyalty to the Confucian tradition did not, however, prevent him from appreciating and even embracing Buddhism. His explanation was simple: Buddhism espoused the same ideas as Confucianism. In Shao-sheng's words:

> When I first studied Confucian texts, I was burdened by literalism. Following the example of Han Yü [768–824], I wrote diatribes against Buddhism. In actuality, I did not know who the Buddha was. Later, when I began to probe the questions of life and death, I was startled by my ignorance and I undertook a serious examination of my past views. For the first time I learned to re-orient myself toward the Mind. I studied the works of my predecessors in the Sung and Ming periods and searched for answers. I began to see the general veins of the teaching of Confucius and Yen Hui. I was particularly impressed with Masters Ch'eng Hao, Lu Hsiang-shan, Wang Yang-ming, and Kao P'an-lung. Using the insights of these four masters, I sought verification in Buddhism and found that they matched seamlessly. . . . My reading of Confucian texts resulted in my grasping of their esoteric meaning. Relying on the boundless I-ching [Book of changes] and its Appendices, and the impartial Chung-yung [Doctrine of the mean], I roam amidst the dharmic ocean of Hua-yen Buddhism. I then realize that this-worldly and other-worldly are mutually penetrating and without obstruction. For the first time I understand that the sages of our land are all great bodhisattvas who teach and expound on the message of deliverance. Yet just because of their difference in name, there has been so much strife and antagonism. Is it not regrettable?[50]

As far as P'eng was concerned, his embrace of Buddhism was not an apostasy. His excursion into the Buddhist realm only confirmed the immutability and universality of the Confucian doctrine. But a close examination of the statement above indicates that he had gone beyond acknowledging Buddhism's validity. He had actually turned the table by dressing the Confucian sages in Buddhist garb and portraying them as bodhisattvas with a message of salvation.

Precisely what did P'eng Shao-sheng find in Buddhism that was attractive to him? P'eng provided the answers in his private letters to friends. In a letter to Wang Chin, he wrote: "The two teachings of East and West are like the sun and the moon. They alternate in their appearance, parallel and do not contradict each other in their path. Their principal and uniform message is to teach people to illuminate their own Mind and to look into their own nature."[51] As in the case of his understanding of Confucianism, P'eng identified in Buddhism the same ultimate message of reaffirming and recognizing the original good nature of humanity. But what precisely should be done in order to effect this recovery of our basically good nature? Shaosheng drew his solution from Mencius (6A:11): "Seek our lost Mind *(ch'iu fang-hsin)*." These three words, he said, "represent the proper and fitting effort of cultivation. They are the most critical and essential gateway to Confucianism and Buddhism."[52]

By now it is quite obvious that P'eng Shao-sheng was an idealist who was most confident about the efficacy of the Mind. It was the Mind that was responsible for human delusion and misery in the first place. Therefore, it had to be the same Mind that could resolve the problem it had created. It was this idealistic view that allowed P'eng to see the relevance of Buddhism in his quest for the Way. Whether it was Ch'an or Pure Land, both of which he studied, the primacy of the Mind was taken for granted. In a colophon to a redaction of the *Vimalakirti Sutra,* P'eng asserted, "All the Buddha realms cannot be detached from the Mind. The Mind itself encompasses all the Buddha realms. Thus it is said, 'If the Mind is pure, the Buddha realms will be pure.' "[53] P'eng's reasoning was that if the purification of the Mind is what it takes to resolve the human predicament, restore the original goodness of humanity, and thereby bring about a universal improvement of the world, then it is worthwhile to pursue it, even though the means may be non-Confucian. This is where P'eng differed from the Lu-Wang school. Although they agreed that the Mind was the focal point of personal cultivation, P'eng fully embraced Buddhism as an efficacious means in the process of Mind cultivation, whereas the Lu-Wang school insisted on the adequacy of the Confucian tradition to attain the same end.

To P'eng, Buddhism provided the simplest and straightest path through which one can recover the original Mind. The Pure Land practice of reciting the Buddha's name *(nien-Fo),* in particular, was regarded by him as most effective. The single-minded invocation, without intellectualization or mediation, was considered by him to be most helpful in training the Mind on one focus. P'eng gushed with excitement when he discussed the practice of *nien-Fo:*

> In recent days I read Master Chu-hung's commentary on the *Amitabha Sutra* and his other writings encouraging people to cultivate the Pure Land. I came to an abrupt realization. I vowed that I will be reborn in the Pure Land in this life, and that I will use the words "Namu Amitabha Buddha" as my support [crutches] on a daily basis. From this day on, there is no longer any need to talk about the extension of knowledge, for the words "Namu Amitabha Buddha" represent the extension of innate knowledge. There is no longer any need for the discussion of preserving the heavenly principle [*ts'un t'ien-li*] either, for the words "Namu Amitabha Buddha" represent the preservation of the heavenly principle.[54]

Nien-Fo is seen here as an undertaking that preempts all metaphysical speculation and philosophical discussion. It is action oriented, not empty philosophizing. It gives form and definition to the Confucian goal of attaining the enlightened Mind. In this connection P'eng expressed some really interesting and radical ideas about the efficacy of *nien-Fo.* In a colophon written for the reissue of a morality text titled *Huo Yen-lo tuan-an* (Sentencing by the living Yen-lo [king of the underworld]),[55] Shao-sheng commented:

> The Buddha is the enlightened one. To be enlightened is to be happy. To remain unenlightened means to suffer. Therefore, for those who wish to remove themselves from suffering, nothing is more urgent than *nien-Fo.* Disloyal ministers and unfilial sons are so because their Mind is deluded. . . . When there is a single flash of enlightenment in their Mind, not even the judgment of the *Ch'un-ch'iu* [Spring and autumn annals] can be passed on them. When the suffering souls in hell focus a single thought on *nien-Fo,* not even the awesomeness of Yen-lo can keep them at bay. . . . The suffering souls in hell are basically all Buddhas. With a single thought of enlightenment, to be followed by another and yet another, they will begin with forced goodness, but end up with nothing but total goodness. Disloyal ministers and unfilial sons are basically all sages. Therefore it is said that people are what they make themselves to be. Is that not so! Is that not so![56]

Like his idealistic predecessors, notably Wang Yang-ming, Shao-sheng had so much faith in the efficacy of the Mind that he found himself taking a

position of extreme moral radicalism. The immoral characters and the suffering souls in hell suffer sanction and punishment because their original
Mind is obscured and deluded. But obscuration or delusion does not mean
irreversible destruction. The moment this obscuration is removed, the original Mind, like the sun emerging from behind a dark cloud, can shine forth
again with undiminished brightness. It is in their sharing of the original
good nature that the sinners are the equal of the sages. For P'eng, the return
to the original good nature can easily be attained through *nien-Fo*. His view
represents the classic position of Ch'an and Pure Land, which advocates
reassuringly that the moment a butcher lays down his knife, he is instanta-
neously a Buddha.

P'eng's moral radicalism should not be confused with moral relativism,
however. By no means was he suggesting, as some later followers of Wang
Yang-ming had done, the total elimination of moral standards, or even the
ultimate relativity of moral standards. On the contrary, he was most ada-
mant in insisting on the immutability and universality of such values as
chung (loyalty) and *hsiao* (filial piety). To him, the original goodness of
human nature lies precisely in its emanation of such values. "There is no
Mind of humanity that does not inherently contain *chung* and *hsiao*," he
declared with certainty.[57] Of the two, Shao-sheng considered the latter to be
the most fundamental. The filial sentiment is so basic and primary that it
informs all teachings, Buddhism included. Thus he reasoned, "Though
there is a difference in teaching between this-worldly and other-worldly,
they are identical in aim—to inculcate filial piety. It is impossible to enter
the Way without embracing this!"[58] He elaborated further: "I have heard the
sutras declare that for humans to serve heaven and earth, ghosts and spirits,
it is best to be filial to the parents. The sutras also regard filial piety as a
basic precept. Therefore among all moral conduct, filial piety comes first in
importance. Yet there are myriad ways to practice filial piety. . . . In the
final analysis, however, nothing surpasses *nien-Fo*. . . . To practice *nien-Fo*
is to honor our parents, the two are not different. To be filial to our parents
is to be filial to the Buddha, the two are identical."[59] Here P'eng is simply
echoing the familiar refrain of all Buddhist apologists since Mou-tzu in the
Eastern Han, namely, that Buddhism is not only not opposed to filial piety,
it is in fact most supportive of filial virtue. Quoting Ch'eng Hao's charge
that Buddhism aspires to eliminate the virtues of *chung-hsiao* and *jen-i*,
P'eng refuted it by pointing out that the Buddha taught his followers to be
mindful of life and of the source of life, hence to focus on the parents of all
living things. Thus the prestige of the parents reaches its greatest heights
with the Buddha.[60]

P'eng Shao-sheng as a Buddhist Apologist

Being a Confucian scholar with a Buddhist bent, or, to put it another way, being a practitioner of Buddhism with a solid grounding in Confucianism, P'eng Shao-sheng was acutely aware of the controversy and the antagonism that existed between the two traditions since the Han dynasty. In an age highly charged with Confucian partisanship, as was the case in the eighteenth century, when much of the prevailing evidential scholarship was aimed at the complete removal of all Buddhist and Taoist elements from the Confucian teaching, P'eng felt obliged to explain and defend his espousal of Buddhist views. His insistence on the identity of the two teachings notwithstanding, he had to justify why that was so, in view of the many apparent contradictions. P'eng's defense was both interesting and noteworthy.[61]

At the crux of the matter is the very issue of human nature itself. The orthodox Confucian position is that human nature is fundamentally good; the traditional Buddhist view is that it is empty. It is this divergence that leads to much debate. As P'eng saw it, the conventional followers of Confucianism and Buddhism were faced with a mutually exclusive choice: if they favor the view of basic goodness, they have to reject the notion of ultimate emptiness, and vice versa. In actuality, P'eng argued, such mutual exclusivity was the product of ignorance and contrivance. For "nature is originally empty, its emptiness is not assigned by the Buddhists. At the same time, nature is originally good, its goodness is equally not designated by the Confucians. It is precisely because of its emptiness that nature is good."[62] For P'eng, then, emptiness is synonymous with goodness. It is the Mind in its empty, pure state that allows it to attain the highest good. Emptiness thus represents the original and ultimate state of the Mind, a harmonious state of the enlightened, unencumbered, and benevolent Mind. This is the Mind of the sage; it is also the Mind of the Buddha.

P'eng was mindful of a serious charge against Buddhism, namely its selfishness and egoism. The Sung-Ming neo-Confucians often accused the Buddhists of being preoccupied with their own salvation, to the neglect of their social obligations and financial responsibilities. P'eng attributed this charge to misunderstanding and ignorance. "The root of selfishness," he contended, "lies in the attachment to the notion of self. Yet the bodhisattvas realize that all the dharma teach about no-self *(wu-wo)*; this is why they can attain their enlightenment. When the root is cut, to what can the branches and leaves attach themselves?"[63] For P'eng Shao-sheng, the bodhisattva is a figure who goes through innumerable incarnations, piling merit on merit, until he arrives at the realization of no-birth *(wu-sheng)*. Yet instead of entering into nirvana, he turns around and plunges back into the murky waters of samsara, tirelessly teaching and coming to the rescue of other beings. As all beings are limitless in number, his vow to save all can never be completely fulfilled. To accuse such a figure of being selfish or egoistic, P'eng reasoned, borders on the ludicrous. It is like the blind man who, having touched but one part of the elephant, declares that he already has the whole picture of the animal.[64]

The selflessness of the Buddhist teaching is given further elaboration by P'eng in the following passage:

> The evil deeds of the suffering multitudes arise from the notion of the self. As there is the delusion of the self, then my body is considered mine, as are my property, wife, children, slaves, servants, land, and houses. . . . Taking note of this, the sages teach the wisdom of no-self, and instruct on the dharma of no-self. Since there is basically no self, letting go becomes possible. . . . The bodhisattvas cultivate themselves through innumerable kalpa. They give up their lives and bodies as if they were dirt. This is why they can go to such lengths as slicing their own flesh to feed the hawk and jumping down a precipice to offer themselves to a hungry tigress. They have been enlightened to the truth of no-self.[65]

Yet another bone of contention between Confucianism and Buddhism was the issue of birth and death. Confucians often accused the Buddhists of being obsessed with matters pertaining to life and death. They charged that the Buddhists use scare tactics to cajole people into subscribing to their faith, such as depicting how horrible death can be without having been saved by the Buddha. In contrast, Confucians like Ch'eng Hao took pride in their equanimity toward life and death, as they regarded such matters as natural and therefore not deserving of extensive discussion. P'eng Shao-sheng objected to such a characterization of the respective positions of the two teachings. He pointed out that Confucius once remarked, "If, in the morning I can hear the Way, I will die content in the evening!" (*Analects* 4:8). Then he asked, "What if one dies without hearing the Way? Will not his life be wasted? Wasting one's life is what the sage fears most. This is why he studies the *Changes* to prolong his life, and why he is so eager to learn that he forgets about old age creeping up on him. Is not his worry for life profound? When the Buddha says that life and death are serious matters, he is trying to urge people to listen to the Way. Is he ever afraid of death?"[66] The Buddhist concern with death is thus explained as an anxiety to attain enlightenment while one is still alive and the constant fear that it may be too late. It is actually a concern for a meaningful life, one that is not lived in vain. In that sense, argues Shao-sheng, it parallels the view of the Confucian sages.

One last favorite Confucian critique of Buddhism was its antisocial, anti-familial stance. P'eng summarized this criticism with a quote from Ku Hsien-ch'eng (1550–1612), the Tung-lin colleague of his hero Kao P'an-lung: "Our sages regard human relationships as concrete. When we talk about Mind and nature, we think of them existing among ruler and minister, father and son, elder and younger brother, and husband and wife. The Buddhists, on the other hand, regard human relations as illusory. When they discourse on Mind and nature, they have them outside of ruler and minister, father and son, elder and younger brother, and husband and wife."[67] To this familiar charge, Shao-sheng's response was quite ingenious. He did not deny that Mind and nature, which he called the Way, exist in human relationships. At the same time, however, he also insisted that the Way, by definition, has to exist outside of human relationships. To him, the Way is universal, all-pervasive, and immutable. It exists before human civilization, if not before creation itself. Although it defines human relations, it is not confined by them. For the Confucians to limit the Way to human relationships is to betray their ignorance of its transcendence. To deny the presence of the Way before the creation of human society and its network of relations is to belie the Confucian profession of faith in the exaltedness of the *tao* itself. What Shao-sheng seems to be arguing is that the Buddhists are capable of beating the Confucians at their own game—that Buddhism can carry Confucian values to their fulfillment better than most exponents of Confucianism can.[68]

This brings us to the final crucial point in P'eng Shao-sheng's defense of Buddhism. Heretofore, his argument centers around the similarity between Confucianism and Buddhism. His justification rests on the basic compatibility in outlook between the two teachings as well as the fundamental identicalness in their goals. Assuming that the argument is sound and convincing, P'eng still has to rationalize why he, as a Confucian scholar, is willing to step beyond Confucianism to embrace the Buddhist faith. If all that Buddhism can offer is something identical to what is already available in Confucianism, why should anyone take the trouble to embrace it? P'eng's discussion of this point fully reveals his basic grasp on the two traditions as well as his own religious preference. The essence of his argument is that Buddhism best realizes the Confucian vision.

Take the love of life, for instance: Shao-sheng noted that Confucians pride themselves for their advocacy of cherishing life and loving things *(hao-sheng, ai-wu)*. Yet they feel no compunction in killing animals, fowls, and fish and eating their meat. How can that be the case? In an essay on abstinence from killing, P'eng presented his justification for strict vegetarianism:

> The Mind of heaven and earth promotes and encourages life. All the furred, feathered, scaled, and shelled creatures in this world, even a single mosquito or a flea, partake of this Mind and this life. In a human body there are eighty four thousand hairs and apertures. Every single one of them represents the life in me. Pluck one hair, needle one aperture, and I will be startled with pain. Why? Because every single hair and aperture is the extension of my life, and therefore is the extension of my Mind as well. He who treasures his body protects every single hair and aperture on it. In doing so, he protects his life and his Mind also. By extension, a gentleman protects every furred, feathered, scaled, and shelled creature, including every mosquito and flea. In doing so, he protects his Mind and his life; because all these creatures are the extension of his life and his Mind. My life is the life of heaven and earth, as is my Mind. To think that a murderous instinct begins with me in this universe, is it not terrifying?[69]

Elsewhere Shao-sheng further explained that in order to realize our benevolence, we must regard the life of all other creatures as precious as our own. We therefore must love their life in the same way we love ours. The abstension from meat eating, as the Buddhists prescribe, is therefore essential to the embodiment of benevolence. To be sure, P'eng conceded, some Buddhists practice vegetarianism because of the promise of spiritual merit and the threat of retribution. For himself, however, he observed a meat-free diet because he was trying to live his own values and to have the peace of mind, knowing that life should be cherished and things should be loved.[70] Thus it is Buddhism that allowed P'eng Shao-sheng to carry his understanding of *jen* to its logical conclusion.

Shao-sheng felt that, although the Confucian tradition espoused a truly noble teaching that cherishes life, it nevertheless has a blind spot when this life-loving doctrine is not applied to the human-animal relationship. In a similar vein, Shao-sheng also took the Confucians to task for what he regarded to be an extremely narrow-minded preoccupation with male offspring in the family. Despite the nobility of the Confucian teaching and the universality of its benevolence, Shao-sheng saw an unhealthy obsession with male children among the conventional Confucian scholars. When one's mind is set so much on the procreation of male children within one's own family, will not the concern for humanity as a whole suffer? In other words, the priority given to progeny, a common Confucian value, may not be entirely compatible with the other values, such as the universal application of benevolence. In an essay titled "Sympathy for an Aquaintance" (min-k'e), Shao-sheng discussed this point at length.[71] "There is a friend," he wrote,

> who laments his failure to produce a son.[72] I pity him and say to him, "There are three kinds of sons. Maybe you only get two and have to make do with the third." He asks, "What do you mean?" I reply, "Ordinary people regard as sons their own sons. The sages and worthies regard as sons other sages and worthies, while the Buddha regards as sons all of humanity. Treating our own sons as sons, we focus only on their physical form [shen]. Treating other sages and worthies as sons, we treasure their Mind [hsin]. But when we treat all of humanity as sons, we acknowledge the physical form of all humanity as our form, and the Mind of all humanity as our Mind."

What Shao-sheng wanted to stress is the different degrees of benevolence one can extend to one's fellow humans. To be kind to one's own kin is natural. To treat well other human beings who are morally upright and similar minded as oneself is noble. But to embrace all humanity, regardless of their kinship ties and their moral standing, is to be compassionate. Once again, it is Buddhism that can carry this universalistic impulse to the fullest extent and is totally nondiscriminating in its promise of salvation. It is this nonexclusive, all-encompassing, and compassionate doctrine of Buddhism that appealed to P'eng Shao-sheng. Buddhism, in short, was to him what Confucianism could have, or should have, become, but did not, and, in order to realize fully the potentiality of the Confucian vision, Shao-sheng had no choice but to cross over to Buddhism.

P'eng's Attitude toward Evidential Scholarship and His Debate with Tai Chen

Given the foregoing intellectual portrayal of P'eng Shao-sheng, it should come as no surprise that he had little sympathy for or kindred spirit with the scholastic style then prevalent in the lower Yangtze valley and throughout China. In a letter to Wang Chin, Shao-sheng complained: "The defect of scholarship in recent times lies in the daily increase in empty, inflated writing. There is no discussion whatsoever of returning to the basics. The inferior scholars mire themselves in examination essays, their dissipation is not worth mentioning. For those who have a rough knowledge of the Six Classics, they often do not study to substantiate themselves, but simply to seek approval from others or to gainsay others. Contentious and cliquish, they dissipate their energies in trivial pursuits [*wan-wu sang-chih*], even though they may be diligent in writing and have accumulated tomes of books."[73]

Shao-sheng's objection to textual analysis was threefold: His first objection was that it was putrid *(fu)*, stale *(suan)*, and unrefined *(su)*.[74] He considered this type of scholarship to be an overreaction to Wang Yang-ming's teaching of the mind. This reaction, moreover, marked the emergence of *tao wen-hsueh* (following inquiry and study) as the sole concern in personal cultivation, to the detriment of another equally important aspect, *tsun te-hsing* (honoring moral nature). This observation, interestingly enough, is similar to what Yü Ying-shih has written about the shift in emphasis within Ch'ing Confucianism.[75] On the relation between *tsun te-hsing* and *tao wen-hsueh*, P'eng Shao-sheng was unequivocal in expressing his view. Repeatedly he insisted on the complementarity of the two and objected to the pursuit of *tao wen-hsueh* without *tsun te-hsing*. "Honoring moral nature and then following inquiry and study," he asserted, "is what is called choosing the good and grasping on to it. Goodness is the substance of moral nature; to choose is the effort of inquiry and study. To grasp it means to honor it. Therefore, following inquiry and study is precisely for the purpose of honoring moral nature. It is impossible to exclude moral nature and seek inquiry and study elsewhere."[76]

It should be noted that, although Shao-sheng maintained that *tao wen-hsueh* cannot be undertaken without *tsun te-hsing,* he did not say that the opposite is impossible. In fact, he probably would argue that the latter should have precedence over the former. This is made clear in his reading notes on Lu Hsiang-shan, which tell us: "The scholarship of Master Lu centers on *tsun te-hsing*. When he discusses the effort of *tsun te-hsing,* he points to self-discipline and self-reflection, moving toward goodness and correcting mistakes. This is the scholarship of Master Yen Hui."[77] There is no mention of *tao wen-hsueh* here. Shao-sheng's preference for Lu Hsiang-shan's emphasis on *tsun te-hsing* is even more clear in a letter he wrote to Sung Tao-yuan, part of which has been quoted earlier. The relevant section reads:

In the past one or two years, after I have re-examined the *Doctrine of the Mean* thoroughly, I am all the more convinced, beyond any doubt, that Master Lu Hsiang-shan's teaching is the authentic teaching of the ancient sages. You complain that Master Lu has excluded inquiry and study, while only stressing moral nature; and you fault him for that. It is because you are not aware that the learning of the sages rests in the restoration of nature, while the effort toward the restoration of nature focuses on the illumination of brilliant virtue. Excluding moral nature, there is no inquiry and study. To insist on it is to be called dissipating one's energy in pursuit of trivial matters.[78]

Once again P'eng uses the phrase *wan-wu sang-chih* (dissipating one's energy in trivial pursuits). For him, to engage in textual exegesis without knowing the purpose, as most evidential scholars of his time seemed to be doing, was to waste one's time on unimportant matters. It was *tao wen-hsueh* without *tsun te-hsing*. Summoning up the authority of Chu Hsi, he noted the inadequacy of this approach: "Master Chu never undertook *tao wen-hsueh* apart from moral nature. Yet later followers of *tao wen-hsueh* avoid mentioning moral nature altogether. . . . Without knowing moral nature while merely engaging in the task of inquiry and study, and yet calling it the teaching of Master Chu, is this not crude?"[79]

P'eng Shao-sheng's position on the relation between the two basic approaches to Confucian cultivation made almost inevitable a confrontation between him and the *k'ao-cheng* scholars of his day. What was unexpected was that the confrontation, when it finally came, involved no less an eminent evidential scholar than Tai Chen. As a philologist and astronomer, Tai was a towering figure in the eighteenth century. Yü Ying-shih's careful study of this intellectual giant also reveals that Tai's philological pursuits were mere tools used by him to realize a fundamentally philosophical goal, that of rediscovering the Way. Bringing his formidable textual analytical skills to bear, Tai argued that the entire Sung-Ming exegesis of the classics had been so tainted by elements of Buddhism and Taoism that it was philologically untenable. The Way of the sages had to be purged of all such heterodox contaminants before it could be restored; his most mature philosophical works, *Yuan-shan* (On goodness) and *Meng-tzu tzu-i shu-cheng* (Evidential explications of the meaning of the terms in the *Mencius*), were written specifically to do that. The approach he adopted in accomplishing this task was *tao wen-hsueh,* the solid and objective tools of contemporary philology. His justification was the exact opposite of what P'eng espoused: "Apart from following inquiry and study, how can we honor moral nature?" he asked.[80]

With such a complete divergence of opininion on the very fundamental approach to personal cultivation, the stage was definitely set for a major debate. The circumstances that led up to the controversy remain, however, somewhat unclear. We know Tai, who began his career as an up-start scholar from the merchant center of Hui-chou, had wanted to gain P'eng Shao-sheng's acquaintance for over ten years. After he finished his *Evidential Explications* in 1777 (only months before his unexpected and premature death), Tai sent it to P'eng, along with his earlier work *Yuan-shan,* for comment. He might have done so at P'eng's request, but it was certainly intended as a gesture of respect and goodwill. That Tai did send to P'eng the two philosophical works of which he was most proud is intriguing. Why would the prominent representative of the prevailing school of philological scholarship seek comment on his works from the stalwart of metaphysical inquiry? Was he hoping to find a sympathetic reader, one who would appreciate the profundity of his thought, as few among his *k'ao-cheng* cohorts could?

P'eng's response was prompt. He made a few opening remarks praising Tai's profound explication of the hidden meaning of the *Shih-ching* and the *Mencius.* Then he continued: "I am ignorant of scholarship. But in terms of the basic approach to learning, I beg to differ. It would be impossible to arbitrarily set up differences on matters we agree on. Yet there are a number of points about which I feel ill at ease, and I would like to get your explication. . . ."[81]

The first point brought up by P'eng was the relation between heaven and humanity.[82] P'eng agreed that it was impossible to discuss heaven apart from humanity, a major argument of Tai in both of his books. But he also reminded Tai that it was equally impossible to discuss humanity apart from heaven, a point neglected in Tai's works. Secondly, P'eng took exception to Tai's discussion of allotment *(fen)* in the context of fate or destiny *(ming).* Apparently Tai defined *ming* in his *Yuan-shan* as "that which is limited to one's allotment." P'eng, however, equated *ming* with *hsing* (nature), and argued that since both are derived from heaven, both should be boundless, as heaven is boundless. To say that *ming* or *hsing* is somehow limited by allotment is to undermine their universality. A third point of contention centered on the distinction made by Tai Chen between the Way of Lao-tzu and the Buddha, and the Way of the sages. To Tai, the former is characterized by no desire *(wu-yü);* the latter is by no delusion *(wu-pi).* P'eng saw total identity between these two terms. "Without desires, one will be authentic *(ch'eng),* and being authentic, clear *(ming).* Similarly, without delusion, one will be clear, and being clear, authentic. There is no authenticity without clarity, or vice versa." Thus the sages' Way is identical to that of the Buddha and Lao-tzu.

P'eng then came to the most crucial point in his letter, which is the relation between moral nature and inquiry and study. P'eng singled out for criticism a passage in Tai's *Evidential Explications,* which states that "moral nature, when aided by inquiry and study, advances into sagely wisdom." Shao-sheng charged that this view of moral nature implies inadequacy, that the moral nature has to be aided by scholarship before it can exhaustively probe the Way. If this is indeed the case, then moral nature is not worth honoring. To P'eng, scholarship adds nothing to moral nature; what it does is simply to enable moral nature to realize its full potential.

The difference between P'eng and Tai is further illustrated by the last point raised in Shao-sheng's letter. Tai Chen is quoted as having stated in his books that "outside of things there are no principles; and apart from form and appearance *(hsing-se),* there is no heavenly nature *(t'ien-hsing).*" P'eng argued that in fact the opposite is true. Comparing things to circles and squares and principles to the compass and the measuring square, P'eng reasoned that just as no circles or squares can be drawn without the compass and the measuring square, there is nothing without the underlying principles. Similarly, comparing form and appearance to waves and heavenly nature to water, he tried to show that just as it is impossible to have waves without water, it is impossible to have form and appearance without their heavenly nature.

In the final analysis, what P'eng found uncomfortable in Tai's works was too great an emphasis on the branch and not the root, on the physical and not on the metaphysical, and on external scholarship and not on inner moral nature. P'eng's attack invited a wrathful reply from Tai. His pride obviously hurt, Tai wrote a lengthy rebuttal in which he not only addressed P'eng's complaints point by point but also launched a comprehensive and scathing attack on P'eng's philosophical foundation and everything it represented. It was a breathtakingly blunt refutation in which Tai made his final assault on the entire Sung-Ming legacy for which P'eng stood. His tone was uncompromising and combative from the outset:

> Confucius said, 'There is no point in people discussing issues together when they follow different ways.' [*Analects* 15:40]. What he meant is that for those whose mind is made up, all discussions are futile. You, sir, are one whose mind is made up. You wish to examine my *Yuan-shan.* I have long heard of you and have respected your moral behavior. For more than ten years now I have tried to make your acquaintance, even though what I have repeatedly presented in

my *Yuan-shan* and additionally my *Evidential Explications on the Mencius* run entirely counter to your Way. Now that you have inquired about my works, I make bold to present my views. In your letter you embrace some of my views as similar to yours, while distinguishing others as different. But for me, I would say that our views are entirely different, without the least bit of similarity!"[83]

Then Tai went on the offensive and charged that all Confucian scholarship since the Sung dynasty had confused and distorted the original teaching of the sages with the thought of Lao-tzu and the Buddha. "Before the Sung dynasty, Confucius and Mencius, and Lao-tzu and the Buddha, were separate and distinct. Since the Sung period, however, the original meaning of all Confucian and Mencian classics has been obscured." Even Ch'eng Hao and Chu Hsi were guilty of such obscuration of the sages' Way. They, like P'eng Shao-sheng in the present day, were attracted to the Buddhist and Taoist teaching when young. Consequently, their reading of the canons were colored by a Buddhist and Taoist bias that made their insights unsound. Though they later realized their folly and returned to the Confucian fold, the damage was already done. The Six Classics and the other canonical texts were so tainted by Buddhist and Taoist explications that they lost their original meaning, thereby allowing the Buddhists and Taoists to masquerade as Confucians. The situation, Tai contended,

is like that of some descendants who, not having seen the likeness of their ancestor, mistakenly paint the likeness of someone else and worship it. What they worship is of course their ancestor, but the likeness is a mistaken one. Yet as long as the reality of worshipping the ancestor is there, even when they miss the likeness, what is the harm? But if someone else attempts to pass off a likeness of his own ancestor as my forbear, and in reality tries to beguile my lineage into becoming his, this is exactly why I was compelled to write my *Evidential Explications*. I did so to smash the error of the painted likeness so as to protect my clan and to preserve my lineage.[84]

The above quote clearly indicates that Tai Chen saw the distinction between Confucianism and the other two teachings of Buddhism and Taoism in highly emotional and personal terms. His puristic partisanship made it inconceivable for him to accept, even as a remote possibility, that Buddhism and Taoism had any claim to the truth. They were to him nothing more than a set of heterodox and alien superstitions.

On the question of *fen* (allotment) and *ming* (destiny or fate), Tai adamantly maintained the accuracy of his interpretation. Using highly technical philological analysis, he identified the root meaning of *ming* as a lord's decree, which always implies limitation and constraint. *Fen* to him meant differentiation and division as a whole. Every part of a whole is by definition also limited by its allotment and therefore cannot aspire to control the whole. Tai also reaffirmed his charge that the Buddhists and Taoists wanted to eradicate all desires, whereas the original Confucians such as Mencius affirmed them.

Tai reacted particularly strongly to P'eng's discussion of authenticity. Because authenticity is closely related to goodness, P'eng's elucidation of the term was perceived by Tai as an implication that Tai himself had been remiss in addressing the ultimate basis of the distinctions between good and evil and between authenticity and falsity—a most serious charge for the author of a book on goodness! Thus Tai was vituperative in response. He pointed out that though P'eng quoted copiously from Ch'eng Hao and Chu Hsi, he should have cited Wang Yang-ming more instead, as Wang was far closer to him in spirit.[85] He remarked: "Now you, sir, subscribe to Lao-tzu, Buddha, Lu Hsiang-shan, and Wang Yang-ming,[86] but you combine them with Confucius, Mencius, the Ch'eng brothers, and Chu Hsi. Not only should Confucius and Mencius not be so slandered, neither should Ch'eng and Chu. Furthermore, since you have also changed the appearance of Lao-tzu and the Buddha into that of Confucius, Mencius, Ch'eng and Chu, I am afraid that even the Buddha and Lao-tzu would feel slandered and would object." He then executed the coup de grace: "What you love is the substance of the Buddha. Yet even though you love its substance, you discard its label. On the other hand, you borrow the label of Confucianism, but change its substance in secret. In both cases you have violated authenticity [*ch'eng*]. You, sir, have stated that 'in matters of scholarship, nothing is more urgent than to examine the subtle difference between good and evil, and to make fast the distinction between authenticity and falsity.' I beg that you first live up to this injunction yourself!"[87]

Tai ended the polemic with a plea that P'eng should seriously probe the words of the classics so that he could see for himself that both in content and appearance, Confucianism shares nothing in common with Buddhism and Taoism. There should not be, he said, any simulated correspondence or dishonest borrowing. Unfortunately, Tai passed away within months of writing his letter to P'eng, thereby putting an end to the lively and stimulating debate. We can only wonder whether it would have continued had he lived.

Conclusion

P'eng Shao-sheng was an anachronism of his time. In an age of increasing professionalism and specialization, he remained serenely amateurish and a generalist. Though by no means a lonely voice crying in the wilderness, he and his handful of friends were definitely in the minority. He was guilty of an ecumenism that was no longer fashionable or tolerable, and his willingness to accept the possibility that traditions other than Confucianism could be vehicles of truth was anathema to most of his contemporaries. He was, of course, treading a very thin line. What he attempted to do was to realize the full implications of the Confucian vision by incorporating other teachings. Far from challenging the fundamental assumptions of the Way of the sages, he was trying to affirm their universality and immutability. His espousal of Buddhism was meant to fill a spiritual gap in the Confucian tradition that had been created by misunderstanding and ignorance. He genuinely believed that "the Way is One." He confided to a friend that, "though there are three teachings, the basis of the Way cannot be divided into three. In entering each teaching, the student must first know this basis."[88]

In embracing Buddhism P'eng automatically aligned himself with the Lu-Wang school of neo-Confucianism. In the intellectual milieu of the eighteenth century, this allegiance to the subjective and metaphysical wing of Confucian studies required courage. To be sure, P'eng's illustrious pedigree and affluent family background allowed him a certain intellectual independence few others could afford. His refusal to accept bureaucratic appointment further insulated him from the constraints of officialdom. Still, his voluntary affiliation with the Lu-Wang school must have at times brought him snickers or even open contempt from his contemporaries, especially considering that his native Ch'ang-chou was deeply involved in evidential scholarship.

P'eng Shao-sheng was no narrow partisan, however. He recognized the validity of the Ch'eng-Chu school and included their ideas in his formulation of a unified Confucian tradition. By temperament he did not possess any of the sectarian mentality that was characteristic of his age. He was therefore a breath of fresh air in the stultifying atmosphere of the Ch'ien-lung era. He was living testimony to the resilience of the teaching of the Mind and to the tenacity of metaphysical inquiry.

Furthermore, his faith in Buddhism was by no means unique, nor was his brand of literati lay devotionalism. Others scholars such as Sung Wen-sen (1611–1702), Pi Tzu-feng (d. 1708), and Chou An-shih (1656–1739) had come before him and had made their own marks on lay Buddhism.[89] But P'eng did much more than they to make Buddhism a genuine alternative for Confucian scholars who were restless and curious. He made Buddhism a respectable haven for many who were conducting their own search for meaning and synthesis. His role in the history of Chinese Buddhism needs to be recognized.

Notes

1. John B. Henderson, *The Development and Decline of Chinese Cosmology* (New York, 1984); Benjamin A. Elman, *From Philosophy to Philology: Intellectual and Social Aspects of Change in Late Imperial China* (Cambridge, Mass., 1984); Yü Ying-shih, "Some Preliminary Observation on the Rise of Ch'ing Confucian Intellectualism," *Tsing-hua Journal of Chinese Studies* 11 (1975): 105–146. See also Yü's *Lun Tai Chen yü Chang Hsueh-ch'eng* (On Tai Chen and Chang Hsueh-ch'eng) (Hong Kong, 1976), pp. 15–30.

2. Liang Ch'i-chiao, *Intellectual Trends in the Ch'ing Period,* trans. Immanuel Hsu (Cambridge, Mass., 1959); Ch'ien Mu, *Chung-kuo chin-san-pai-nien hsueh-shu-shih* (Chinese intellectual history in the past three hundred years), 2 vols. (Taipei, 1972).

3. *Tzu:* Ch'ih-mu, *Hao:* Yun-ch'u. A brief biography of him can be found in Arthur Hummel, ed., *Eminent Chinese of the Ch'ing Period* (reprint, Taipei, 1970), pp. 614–615. The following works treat P'eng's ideas in some detail: (1) Ogawa Kanichi, "Koji bukkyo no kinseiteki hatten" (The modern development of literati Buddhism) *Ryukoku daigaku ronshu* 339 (1951): 46–75; (2) Lu Pao-ch'ien, "Ch'ien-lung shih-tai chih shih-lin Fo-hsueh" (Literati Buddhism in the Ch'ien-lung period), in *Chung-kuo Fo-chiao-shih lun-chi* (Symposium on Chinese Buddhist history) (Taipei, 1977) 6:319–343; and (3) Makita Tairyo, "Koji bukkyo ni okeru Hosaishin no chii" (P'eng Chi-ch'ing's place in the history of literati Buddhism), in his *Chugoku bukkyoshi kenkyu* (Study of the history of Chinese Buddhism) (Tokyo, 1984) 2:270–289.

4. Elman, *From Philosophy to Philology,* p. 91.

5. See the "Biographies of the P'eng family," in *Erh-lin-chü chi* (Collected essays of the Erh-lin residence) (hereafter ELCC), 23:1a.

6. P'eng Ting-ch'iu has a biography in Hummel, *Eminent Chinese,* pp. 616–617.

7. Ibid.

8. ELCC 18:9b.

9. Ibid. 18:19a.

10. Ibid. 22:16a–18a.

11. P'eng Shao-sheng wrote a biography of his wife and included it in his *I-hsing-chü chi* (Collected essays of the one act residence) (hereafter IHCC), 7:14b–16a.

12. ELCC 3:14a.

13. See his brief autobiography, "Chih-kuei-tzu chuan" (Biography of the master who knows to return), in IHCC, preface, 1a–b.

14. P'eng admitted in a colophon to *Wang-tzu wen-lu* (Wang Chin's collected essays) that his most compatible lifelong friends were these three. ELCC 6:8a.

15. ELCC 22:1a–2a.

16. IHCC 5:9b.

17. Elman, *From Philosophy to Philology*, chap. 3.

18. ELCC 5:5a.

19. Ibid. 23:8b–9a.

20. Hummel, *Eminent Chinese*, p. 617.

21. ELCC 7:10a; also 10:8b. For Chu-hung's promotion of releasing life, see Kristen Yu Greenblatt, "Chu-hung and Lay Buddhism in the Late Ming," in William Theodore de Bary, ed., *The Unfolding of Neo-Confucianism* (New York, 1975), pp. 93–140.

22. ELCC 18:18b.

23. IHCC 3:16b.

24. Ibid. 5:23b–24b. Founded during the reign of Emperor Shun-chih in the Early Ch'ing, the altar was at first dedicated to the worship of Hsuan-wu, the martial deity; later it also included the Mother of the Dipper and Lord Wen-ch'ang.

25. Ibid. 6:4b–18b.

26. Ibid., preface, 1a–b.

27. Shao-sheng wrote a preface to the "Recorded Sayings of Shih-ting," see IHCC 3:22a–23a.

28. IHCC, preface, 1b.

29. Ibid.

30. *Zoku zokyo* (Supplement to the Buddhist Tripitaka) 149:791–1012.

31. ELCC 6:9b–10a.

32. Ibid. 10:4a–b.

33. Ibid. 10:5a.

34. P'eng's letter to Tai is included in ELCC 3:16a–19a. Tai's reply is reproduced in an appendix to an edition of *Yuan-shan* (On goodness) and *Meng-tzu tzu-i shu-cheng* (Evidential explications of the meaning of the terms in *Mencius*) (Shanghai, 1956).

35. IHCC 4:3a–b.

36. He wrote an essay to commemorate the occasion, and explained that the term *i-hsing* was derived from *i-hsing san-mei* (single act focused on *samadhi*).

37. Kung Tzu-chen styled himself Huai-kuei tzu (master who is nostalgic about returning) in clear reference to P'eng's name of Chih-kuei tzu.

38. *Zoku zokyo* 150:211–257.

39. Both can be found in *Zoku zokyo* 104:149–178.

40. ELCC 5:9b.

41. Ibid. 1:9b.

42. Ibid. 2:7b.

43. Ibid. 3:14a–b.

44. See his reading notes on the three: ELCC 2:1a–b, 2b–3a, 3a–b.

45. Ibid. 3:14a.

46. At the same time, however, he did recognize that Wang's later followers lost sight of the original intent of Wang and adulterated his teaching. See ELCC 2:3b.

47. Similarly, P'eng faulted the followers of Chu Hsi for having failed to grasp the substance of Chu's thought. They have also deviated from the Way. ELCC 2:2b.

48. ELCC 2:3b–4a.

49. Shao-sheng was undoubtedly favorable in his assessment of Kao's scholarship because of his great-grandfather's admiration for Kao.

50. *Zoku zokyo* 104:149.

51. IHCC 4:7a.

52. Ibid. 4:4a.

53. Ibid. 1:22b–23a.

54. Ibid. 4:1a.

55. Makita Tairyo devotes a chapter to this sixteenth-century morality book in his *Chugoku bukkyoshi kenkyu* 2:254–269.

56. IHCC 3:28a–b.

57. ELCC 9:9b.

58. IHCC 1:12a–b.

59. Ibid. 1:4a.

60. *Zoku zokyo* 104:149–150.

61. Ibid., p. 151.

62. ELCC 10:9a.

63. IHCC 3:1b–2a.

64. Ibid. 3:1b.

65. Ibid. 3:32b.

66. "I-ch'eng chueh-i lun," in *Zoku zokyo* 104:149.

67. Ibid., p. 163.

68. Ibid.

69. ELCC 2:12a–b.

70. Ibid. 6:2a.

71. IHCC 2:25a.

72. It should be noted that Shao-sheng himself had no son either. Thus the essay has even more significance. It was written as much for his friend as it was for himself.

73. ELCC 3:15a–b.

74. Ibid. 3:4b.

75. In addition to the works listed in n. 1, above, Yü also wrote the following: "Ts'ung Sung-Ming ju-hsueh ti fa-chan lun Ch'ing-tai ssu-hsiang-shih" (Ch'ing intellectual history from the perspective of the development of Sung-Ming Confucianism), in *Chung-kuo hsueh-jen* 2 (September 1970): 19–41; "Ch'ing-tai ssu-hsiang-shih ti i-ko hsin-chieh-shih" (A new interpretation of Ch'ing intellectual history), in *Chung-kuo che-hsueh ssu-hsiang lun-chi: Ch'ing-tai p'ien* (Collected essays on Chinese philosophical thought: The Ch'ing period), ed. Hsiang Wei-hsin and Liu Fu-tseng (Taipei, 1977), pp. 11–48.

76. ELCC 2:10b; 4:16b; 1:12a–b.

77. Ibid. 2:2b.

78. Ibid. 3:14a–b.

79. Ibid. 5:4b–5a.

80. *Tai Chen wen-chi,* quoted in Yü Ying-shih, *Lun Tai Chen yü Chang Hsueh-ch'eng,* p. 20.

81. ELCC 3:17a; also *Meng-tzu tzu-i shu-cheng,* p. 96.

82. All subsequent discussion concerning P'eng's letter to Tai can be found in ELCC 3:17a–19a, and *Yuan-shan,* pp. 96–98.

83. All subsequent discussion of Tai's rebuttal can be found in *Yuan-shan* (see n. 34, above), pp. 87–96.

84. Ibid., p. 89.

85. Ibid., p. 93.

86. Yü Ying-shih curiously labels P'eng an obscurantist defender of the Ch'eng-Chu tradition. See his *Lun Tai Chen,* pp. 96, 102, 106–107.

87. *Yuan-shan* (n. 34, above), p. 95.

88. IHCC 4:15b–16a.

89. Together with P'eng, they were the four most prominent literati Buddhists in the High Ch'ing. Cf. Ogawa Kanichi, "Koji bukkyo no kinseiteki hatten," pp. 53–54.

6

Ch'ing Cosmology and Popular Precepts

SAN-PAO LI

The complexity of traditional Chinese culture defies any effort to treat it simply as a monolith. However, general patterns of beliefs and values can be traced and delineated if a sufficiently wide range of literature produced or cherished by members of various Chinese social groups can be identified. This essay is an effort to delineate such patterns. It deals with a cosmology and related values that persisted long after the passing of the imperial era. The hypothesis presented in this study is that by the Ch'ing period, if not earlier, basic elements of Confucian cosmology and ethics had made their way through a variety of channels not only to the literati but also to merchants and peasants, women as well as men. In other words, there was a broad consensus on basic beliefs and values that the commoners shared with the elite. These patterns of meaning seem to have overridden not only educational and class divisions but also regional differences, at least among the Han ethnic majority.

The basic belief system of the elite was, of course, produced and maintained by the scholars. But, through the government's deliberate cultural policy and the elite's self-conscious efforts, the moral values of this system were constantly promoted among the lower strata of Chinese society, both in the cities and in the countryside. There were, to be sure, definite limits to the effectiveness of such efforts. Nonetheless, the values promoted proved to be fully harmonious with traditional cosmological beliefs, including those of popular religion.[1] Furthermore, cultural integration proceeded in both directions. Writing of the late Ming period, Tadao Sakai opined that it was no longer "a question of traditional Confucianism being disseminated downward but of popular thought penetrating upward."[2]

This set of widely accepted values could be instilled into the minds of the very young through formal education, at least for those who could afford it. But for financially disadvantaged families, informal education could also introduce an ethos that was fundamentally Confucian. For example, the popular collection of proverbs, *Hsi-shih hsien-wen* (Sayings of virtuous men of antiquity), was often printed as an integral part of almanacs *(li-shu* or *t'ung-shu),* which may be compared to the family Bible of the devout in Western society. Almanacs were perhaps the most widely distributed books in all China during late imperial times, particularly the Ch'ing period.[3] The *Hsun-meng chiao-erh ching* (Elementary instructions for children), a primer of about nine pages, was apparently designed as an elementary reader for peasants. It contains a relatively lengthy section on basic agricultural knowledge and skills, emphasizes family ethics, and exhorts all children to study and pursue a morally acceptable life.[4]

Of course, most peasants in traditional China had no opportunity for formal education. Yet a market still existed for primers such as the *Hsun-meng chiao-erh ching.* Referring to South China in late imperial times, Wolfram Eberhard has observed that in rural communities, where there was a large population of the uneducated, one could still find "numerous sermons of moralistic literature, elaborating in the most elementary way upon the basic moral principles of Chinese ethics—often illustrated with brief stories which describe good or bad deeds and their consequences."[5] Daniel Harrison Kulp discovered in 1923—eighteen years after the traditional civil service examinations had been abolished—that even the poor peasants in Phenix Village, Kwangtung recognized the magical potency and benefit of studying the Four Books and the Five Classics.[6]

As late as 1941, according to a survey conducted in Shanghai—a far more modern environment than most Chinese cities of the period—popular primers such as the *San-tzu ching* (The trimetrical classic), the *Ch'ien-tzu wen* (The thousand-character reader), the *Pai-chia hsing* (The hundred surnames), the Four Books of Confucianism, and children's illustrated glossaries *(tsa-tzu)* constituted from five percent to ten percent of the street book venders' total stock.[7] These materials were meant to be basic primers for the young and were used extensively before 1949 by small-town or village teachers and tutors.[8] In addition to introducing the young to a basic stock of Chinese characters, such works contain Confucian lessons on the universe and its components, China's past, its illustrious historical personalities, and moral precepts for proper conduct, including hortatory sentiments concerning filial piety *(hsiao)* and relationships between siblings.

The popular elementary readers, in use in the late imperial period, together with some ballads and children's songs that must have gained popularity long before the present century, have been exploited in this paper.

Such materials must have served to instill and maintain certain values and attitudes among the population at large. It is justifiable to assume that a large majority of people living in late imperial China were, to some degree, exposed to the precepts inherent in Confucian cosmology and ethics and hence had an emotional commitment to Confucian orthodoxy, if not an intellectual one.

Orthodox Cosmology: Harmonious Hierarchy

Students of Chinese history are aware that traditional Chinese cosmology has as its most distinctive feature a view of the cosmos as an organic whole in which heaven, earth, and man are part of a single world, each merging and interacting with the other. Although much has been written about this theory of cosmic unity, there is yet another unique feature of the Chinese worldview that, I believe, has not been fully examined—that is, the inseparable relation of cosmology, ethics, and religion, which overlap to such a degree that each contains substantial elements of the other two. This is a topic of immense scope and only a brief treatment can be attempted here.

At the basis of Chinese cosmology is the concept of order and harmony. The cosmos in the Chinese conception is a self-contained, self-operating organism. Everything is an integral part, and only a part, of a colossal cosmic pattern. The harmonious state of the universe is achieved not from the orders of a superior authority external to individual things but because things spontaneously obey the internal dictates of their own nature. Thus, the universe functions the way it does because it is the nature of the universal organism that it should do so, and for no other reason. The cosmic harmony is, in a sense, preestablished, and Confucian moral and social categories became rooted in a cosmology developed by seeking symmetries in natural phenomena. "A true Confucianist," observed Professor Eberhard, "is not afraid of deities, ghosts, or spirits, but he is afraid of upsetting the cosmic or social order."[9] The realm of nature and that of man were woven inextricably into a single seamless fabric.

This notion of harmonious hierarchy has been characteristic of the Chinese moral culture. Relationships among family members were hierarchical. Yet until recent decades, few Chinese had not heard of the proverb: "What is of utmost importance to a family is harmony" *(i-chia chih chi tsai-yü ho)*.[10] Most Chinese, rural and urban, were exhorted that harmony within a household can be attained only when its members are willing to accept and to maintain the hierarchical status differentiation existing between father and son and between husband and wife. Such is the pattern of the cosmos—of heaven being high and earth low, of *yang* being strong and *yin* weak. It is a common argument in the literature I have surveyed that the responsibility lies with the parents to educate their children so that they may become familiar with the teachings of the sages and be cognizant of the heavenly principles *(t'ien-li)*.[11] There was no clear demarcation between cosmology and ethics in the Chinese tradition. The physical, natural order and the social, moral order were identical and often spoken of as one and the same.

Proper rituals and sacrifices offered to the ancestors were also considered conducive to such an understanding of the cosmic order.[12] Ancestor veneration and filial piety toward the living parents were believed to be harmony producing and thus played an important role in maintaining the stability of the universe. Popular religion, including popular Buddhism and Taoism, did not challenge the ancestral rites and often assisted in the family-centered ceremonies and sacrifices.[13] Consequently, the Chinese concept of spirituality is defined as the fullest possible development of the ethical character of the individual.[14]

According to the theories advanced in the *I-ching* (Book of changes), which were assimilated by many popular Chinese faiths, there is no isolated occurrence but only concurrence. Heaven, earth, and man are the three dimensions simultaneously involved in any given pattern of activity. All categories such as heaven and man, life and death, good and evil are not diametrical opposites but rather interrelated aspects of a continuum. Underlying the trigrams and hexagrams in the *Book of Changes* is the perceived truth that things are groups of relations. Time is not recognized as an abstract addition of quantitatively equal and qualitatively indistinguishable units. Space, too, in the traditional Chinese conception, is heterogeneous and hierarchical. It is not conceived as an undifferentiated and homogeneous medium similar to that described by Newton and Galileo. Everything in the universe is assigned its specific quality, function, and status, as well as value, all contributing to the grand cosmic harmony. Disturbances in the one realm result in corresponding disturbances in the other. Abnormal phenomena in the realm of nature are positive evidence of irregularities in human society. The failure of human beings to fulfill natural social obligations does violence to the cosmic harmony and is hence unforgivable.[15]

Yin and *yang* were originally conceived as two equally necessary cosmic forces, mutually complementing each other, neither ever permanently triumphing in their eternal cosmic interplay. But *yin* was regarded as definitely inferior to *yang,* just as earth was low and humble and heaven was high and exalted *(t'ien-tsun ti-pei)*.[16] By extension, different human estates were believed to be fixed and predestined. Tung Chung-shu (c. 179–c. 104 B.C.), for example, regarded the inequality between *yin* and *yang* as justification for inequalities within the human social order. Patterning after nature *(fa-t'ien)* was a concept that informed the thought of many elite thinkers. This concept also had a pervasive influence among commoners, who generally believed the proverb: "Those who obey the decrees of Heaven will prosper while those who defy them will perish" *(Shun-t'ien-che ts'un ni-t'ien-che wang)*.[17] In the minds of many, one's present blessings or misfortunes were determined in a previous existence *(ch'ien-sheng fen-ting)*.[18] In fact, the concepts of *fen* (status) and *ming* (fate) became so dominant in Chinese culture that they were hardly questioned. "Accept your appointed status and be content with your destiny" *(shou-fen an-ming)* and "Listen to heaven and follow your fate" *(t'ing-t'ien yu-ming)* are two expressions that were widely circulated in late imperial times and that still retain their potency today.[19]

Confucian Ethics in Popular Perspective

There are two main dimensions of Confucian morality: altruism based on the concept of humanity *(jen)* and the social obligations prescribed in specific human relationships. Confucian humanism includes a concern that extends to society at large. But, although altruism toward society as a whole always existed in Confucian morality, there was for the superior man *(chün-tzu)* a more immediate and indeed prior concern—namely, the fulfillment of social obligations inherent in specific human relationships. Students of Confucian ethics are aware that notions such as *jen* and *li* (ritual), cannot merely be regarded as forms, devoid of dynamic qualities and ethical content. In fact, it is the very capability of an individual to maintain functionally a creative tension between his inner morality *(jen)* and its external manifestation *(li)* that enables him to become a normative paradigmatic being *(chün-tzu)*.[20] *Jen* is a potential virtue intrinsic to every human being; it is the primary focus of Confucian ethics and a unifying principle of particular Confucian virtues. Yet as Professor Mou Tsung-san and others have argued, this internal criterion of Confucian morality must necessarily be externalized and actualized in concrete and specific social contexts in order to maintain its viability.

The concepts of *jen* and *li* underwent many changes over time, of course, and accumulated several different layers of meaning. Nonetheless, by late imperial times, we can identify certain common denominators in Confucian social morality. Among the most important concrete manifestations of *jen* and *li* in Chinese society were the values of *chung* (loyalty to the monarch), *hsiao* (filial piety), *chieh* (integrity and chastity), and *i* (a sense of obligation). Let us consider them in turn.

Loyalty to the Monarch

Of these assorted virtues, *chung* was more obviously relevant to the elite who became degree holders and officials than to the common people. Yet it was also a popular precept that figured in folklore and in popular elementary readers. The tragic heroism of the loyalist official Yueh Fei (1103–1141) was well known to virtually all Chinese. Regardless of the authenticity of authorship of the poem titled "Man-chiang-hung" (Redness all across the river), it represents a subgenre of patriotic poetry, exalting the virtue of loyalty to the monarch. The spirit of Yueh Fei is expressed in the widely known popular phrase, "utmost loyalty in repayment to the state" *(ching-chung pao-kuo),* which according to legend was tattooed on his back by his mother and was engraved on a stele south of his tomb in 1535 in commemoration of his loyal conduct. Here, the long-standing Chinese social concept of *pao* (repaying kindness) reinforces loyalty as a virtue. By the Ming period, if not before, *chung* implied a personal commitment unto death should one enter the service of the emperor.[21]

Huang Tao-chou (1585–1646), one of the Ming loyalists who was executed by the Manchus, wrote a famous couplet before his death: "Eternally valid are the Three Bonds and Five Constant Virtues; forever exalted are loyalty and duty" *(Kang-ch'ang wan-ku chung-i ch'ien-ch'iu).* The prince of T'ang, of the remnant Ming regime, canonized him posthumously with the title *chung-lieh* (loyal and illustrious), and 130 years after his heroic death the Ch'ien-lung emperor granted him the title *chung-tuan* (loyal and upright), testifying to Manchu support for Confucian ethics, even when practiced by Ming loyalists. In 1825, during the Tao-kuang reign, Huang's name was entered in the Temple of Confucius.[22] The foster mother of Ku Yen-wu, a woman née Wang, was remembered not only for her influence on Ku, the famous Ming loyalist, but also for her own heroic actions. When she learned that the occupation of the county of Ch'ang-shu by Ch'ing troops was imminent, she began to starve herself and died fifteen days later. According to Ku's own account, she said to her adopted son with her last breath, "Although only a woman, I have received favor from the [Ming] dynasty; to perish with the dynasty is no more than my duty. . . ."[23]

The moral sentiments behind the concept of loyalty to the monarch continued to be potent throughout the Ch'ing period. It has been persuasively argued that it was the loyalty to the monarch that sustained Ch'ing imperial authority and made possible the T'ung-chih Restoration in the nineteenth century.[24] From a popular perspective, it seems certain that, even in the period of the rampant mid-nineteenth-century rebellions, loyalty to the monarch was not absent from popular consciousness. Popular precepts not only called for obeying the law and paying taxes promptly but also instilled the sanctity of the imperial status. "The sky never has two suns, and the state never two rulers" *(T'ien wu erh jih ming wu erh wang)* was a common proverb in the Late Ch'ing period.[25] The *San-tzu ching* exhorted, "The monarch should show respect and the subject should be loyal" *(Chün tse ching ch'en tse chung).*[26] In the *Hsi-shih hsien-wen,* readers are reminded, "Once a monarch, he will be ruler all his life" *(i-jih wei chün chung-sheng wei chu).*[27] Loyalty to the monarch was in fact regarded as a logical extension and a higher manifestation of filial piety, hence the saying, "extending filial devotion to loyalty for the monarch" *(i-hsiao tso chung).*[28] In fact, *chung* is defined in the imperially sanctioned and extremely influential *Hsiao-ching* as "serving the monarch with filial piety" *(i hsiao shih chün).*[29] The proverb "Loyal ministers must be sought in the families that produce filial sons" *(ch'iu chung-ch'en pi yü hsiao-tzu chih men)* gained widespread circulation in Ch'ing times.[30] The *Ch'ien-tzu wen,* for its part, advises its countless young readers that "in being loyal to the monarch, one must devote all of one's being" *(chung tse chin-ming).*[31] Through such sayings, as well as folktales and operas that praised *chung* as the loftiest virtue, loyalty to the monarch entered popular consciousness.

Filial Piety

Even more deeply imbedded than *chung* in the popular consciousness was of course the precept of *hsiao*—filial piety. The *Hsiao-ching* states in its opening chapter that filial piety is the root of all virtues *(te-chih-pen).*[32] It is the warp of heaven's fabric *(t'ien-ching)* and the principle of earth *(ti-i).*[33] Filial piety was regarded as an axiomatic, absolute, and constant virtue, an imperative in human existence. The *Hsiao-ching* also states, "Veneration of the father is the utmost form of filial piety, and to identify him as heaven [*p'ei-t'ien*] is the epitome of veneration."[34] "The attitude of a sage toward heaven and earth," says Chu Hsi, "is not dissimilar to that of a child toward his/her parents."[35] Reverence shown to one's parents should, therefore, not be different from that shown to heaven and earth.[36] Among the major precepts expounded by the influential Ming philosopher Wang Yang-ming (1472–1529) was that of *liang-chih* (innate knowing faculty), which, on the surface, seems to connote subjectivity and even individuality. This innate knowing faculty may be understood as the innermost and indissoluble reality of man. Yet it certainly does not imply the need to set oneself against everything externally imposed on him. Wang did not formulate a philosophy in which the breaking away from social obligations was a prerequisite for self-sufficiency and the full realization of oneself. In fact, Wang accepted without question the concrete implications of Confucian ethics, whereby the innermost reality was linked to specific human relationships. Wang illustrated his principle of innate knowledge repeatedly with reference to the virtue of filial piety. The true meaning of human existence, he believed, should be sought in the context of human relations. To Wang, filial piety was so deeply rooted in human nature that "to expunge it would be to deny the very foundation of humanity."[37]

In the *Book of Changes* heaven and earth are clearly identified cosmologically as father and mother respectively *(ch'ien wei fu k'un wei mu)*.[38] This powerful symbolism was often taken literally by people in late imperial China. Fan Hung-ssu, for example, wrote in his *Tso-jen ching* (The mirror of human conduct) that "the parent is my heaven and the monarch of my family."[39] The authority of the parents was thought to be near absolute, if not indeed absolute. As a result of this belief, religiosity was fused into ethics.

For obvious economic reasons peasant families recognized the importance of filial duties on the part of the young. Devotion of the sons assured greater productivity for the household and the security of the parents in their old age. Filial piety is given the highest priority among all virtues in the *Hsi-shih hsien-wen,* which states, "In a thousand classics and a myriad of books, the virtue of filial piety is the most important of all" *(Ch'ien-ching wan-tien hsiao i wei hsien)*.[40] Even learning *(hsueh),* greatly valued by the Chinese, was of secondary importance in the *San-tzu ching*. The performance of filial duties and the demonstration of brotherly love were more essential *(shou hsiao-t'i tz'u chien-wen)*.[41] In the minds of many, a thorough comprehension of the content of *Hsiao-ching* should be accomplished before one took up other classics.[42] The elementary primer, *Hsun-meng chiao-erh ching,* contains a rather lengthy discussion of *hsiao,* part of which reads:

Be filial to your parents. . . .

Filial sons are kindly advised to maintain a pleasant appearance and to show no anger.

Treat your parents with genuine understanding.

Do not travel far when your parents are advanced in age.

Filial sons will consequently perpetuate their names.

Meng Tsung's tears [moved Heaven and Earth and] caused bamboo shoots to grow out of season [when his mother yearned for them] on a wintry day.

Wang Hsiang laid his body on the numbingly freezing ice for his mother [in an attempt to catch carp desired by his mother].

Tung Yung sold himself [to raise money] so he could properly bury his father. Heaven sent down an immortal to wed him [in response to his filial act].

It is only obvious that among a hundred acts, filial conduct is the greatest of all.

Heaven never fails to respond to people who are filial. . . .

Your parents are indeed living Buddhas. . . .

They are high as heaven.

Their kindness is too great to be repaid even with one's own life.[43]

Meng Tsung (of the Three Kingdoms period), Wang Hsiang (Chin dynasty), and Tung Yung (Han dynasty) are among the best-known paragons of filial piety. Stories of Tzu Lu and Tseng Shen (both disciples of Confucius), Huang Hsiang, Lu Chi, and Ting Lan (all of the Han dynasty) are standard entries in the numerous versions of Kuo Chü-ching's *Erh-shih-ssu hsiao* (The twenty-four examples of filial piety) and in a variety of other popular readers, such as the *San-tzu ching, Jen-sheng pi-tu* (Necessary reading for everyone), *Ku yao-yen* (Ancient folklore and proverbs), and *Hsiao-hsueh chi-chieh* (Annotations on elementary education [by Chu Hsi]).[44] Stories of exemplary filial acts were often printed in popular booklets and primers for children, and illustrated versions of the *Erh-shih-ssu hsiao* commonly appeared in Ch'ing period almanacs.[45]

Filial devotion is a ubiquitous theme in popular literature of all sorts. The phrase "the kindness of parents is profound" *(fu-mu en-shen)* can be found in both the *Hsi-shih hsien-wen* and the *Jen-sheng pi-tu.*[46] Some works even stressed that a nonhuman mammal or a bird would repay parental kindness. A lamb, out of filial piety, would suck its mother's milk while kneeling *(yang yu kuei-ju chih en);* a raven would feed its parents when they are too old to find food for themselves *(ya yu fan-pu chih i).*[47] These stories, abbreviated in the form of proverbs, gained wide circulation, and terms derived from them are used even today as synonyms for filial piety.[48] Children's songs collected from Fukien include the following lines: "Young roosters are raised so that they will crow at dawn. Puppies are raised so that they will bark [to alert their owners of danger]. Sons are raised so that they will provide when the father is old."[49]

Among the traditional marriage customs observed by the people of Ch'ao-chou, Kwangtung, was the practice of asking the bride to step on firecrackers, an auspicious act designed to encourage the arrival of a male child. But at the same time the new bride was also reminded of one of her major responsibilities, that is, to be filial to her new parents-in-law. The "Song of Firecracker Stepping" (T'a huo-yen shih) reads:

> The bride steps on the firecrackers,
> To obtain early a ch'i-lin—a male child;
> The husband sings and the wife follows, two with one heart.
> Be diligent in carrying out filial duties toward the parents-in-law.[50]

A children's song that unfailingly arouses filial sentiment among the young, collected from Chekiang province and titled "A Round-Shaped Fruit" (I-ko yuan-kuo), has an almost identical version in Fukien:

> A round-shaped fruit, spherical and rotund,
> The shell is brown and the pulp sweet;
> With living parents one's life is as sweet as honey,
> Without them, life is as bitter as huang-lien [coptis japonica].[51]

Songs belonging to this genre are too numerous to cite.[52] The subtle didactic role played by this type of literature in molding Chinese mentality is intriguing. Expressions related to the virtue filial piety are ubiquitous. Filial piety was indeed the supreme virtue even from the popular perspective. It was believed that "failure to perform filial duties toward one's parents would render all religious worship futile" (pu hsiao fu-mu ching shen wu-i).[53]

Female Chastity

The relationship between parents and children was, of course, most important to the family. But the relationship between husband and wife was no less emphasized. Indeed, Chang Huang of the Ming dynasty argued in his "Essay on the Ordering of the Family" (Cheng-chia lun) that "the relationship between husband and wife must be properly maintained before the father can be loving, the son filial, the elder brother kind, and the younger brother respectful."[54] It was believed that a wife demonstrating moral integrity and chastity would be able to arrest the family from decline *(chia-p'in ssu hsien-ch'i)*, just as a capable general could restore peace for an empire in turmoil *(kuo-luan ssu liang-chiang)*. These concepts appear in at least two popular readers, the *Jen-sheng pi-tu* and the *Hsi-shih hsien-wen*.[55]

How was the pivotal role of a wife defined in the orthodox fashion? In addition to loyalty to the monarch and filial piety, Confucianism also championed fidelity and submission *(chen-shun)* on the part of the wife. Her obligations and those of the husband were not reciprocal. Because each represented one of the two cosmic principles of *yin* and *yang,* they possessed diametrically different sets of attributes and responsibilities. Just as these two cosmic forces *(erh-i)* operated always in perfect spontaneity, each following the dictates of its respective characteristics, husbands and wives must play their respective roles without transgressing each other's.[56] According to a popular proverb, "As *yin* and *yang* are of a different nature, so male and female behave differently" *(yin-yang shu-hsing nan-nü i-hsing)*.[57] Those who failed to recognize such role distinctions were no different from animals *(yü ch'in-shou wu-i)*.[58]

The family prospers, according to the *I-ching,* when "the females of the family behave properly" *(nü-chen)*.[59] The *Ch'ien-tzu wen* teaches that chastity and integrity are to be cherished by women *(nü mu chen-lieh),* whereas the capable and the virtuous are to be emulated by men *(nan hsiao ts'ai-liang)*.[60] Based on Ch'eng I's commentary on the *I-ching, chen* (chastity) is, in actuality, synonymous with *cheng* (orthodox). Hsu Chen-chi of the Ming dynasty reiterated this position in his *Chih-yen* (Straightforward remarks): "The orthodox code of female behavior requires women to demonstrate their virtue of submissiveness *(jou-te)* for the sake of maintaining harmony in the family.[61] This submissive role of women and the three stages of their subordination *(san-ts'ung)* had long-standing classical roots in works such as the *Li-chi* (Record of ritual) and *I-li* (Decorum and ritual). The theme of submissiveness for women was constantly inculcated into young minds through works such as the *Hui-t'u nü-erh ching* (Illustrated classic for girls) as well as the *Hsun-meng chiao-erh ching, Jen-sheng pi-tu,* and *Hsi-shih hsien-wen*.[62] A wife was taught to regard her husband as "heaven"; his position was supreme and not to be challenged.[63]

Although not without exceptions, the remarriage of a woman was generally regarded as disgraceful and detrimental to her moral integrity. Suicide as a protest against enforced remarriage not only was not discouraged but was recognized as a virtuous and heroic act, to be rewarded by the state. Biographies of "women of integrity" can be found in almost all Ming-Ch'ing gazetteers, and during the Ch'ing period, temples of fidelity and filiality *(chieh-hsiao tz'u)* appeared throughout the empire—one in each county by imperial order. Women who had demonstrated the virtue of chastity and filial piety were honored during the sacrifices in spring and in autumn.

Dutifulness

Having examined the cosmologically grounded concepts of *chung, hsiao,* and *chieh,* we must now consider the precept of *i* (a sense of duty, often translated as "righteousness"). In terms of moral philosophy, *i* may be regarded as a normative criterion applicable to all Confucian virtues and obligations. Used adverbially, *i* indicates that one puts into practice all the specific virtues, including reverence and deference. Any failure to actualize a potential virtue or an obligation, and any infraction against loyalty to the monarch, filial piety, chastity, or even the principle of faithfulness *(hsin)* with respect to friends, disqualifies a person from being considered dutiful. That person's conduct therefore becomes morally unacceptable. A superior person *(chün-tzu)* is expected to adhere conscientiously to the prescriptions of proper behavior at all times. In the Confucian scheme of values, *i* is a "pervasive mode of living which gives meaning to every area of human conduct."[64] Ontologically speaking, when *i* is fully cultivated and developed to the utmost, it should be as extensive as the entire universe—what Mencius called the vast, overflowing inner vital force *(hao-jan chih ch'i).*[65] It is in this sense that Wen T'ien-hsiang (1236–1282), a Sung loyalist much remembered in Ming-Ch'ing times, wrote in his celebrated "Song of the Spirit of Rectitude" *(Cheng-ch'i ko):*

The universe is suffused with [this spirit]. . . .
When an individual is abundantly permeated by this spirit, [his exemplary
    conduct] will forever be remembered. . . .
The earth is sustained by this spirit, and so are the pillars of heaven.
The maintenance of the Three Bonds is contingent upon the existence of this
    spirit.
It is the very root of morality.[66]

I, as compared with the more universalistic but less tangible *jen,* imposes on each person a strong sense of specific obligation. Those who fail to actualize in entirety the Confucian virtues, hence failing to fulfill their sense of obligation, are regarded as undutiful or wayward. This should create in them a sense of shame and disgrace. Mencius had said that "the feeling of shame and dislike is the beginning of *i*."[67] *I* is, therefore, a natural moral imperative. Until concrete obligations are observed or fulfilled, one cannot aspire to the larger concerns of society.

Confucian Relationships

As should already be apparent, the above-mentioned values invariably operated within the framework of the so-called Three Bonds *(san-kang)* and Five Relationships *(wu-lun)* of Confucianism. The Three Bonds referred to the hierarchical obligations of rulers and subjects, husbands and wives, and fathers and sons (or more generally, parents and children). The Five Relationships included the Three Bonds, plus two other networks of obligation —those between younger and older brothers and those between friends. On the whole, these relationships, with the exception of the last, emphasized unilateral obligations more than reciprocity.

The Confucian classics naturally underscored the crucial importance of maintaining order within the family. The "Commentary on the Decision" of the thirty-seventh hexagram of the *I-ching*—designated "Family," *(chia-jen)* —echoes the famous lines of the *Analects,* "Let the sovereign be a sovereign, the subject a subject, the father a father and the son a son" *(Chün-chün ch'en-ch'en fu-fu tzu-tzu)*. It states: "Among the members of the family there are strict rulers; these are the parents. When the father is in truth a father and the son a son, when the elder brother is an elder brother and the younger brother a younger brother, the husband a husband and the wife a wife, then the house is on the right way."[68] Mencius defined the teachings *(chiao)* appropriate to each of the Five Relationships: between father and son, there should be affection; between sovereign and minister, there should be righteousness; between husband and wife, there should be attention to their separate functions; between old and young, there should be a proper order; and between friends, there should be faithfulness.[69] The *Chung-yung* (Doctrine of the mean) explains that the duties of the Five Relationships constitute the universal way of the world *(t'ien-hsia chih ta-tao)*. The concept of *yung* (commonality) in particular implies behavioral constancy because each individual has an evaluating mind that makes such behavior both possible and imperative. Not surprisingly, Chu Hsi devotes special attention to the Five Relationships in the first half of his commentary to the *Chung-yung*.[70]

Although the Five Relationships should be understood as implying mutual obligations, they were, at least by late imperial times, plainly qualified by two important Confucian doctrines: propriety *(li)* and the rectification of names *(cheng-ming)*.[71] The term *cheng-lun* (rectifying personal relationships), applies to the proper behavior of one person toward another within the specific nexus of the Five Relationships. For Chu Hsi, the observance of proper interpersonal relationships should be as natural and spontaneous as "a person who waves a fan to cool himself when hot" *(jen-je tzu-hui yao-shan)*.[72] Fang Hsiao-ju, the respected scholar of the Early Ming, devoted an entire chapter to proper human relationships in his *Hou-ch'eng tsa chieh* (Miscellaneous exhortations of Hou-ch'eng).[73]

In the popular elementary readers of the Ming and Ch'ing periods, the Five Relationships receive prominent treatment. In the *San-tzu ching,* for example, we read: "In the human relationships, kindness should exist between father and son, and obedience between husband and wife. The older brother should be friendly, and the younger respectful. The proper order of the old and the young is not to be upset. Those who share common virtue shall become friends. The ruler should show respect to his ministers, and the ministers should be loyal to the ruler. These ten obligations are to be universally observed. Elementary primers must all give due emphasis to them."[74] The *Ch'ien-tzu wen,* never repeating a character, devotes twelve key sentences to these obligations; and the *Chu-tzu chih-chia ko-yen* (Family instructions of Master Chu) warns that, "when violence is done to the proper personal relationships and to the constant virtues [*jen, i, li, chih,* and *hsin*], destruction is imminent" *(lun-ch'ang kuai-ch'uan li-chien hsiao-wang)*.[75]

Although emphasizing the concept of the Five Relationships, popular primers also exhorted their readers to give proper attention to blood relatives of the patrilineal line other than one's father and one's elder brothers. The *San-tzu ching* informs its impressionable young readers: "Your great-great-grandfather, great-grandfather, and grandfather; your father and yourself; and your sons, grandsons, great-grandsons, and great-great-grandsons—these form a lineage of nine generations, tied together by personal relations [*jen chih lun*]."[76] The *Ch'ien-tzu wen* urges the extension of Confucian particularistic ethics at least to paternal cousins: "All the paternal aunts and uncles [produce] nephews who are comparable to your sons. Think solicitously of your brothers who are linked to you like air and the tree's branches."[77]

Of the Five Relationships, the first three were clearly primary. The concept of *san-kang,* which goes back at least to the Han dynasty, became particularly prominent from the Sung dynasty onward. Many classic Chinese novels illustrate the theme of virtuous persons who devote themselves unilaterally to their superiors within the framework of the Three Bonds—such as ministers who remain unstintingly loyal to unworthy rulers, and wives who remain faithful to husbands who are scoundrels, espousing chaste widowhood after their husbands' deaths and devoting themselves to rearing their offspring and honoring their family name. From an orthodox Confucian standpoint, a person could preserve his or her individual dignity only by submission to a person of superior status in a particular bond. Moral self-realization became identical with "the suppression of one's deep-seated instincts for the maintenance of social decorum."[78]

The literal meaning of *kang* is the major cord in a net to which all the other strings are attached. The *san-kang* could therefore be regarded as the three major cords tying together the entire structure of Confucian ethics. In the *San-tzu ching,* immediately after mentioning the *san-ts'ai* (cosmic triad) (heaven, earth, and man) and the *san-kuang* or three celestial bodies (the sun, the moon, and the stars), the Three Bonds are introduced, suggesting a clear parallelism between cosmic phenomena and specific human relationships.[79] The sublime duties they entailed could, under certain circumstances, call for martyrdom: "The minister sacrifices his life for the monarch, and the wife dies for her husband" (*Ch'en wei chün ssu ch'i wei fu wang*) is a standard entry in the *Ku yao-yen* and other similar collections of proverbs.[80]

Naturally the rigid requirements of ritual *(li)* strengthened the hierarchical imperatives of the *san-kang.* Old and young, superior and inferior *(chang-yu tsun-pei)* were distinctions that self-evidently demanded ritual recognition in China. According to many family instructions *(chia-hsun),* a sense of hierarchy should be instilled into the minds of the young by the age of eight at the latest.[81] According to the popular elementary reader *Ch'ien-tzu wen,* which drew heavily on classical inspiration, music *(yueh)* was to inspire the respect of the inferior for the superior; ritual *(li)* had no other purpose than to help internalize this sense of respect.[82] The combination of proper ritual and unilateral obligations according to the Three Bonds characterized Chinese culture from at least the Sung dynasty onward. Loyalty to a fallen dynasty called for martyrdom or at least eremitism on the part of those who had received imperial appointment.[83] Filial piety came to mean utter obedience as well as loving devotion. Strict and meticulous rules governing mourning became obligatory, "at times," according to Frederick Mote, "to the complete extinction of the humane content."[84]

A few Ch'ing intellectuals, notably Yen Yuan (1635–1704), discovered that the rules laid down in the *Family Rituals (Chia li),* traditionally ascribed to Chu Hsi, were not entirely in accordance with the original canon, including the *Li-chi.* This discovery prompted Yen to become suspicious of the reliability of the Sung philosophers' interpretations, a suspicion also engendered by *k'ao-cheng* scholarship, which Yen, however, felt was overly pedantic.[85] But skepticism such as Yen's was confined to elite circles and was vastly overshadowed in China as a whole by the wide dissemination of traditional precepts among the population at large. Far more influential than Yen was Chu Yung-ch'un, whose *Chu-tzu chih-chia ko-yen* argued powerfully that inherited rules concerning mourning ought to be strictly enforced and backed by stern exhortations *(fa-su tz'u-yen).*[86] The universal practice of ancestor worship and certain common elements of marriage ritual, as well as the sacredness of imperial rituals performed by the Son of Heaven himself, allowed the Three Bonds to penetrate every level of traditional Chinese religion.

Popular Values and the Three Teachings

No single factor can explain the enduring power of Confucian values. In truth, their strength derived from a complex interaction of mutually supporting ideas and institutions in traditional Chinese society, including not only the family and clan system, and the state structure with its propaganda mechanisms, legal apparatus, and official worship, but also institutional Buddhism and sectarian Taoism, not to mention popular religious practices. Even the most lofty and abstract Confucian concepts were always rooted in concrete social realities.

Jen, for example, as a truly cosmic virtue, was supposed to encompass all humanity. Ideally, it produced benevolent government policies as well as charitable acts within individual Chinese communities. But as Chu Hsi and others insisted, following Mencius, *jen* had to start with filial piety and respect for senior relatives. Duty *(i)* came to be inextricably linked with the Five Relationships and the Three Bonds, as did *li* (proper decorum or ritual), which bolstered the sanctity of social and political distinctions and helped individuals first to internalize, and then express externally, their moral responsibilities. *Chih,* as humane wisdom or intelligence, established the criterion for the only kind of education that really mattered in late imperial times—moral learning, institutionally reinforced by the civil-service examination system.

These four values, together with faithfulness *(hsin),* constituted the Five

Constant Virtues *(wu-ch'ang)*. They were always manifest in social action and could not be compromised or confused in any manner *(pu jung wen)*.[87] Popular readers of the Ch'ing period constantly touted the importance of moral education. The *Hsi-shih hsien-wen* states, for example, that "wealth is as worthless as dung and dirt, while the virtues of *jen* and *i* are worth a thousand pieces of gold" *(Ch'ien-ts'ai ju fen-t'u jen-i chih ch'ien-chin)*.[88] Although the emphasis in this case appears to be on universalistic moral imperatives, the general thrust of popular Confucianism was to emphasize the family as the matrix of morality. According to the *Ch'ien-tzu wen,* we receive not only our physical body and our four limbs *(ssu-ta)* but also the Five Constant Virtues from our parents—all the more reason, then, that we must nourish these naturally endowed moral qualities with the utmost reverence *(kung-wei chü-yang)*, and under no circumstances inflict harm on them.[89] From a Confucian standpoint, the Three Bonds and Five Constant Virtues themselves constituted morality.[90] When they were properly maintained, most Chinese believed, peace would prevail in the entire cosmos, both in heaven *(t'ien-ching lai-i-ch'ing)* and on earth *(ti-wei lai-i-ning)*.[91]

Popular ballads attest to the pervasiveness of moral concerns in traditional Chinese society. Two songs, both gathered in Fukien, illustrate the point. One ballad, about marriage, is titled "Happiness Abides as the Door Is Being Knocked" *(Shou-p'ai fang-men hsi-ch'i ch'ang):*

Happiness abides at the knocking of the door.
Two families are joined and the
Five Constant Virtues prevail.
Like fish swimming in the water, affection and love deepen and abound.
Like plum branches on the mountain top, blossoming year after year without
    ceasing.[92]

Here the Five Constant Virtues are regarded as the ultimate source of lasting marital happinesss. A second ballad, titled "Unto the Tenth Kerchief Embroider the Yellow Chrysanthemum" *(Shih-t'iao shou-chin hsiu chü-huang),* seems to express subtle resentment regarding the Three Bonds and Five Constant Virtues, but the singer, a woman, nonetheless realizes that they are inescapable moral imperatives:

The yellow chrysanthemum is embroidered unto the tenth kerchief.
I know so well the Three Bonds and the Five Constant Virtues.
My youth and beauty are long gone.
I keep myself chaste now and leave behind a good name.[93]

These cultural norms were regarded as correct not only by Confucians but also by many, if not most, Buddhists and Taoists in Ch'ing dynasty China. Although Buddhism's concern was supposed to extend to all humanity, and indeed to all sentient beings, it had nevertheless come to terms with the specific obligations of the Three Bonds.[94] In morality books *(shan-shu)* of both Taoist and Buddhist inspiration, there was more than "an embryonic recognition that morality appropriate for the common people has to take into account their actual statuses and functions."[95] Significantly, these books were "read and memorized by the middle and lower classes" in China, and their self-conscious appeal to the common denominator of Confucian ethics was especially conspicuous in works such as the *T'ai-shang kan-ying p'ien* (Treatise of the most exalted one on moral retribution) and the *Pu-fei-ch'ien kung-te li* (Meritorious deeds at no cost).[96] In these books, hierarchical differentiation in social and moral terms is clearly recognized, and such virtues as loyalty to the monarch, filial piety, chastity, propriety, and dutifulness are bolstered by a belief in supernatural retribution *(pao-ying).*[97] This combination of Confucian moral precepts and popular Buddhist and Taoist religious beliefs can also be found in works such as the *Hsi-shih hsien-wen,* the *Hsun-meng chiao erh-ching,* and the *Jen-sheng pi-tu.*[98]

At the top of traditional Chinese society, the emperors of both the Ming and Ch'ing dynasties endorsed not only Ch'eng-Chu metaphysics but also specific ethical obligations. The founder of the Ming dynasty, for example, wrote a preface in 1374 to a work titled *Hsiao-tz'u lu* (Record of filial piety and parental kindness), thus indicating his approval. Emperor Hsuan-tsung (r. 1426–1436) published a work of sixty-two *chüan,* supposedly authored by himself, titled the *Wu-lun shu* (Book of the Five Relationships). The early Ch'ing rulers also made great efforts to inculcate familiar ethical precepts among the people. The Shun-chih emperor initiated no less than fifteen works of this sort, including two on the *Classic of Filial Piety: Hsiao-ching chu* (Commentaries on the *Classic of Filial Piety,* 1656) and *Hsiao-ching yen-i* (Exposition and amplification of the *Classic of Filial Piety,* completed after his death in 1682 and printed in 1690). Two others are on the proper conduct of officials: *Jen-ch'en ching hsin lu* (Notes on the vigilance of officials, 1655) and *Tzu-cheng yao-lan* (Essentials of government, 1655). He also commissioned a book to serve as a guide for women: *Nei-tse yen-i* (Exposition on rules for inside the household, 1656).[99]

The K'ang-hsi emperor issued his famous Sacred Edict in 1670. It was supposed to be read aloud by officials and village elders in public meetings twice a month in all rural localities. The first of the sixteen maxims that comprise the Sacred Edict is "Esteem most highly filial piety and brotherly respect in order to give due importance to human relations." The second maxim reads, "Respect kin in order to display the excellence of harmony." The third states, "Let concord abound among those who dwell in the same neighborhood in order to prevent litigation." The seventh maxim says simply, "Expel heterodoxy in order to improve customs." Even more effectively publicized was the *Sheng-yü kuang-hsun,* an amplification of K'ang-hsi's Sacred Edict by his son, the Yung-cheng emperor, and published in 1724. The *Sheng-yü kuang-hsun* came to be disseminated in a number of popularized versions, some written in the vernacular.[100] The semimonthly ritual of expounding these maxims to the illiterate populace was among the major responsibilities of the gentry, especially the lower degree holders, although the effectiveness of this exercise has been questioned.[101]

The unilateral obligations and rigid status differentiation based on the Five Relationships and especially the Three Bonds received powerful sanction from law in imperial China. As Ch'ü T'ung-tsu demonstrates in his classic study, Confucian particularism, as opposed to Legalist universalism, was written directly into the imperial law codes.[102] Legal equality between the sexes had no place in traditional China, and, if a marriage bond had to be broken, the husband and his family initiated it.[103] A concubine not only served her husband with single-minded devotion but also was expected to respect and obey the legitimate wife of the husband, as well as her father-in-law or mother-in-law. Filial piety was a legal as well as moral obligation. Unfilial acts were punishable with the greatest severity, as was any act suggesting disloyalty against the monarch.[104] Although Ch'ü prefers to characterize the Chinese legal tradition as dominated by Confucian *li* (which he defines as "the rules of behavior varying in accordance with one's status defined in the various forms of social relationships"), these rules of behavior, as expressed in law, invariably upheld the Three Bonds.[105]

Above all, the state sought to maintain order *(chih)* and to eradicate all potential sources of disorder *(luan)*. Thus, the objective of elementary education was to prevent young children from slipping into heterodoxical teachings *(fu na yü hsieh)*.[106] Yu-liao-weng, in his postscript to the *Yang-meng san-tzu ching*—an enlarged version of the *Trimetrical Classic* authored by the noted Ch'ing scholar, Chiang Ch'ien—commended the work for its effort to nurture the moral integrity *(cheng)* of young children through rhymed verses and easily understood prose."[107] The primers discussed in this essay did not aim at intellectual profundity and trenchant philosophical exposition; they were meant, following Chu Hsi's design, to fill the ears and stuff the stomachs *(ying-erh ch'ung-fu)* of children.[108] As propaganda tracts they pulled no punches. A proverb in the *Hsi-shih hsien-wen* advised baldly that it was "better to be orthodox and poor than heterodox and well-to-do."[109] The *Hsun-meng chiao-erh ching,* for its part, drove home the point that children must associate themselves with morally exemplary people *(yu-tao shih),* so that their speech and conduct do not deviate from the orthodox way *(cheng-tao).*[110]

Although fundamentally down-to-earth, elementary primers did not always shy away from neo-Confucian metaphysics. Thus, for example, we find the *Hsun-meng chiao-erh ching* linking morality and cosmology in the following way: "Heaven's principle [*t'ien-li*]," it asserts, "grows out of conscience [*liang-hsin*], and conscience is born of heavenly principle. With these four words, *t'ien-li liang-hsin,* good and bad people are to be distinguished."[111] In the end, human conscience, however exalted its origins, inevitably came to be conditioned by concrete notions of a harmonious hierarchy with differentiated personal status *(fen)* as its foundation. By late imperial times, a complex of powerful cosmological, ethical, and religious ideas and concepts merged into an overwhelmingly strong intellectual and emotional force, whose influence could perhaps be escaped only by the most defiant or the most desperate members of Chinese society.

Notes

Abbreviations

CCKY   Chu Yung-ch'un (Ch'ing dynasty), *Chu-tzu chih-chia ko-yen* (Family instructions of Master Chu) (Taipei, 1951). *Chu-tzu chia-hsun* is a different title of the same book.

CEC   *Hsun-meng chiao-erh-ching* (Instructions for children: An elementary primer) (Hsinchu, 1966). This is a reprint of *Hsiao-hsueh chiao-erh-ching,* published in 1925.

CTW   Chou Hsing-ssu (Liang dynasty); Chiang Shou-ch'eng annotated, *Ch'ien-tzu-wen chu-chieh* (Annotated thousand-character classic) (Taichung, 1968).

HC   *K'ung-tzu hsiao-ching* (Confucius' classic of filial piety) (reprint, Taipei, 1971).

HSHW   *Chu-chieh pai-hua tseng-kuang hsi-shih hsien-wen* (Collection of sayings of ancient virtuous men: Annotated vernacular edition) (Kaohsiung, 1978).

JSPT   *Hsin-t'i jen-sheng pi-tu* (Necessary reading for everyone: New-type ed.)
            2 vols. (Shanghai, 1930). This book is based on *Hsi-shih hsien-wen.*
KYY   Tu Wen-lan (Ch'ing dynasty), collected and compiled, *Ku yao-yen*
            (Ancient folklore and proverbs) (Beijing, 1958, based on Man-t'o-lo
            hua-ko ts'ung-shu ed.).
MSTS: CF   Lou Tzu-k'uang, ed., *Kuo-li Pei-ching ta-hsueh Chung-kuo min-su
            hsueh-hui Min-su ts'ung-shu, chuan-hao 4. Chia-fan p'ien, no. 1, Chia-
            fan tsung-lun* (Supplement of folklore and folk literature series of
            National Beijing University and Chinese Association for Folklore, set 4,
            Chinese family customs, no. 1, general model of the family; reprint,
            Taipei, 1979).
MSTS: CT   *Min-su ts'ung-shu: Chiao-tzu tien-fan,* set 4, no. 2 of the above series.
MSTS: FM   *Min-su ts'ung-shu: Fu-mu,* set 4, no. 4 of the above series.
MSTS: FT   *Min-su ts'ung-shu: Fu yü tzu,* set 4, no. 5 of the above series.
NEC   *Hui-t'u nü-erh-ching* (Illustrated classic for girls) (Taichung, 1968).
STC   Wang Ying-lin (?) (Sung dynasty), *Tseng-pu san-tzu-ching* (The trimet-
            rical classic: Amplified edition) 10th printing (Hsinchu, 1974).

1. See inter alia Richard J. Smith, *China's Cultural Heritage: The Ch'ing Dynasty, 1644–1912* (Boulder, Colo., 1983), esp. pp. 108–120, 144–155.

2. William Theodore de Bary, *Self and Society in Ming Thought* (New York, 1970), p. 331.

3. *Hsi-shih hsien-wen* is a collection of proverbs, aphorisms, adages, and maxims. It has been impossible to determine when the earliest version of this work appeared. By virtue of the popularity of this work, it has been printed and enlarged repeatedly in China during the past centuries. On almanacs and their cultural significance, see R. J. Smith's contribution to this volume; also his *Fortune-tellers and Philosophers: Divination in Traditional Chinese Society* (Boulder, Colo., 1991).

4. The authorship and the date of the first appearance of *Hsun-meng chiao-erh ching* cannot be determined. There can be little doubt, however, that this work has been in existence for centuries. It gained wide circulation by the end of the Ch'ing dynasty and is included in the list of traditionally popular educational materials in Chang Chih-kung, *Ch'uan-t'ung yü-wen chiao-yü ch'u-t'an* (A preliminary study of traditional language instruction) (Shanghai, 1962).

5. Wolfram Eberhard, *Moral and Social Values of the Chinese: Collected Essays* (Taipei, 1971), p. 191.

6. Daniel Harrison Kulp, *Country Life in South China: The Sociology of Familism: Phenix Village, Kwantung, China* (New York, 1925), pp. 222–223.

7. Evelyn Sakakida Rawski, *Education and Popular Literacy in Ch'ing China* (Ann Arbor, 1979), pp. 177–178, 252 n. 81.

8. The *San-tzu ching* is traditionally ascribed to Wang Ying-lin (T. Po-hou) of

the Sung dynasty. For a list of different popular versions of this work, see Chang Chih-kung, *Ch'uan-t'ung yü-wen chiao-yü ch'u-t'an,* pp. 158–159. The *Ch'ien-tzu wen* was authored by Chou Hsing-ssu of the Liang dynasty. A list of various annotated editions and versions is found in Chang Chih-kung, pp. 154–157. The *Pai-chia hsing* is most likely a work of the early Sung. The village books *(ts'un-shu)* mentioned in one of the poems of Lu Yu (1125–1210) must have referred to primers such as the *Pai-chia hsing,* which begins with Chao, the name of the imperial house of Sung.

9. Wolfram Eberhard, *Guilt and Sin in Traditional China* (Berkeley, Calif., 1967), p. 124.

10. This phrase is included both in *Hsi-shih hsien-wen* and *Jen-sheng pi-tu.* See HSHW, p. 26; and JSPT 1:1.

11. See the discussion of the Three Bonds and Five Constant Virtues, below.

12. See the passage of Chu Hsi's *Chin-ssu lu* (Reflections on things at hand), quoted in MSTS: CF, p. 138.

13. See the discussion in Smith, *China's Cultural Heritage.*

14. Charles A. Moore, ed., *The Chinese Mind: Essentials of Chinese Philosophy and Culture* (Honolulu, 1967), p. 5.

15. See Wolfram Eberhard, "The Political Function of Astronomy and Astronomers in Han China," in *Chinese Thought and Institutions,* ed. John K. Fairbank (Chicago, 1957), pp. 33–70; and Hans Bielenstein, "An Interpretation of the Portents in the Ts'ien-Han-Shu," *Bulletin of the Museum of Far Eastern Antiquities* 22 (1950): 127–143.

16. This popular expression can also be found in Clifford H. Plopper, *Chinese Religion As Seen through the Proverbs* (New York, 1969), p. 24.

17. This proverb is included both in *Jen-sheng pi-tu and Hsi-shih hsien-wen.* See JSPT 2:86; and HSHW, p. 76.

18. Plopper, *Chinese Religion,* p. 292.

19. These proverbs are found in ibid., pp. 74 and 293, respectively.

20. Wei-ming Tu, "The Creative Tension between *Jen* and *Li,*" *Philosophy East and West* 18, nos. 1–2 (January–April 1968): 29–39; Wei-ming Tu, "*Li* as a Process of Humanization," *Philosophy East and West* 22, no. 2 (April 1972): 187–201; and Antonio S. Cua, "Reflections on the Structure of Confucian Ethics," *Philosophy East and West* 21, no. 2 (April 1977): 125–140.

21. For the concept of *pao,* see Lien-sheng Yang, "The Concept of *Pao* as a Basis for Social Relations in China," in *Chinese Thought and Institutions,* ed. John K. Fairbank, pp. 291–309; also Lien-sheng Yang, *Excursions in Sinology* (Cambridge, Mass., 1969), pp. 3–23.

22. For a biography of Huang Tao-chou, see Arthur W. Hummel, ed., *Eminent Chinese of the Ch'ing Period, 1644–1912* (Washington, D.C., 1943–1944), pp. 345–347.

23. Willard J. Peterson, "The Life of Ku-Yen-wu (1613–1682)," *Harvard Journal of Asiatic Studies,* 28 (1968): 142.

24. Kwang-Ching Liu, "Wan-Ch'ing tu-fu ch'üan-li wen-t'i shang-ch'ueh" (The limits of regional power in the late Ch'ing period: A reappraisal), *The Tsing Hua Journal of Chinese Studies,* n.s. 10, no. 2 (July 1974): 180–181, 196 n. 24, 197 n. 25, 213.

25. See Arthur H. Smith, *Proverbs and Common Sayings from the Chinese* (New York, 1965), p. 43.

26. STC, p. 3.

27. This phrase is also found, among several editions, in a 1969 edition of the *Hsi-shih hsien-wen* published by the Li-hsing shu-chü in Taiwan.

28. Fung Yu-lan, "The Philosophy at the Basis of Traditional Chinese Society," in *Ideological Differences and World Order,* ed. F. S. C. Northrop (New Haven, 1949), p. 28.

29. HC5; MSTS: FM, pp. 65–66.

30. KYY, pp. 834, 912.

31. CTW, p. 7.

32. HC1; and MSTS: FM, p. 63. See also Fung, "The Philosophy at the Basis of Traditional Chinese Society," p. 26.

33. HC7; and MSTS: FM, pp. 66–67.

34. See HC9; MSTS: FT, pp. 89–90; MSTS: FM, pp. 68–69.

35. MSTS: FM, p. 148.

36. Yuan Hung expressed a similar view in his *Hou-Han chi.* See Yü Ying-shih, *"Ming-chiao wei-chi yü Wei-Chin shih-feng ti chuan-pien,"* in *Shih-huo yueh-k'an,* n.s. 9, nos. 7 and 8 (November 1979): 248; Ssu-ma Kuang, *Su-shui chai,* in *MSTS: CF,* p. 125.

37. Tu Wei-ming, *Neo-Confucian Thought in Action: Wang Yang-ming's Youth (1472–1509)* (Berkeley, Calif.: 1976), p. 59. See also Julia Ching, trans., *The Philosophical Letters of Wang Yang-ming* (Canberra, 1972); William Theodore de Bary, "Individualism and Humanitarianism in Late Ming Thought," in *Self and Society in Ming Thought,* pp. 145–247; Wei-ming Tu, "Subjectivity and Ontological Reality —An Interpretation of Wang Yang-ming's Mode of Thinking," *Philosophy East and West* 23, nos. 1–2 (January and April 1973): 187–205; David S. Nivison, "Protest against Conventions and Conventions of Protest," in *The Confucian Persuasion,* ed. Arthur F. Wright (Stanford, 1960), p. 180.

38. MSTS: FM, p. 1.

39. Ibid., p. 163. See also Chia-yü collected in MSTS: FM, pp. 79–80.

40. HSHW, p. 83.

41. STC, p. 1b.

42. Ibid., p. 3b.

43. CEC, pp. 4–5.

44. See STC, p. 1b; KYY, pp. 90, 650–660; JSPT, 2:2; Chang Po-hsing, *Hsiao-hsueh chi-chieh* (Annotated materials for elementary education), in *Ts'ung-shu chi-ch'eng,* ed. Wang Yun-wu (Shanghai, 1937) 983:94.

45. Eberhard, *Moral and Social Values of the Chinese,* p. 200.

46. HSHW, p. 47; and JSPT, p. 10.

47. HSHW, p. 66.

48. See, e.g., KYY, p. 332.

49. Yun-sheng Hsieh, *Min-ko chia-chi* (Songs from Fukien, pt. 1), in Lou Tzu-k'uang and Yuan Chang-rui, eds., *Chung-shan ta-hsueh min-su ts'ung-shu,* vol. 13, Folklore Series of National Sun Yat-sen University (1928; reprint, Canton, 1969).

50. *Hun-yin ko-yao yü hun-su* (Marriage songs and customs), p. 94. A similar song, titled "San-jih pai-shen shih" (Hymn of worshipping god for three days), contains the same message. See ibid., p. 96.

51. Chu T'ien-min, *Ko-sheng t'ung-yao chi* (Children's songs from various provinces) (1923), p. 49; and Hsieh Yun-sheng, *Min-ko chia-chi,* pp. 161–162.

52. For further examples, see Chu T'ien-min, *Ko-sheng t'ung-yao chi* (Ballads from Foochow, pt. 1), pp. 151–153.

53. JSPT 1:14b.

54. MSTS: CF, pp. 274–275.

55. JSPT, 2:6b; and HSHW, p. 87.

56. See the passage in Hsun Yueh's *Shen chien* (Extended reflections), collected in MSTS: CF, pp. 95–96. For a study of *Shen-chien,* see Ch'i-yun Ch'en, *Hsün Yüeh and the Mind of the Late Han China: A Translation of the Shen-Chien with Introduction and Annotations* (Princeton, N.J., 1980).

57. KYY, p. 93.

58. See Ts'ao Tuan's *Yeh-hsing chu* (Candles for strolling at night), collected in MSTS: CF, p. 281.

59. MSTS: CF, p. 67.

60. CYW, p. 5.

61. MSTS: CF, p. 268.

62. NEC, pp. 5b, 13; JSPT 2:10, 2:12; and HSHW, p. 36.

63. NEC, p. 4. See also T'ung-tsu Ch'ü, *Han Social Structure* (Seattle, 1972), pp. 41 n. 39, 50, 50 n. 5.

64. Chung-ying Cheng, "On *Yi* as a Universal Principle of Specific Application in Confucian Morality," *Philosophy East and West* 22, no. 3 (July 1972): 276.

65. See *Mencius* 2A:2. For James Legge's translation, see *The Chinese Classics* 2:190.

66. Wen T'ien-hsiang's *Cheng-ch'i ko* is found in a great number of anthologies and textbooks. See, e.g., *Ku-chin wen-hsuan* (Weekly anthology of ancient and modern Chinese literature) 51 (September 8, 1952), reprinted in *Chu-yin hsiang-chieh ku-chin wen-hsuan,* ed. Liang Jung-jo, et al. 17th ed. (Taipei, 1976) 1:241.

67. *Mencius* 2A:6. See Legge, *The Chinese Classics* 2:203.

68. For the hexagram, see Richard Wilhelm, trans., *The I Ching or Book of Changes* (Princeton, N.J., 1967), p. 570. The commentary on this hexagram is included in the *Min-su ts'ung-shu*. See MSTS: CF, pp. 68, 277.

69. *Mencius* 3A:4. See Legge, *The Chinese Classics* 2:251–252. Interestingly, besides these officially recognized human relations, there seems to have evolved from the concept of *pao* a relation between master and disciple or teacher and student. Curious and unusual as it was, a Manchu officer, out of gratitude toward his deceased teacher, actually entertained the idea of committing suicide so as to serve him in the next world. For this particular case, see Derk Bodde and Clarence Morris, *Law in Imperial China: Exemplified by 190 Ch'ing Dynasty Cases* (Cambridge, Mass., 1967), pp. 166, 440–441.

70. For the problem of dating and authorship of the *Chung-yung*, see Tu Wei-ming, *Centrality and Commonality: An Essay on Chung-yung* (Honolulu, 1976), pp. 13–15, 21–22. For the central theme expounded in *Chung-yung*, see Hsu Fu-kuan, *Chung-kuo jen-hsing-lun shih: Hsien Ch'in p'ien* (The history of the Chinese philosophy of human nature: The pre-Ch'in period) (Taichung, 1963), pp. 103–160. The mention of the five human relations in *Chung-yung* is found in chap. 20. See Legge, *The Chinese Classics* 2:406–407.

71. For quotations from the various chapters of the *Li-chi* in which the proper "order" is discussed, see, e.g., MSTS: FM, p. 27; MSTS: CF, pp. 86–87; and MSTS: CT, p. 10. For an excellent discussion of the definition of *ming-chiao*, see Ying-shih Yü, "*Ming-chiao wei-chi*," pp. 1–22.

72. MSTS: FT, p. 116.

73. MSTS: CT, p. 249.

74. STC, p. 3.

75. CCKY, p. 45. See also Plopper, *Chinese Religion*, p. 232.

76. STC, p. 2b–3.

77. CTW, pp. 9–10.

78. See the appendix, "Society and Self in the Chinese Short Story," in C. T. Hsia, *The Classic Chinese Novel: A Critical Introduction* (New York, 1968), p. 301.

79. STC, p. 2.

80. See the heroic story included in the *Ch'ien-t'ang i-shih* of Liu I-ch'ing (Yuan dynasty). KKY, p. 319; MSTS: FT, p. 239.

81. This is prescribed in the "Nei-tse" (Inner regulations) of the *Li-chi*. See MSTS: CT, p. 10. Fang Hsiao-ju, in his *Mien-hsueh shih,* also emphasizes this. See MSTS: CT, p. 237.

82. CTW, p. 9.

83. Frederick W. Mote, "Confucian Eremitism in the Yuan Period," in *The Confucian Persuasion,* ed. Arthur F. Wright, pp. 202–240. The possible ambiguities between voluntary and compulsory eremitism are discussed in Willard J. Peterson, "The Life of Ku Yen-wu," pt. 1, pp. 143 n. 131, 143–144.

84. Mote, "Confucian Eremitism," p. 232.

85. Wang Mao-hung, in his *Pai-t'ien tsa-chu,* contends that the authorship of this work, which is generally attributed to Chu Hsi, is questionable. For Yen Yuan's biography, see Hummel, *Eminent Chinese of the Ch'ing Period,* pp. 912–915.

86. See CCKY, p. 5; MSTS: CT, p. 117; MSTS: FT, p. 27; MSTS: CF, pp. 181, 255, 295.

87. STC, p. 2b.

88. HSHW, p. 21.

89. CTW, p. 5.

90. See Fung, "The Philosophy at the Basis of Traditional Chinese Society," p. 26.

91. For an excellent discussion on the problem of the Three Bonds and Five Constant Virtues, see Chang Huang's *T'u-shu pien,* collected in the *Min-su ts'ung-shu.* MSTS: CF, pp. 273–274.

92. Wei Ying-ch'i, comp., *Chung-shan ta-hsueh min-su ts'ung-shu, no.8: Fu-chou ko-yao chia-chi,* no. 8, Chungshan University Folklore Series, Ballads from Foochow, (Canton, 1928), pt. 1, p. 128.

93. Ibid., p. 142.

94. On Buddhism and Taoism, see Smith, *China's Cultural Heritage,* chap. 7.

95. Tadao Saki, "Confucianism and Popular Educational Works," in William Theodore de Bary, in *Self and Society in Ming Thought,* p. 346. See also Evelyn Sakakida Rawski, *Education and Popular Literature in Ch'ing China,* p. 51.

96. Eberhard, *Guilt and Sin in Traditional China,* p. 118.

97. For the type of moral practice recommended by *Pu-fei-ch'ien kung-te li,* see de Bary, *Self and Society in Ming Thought,* pp. 352–361.

98. See HSHW, pp. 48, 62; CEC, p. 8; JSPT 1:1; JSPT 2:9, 11.

99. Hummel, *Eminent Chinese of the Ch'ing Period,* p. 258.

100. For K'ang-hsi's "Sacred Edict," see James Legge, "Imperial Confucianism," in *The China Review* 1 (1878): 147–158, 223–235, 299–310, and 363–374. An extract of William Milne's translation of the Sixteen Maxims, which appeared in *The Chinese Repository,* is quoted in Chung-li Chang, *The Chinese Gentry: Studies on Their Role in Nineteenth-Century Chinese Society* (Seattle, 1967), p. 65 n. 285. A brief discussion of the different editions of the Sacred Edict is found in Hummel, *Eminent Chinese of the Ch'ing Period,* p. 329. For the wide circulation and popularity of *Sheng-yü kuang-hsun,* see Meng Hsien-ch'eng, *Chung-kuo ku-tai chiao-yu tzu-liao* (Sources of traditional Chinese education) (Beijing, 1964), p. 269.

101. See Chung-li Chang, *The Chinese Gentry,* p. 65 n. 287. For different definitions of the term "gentry" of nineteenth-century China, see also Ping-ti Ho, *The Ladder of Success in Imperial China: Aspects of Social Mobility, 1368–1911* (New York, 1967); and T'ung-tsu Ch'ü, *Local Government in China under the Ch'ing* (Cambridge, Mass., 1970).

102. See T'ung-tsu Ch'ü, *Law and Society in Traditional China* (Paris, 1965), pp. 267–289.

103. Ibid., p. 118.

104. Ibid., p. 126.

105. Ibid., pp. 230–231.

106. MSTS: CT, p. 186.

107. See Chiang Ch'ien, *Yang-meng san-tzu ching* (The trimetrical classic for rearing children) (reprint, Taipei, 1963), postscript.

108. See his *Chin-ssu lu,* collected in MSTS: CT, p. 81; and *Hsing-li hui-t'ung,* collected in MSTS: CT, pp. 85–86.

109. HSHW, p. 36.

110. CEC, p. 6b.

111. Ibid., pp. 6b–7.

7

Divination in Ch'ing Dynasty China

RICHARD J. SMITH

In a widely read essay titled "An Inquiry into Fate" *(Yuan-ming)*, the Ch'ing scholar Ch'üan Tsu-wang (1705–1755) expressed the ambivalence of both his time and his social class toward the problem of destiny and divination. On the one hand, he had to acknowledge that "the ancients spoke a great deal about fate." On the other, he was quick to point out that talk of good and bad fortune by astrologers and other soothsayers was "unworthy of belief." Citing Huang Tsung-hsi (1610–1695) and other authorities, he went on to say that, although divination systems based on simple calculations of time of birth could not possibly yield a satisfactory discussion of destiny, there were simply too many examples of wise men who believed in fortune-telling techniques to dismiss divination out of hand.

Ch'üan's fundamental position, derived from orthodox neo-Confucianism, was that although heaven endowed man with his nature, it had no actual control over his actions. Surely, he argued, the will of heaven was that every man be a sage and that virtuous government by sage-rulers would bring peace to the world. Heaven also undoubtedly wanted all people on earth to be healthy, strong, and properly provided for. Yet not everyone was a sage; villains often ruled despotically. The virtuous might well suffer from cold, hunger, and premature death; villains might live long and comfortable lives. "These things," he claimed, "heaven can do nothing about."

Ch'üan's purpose was, of course, to show that what appear to be blessings *(fu)* and calamities *(huo)* are nothing more than ephemeral phenomena, "like morning dew and melting icebergs." History ultimately reveals good and evil, and humans are therefore bound to strive relentlessly for sagehood. Superior men, he asserted, refer to fate only in certain unavoidable situations—such as Confucius did in the face of Po-niu's fatal illness (*Lun-yü* 6:8) or in the case of Kung-po Liao's slander of Tzu-lu (*Lun-yü* 14:38). Such remarks were not at all, he emphasized, like the predictions of fortune-tellers.[1] Of course Ch'üan knew perfectly well that Confucius said much more about fate, as did Mencius and a great number of other prominent thinkers.[2] But to include these references, or even to allude to the range of opinion that they represented, would have made his essay too intellectually untidy; for in truth, Confucian scholars, both during the Ch'ing period and at earlier times, were profoundly uncertain about exactly how to know fate *(chih-ming)*, as Confucius advised (see *Lun-yü* 20:3)—not to mention what to do with the knowledge acquired.[3]

This much was indisputable: techniques of divination had abundant sanction in the classical literature. Indeed, all canonical works in the Confucian tradition mention the phenomenon. The hallowed *I-ching* (Book of changes) actually began as a fortune-telling text, and it continued to represent the orthodox tradition of divination throughout the imperial era (see below). Works such as the *Tso-chuan* (Commentary of Tso) contain numerous references to the use of the turtle shell and milfoil stalk, as well as other mantic techniques, including dream interpretation, to determine good and bad fortune *(chi-hsiung)*; and the *Li-chi* tells us simply: "By means of divination the former sage-kings caused the people to have faith in the seasons and the times, to respect spiritual beings, to fear laws and orders, and to elucidate and settle doubts and suspicions."[4]

To be sure, the rational tradition of neo-Confucianism downplayed the supernatural world of ghosts and spirits *(kuei-shen)*—despite their prominent appearance in the classical literature, and at least a few Ch'ing scholars, such as Wang Fu-chih (1619–1692), took pains to point out that prevailing cosmologies derived from the *Shu-ching* (Classic of history) were in fact distortions concocted by later generations of fortune-tellers and numerologists. Moreover, we know that the editors of the massive Ch'ing literary project known as the *Ssu-k'u ch'üan-shu* (Complete collection of the Four Treasuries) made a special effort to disassociate mantic works based on the *I-ching* from the classic itself, in order to distinguish the orthodox Confucian tradition from the Taoist tradition of magical practices.[5]

In everyday life, however, the distinction between the two often became hopelessly blurred, if not obliterated. This was particularly true for those at the end of the Chinese social spectrum whose interests and outlook were seldom represented in the *Ssu-k'u ch'üan-shu*—commoners, especially peasants. For these unnamed actors in China's ongoing drama, the line between Confucian orthodoxy and Taoist magic was not worth drawing—at least not in most day-to-day affairs. As a result, in the Ch'ing period—and indeed throughout China's imperial history—peasants and other commoners persistently sought to know as much about the future as possible, and to do as much as they could about it, by whatever means. For the traditionally disadvantaged throughout the realm, any advantage worth possessing was worth investigating.[6]

This essay, based in part on research for a longer, book-length study, examines the phenomenon of divination in the Ch'ing dynasty from a popular as well as an elite perspective and seeks to identify a relation between the two. It attempts to show not only the prevalence of divination in late imperial times but also the variety of forms that it took and the social and political significance that it had.

Ch'ing Attitudes toward Divination

Surprisingly, comparatively little modern scholarship has been done on either the theory or the practice of Chinese divination in late imperial times.[7] One reason is that most forms of fortune-telling have been regarded by twentieth-century Chinese intellectuals as nothing more than popular superstition *(mi-hsin)*, unworthy of serious study. This attitude is reflected in the following quotation from a highly regarded anthology of Chinese writings: "While educated Chinese have paid homage only to Heaven and their ancestors, and sometimes to Confucius, Buddha, Lao Tzu, and a few other historical personages, the common people have believed in the existence of thirty-three Buddhist Heavens, eighty-one Taoist Heavens, and eighteen Buddhist hells, and put faith in astrology, almanacs, dream interpretation, geomancy, witchcraft, phrenology, palmistry, the recalling of the soul, fortune telling in all forms, charms, magic, and many other varieties of superstition."[8]

In fact, however, divination was not simply a preoccupation of the common people. Virtually everyone in traditional China believed in divination. The problem was not whether to believe in it, but whom to believe. In the words of a popular proverb: "Do not say that King Wen's hexagrams are ineffective *[buling]*; fear only that the fortune-teller's reading is untrue *[buzhen]*."[9] It was specialization and professionalism that stigmatized divination, not the theory itself. From an elite standpoint, fortune-telling—like medicine, husbandry, gardening, and a number of other specialized, nonscholarly pursuits—was a minor employment *(hsiao-tao)*,[10] to be learned by Confucian gentlemen for the benefit of their own families, perhaps, but not left to mean people *(hsiao-jen)*, who were concerned only with profit.[11] This elitist view of divination was also reflected in a well-known adage in Ch'ing China attributed to the Sung scholar Chang Tsai: "The *I-ching* is for consultation by the superior man, not the mean man."[12]

But the complexities of calculating fate *(suan-ming, shu-ming,* etc.) kept professional divination specialists in great demand—not only in religious temples and private homes but also in businesses, and even the yamens of Ch'ing officials. These complexities had to do with an enormous array of cosmic variables, including the phases of change associated with *yin* and *yang,* the sun and the moon, the four seasons, the five elements or activities *(wu-hsing)* and their numerous correlations (including the five planets), the six cardinal points *(liu-ho);* the eight trigrams *(pa-kua),* the nine palaces *(chiu-kung),* the ten heavenly stems and twelve earthly branches, the twenty-four solar periods *(erh-shih-ssu ch'i),* the twenty-eight lunar lodges *(erh-shih-pa hsiu),* the sixty-four hexagrams *(liu-shih-ssu kua),* and over two hundred auspicious and inauspicious stars *(hsing).*[13]

The way in which these and other cosmic forces interacted with one another varied according to different divination systems, and, not surprisingly, many of these systems overlapped or intersected.[14] But the most sophisticated exponents of fortune-telling in Ch'ing times generally took all such variables into account. Complicating an already complex picture of the future were Buddhist concepts of karma, and sectarian Taoist ideas of merits and demerits *(kung-kuo).* These notions, although disparaged by many Ch'ing intellectuals, were widely held and, predicated on the assumption that the past, present, and future, were linked in a morally grounded chain of causation. In a sense, they accorded with the traditional idea of fate following behavior *(sui-ming)*—one of several early Chinese concepts of fate in addition to regular fate *(cheng-ming),* also known as fate received (from heaven; *shou-ming).* Meanwhile, the Maitreya Buddhist idea of a heavenly destiny *(t'ien-yun),* like Shao Yung's notion of rhythms of fate *(yun-hui),* implicated not only individuals but also the entire world in predictable patterns of cosmic change.[15]

Although considerable debate existed among both scholars and professional fortune-tellers over the question of exactly how to know fate, and over which cosmic variables were most important, there was widespread agreement in Ch'ing society on most of the variables themselves and a shared faith that fate could in fact be known. In a certain sense, Chinese divination may be compared to modern stock-market speculation based on commonly held economic theories or principles but reflecting different particular emphases. As with traditional Chinese doctors (or modern Western stockbrokers, for that matter), a number of competing specialists might be consulted in any given situation.[16]

Assuming that one's fate could be known, the question was then; What could be done about it? Did one simply accept destiny passively? Philosophical Taoism argued yes: "Rest with fate (an-ming)," argued Chuang-tzu. But the answer for orthodox Confucians, as Ch'üan Tsu-wang's essay suggests, was quite the opposite. In the Confucian tradition, it was not enough simply to know fate, or to rest satisfied with fate; one also had to establish fate (li-ming)—that is, devise a moral strategy for contending with predestined situations. In the words of the great Ch'ing scholar T'ang Chien: "He who knows fate will cultivate the Way [tao]; he who [merely] relies on fate will do harm to the Way."[17]

It is true that both classical sources and a large number of popular proverbs from the Ch'ing period suggest the inevitability of fate in realms such as birth and death, sickness and health, wealth and blessings, marriage and children, official rank and scholarly achievement. But the evidence suggests that on the whole this type of fatalism did not cripple self-reliance. Individuals continually strived to achieve status and material benefits, as well as health and longevity, through both self-exertion and the use of religious agents, including Taoist priests, Buddhist monks, magicians, sorcerers, and shamans.[18]

Of course, as a matter of principle Chinese elites distrusted all such religious specialists and regularly denounced their deceitful and self-interested behavior. The same tended to be true of diviners. As if this were not enough of a problem for exponents of the mantic arts, the Ch'ing period witnessed a number of particularly vigorous and powerful attacks by Chinese scholars on inherited cosmological assumptions. Some authorities have argued, for example, that "technical and empirical studies" by savants of the seventeenth and eighteenth centuries in areas such as philology, astronomy, and geology had a profoundly subversive effect, contributing not only to a marked decline of the traditional cosmology but also to "more or less popular criticism" of at least a few of the more prevalent forms of Chinese divination.[19] Although there can be no doubt that k'ao-cheng scholarship had important implications in many realms of intellectual life, I have found no evidence to suggest a decline of Ch'ing interest in fortune-telling compared to previous eras. On the contrary, it flourished throughout the period, and may even have experienced a surge of popularity in the nineteenth century parallel to the revival of Buddhism in the midst of precipitous dynastic decline.

Ch'ing interest in divination can be measured in a variety of ways. One is the attention devoted to the subject in the section on arts and occupations (i-shu tien) in the massive, imperially commissioned encyclopedia titled Ku-

chin t'u-shu chi-ch'eng (Compendium of writings and illustrations, past and present), first published in 1725. This work contains several large subsections *(pu)*—over 280 *chüan* in all—devoted to various theories, techniques, and famous exponents of divination.[20] Other sources of the period, from local gazetteers and the *Ta-Ch'ing hui-tien* (Collected statutes of the great Ch'ing dynasty) to legal cases and anecdotal accounts such as the *Ch'ing-pai lei-ch'ao* (Classified anecdotes from the Ch'ing), also attest to a widespread interest in various fortune-telling techniques on the part of the Chinese at all levels of society.[21] Furthermore, short stories, plays, and novels of Ch'ing times reflect the social importance of divining techniques—even if fortune-tellers themselves are often made out to be the objects of elite derision.[22]

The observations of foreigners provide another index of the prevalence of divination in late imperial times. The remarks of S. W. Williams, a long-time resident of nineteenth-century China, are typical in tone and substance: "No people are more enslaved by fear of the unknown than the Chinese, and none resort more frequently to sortilege to ascertain whether an enterprise will be successful or a proposed remedy avail to a cure. This desire actuates all classes, and thousands and myriads of persons take advantage of it to their own profit." William Milne asserted in 1820 that "astrology, divination, geomancy and necromancy every where prevail [in China]." John Nevius, another experienced observer of China, stated in 1869 that a belief in fortune-telling was "of universal prevalence" among the Chinese." Similarly, A. P. Parker claimed in 1888 that fortune-telling in China was "universally believed in"; and at the end of the century, Arthur Smith remarked that "the number of Chinese who make a living out of . . . [divination] is past all estimation."[23]

The most influential work on divination in China for well over two thousand years was, of course, the *I-ching*. Scholars consulted the vaunted classic on matters both weighty and trivial, and it was commonly said in the Ch'ing period: "If you read the *I-ching* you will know how to calculate [the future] with hexagrams." Nearly everyone in traditional China had occasion to use the document in some form, at some time—from the emperor and his advisers at court, to the lowliest peasant consulting a street-stall diviner.[24] A number of Ch'ing intellectuals chose to emphasize the moral value of the *I-ching* over its utility as a book of divination (a long-standing debate); and several scholars—notably Mao Ch'i-ling (1623–1716) and Hu Wei (1633–1714)—questioned the authenticity of certain post-Han accretions to the work.[25] But the *I-ching* retained enormous scriptural authority as an explanation of time, change, and causality.[26]

The highly influential neo-Confucian compilation known as the *Chin-ssu lu* (Reflections on things at hand), informs us, for example, that the *I-ching* is "comprehensive, great, and perfect. It is intended to bring about accord with the principle of . . . [human] nature and destiny, to penetrate the causes of the hidden and the manifest, to reveal completely the nature of things and affairs, and to show the way to open resources and to accomplish great undertakings."[27] Similarly, the *Ssu-k'u ch'üan-shu tsung-mu* (Index to the complete collection of the Four Treasuries) states: "The way of the *I-ching* is broad and great. It encompasses everything, including astronomy, geography, music, military methods, the study of rhymes, numerical calculations and alchemy."[28]

Even Wang Fu-chih, who railed against many aspects of the inherited cosmology and felt that Chu Hsi's emphasis on the *I-ching* as a book of divination made it appear to be little more than a trivial manual for fortune-tellers *(fang-shu chih I),* had enormous esteem for the cryptic classic. "It is," he wrote, "the manifestation of the Heavenly Way, the unexpressed form of nature, and the showcase for sagely achievement. *Yin* and *yang,* movement and stillness, darkness and brightness, withdrawing and extending—all these are inherent in it. Spirit [*shen*] operates within it; the refined subtlety of ritual and music is stored in it; the transformative capacity of ghosts and spirits [*kuei-shen*] emerges from it. The great utility [*ta-yung*] of humaneness and right behavior issues forth from it; and the calculation [*shu*] of order and disorder, good and bad luck, life and death is in accordance with it."[29]

The fundamental assumption of the *I-ching* was that the universe was intelligible—that fate or destiny (*ming, yun, ming-yun,* etc.) could be known. The "Discussion of the Trigrams" *(Shuo-kua)* states: "In ancient times the holy sages made the *I-ching* in order to follow the principle of their nature [*hsing*] and of fate [*ming*]. They established the *tao* of heaven and called it *yin* and *yang;* they established the *tao* of earth and called it the yielding and the firm; they established the *tao* of man and called it humaneness and right behavior." According to the *Shuo-kua,* by following the way *(tao),* correctly ordering their behavior, investigating principle to the utmost *(chiung-li),* and exhausting their nature *(chin-hsing)* the sages arrived at a complete understanding of destiny.[30]

The sixty-four hexagrams of the *I-ching* and their constituent trigrams and individual lines, together with written decisions *(t'uan),* appended judgments *(hsi-tz'u,* or *hsiao-tz'u)* and commentaries, reflected and explained various predestined situations evolving out of the natural patterns and processes of eternal cosmic change. According to the "Great Commentary" *(Ta-chuan* or *Hsi-tz'u chuan)*, the *I-ching* served as a kind of medium that allowed the person consulting it to establish a spiritual link with heaven and to be able divine the future by means of the tortoise shell and milfoil stalks, through the interpretation of omens, by observing the planets and stars, and by means of numerical devices such as the "Yellow River Chart" *(Ho-t'u)* and "Lo River Writing" *(Lo-shu)*.[31]

Ch'ing Divination Practices

Commoners and scholars alike believed that most Chinese mantic techniques were related in some way to the *I-ching*.[32] The pervasive use of trigrams and hexagrams as explanatory symbols in a variety of fortune-telling schemes naturally reinforced this belief. So did the many correlative systems that linked the symbols of the *I-ching* with the forces of *yin* and *yang,* the five elements or phases of change, and the system of stems and branches of the ancient sexagenary cycle.[33] Among the most popular of these numerologically oriented systems were six direction divination *(liu-jen),* the method of calculation known simply as the great one *(t'ai-i),* and hidden stems expertise *(ch'i-men tun-chia)*.[34]

Other popular divining schemes—all at least a thousand years old (and most more than two thousand years old) by Ch'ing times—included fate extrapolation *(t'ui-ming),* the interpretation of auspicious or inauspicious omens *(chi-hsiung chih chao),* dream divination *(meng-chan),* physiognomy *(hsiang-jen, hsiang-mien, k'an-hsiang,* etc.), word analysis *(ch'ai-tzu* or *ts'e-tzu),* meteorological divination *(chan-hou),* geomancy *(k'an-yü, feng-shui,* etc.), spirit writing *(fu-chi),* the use of bamboo or wooden blocks *(chih-chiao pei-chiao),* and the interpretation of messages connected with bamboo sticks *(ch'ien-pu).* Individuals also consulted official state calendars and popular almanacs for daily guidance, and occasionally asked deceased ancestors and other spirits *(shen)* for advice concerning the future.[35]

The eight natal characters *(pa-tzu)*—one stem and branch combination each for the year, month, day, and hour of birth—were considered especially revealing. Although several different techniques of fate calculation based on birth dates existed during Ch'ing times, the most commonly used was the system of Hsu Tzu-p'ing, developed during the Sung dynasty, in which eight characters were grouped into four units of two each (known as the four pillars, *ssu-chu).* These characters reflected both cosmological and social relationships. Each stem and branch, for example, was designated *yang* or *yin,* and correlated with one of the so-called five elements or activities, as well as a particular season and a twelve-stage developmental cycle extending from prenatal life in the womb *(t'ai)* to extinction *(chueh).* The four pillars were generally correlated with one's ancestors, parents, spouse (if married), and son(s). Many fortune-tellers placed particular emphasis on the idea of an operational force *(yung-shen)* that determined whether the correlations would be creative or destructive, harmonious or antagonistic—not only for the individual under consideration but also for other individuals with whom the principal party might be involved.[36]

Regardless of the method employed, and whether or not all eight characters were taken fully into account, few Chinese of any social class were inclined to dismiss birth dates as irrelevant to future affairs—particularly in matters such as marriage. Evidence from local gazetteers, as well as from handbooks on etiquette and the testimony of contemporary observers, both Chinese and foreign, indicates that practices such as fate extrapolation, the selection of lucky days *(hsuan-tse)* and the exchange of the eight characters in marriage ritual were extremely prevalent throughout the Ch'ing empire, from Ch'u-hsiung district in remote Yunnan province, to Liao-yang in Manchuria (Liao-ning).[37] It is true that Wolfram Eberhard's study of over 3,700 married couples from the Jung clan of Kwangtung province in the period from 1600 and 1899 concludes that the members of this clan, at least, "did not let themselves be influenced by the auspicious and inauspicious combinations of signs in their selection of marriage partners." But his investigation, which also contains data from modern-day Taiwan, considers only the year of birth (associated with one of twelve cyclical animals) as an index of marital compatability, thus oversimplifying a very complex process by which families contemplating marriage negotiated the future of their children.[38]

A sensitivity to omens was pervasive in traditional China—especially at the top, where emperors and dynasties depended on heaven's mandate *(t'ien-ming)* for legitimacy. Auspicious signs *(fu-jui, hsiang-jui,* etc.), such as the appearance of colored vapors, bright lights, rare animals, unusual plants, strange stones, sweet dew, and so forth, reflected heaven's pleasure and portended joyful events; calamities *(tsai-i),* such as unanticipated eclipses and similar celestial anomalies, earthquakes, floods, and other natural disasters indicated heaven's displeasure, and perhaps even loss of the mandate. The Ch'ing dynasty, like all of its imperial predecessors, dutifully recorded all unusual signs from heaven, and the Manchu emperors took them very seriously.[39] About a third of the imperial amnesties granted from the early seventeenth century to the late nineteenth century were justified as a means of restoring harmony to the natural order after portents indicated that it had been disrupted by human excesses.[40]

To be sure, the K'ang-hsi emperor—arguably the most scientific and skeptical of all the Manchu rulers—might assert that, although the dynastic histories were full of accounts of omens, they were of no help in governing the country, that "the best omens were good harvests and contented people."[41] But the "Respecting Heaven" *(ching-tien)* sections of the *Ta Ch'ing shih-ch'ao sheng-hsun* (Sacred instructions for ten reigns of the great Ch'ing) provide numerous instances in which he, like both his predecessors and successors, registers great concern over portents, is moved to self-examination because of them, and admonishes his officials to rectify their administration as a result. Scholars might disagree over whether the sovereign's self-cultivation could actually prevent anomalous events from occurring, as Chu Hsi seems to have believed, but few doubted that a relation existed between portents and the need for an immediate imperial response to the messages they conveyed.[42]

At less exalted levels, heavenly portents were also taken seriously, along with less dramatic signs, such as birdcalls *(niao-chiao),* the residue or shape of lamp wicks *(teng-hua),* and various body sensations (itching, tingling, sneezing, etc.).[43] The *Ch'ing-pai lei-ch'ao* devotes considerable attention to the interpretation of various kinds of natural and supernatural omens, as do other Ch'ing sources, both Chinese and Western. Many anecdotes involve scholars and at least a few famous officials.[44]

Dreams had special significance in Chinese society and were classified in treatises on the subject according to various broad categories, such as those pertaining to heaven, the sun and the moon, thunder and rain (and related phenomena), mountains and streams (a category including roads, earth, and rocks), shapes and sounds, food and clothing, utensils, wealth and property, writing implements and scrolls, the civil service examinations, supernatural things and occurrences, longevity, various plants and animals, giving and receiving, and certain vague indications *(fan-yü).*[45] Undoubtedly the most popular Ch'ing work on dream divination was the *Chou-kung chieh-meng* (Dream interpetations of the Duke of Chou), published in a great many versions and widely disseminated in almanacs empirewide, usually in simplified form.[46]

Ch'ing accounts of dream divination abound. Often people prayed for dreams *(ch'i-meng)* and spent the night in local temples in hopes of receiving clues to the future. Justus Doolittle writes of Fukien in the mid-nineteenth century: "Many people, in case they find great difficulty in deciding what course to take in regard to an important subject under consideration, visit some popular temple and, having burned incense and candles, beg the divinity worshipped to favor them with a dream shedding light on the subject of their perplexity, which they briefly state."[47] Of the literally dozens of stories on dream divination in the *Ch'ing-pai lei-ch'ao,* no less than ten focus on "praying for dreams." Significantly, most of the individuals involved in seeking them are highly reputable scholars—among them, such Ch'ing notables as Li Kuang-ti (1642–1718), Chiang I (1631–1687), Chang Ying (1638–1708), and Hsu Pen (1683–1747).[48]

Most Chinese believed that the physical appearance of individuals could yield important clues regarding both character and destiny. Elites as well as commoners held this view. John Gray writes, for instance, "It is surprising to find what a number of respectable and influential men throughout the empire resort to professors of the art [of physiognomy]." The *Ch'ing-pai lei-ch'ao,* local gazetteers, and other sources indicate that a great many Ch'ing civil and military officials relied on physiognomers for advice, and a number of Chinese scholars actually practiced the art—including such high-ranking individuals as Chi Huang (1711–1794), Tseng Kuo-fan (1811–1872), Shen Pao-chen (1820–1879), Liu Ming-ch'uan (1836–1896), Li Wen-t'ien (1834–1895), and Chao Shu-ch'iao (d. 1900).[49]

The social importance of impressive features in Ch'ing China can scarcely be underestimated. In the first place, physiognomic stereotypes unquestionably influenced the way people at all levels responded to one another. These stereotypes were reinforced not only in popular proverbs but also in folktales and novels. At least some almanacs, like all physiognomy manuals, depicted different types of faces, as did public displays that advertised the skills of professional physiognomers "with painted representations of the human countenance."[50] Facial streotypes could even affect a person's bureaucratic career. A middle degree holder *(chü-jen),* for example, could enter Ch'ing official life at a comparatively high level after failing the *chin-shih* examination three times if he possessed what was considered to be the right kind of face. Professional physiognomers generally focused primary attention on the hands and basic facial characteristics of their clients (ears, forehead, eyebrows, eyes, nose, cheeks, mouth, chin, and complexion), but they might also pay attention to other parts of the body, as well as movements, vocal sounds, and even urine and excrement.[51]

Closely related to physiognomy in its emphasis on visual interpetation *(hsiang)* was the art of fathoming or dissecting written characters, a technique employed not only as a separate category of divination but also in conjunction with dream analysis. The great Ch'ing scholar Chi Yun (1724–1805) once described the omens of word analysis as developing from the same sort of spiritual communication as the selection of milfoil stalks in *I-ching* divination or the use of oracle bones.[52] For the convenience of illiterate or semiliterate commoners, professional fortune-tellers provided a limited number of characters to be chosen by clients and interpreted, but elites generally wrote their own word choice down. The logic of word analysis, like that of dream interpretation, physiognomy, and most other forms of Chinese divination, was inveterately associational, allowing, perhaps even compelling, diviners to link all relevant concepts, cosmological as well of personal, to the client. Stories surrounding the dissection of characters circulated widely in Ch'ing China, and many involved famous scholars and officials such as Chang Ying (1638–1708), adviser to the K'ang-hsi emperor.[53]

The heightened attunement of the Chinese to shapes influenced other Chinese divination techniques, from the analysis of "chops" or seals *(yin-hsiang)* to meteorological divination, known generically as *chan-hou.* *Chan-hou* techniques, like those of seal interpretation, were not, of course, as obviously psychological in orientation as word analysis, which involved a degree of conscious or unconscious choice, and they relied to a far greater extent on explicit stem-branch correlations and astrological configurations in the process of making predictions. Furthermore, the category *chan-hou* included a number of nonvisual divination methods, such as the analysis of wind sounds *(feng-chiao,* lit. "wind corners") as part of its repertoire. Nonetheless, techniques such as observing the rain *(hsiang-yü),* watching the vapors *(wang-ch'i* or *wang-hou),* and divining from clouds *(chan-yun)* required the same careful attention to visual detail required of physiognomy, word analysis, and geomancy.[54]

Geomancy or siting—the Chinese practice of selecting auspicious locations for tombs, houses, and other structures—took many forms and went by a variety of names in the Ch'ing period. There were numerous schools and subschools of the art, but all had a common goal: to harmonize dwellings for both the living and the dead with the immediate physical environment as well as the larger cosmic scheme. Geomancy thus shared with traditional Chinese medicine a concern with maintaining a harmonious *yin-yang* equilibrium in the midst of constant change. A given location, like the human body, represented a microcosm of the universe, which naturally required a balance of cosmic energy *(ch'i)* for proper functioning. As specialists in siting, geomancers, often known as *feng-shui* masters *(feng-shui hsien-sheng)* were, in effect, doctors of the earth, and a great many were conversant in traditional Chinese medicine.[55] As with physiognomy, *feng-shui* divination both reflected and encouraged a certain aesthetic logic, but the calculations of geomancers usually involved much more than simply a visual analysis of topography. Cosmological calculations required a compass, or *lo-p'an*—a complex device used by most *feng-shui* specialists that included virtually every major symbol used by the traditional Chinese in dealing with space and time.

Practitioners of geomancy in Ch'ing times ranged from high officials such as Chao Chih-hsin (1662–1744), Li Wen-t'ien (1834–1895), and Chang Chih-tung (1837–1909) to commoners whose names are forever lost to history. According to the *Ch'ing-pai lei-ch'ao,* some emperor's were considered conversant in the art, and, despite regulations in some monasteries prohibiting the practice of geomancy and certain other forms of divination, there were a number of Buddhist and sectarian Taoist *feng-shui* practitioners, including the eminent Ch'an abbot Hsu-yun (1840–1959).

The clients of *feng-shui* specialists likewise spanned the entire Chinese social spectrum. Emperors, empresses and members of the imperial household used them, as did civil and military officials at all levels of administration.[56] Throughout the empire, individual families, clans, villages, and whole cities employed geomancers, since filial sons wanted to do all they could for their deceased parents (and themselves), and larger corporate entities could not afford to neglect geomantic factors that might affect their collective scholarly fortunes. Among the many famous officials who utilized *feng-shui* specialists in their personal lives were Ch'en Hung-mou (1696–1771), Wei Yuan (1794–1856), T'ao Chu (1779–1839), Tseng Kuo-fan, and Ting Jih-ch'ang (1823–1882).[57]

Geomancy was a subdued and rather private form of divination, but many other forms were more public, and at least a few entailed colorful and highly visible dramatic action. Spirit writing, in particular, involved elaborate ritualized preparations—including the offering of incense, ceremonial bowing, and prayers of petition—prior to the actual descent of a spirit into the diviner's stick. The ritual of divination itself, which, like all other forms of divination I have discussed, can still be seen in Taiwan and Hong Kong today, consisted of furious bursts of stick writing by the medium (often a Taoist priest) in response to written questions solicited orally from petitioners. The spirit's esoteric written message was then read aloud, transcribed, and given to the petitioner.[58]

During the Ch'ing period, spirit writing enjoyed widespread popularity. According to Hsu Ti-shan, in Ming-Ch'ing China there was a spirit-writing altar *(chi-t'an)* in virtually every prefectural and district-level city. And as interest in *fu-chi* divination grew, specialists began to operate in private homes and ancestral halls as well as temples. There were even spirit-writing clubs for various strata of Chinese society. Hsu tells us that particularly in provinces such as Kiangsu and Chekiang, where the scholarly fashion *(wen-feng)* prevailed, the attitude was simply that, "if one did not believe in *fu-chi* spirits, one could not be successful in the examinations." He goes on to say that the questions asked of spirits regarding the examinations might affect one's entire career and that even after scholars had attained official positions they would still think of *fu-chi* divination whenever faced with a difficult decision.[59]

In part, Ch'ing scholars esteemed *fu-chi* divination for its self-consciously moral emphasis—although most other Chinese mantic messages also had explicitly ethical content. They also enjoyed the elaborate wordplay of spirit writing. In many instances, interpretation of a *fu-chi* revelation, like that of a dream, required skills closely akin to, if not identical with, conventional word analysis. Sometimes the conversation between a *fu-chi* spirit and his interlocutor took the form of an effort to match couplets *(tui-tui);* and scholarly patrons were occasionally moved to impose specific stylistic requirements on the poetry of a spirit. But the primary reason *fu-chi* divination attracted the attention of Ch'ing scholars was its utility in answering questions of ultimate importance to them. These included matters of life and death, sickness and health, problems of civil and military administration, and career issues. Not surprisingly, a number of scholars asked *fu-chi* spirits for assistance in the civil service examination system—either advice on how to write better essays or information concerning the questions themselves.[60]

The *Ch'ing-pai lei-ch'ao,* Hsu Ti-shan's collection of anecdotes on spirit writing, and other sources provide a wealth of information on the use of *fu-chi* divination in the Ch'ing period. Like professional fortune-tellers, *fu-chi* spirit mediums predicted disasters such as droughts, floods, epidemics, and rebellions. They also advised individuals on how to conduct their lives for maximum personal advantage, assisted officials in their administrative affairs (including legal decisions), and helped them defeat pirates and bandits. Among the many high-ranking Ch'ing officials who relied on *fu-chi* oracles were P'eng Ting-ch'iu (1645–1719), Yeh Ming-ch'en (1807–1859), and Tseng Kuo-fan.[61] Women did not normally engage in spirit writing.

They did, however, perform most other shamanistic functions—primarily for members of their own sex. These services included healing, fortune-telling, and the performance of exorcisms and magic. A number of women specialized in communicating directly with the dead—perhaps because so many unplaced spirits *(kuei)* in traditional China were female ghosts who had an axe to grind with the oppressive patriarchal society that caused them so much misery in life.[62]

Ch'ing elites tended to be particularly critical of women shamans and their allegedly foolish woman followers. But all spirit mediums proved threatening to the scholarly class—not only because of their willingness to flout Chinese social norms openly but also because of their social power. They could, for example, criticize local power holders or ask officials for the redress of grievances *(shen-yuan)* in the name of the gods. And even when shamanistic oracles worked to the advantage of the elite—such as when a local spirit writer advised thousands of angry and recalcitrant peasants that they should honor the wishes of the local magistrate, who had canceled a procession honoring the Ch'ing-pu (Kiangsu) city god on his "birthday"—the scholarly class could hardly fail to recognize the political implications of such utterances.[63]

Of course a number of Chinese fortune-telling techniques, such as the use of bamboo blocks *(chiao)* in homes and temples, and divination by means of bamboo sticks *(ch'ien)* at religious shrines, required no supernatural intervention and little, if any, formal education. Not surprisingly, such techniques tended to be undertaken primarily by unlettered women, for whom trips to local temples represented one of the few forms of nondomestic recreation available to them.[64] But women were not the only people to employ such humble methods of divination. The great Ch'ing scholar Yen Yuan (1635–1704), for example, resorted to *ch'ien* sticks in an effort to locate his father, from whom he had been separated since the age of three, during the Manchu conquest. Other prominent Ch'ing elites who are known to have practiced *ch'ien* divination at one time or another include Wang Shih-chen (1634–1711), Han T'an (1637–1704), Pi Yuan (1730–1797), and En-ming (1846–1907).[65]

Divination and Official Orthodoxy

If individual Chinese were preoccupied with fate, the Ch'ing government was positively obsessive about it. The reasons are not difficult to find. In the first place, imperial legitimacy was viewed, in large measure, as a matter of predicting the future correctly—whether in terms of anticipating events such as eclipses, interpreting portents, or selecting auspicious days for conducting all-important state rituals. Because failure to perform these functions satisfactorily called into question the regime's right to rule by virtue of the heavenly mandate, activities such as regulating the calendar (chih-li) and fixing the time (shou-shih or shih-ling) assumed special importance to every dynasty. Not surprisingly, throughout the imperial era divination often played a significant role in dynastic transitions—not least in the changeover from Ming to Ch'ing.[66]

The state calendar, compiled by the Imperial Bureau of Astronomy (Ch'in-t'ien chien) in conjunction with the Board of Rites (Li-pu), and issued annually at the year's end after review by the emperor himself, was the single most visible index of imperial legitimacy. Throughout the Ch'ing period, the collected statutes specifically outlawed unauthorized versions of the official calendar, and certain editions of the work carried an explicit warning on the cover to the effect that those who forged copies of the calendar were subject to decapitation, and that those who informed on such persons would receive an imperial reward of fifty taels. Calendars that did not carry an official seal were considered to be private and, therefore, strictly speaking, illegal.[67]

Privately published almanacs, many based closely on the imperial calendrical model and all reflecting the same orthodox cosmology, circulated freely throughout the Ch'ing period.[68] They generally had auspicious red covers rather than imperial yellow ones, and they possessed a number of pages of written text in addition to the standard columns, charts, and diagrams of their official counterparts. Many contained popular wood-block prints not to be found in calendars, such as depictions of the two dozen or so difficult or dangerous passes (kuan) that might be encountered by Chinese children, or annotated pictures of the twenty-eight asterisms and their general influence on life situations. And every almanac I have seen (not to mention at least a few works designated calendars [Shih-hsien shu]) included illustrations of the spring ox (ch'un-niu) and its herdsman (shen-t'ung or mang-shen), whose rich color symbolism—supposedly indicating agricultural prospects for the new year—was evocative, instructive, and nearly universal in traditional China.[69]

Other common elements in almanacs—particularly in the late Ch'ing period—were folk stories, morality tales (such as the "Twenty-Four Examples of Filial Piety," Erh-shih-ssu hsiao), and popular religious materials. Almanacs might also include practical advice on matters relating to agriculture, business, health, proper etiquette, and, of course, omens and techniques of divination. By the early twentieth century, a number of these works had become conduits for new information on recent educational and political changes, modern science and technology, and news regarding foreign nations. Photographs of Chinese political leaders, such as the notorious Prince Ch'ing and other Manchu nobles, began to adorn their pages.[70]

At the core of all state calendars and annual almanacs was a month-by-month, day-by-day breakdown of the entire year, designed to coordinate and control certain aspects of Chinese political, social, ritual, and economic life. Generally, each column, whether for the month as a whole or for the individual days within each month, indicates the particular spiritual influences, agents, asterisms, and other cosmic variables affecting that particular time. The positive spiritual influences (shen) normally appear at the top of each column, and the negative spirits (sha) at the bottom. For each day—with only a few exceptions in any given year—there are a certain number of activities designated appropriate (i, i.e., auspicious) or inappropriate (pu-i, inauspicious). Designated activities of this sort were categorized and included in the Ch'ing collected statutes. Sixty-seven matters fell under the rubric imperial use (yü-yung), thirty-seven under people's use (min-yung), and sixty under almanac selection (t'ung-shu hsuan-tse).[71]

Of the sixty-seven categories of imperial concern identified in the Ch'ing collected statutes, a great number dealt with general administrative and ritual matters, such as various forms of sacrifice and prayer, the submission of documents, the promulgation of edicts, the bestowal of favors and awards, personnel matters, diplomatic and military affairs, and events such as banquets. On a more personal level, the calendar provided guidance in choosing days for educational activities, domestic rituals, health, business decisions, and the solicitation and adoption of suggestions and advice. Among mundane activities regulated by the calendar we find bathing and grooming, cutting out clothes, household cleaning and decoration, establishing a new bed, discarding things, moving things (pan-i), traveling, breaking ground, well digging, construction and repair, hunting, fishing, trapping, planting, cutting wood, and herding animals.

The thirty-seven activities designated for the people, encompass vitually all of the major personal and mundane matters indicated above. This category also includes a few additional mundane items, such as visiting and receiving relatives and friends, as well as important ritual and administrative acts such as carrying out sacrifices, submitting a memorial to the throne, assuming an official post, and arranging for burials (the last not expressly specified in the imperial list). The almanac category, although listed last, seems to stand midway between the two previously mentioned sets of concerns. It includes most of the major categories of activity noted above but omits those that are obviously the exclusive prerogatives of the emperor. At the same time, it is especially specific about certain personal and mundane affairs. It indicates, for example, particular stages of marriage ritual, the treatment of particular afflictions, and the use of particular medical remedies. It also mentions a few activities not included in either of the preceding categories, such as constructing, opening, and repairing storehouses and granaries, fermenting liquor, smelting metals, and crossing the water by boat or other means.[72]

How seriously, one might ask, did Ch'ing elites take the divinatory stipulations of calendars and almanacs? Positive evidence is difficult to come by in Chinese sources, because most people seem to have taken the predictions of these publications for granted—rather like weather forecasts in the modern West, which are seldom worthy of a recorded remark. We know, however, from diaries, correspondence, dedicatory inscriptions, and other sources that Ch'ing scholars and officials were acutely aware of auspicious and inauspicious days. We also know that almanacs remained among the most widely circulated books in the entire Chinese empire in late imperial times and that official calendars were always in short supply. At least one late Ch'ing ritual handbook asserts categorically that "no household is complete without an almanac."[73]

Furthermore, Western observers continually remarked on the prevalence and pervasive influence of calendars and almanacs. A report by the Society for the Diffusion of Useful Knowledge in China (November 21, 1838), referring to "the almost universal demand" for these books among all classes of Chinese, echoes the views of a great many other informed foreigners— from Matteo Ricci in the early seventeenth century to Robert Hart in the late nineteenth. A. P. Parker, an astute student of Chinese calendrical science in the 1880s tells us that "the astrological part [of the official calendar] is universally believed in, though there seems to be considerable difference in the practice of the details by different persons—some considering it necessary to be careful about the times and places of carrying out the most important affairs of life, such as marriage, burial, house-building, &c., while others believe it necessary to be careful as to the time and place for the most commonplace details of everyday life, such as opening a shop, entering school, going on a journey, giving an entertainment, sweeping the floor, shaving the head, taking a bath, &c."[74]

As long as almanacs and unofficial versions of the calendar reflected orthodox views and reinforced imperial legitimacy, they could be tolerated; but if not, the state suppressed them with a vengeance. This was naturally true of calendars produced by contenders for political power, such as the Yung-li emperor of the Southern Ming during the latter half of the seventeenth century, or the Taiping rebels of the mid-nineteenth century. But it was also true of certain privately printed heretical *(hsieh)* almanacs such as the early nineteenth-century handbook titled *San-Fo ying-chieh t'ung-kuan t'ung-shu* (Comprehensive almanac for responding to the *kalpas* of the three Buddhas [past, present, and future])—used by Lin Ch'ing of the Eight Trigrams sect to, in the Chia-ch'ing emperor's words, "deceive the people" and "violate the authority of Heaven." After discovery of this document, the emperor ordered all copies destroyed, and engaged in a relentless search for the authors and publishers.[75]

In the same spirit, and for the same reasons, the Ch'ing legal code prescribed severe penalties for ritual activities deemed subversive (or potentially subversive) of the throne's claim to universal cosmic authority. It proscribed private worship of heaven or the North Star (the exclusive prerogatives of the emperor) and forbade the keeping of astronomical instruments and charts at home. *Yin* and *yang* fortune-tellers *(yin-yang shu-shih)* were prohibited from entering the houses of civil and military officers and falsely prophesying *(wang-yen)* fortune or misfortune. Magicians, shamans, and other ritual specialists were forbidden to summon heretical spirits *(hsieh-shen)*, write charms, carry idols, pray to saints, offer incense, hold night meetings, perform heretical arts *(hsieh-shu)*, write books on sorcery *(yao-shu)*, or promote heretical formulas *(hsieh-yen)*. Although these and other heretical crimes were never rigorously defined, and not always strictly enforced, their statutory existence, together with evidence from other sources, suggests the state's awareness of the link between divination and imperial legitimacy. From the standpoint of the government, to surrender authority concerning the future to nonorthodox ritual agents was to compromise the very foundations of imperial rule.[76]

What the Ch'ing rulers feared most was the capacity of individuals outside the state's direct sphere of control to manipulate and mobilize the masses. The preface to the dynasty's official divination manual known as the *Hsieh-chi pien-fang chi* (Book for calendrical calculations) reflects this persistent anxiety: "Specialists of the occult arts [*fang-shih*] talk of good luck and bad luck, calamities and blessings, and frighten the people into having no standards of behavior."[77] The government's fear extended not only to professional fortune-tellers and magicians but also to millenarian cults such as the White Lotus Society, which drew on orthodox cosmological symbols—including the eight trigrams, the nine palaces, the ten stems and twelve branches, and the twenty-eight constellations—but placed them in a heretical framework: the advent of the Maitreya Buddha. Prophecy, under such circumstances, was a form of divination that had enormously threatening political potential.[78]

To be sure, divination did not have to be dangerous to invite criticism. As I have already indicated, throughout the late imperial era—and, in fact, well before—a number of influential Chinese intellectuals assailed divining practices such as fate extrapolation, physiognomy, the selection of lucky and unlucky days, and especially geomancy. The famous late Ch'ing compendium known as the *Huang-ch'ao ching-shih wen-pien* (Writings on statecraft from the present dynasty) contains several critical essays on these and related topics by scholars such as Ku Yen-wu (1613–1682), Lu Shih-i (1611–1672), Feng Ching (1652–1715), and Ch'üan Tsu-wang.[79]

These essays reflect the major concerns of the Ch'ing elite with respect to divination. One widely shared fear was that blind acceptance of fate on the part of commoners would diminish their impulse toward moral improvement and self-reliance. Another was that false prophecy could easily delude people into creating disorder *(huo-jen tso-luan)*—that is, into instigating rebellion. A third concern was that many mantic practices generated or exacerbated social tensions and led to breaches of etiquette (such as late burials, in the case of geomancy). Finally, in the eyes of many scholars, fortune-tellers were simply unreliable. Ku underscored the divergent and often misleading interpretations of diviners; Lu questioned the validity of astrological predictions and portent interpretations because they were unscientific ("Western studies," he reports, "say absolutely nothing about divination"). Ch'üan, following Huang Tsung-hsi, argued that "many people are born on the same day, yet some are fortunate and some are not; some will enjoy longevity and others will die young." And Feng, in an essay titled "Refuting the Theories of *Yin-Yang* Soothsayers" *(Po yin-yang chia yen)*, maintained that skill with esoteric numerical calculations was "not equal to an understanding of the principles of things."[80]

Significantly, although Lu's reference to Western science was rather unusual, none of these criticisms of divination were new. In fact, they followed closely the lines of attack crafted centuries before by individuals such as Hsun-tzu in the Late Chou, Wang Ch'ung in the Han, and Lü Ts'ai in the T'ang—all of whom are excerpted in various sections on divination in the

T'u-shu chi-ch'eng. Like their ancient predecessors, not to mention their more orthodox neo-Confucian contemporaries, Ch'ing *k'ao-cheng* scholars had no quarrel with the idea of divination itself, for the practice had far too long and illustrious a pedigree in China's classical tradition to ignore. Rather, their hostility was directed toward specific misapplications of the practice—especially by professional fortune-tellers who were not by definition members of the orthodox elite. As in the case of religion, the Ch'ing elite made a sharp (though somewhat artificial) distinction between their own enlightened beliefs and the crude customs of the popular masses. The bias against divination was essentially a class prejudice, masked by the rhetoric of Confucian morality.[81]

In any case, scholarly criticisms of divination had little effect. Even the charge that fortune-tellers made inaccurate predictions fell on essentially deaf ears. The very complexity of most Chinese divination systems provided conceptual flexibility, and contributed to their self-confirming character. Wrong prognostications did not invalidate the idea that fate could be known (an article of Confucian faith, after all, encouraged by the *I-ching* itself); they merely indicated that someone had misinterpreted the huge number of cosmic variables involved, or that either the diviner or the client was insufficiently "sincere."[82] Furthermore, as I have indicated, many Ch'ing scholars employed the same mantic methods that they decried. A popular book by Wang Wei-te, published in 1709 and titled *Pu-shih cheng-tsung* (Orthodox milfoil divination), castigates members of the Chinese elite for affecting a disdain for divination, only to use it surreptitiously through the agency of friends or servants.[83] The imperial government displayed the same sort of hypocrisy, denouncing the practices it regularly relied on. The official commentary to the Ch'ing legal code, for instance, describes geomancy as "basically absurd and false, unworthy of belief." Yet we know that the throne and members of the imperial household, as well as civil and military officials, used *feng-shui* specialists all the time, as they did many other kinds of diviners and divining techniques.[84]

The Persistence of Divination

Hypocrisy aside, how do we account for the longevity and pervasiveness of divination in China? One answer might be China's comparative disinterest in modern (Western) science. While "scientific" *k'ao-cheng* scholarship in the seventeenth and eighteenth centuries brought a new epistemology to China, and with it, "a fundamental pattern of intellectual change," it certainly did not have the same effect on magic and divination that Keith Thomas ascribes to the roughly contemporary "scientific and philosophical revolution" in Europe.[85] Nor have all premodern societies embraced the mantic arts with equal enthusiasm. In fact, two of the cultures of the world least interested in divination appear to be the traditional Australian Aborigines and the American Plains Indians.[86]

A more likely explanation for the staying power of divination in China is simply that it both embodied and reflected many of the most fundamental features of traditional Chinese civilization. Although it always had a certain heterodox potential, it was not fundamentally a countercultural phenomenon. On the contrary, it remained an integral part of the most important state and domestic rituals—from official sacrifices to life-cycle ceremonies—throughout the imperial era.

Enjoying abundant classical sanction and a long history, Chinese mantic practices followed the main contours of traditional Chinese thought. Most forms of Ch'ing divination were eclectic, "spiritual," associational, intuitive, tradition bound, and highly moralistic. These qualities fit comfortably in a syncretic society whose dominant class esteemed ancient Confucian values, relied heavily on correlational logic, believed in a spiritual link between heaven, earth, and man (which made divination possible, after all), and saw knowing as an activity in which "the rational operations of the intellect were not sharply disconnected from what we [Westerners] would call intuition, imagination, illumination, ecstacy, aesthetic perception, ethical commitment, or sensuous experience."[87] The *I-ching* epitomized both the philosophical and the mantic traditions of China, establishing a crucial epistemological link between the two. Although it possessed a kind of biblical authority, it pointed to a very different path of cosmological and ontological understanding.

In more mundane terms, divination had a decidedly visceral appeal. Ch'ing fortune-tellers invariably employed a colorful and universally resonant symbolism that remained deeply imbedded in the consciousness of Chinese at all levels of society. Allusions to historical, classical, and mythological figures in prophetic statements evoked powerful responses in clients, as did references to certain symbolic colors, numbers, plants, and animals. Furthermore, fortune-tellers invariably surrounded themselves with culturally familiar paraphernalia. Even the most rudimentary fortune-telling table on the street would generally be adorned with writing materials, books, and calligraphic inscriptions—the marks of scholarly refinement and moral cultivation. More elaborate settings in homes or at divination parlors might boast religious icons or spirit tablets, as well as incense and candles. Visual representations of cosmic power such as the *T'ai-chi t'u* (Diagram of the Supreme Ultimate) and the eight trigrams, which often adorned divination handbooks, almanacs, and fortune-telling stalls, were also ubiquitous as decorative elements (and charms) in elite and commoner households alike.

The rituals of divination were likewise satisfying and culturally familiar to all clients. Ceremonies such as the burning of incense, which invested divinatory procedures with a mystical if not a magical aura, had a truly universal appeal. The use of writing by diviners not only enhanced their social prestige but also gave them cosmic leverage, because so many Chinese believed that written words had magical power. Meanwhile, the theatrical performance of fortune-tellers contributed to their public allure. In several respects patronizing a diviner was like watching a play, or even participating in one. Dramatic forms of divination such as spirit writing and other types of spirit possession held audiences literally spellbound; but even the more subdued rituals of physiognomy, fate extrapolation, and word analysis attracted passersby on the streets, in marketplaces, and at temples throughout China. Although private fortune-telling parlors existed, and a number of people consulted diviners in the privacy of their homes, Chinese divination was fundamentally a public affair. This was yet another reason why most Ch'ing subjects simply took it for granted.

The close link between divination and traditional Chinese medicine probably contributed to the tenacity of both. Despite the great diversity of medical and mantic theory in late imperial times, doctors and diviners shared many of the same cosmological assumptions about systematic correspondence as well as demonology.[88] And, although the Confucian classics and a number of popular proverbs emphasized that health and longevity were predestined, few individuals in Ch'ing China accepted their fate passively. Most people believed that they could modify their fate, either by moral or magical means. In fact, the two sources of power were closely related. For the elite, the same spiritual capacity that made foreknowledge possible, gave those who had developed their sincerity to the utmost the ability to transform their own lives in concert with heaven and earth. Theirs was a kind of cosmological mind magic, sanctioned by no less authority than the *Chungyung*. For commoners, charms and the advice of soothsayers might do the trick.

On the other hand, the idea of inescapable destiny occasionally served as a convenient explanation for adversity and disappointment. Thus, we find that even Tseng Kuo-fan, a staunch Confucian and certainly no slouch, once remarked during a difficult phase of the Taiping Rebellion that fate determined seventy percent of a situation, leaving only thirty percent to man's exertions. And Kuo Sung-t'ao (1818–1891), a hardworking and dedicated scholar who had the misfortune to assume a career in late Ch'ing foreign affairs, went so far as to ask that his obituary end with the following remark: "I don't believe in books; I believe in luck" *(pu-hsin shu hsin ch'i-yun)*.[89]

Another point to keep in mind is that in Ch'ing China, divination did not stand as starkly opposed to either science or religion as it did in seventeenth- and eighteenth-century Europe. To be sure, Chinese scholars in the late imperial era were well aware of the expanding parameters of knowledge about the natural world, and of an increasing ability to predict accurately. But scientifically minded individuals of the Ch'ing period had neither a religious belief in order of the sort that inspired their European contemporaries, nor did they hold the conviction that in time all phenomena would yield their ultimate secrets. The typical belief was that "natural processes wove a pattern of constant relations too subtle and too multivariant to be understood completely by what we would call empirical investigation or mathematical analysis. Scientific explanation merely expressed, for finite and practical human purposes, partial and indirect views of that fabric."[90]

The influential Sung dynasty scientist Shen Kua (1031–1095) articulated this notion in the following way: "Those in the world who speak of the regularities underlying phenomena, it seems, manage to apprehend their crude traces. But these regularities have their very subtle aspect, which those who rely on mathematical astronomy cannot know of. Still, even these are nothing more than traces. As for the spiritual processes described in the *Book of Changes* . . . [which] penetrate every situation in the realm, mere traces have nothing to do with them. This spiritual state by which foreknowledge is attained can hardly be sought through traces, of which in any case only the cruder sort are attainable."[91]

Divination thus often passed for science in Ch'ing times. Although the period witnessed a revival of interest in mathematics, mathematical astronomy, and geography, stimulated in part by the Jesuit educational effort, astrology remained integral to the Chinese scientific tradition. The Jesuits themselves practiced divination in the Imperial Bureau of Astronomy.[92] Chinese fortune-telling techniques, like all such self-confirming methods, could not be falsified, but they at least involved generalizations based on observation as well as a kind of experimentation that required verification *(cheng)*. Furthermore, and more importantly, divination categorized and explained experience in culturally significant ways. The elaborate schemes used by fortune-tellers to analyze heavenly phenomena, earthly forms, personality types, and so forth were undoubtedly more generally well known and persuasive than other systems of scientific expanation available in Ch'ing dynasty China. To the extent that science can be viewed as an ordering device for managing data, divination served Chinese scientific purposes nicely. Certainly this was true, for better or worse, of the hallowed *I-ching*.[93]

The spiritual preoccupations of diviners did not necessarily preclude scientific investigation. It is true that experts in wind, rain, and cloud divination—like other types of Chinese fortune-tellers (and most of the rest of the Ch'ing population)—believed in the influence of supernatural forces. But they were also close and insightful students of meteorology. Exponents of *ch'i-men tun-chia* and other numerological systems, although concerned primarily with cosmological calculations to determine auspicious times and locations, often studied military science as part of their training. Geomancers used mystical compasses to identify lucky sites and times for building and making repairs, but they also knew a great deal about land forms and hydraulic systems—information of value in public works as well as military affairs. In all, geomancy probably exerted a more profound influence on the physical environment, and the way the Chinese responded to it, than most other natural sciences of the time.

An especially significant reason for the prevalence and persistence of divination in Ch'ing China was the multifaceted social role it played. In the first place, it contributed to social order by regulating the rituals and rhythms of daily life. Few devices were more powerful as mechanisms for structuring society than the stipulations regarding lucky and unlucky days in Chinese calendars and almanacs. Divination also conduced to social stability by depersonalizing difficult decisions and validating status distinctions —most notably in situations related to marriage and mortuary ritual.[94] It is true, of course, that practices such as geomancy could prove socially disruptive, as elite critics had long claimed, but the social advantages of these practices, both for individuals and for corporate entities, far outweighed the liabilities. For this reason, elites themselves availed of divination under all sorts of circumstances.

Moreover, Chinese fortune-tellers served as the functional equivalent of modern-day psychologists. As therapists and personal counselors, they helped individuals in China to cope with their anxieties, whether inspired by bureaucratic problems, the examination system, or more mundane concerns. Divination clarified the source and nature of difficulties, alleviated doubt, and invested lives with longed-for meaning. It also empowered people with a special kind of cosmic knowledge and perhaps endowed them with greater self-confidence and a more profound sense of personal identity. The optimistic thrust of techniques such as *ch'ien* divination and dreambook interpretation provided hope in time of uncertainty and fear, as did geomancy, with its alluring promise of cosmic control.[95] Exponents of fate extrapolation and physiognomy gave individuals a glimpse of their long-term future, as well as concrete advice on how to contend with seemingly inescapable problems. Methods such as word analysis did the same for more immediate issues; personal consultation of the *I-ching* offered ways of "resolving doubts" that emphasized introspection and personal initiative. By various means, not all equally effective, divination in Ch'ing China restored "value and significance to lives in crisis."[96]

But fortune-tellers were more than personal therapists. In a society such as China's, where so many aspects of life and thought hinged on compromise and concilliation, and where intermediaries were essential to all forms of social intercourse, diviners proved to be cultural middlemen par excellence, mediating not only between the client and the cosmos, and between Confucian, Buddhist, and Taoist versions of reality, but also between contending elements within their own local communities, from quarreling couples to feuding clans.[97] Some relied primarily on their psychological skills and verbal ability to settle disputes. Others made use of their comparatively intimate knowledge of the personal histories and local connections of many community members. Still others, notably shamans, in calling on supernatural authority to develop and maintain group consensus, brought "order out of confusion."[98]

Diviners also helped bridge the gap between commoners and the elite in Ch'ing dynasty China. By summoning up visions of orthodox heroes and urging clients to embrace conventional values, fortune-tellers reinforced the dominant literati culture. For this reason, among others, they periodically received commendation by local officials for their skill as prognosticators. P'eng T'ien-lun, for one, got an honorific plaque that read, "He is able to know the future" *(k'o-i ch'ien-chih)*—a phrase instantly recalling the rare and admirable quality of foreknowledge touted by Mencius.[99] But the process of cultural transmission was not one of downward movement only. Popular values also found their way to the upper levels of Chinese society in the course of divination. Although the exact nature of this two-way interaction cannot be documented with precision, we know that at least some fortune-tellers had both elites and commoners as clients and that a number of non-elite diviners enjoyed close relations with the literati by virtue of their unusual and much-coveted skills.[100] Furthermore, it is clear that certain divinatory media, spirit writing in particular, conveyed messages that were suffused with elements from the Chinese folk tradition as well as Confucian high culture.[101]

The special talents of diviners, from weather prediction and siting to the evaluation of personnel, made them valuable not only to Ch'ing officials but also to the leaders of their own communities. Fortune-tellers helped to maintain the mechanisms of local defense and control, undertook famine relief, managed schools, and supervised public works projects. Some used their special talents to help neighbors find lost or stolen property; others provided free advice and medical assistance to their local areas in times of crisis. These altruistic activities helped diviners to overcome the common stereotype of being devious and selfish and brought them more fully into the mainstream of Chinese community life.[102]

Finally, in attempting to account for the remarkable staying power of divination in China, we should bear in mind institutional factors: For one, the Ch'ing religious establishment did not actively attempt to suppress divination in the fashion of the Christian church in the West. Rather, Buddhist and Taoist temples and monasteries supported a wide range of divinatory activity, undertaken by professional fortune-tellers as well as private individuals.[103] Chinese clerics did not have the institutional power to challenge established mantic practices, even if they had the will, for the church in China remained ever subordinate to the imperial state. The Ch'ing government, for its part, reinforced the inherited cosmology and sanctified orthodox mantic practices at all levels. Edicts and other official announcements constantly referred to auspicious and inauspicious dates, times, events, and omens; the state calendar institutionalized divination empire-wide by designating certain days as appropriate and inappropriate for various activities; and bureaucrats availed of divination in all kinds of civil and military situations.[104] Without fully realizing it, the Ch'ing government was as much in the grip of the future as it was of the past. For the emperor to dispense with divination would be to abandon his cosmological claim to kingship—an abdication of his role as mediator between heaven and earth.[105]

When the Ch'ing dynasty finally fell in 1911–1912, state-sponsored cosmology suffered a mortal blow. But the overthrow of the Ch'ing and the destruction of the imperial system had far less to do with the decline of correlative cosmology than with the rise of modern Chinese nationalism. Put another way, it was a new, politically inspired assault on the idea of cosmo-logical kingship, rather than the Early Ch'ing critique of correlative cosmol-ogy, that spelled the end of the official worldview. The production of a new state calendar for the republic in 1912, with its vigorous denunciations of the old Ch'ing calendar's superstitions *(mi-hsin),* does not warrant the con-clusion that the inherited cosmology had already died. In fact, the revolu-tionary government's self-conscious repudiation of the inherited cosmology may be viewed precisely as an effort to eradicate a still-dangerous potential source of imperial authority.[106]

Seen in this light, C. T. Hsia's assertion that notions such as *yin* and *yang* and *wu-hsing* were unworthy of attention by "May Fourth period champi-ons of the new culture" because of their "dwindling influence and utility" is rather misleading.[107] It is true, of course, that Chinese intellectuals increas-ingly came to see science and technology, modern techniques of political participation, and other forms of new knowledge, as the key to solving Chi-na's manifold problems. But the New Culture Movement's assault on Chi-nese tradition certainly included elements of cosmological criticism. In an article titled "*Yin-yang* Soothsaying," for example, Ch'en Tu-hsiu wrote in 1918 that only by first casting away heretical practices such as geomancy, fortune-telling, spirit writing, and the use of charms, spells, and alchemy, could the Chinese people begin to put their minds right *(cheng jen-hsin).* And, as late as 1934, Lu Hsun wrote a piece titled "Fate," in which he casti-gated the Chinese people for their superstitious belief in monks, priests, shamans, astrologers, and geomancers.[108] Ch'en and Lu Hsun were not attacking straw men, for old-style mantic techniques and cosmological assumptions remained in force, not only during the New Culture Movement but throughout the republican era.[109]

Today, in environments such as Hong Kong and Taiwan, fortune-tellers continue to enjoy extraordinary popularity—despite the pervasive influence of modern science and the attractiveness of certain Western intellectual fash-ions. Even on the Chinese mainland, after four decades of suppression, evi-dence abounds of traditional forms of divination in cities as well as the countryside.[110] In part, we may assume that the sustained appeal of fortune-tellers is related to the same set of cultural, social, and psychological factors that operated with such force in Ch'ing times. But we may also hypothesize that the old cosmology has remarkable staying power. Although propor-tionally there are no doubt fewer Chinese in any one place today who take the predictions of fortune-tellers as seriously as their forbearers in the Ch'ing dynasty, many continue to find attractive the ancient notion of a spiritual resonance between heaven and man, a special kind of cosmic connection. And, although some modern Chinese feel the need to choose between what they have come to view as two utterly incompatible cosmologies, many do not. To them, recourse to fortune-tellers and the use of charms are no more inherently unmodern or unscientific activities than the Western habit of praying to God for guidance and assistance.

In other words, the Western tendency to distinguish sharply between scientific "rationality" and primitive "superstition" may prevent us from appreciating the degree to which the two types of thought might be made to fit under certain sets of circumstances. For example, the discovery by modern astronomers of new stars and planets that have no place in traditional Chinese astrology does not negate the idea of celestial influences on fate, because the vast majority of Chinese star spirits are unembodied, and their ultimate power is determined by an elaborate interplay of cosmic forces that Western science does not recognize. Significantly, many of these forces—notably *yin* and *yang* and the *wu-hsing*—seem to operate with predictable and powerful effect in traditional Chinese medicine.

Notes

Abbreviations

CC	James Legge, *The Chinese Classics* (London and Oxford, 1893–1895).
CPLC	Hsu K'o, *Ch'ing-pai lei-ch'ao* (Classified anecdotes from the Ch'ing) (Shanghai, 1916).
HCCS-WHP	Ko Shih-chün, *Huang-ch'ao ching-shih wen hsu-pien* (Supplement to the writings on statecraft from the present dynasty) (Shanghai, 1888).
HCCSWP	Ho Ch'ang-ling, *Huang-ch'ao ching-shih wen-pien* (Writings on statecraft from the present dynasty) (1826).
HCCS-WPHP	Sheng K'ang, *Huang-ch'ao ching-shih wen-pien hsu-pien* (Additional supplement to the writings on statecraft from the present dynasty) (Wuchin, 1897).
HCPFS	Yin Lu, *Ch'in-ting hsieh-chi pien-fang shu* (Imperially approved book for calendrical calculations) (Beijing, 1724; reprint, Taipei, 1974).
HPCTCC	Shih-chieh shu-chü pien-chi pu, ed., *Hsin-pien chu-tzu chi-ch'eng* (New edition of the compendium on philosophers) (Taipei, 1974).
ICCC	Yen Ling-feng, ed., *I-ching chi-ch'eng* (Compendium on the *Book of Changes*) (Taipei, 1975).
SKCSTM	Chi Yun, *Ch'in-ting ssu-k'u ch'uan-shu tsung-mu* (Reviews from the complete collection of the Four Treasuries) (reprint; Taipei, 1970).

TSCC   Chiang T'ing-hsi, *Ch'in-ting ku-chin t'u-shu chi-ch'eng* (Imperially approved compendium of writings and illustrations, past and present) (reprint; Taipei, 1977).

TSCCHP   Hsin-wen-feng ch'u-pan kung-ssu pien-chi pu, comp., *Ts'ung-shu chi-ch'eng hsin-pien* (New edition of the complete collectanea) (Taipei, 1986).

WHL   Wu Jung-kuang, *Wu-hsueh lu* (Record of my studies) (1832).

Research for this chapter has been generously supported by grants from the Pacific Cultural Foundation and Rice University.

1. Ch'üan's essay is reprinted in HCCSWP 69:15b–16a.

2. See CC: *Lun-yü*, II. 4; VI. 2; IX. 1, 5–6; XI. 6; XII. 5; XVI. 8; XX. 1, 3; *Meng-tzu* II. 1. iv; IV. 1. iv, viii; V. 1. v–viii; VI. 1. vii; VI. 2. xv; VII. 1. i–ii. Cf. Ma Hsu-lun, "Shuo-ming" (Discussing fate), *Hsueh-lin* 9 (1941): 15–34; Wei Cheng-t'ung, *Chung-kuo ti chih-hui* (The wisdom of China) (Taipei, 1974), pp. 181–184.

3. On the ambivalence of Ch'ing scholars, see HCCSWP 69:15b–16a; also CC 3:338–339 n. 31. For indications of Chinese attitudes toward fate over time, consult Fung Yu-lan, *A History of Chinese Philosophy,* ed. Derk Bodde (Princeton, N.J., 1952) 1:30–31, 86, 129, 181, 224–225, 237, 285, 293, 313, 370, 374–375, 384–385; 2:30, 46, 60, 62, 71–75, 125–130, 162, 191–193, 195, 417–418, 421, 446, 453, 466, 494, 514, 516, 527, 531, 592, 631, 650; also nn. 15–18, 89, below.

4. Ch'u Chai and Winberg Chai, eds., *Li Chi: Book of Rites* (New Hyde Park, N.Y., 1967) 1:94 (modified after consulting the Chinese original). For other *Li-chi* references to divination, consult ibid. 1:92, 94, 103, 119, 235, 259, 297–298, 380–381, 367, 385–386, 428–429, 472; 2:4, 51, 53–54, 71, 74, 84, 135–136, 156, 223, 233, 289, 295, 349, 363.

5. SKCSTM 146:8b. On the issue of Confucian rationalism, see, e.g., Hsu Fu-kuan, "Chu Hsi and the Ch'eng Brothers," in *Chu Hsi and Neo-Confucianism,* ed. Wing-tsit Chan, pp. 52–55 (Honolulu, 1986); for a Ch'ing period illustration, see the two-part essay by Chou Yuan-ting titled "An Essay on Ghosts and Spirits *(kuei-shen p'ien),*" in HCCSWHP 61:2a–3a.

6. On commoners, see WHL 9:10a; also n. 8, below. Cf. Liu Chih-wan, *Chung-kuo min-chien hsin-yang lun-chi* (Collected essays on popular beliefs in China) (Taipei, 1974), passim; and Wolfram Eberhard, "Fatalism in the Life of the Common Man in Non-Communist China," in *Moral and Social Values of the Chinese,* ed. Wolfram Eberhard (Taipei, 1971).

7. A noteworthy exception is Yuan Shu-shan, whose *Chung-kuo li-tai pu-jen chuan* (Biographies of diviners in China by dynastic periods) (Shanghai, 1948) is an indispensable resource. I have just completed a book, inspired in part by Yuan's work, titled *Fortune-tellers and Philosophers: Divination in Traditional Chinese*

Society (Boulder, Colo., 1991), which overlaps with, and expands on, many of the themes and arguments of this essay. See also Hung P'i-mo and Chiang Yü-chen, *Chung-kuo ku-tai suan-ming shu* (The divinatory arts of ancient China) (Shanghai, 1990).

8. See W. T. de Bary, et al., eds., *Sources of Chinese Tradition* (New York and London, 1964) 2:286. Cf. Marjorie Topley in *Some Traditional Chinese Ideas and Conceptions in Hong Kong Social Life Today,* ed. Marjorie Topley (Hong Kong, 1967), pp. 13ff.

9. C. Wilfred Allan, *A Collection of Chinese Proverbs* (Shanghai, 1926), p. 179; cf. *Ch'i-hsien chih* (Gazetteer of Ch'i-hsien) (Honan, 1788), *jen-wu,* 18: 18b–19b, which expresses a similar view.

10. The introductory sections on technicians *(fang-chi)* in local gazetteers often refer to Tzu-hsia's famous remark on *hsiao-tao* in the *Analects.* See also Lu Yao's essay, "Technical Arts" in HCCSWP 69:13b–14a.

11. See, e.g., the preface to Ou-yang Ch'un's *Feng-shui i-shu* (Geomancy, bk. 1; 1814), 7a.

12. See Wang Fu-chih's *Chou-i nei-chuan fa-li* (Introduction to the inner commentary of the Chou changes), reprinted in ICCC 141:3b.

13. For a complete inventory of terms and relationships, consult HCPFS vols. 1–10. See also n. 68, below.

14. See Chang Yao-wen, *Wu-shu chan-pu ch'üan-shu* (Complete book on five arts divination) (Taipei, n.d.) esp. pp. 2–28.

15. On different Chinese concepts of fate, see Wang Ch'ung's "An Essay on the Meaning of Fate" *(Ming-i p'ien), Lun-heng,* in HPCTCC 7:11–13. On heavenly destiny, consult Daniel Overmyer, "Folk Buddhist Religion: Creation and Eschatology in Medieval China," *History of Religions* 12, no. 1 (August, 1972): 65.

16. Smith, "Knowing Fate," p. 170. Nathan Sivin makes a similar point in "Science and Medicine in Chinese History," in *Heritage of China: Contemporary Perspectives on Chinese Civilization,* ed. Paul S. Ropp (Berkeley, Los Angeles, and Oxford, 1990), p. 180.

17. T'ang Chien is cited in Richard J. Smith, *China's Cultural Heritage: The Ch'ing Dynasty, 1644–1912* (Boulder, Colo., 1983), pp. 120–121.

18. For an illustration of the elite's disdain for commoners who are "not content with right behavior and fate" *(pu-an i-ming),* and who "flatter spirits to seek blessings," consult WHL 9:10a.

19. For examples of Ch'ing critiques of cosmology and divination, see John Henderson, *The Development and Decline of Chinese Cosmology* (New York, 1984), pp. 108, 168, 159, 178–197, 207–225; Paul Ropp, *Dissent in Early Modern China* (Ann Arbor, 1981), pp. 161–165, 171–179, 183–187, 189, 232. See also n. 79 below.

20. TSCC 47:5681–7135; 48:7136–7854. This does not include material on the *I-ching* in the section on classics *(ching-chi tien),* on extraterrestrial phenomena in

the section on heaven *(ch'ien-hsiang tien)*, on spirits in the section devoted to the supernatural *(shen-i tien)*, and on local divination practices, recorded in gazetteers, in the section on political divisions *(chih-fang tien)*. For examples of regional variation in customs related to divination (usually described as superstitions [*mi-hsin*]), consult Hu P'u-an, comp., *Chung-kuo ch'üan-kuo feng-su chih* (On treatise on Chinese national customs) (reprint; Taipei, 1968), passim. Generally speaking, southerners—the Cantonese in particular—were viewed as "most inclined to believe in spirits and ghosts." See, e.g., HCCSWHP 61:8b.

21. The CPLC's sections on technicians *(fang-chi lei)* and superstitions *(mi-hsin lei)* provide a vast amount of material related to divination. On the collected statutes and other official sources, consult my "Note on Qing Dynasty Calendars," *Late Imperial China* 9, no. 1 (June 1988).

22. Novels such as *Hung-lou meng* (Dream of the red chamber), *Ju-lin wai-shih* (The scholars), and *Hsi-yu chi* (Journey to the west) provide numerous illustrations of this basic point. See Hung and Chiang, *Chung-kuo ku-tai suan-ming shu,* pp. 235–243. For fortune-tellers as objects of derision, see Ropp, *Dissent in Early Modern China* (n. 19, above).

23. S. W. Williams, *The Middle Kingdom* (New York, 1883) 2:260; William Milne, *Retrospect of the First Ten Years of the Protestant Mission to China* (Malacca, 1920); John Nevius, *China and the Chinese* (New York, 1869); A. P. Parker, "The Chinese Almanac," *Chinese Recorder* 19, no. 2 (1888): 66; Arthur Smith, *Chinese Characteristics* (1894), p. 164. See also Henrietta Shuck, *Scenes in China* (Philadelphia, 1853), p. 71; N. B. Dennys, *The Folk-Lore of China* (London and Hong Kong, 1876), pp. 56–57; J. H. Gray, *China: A History of the Laws, Manners and Customs of the People* (London, 1878) 2:2; Robert K. Douglas, *China* (London, 1882), p. 289; R. F. Johnston, *Lion and Dragon in Northern China* (New York, 1910), p. 175; CC 3:335 n. 19; and Henri Doré, *Researches into Chinese Superstitions,* trans. M. Kennelly (Shanghai, 1914–1933) 4: introduction, 321–379.

24. See Richard J. Smith, "The Significance of the *Yijing* in World Culture," *Proceedings of the Sixth International Conference on I-ching Studies* (Shizuoka, Japan, 1989); also Richard J. Smith, "Qing Dynasty *Yijing* Specialists in Yuan Shushan's *Zhongguo lidai buren zhuan*," *Zhouyi Network* (1990): 13–30.

25. For a convenient and illuminating overview of iconoclastic Ch'ing scholarship on the *I-ching,* consult Benjamin Elman, *Classicism, Politics, and Kinship: The Ch'ang-chou School of New Text Confucianism in Late Imperial China* (Berkeley, Los Angeles, and Oxford, 1990), esp. chap. 4. See also n. 26, below.

26. Toda Toyosaburo, "Sincho ekigaku Kanken" (Ch'ing dynasty scholarship on the *I-ching*), *Hiroshima daigaku bungakubu kiyo,* 22, no. 1 (March 1963): 99–128.

27. Wing-tsit Chan, trans., *Reflections on Things at Hand* (New York, 1967), pp. vii, 108.

28. SKCSTM 1:3a.

29. Cited in Toda, "Sincho ekigaku Kanken," p. 104.

30. Richard Wilhelm, trans., *The I Ching or Book of Changes* (New York, 1967), pp. 262–264.

31. Wilhelm, *The I Ching,* pp. 320–321. Although Mao Ch'i-ling and other Ch'ing scholars had conclusively demonstrated that existing versions of the *Ho-t'u* and *Lo-shu* were added to the *I-ching* only in the Sung period, the diagrams continued to be linked to the classic by many individuals, commoners and scholars alike. See Smith, "Qing Dynasty *Yijing* Specialists"; also Michael Saso, "What Is the *Ho-t'u?*" *History of Religions* 17, nos. 3–4 (February-May 1978): 399–416.

32. See SKCSTM 109:18a–20b; also ibid., 109:43b–45b; 111:15b–24a; 111:41a–49b.

33. On traditional correlative systems involving these variables, consult Henderson, pp. 7–20, 23ff.

34. See TSCC, 48:7136–7438.

35. As indicated in n. 7, above, I have analyzed in some detail these and other divination systems in *Fortune-tellers and Philosophers.* For useful summaries in Chinese, consult Chang Yao-wen, and Yuan Shu-shan, *Shu pu-shih hsing-hsiang hsueh* (On the study of divination) (Shanghai, 1926).

36. See TSCC 47:5919ff., esp. the Ming work *San-ming t'ung-hui* (Comprehensive compilation on the three fates), pp. 6175–6517.

37. See, e.g., *Ch'u-hsiung hsien-chih* (Gazetteer of Ch'u-hsiung County) (Yunnan, 1909), *ti-li* 2:23b; *Liao-yang hsien-chih* (Gazetteer of Liao-yang County) (Liaoning, 1918), *feng-wu men, fengsu,* p. 30a.

38. Wolfram Eberhard, "Auspicious Marriages, in *Studies in Chinese Folklore and Related Essays,* ed. Wolfram Eberhard (Bloomington, 1970). Cf. Yuan, *Shu pu-shih hsing-hsiang hsueh* 5:20bff.

39. Ch'en Kao-yung, *Chung-kuo li-tai t'ien-tsai jen-huo piao* (Chart of heavenly calamities and human misfortunes in China by dynastic period) (Shanghai, 1939), provides a convenient chronology from Ch'in times onward. For some indications of the importance of omens to the imperial government in the Ch'ing period, see Ch'ing-shih pien-tsuan wei-yuan-hui, ed. *Ch'ing-shih* (History of the Ch'ing) (Taipei, 1961), *pen-chi* 1:32; *tsai-i chih* 1:655–723; etc. See also n. 42, below.

40. Thomas Metzger, *Escape from Predicament: Neo-Confucianism and China's Evolving Culture* (New York, 1977), p. 51.

41. Jonathan Spence, *Emperor of China: Self-Portrait of K'ang-hsi* (New York, 1975), p. 52; also p. 150; cf. p. 174.

42. See, e.g., *Ta-Ch'ing shih-ch'ao sheng-hsun* (Sacred instructions for ten reigns of the great Ch'ing) (Peking, 1880), K'ang-hsi, *ching-t'ien* 10:7a, 10:1aff., esp. pp. 8a–b. Cf. ibid., T'ung-chih, *ching-t'ien* 11:1aff.

43. Local gazetteers invariably recorded portents, and many included discussions of *fen-yeh* (allocated field) systems that linked specific terrestrial areas with their celestial counterparts. A typical entry, which refers to the cosmological author-

ity of the *I-ching* and emphasizes the principle of a "resonance [*kan-ying*] between heaven and man," can be found in the *Huang-p'o hsien-chih* (Gazetteer of Huang-p'o County) (Hupei, 1871), *t'ien-wen chih* 1:9a–b. Almanacs often included information on interpreting portents such as birdcalls and body sensations. See Richard J. Smith, *Chinese Almanacs* (Hong Kong, 1992).

44. See CPLC, *mi-hsin,* pp. 46ff.

45. See, e.g., the influential Ming work by Ch'en Shih-yuan titled *Meng-chan i-chih* (An easy guide to dream divination), in TSCCHP 25:322ff.

46. The earliest version I have seen, which corresponds closely with comprehensive contemporary editions of the work, has almost a thousand seven-character dream interpretations under a total of twenty-seven overlapping categories. It is contained in a fragment of the British Museum's *Yü-hsi chi kuang-chi* (Comprehensive version of the Jade Casket Record) (c. 1700). For dream divination sections in almanacs, consult Smith, *Chinese Almanacs.*

47. See Justus Doolittle, *Social Life of the Chinese* (New York, 1865) 2:130.

48. CPLC, *mi-hsin,* pp. 75, 79, 86, 87, 95, 96, 106, 119, 120.

49. Gray, *China: A History,* 2:3. The primary text for physiognomy was the Ming work *Shen-hsiang ch'üan-pien* (Complete guide to spirtual observation), compiled by Yuan Chung-che and reprinted in the TSCC.

50. On these and other notables, see Yuan, *Chung-kuo li-tai pu-jen chuan* 3:19; 14:27–28; 18:10–11; 18:21; 30:21–22; 33:8–9; etc. On the role played by physiognomers in administrative affairs, consult ibid. 14:25; 14:27–28; 27:10; 33:22–23; CPLC, *fang-chi,* pp. 79, 84–85, 118ff., esp. 121, 123, 124, 125–126, 131.

51. TSCCHP 25:113–115; also Topley, *Some Traditional Chinese Ideas,* p. 61.

52. Cited in Yuan, *Chung-kuo li-tai pu-jen chuan* 21:3–4; cf. ibid. 20:29–30. On character dissection in dream analysis, see TSCCHP 25:332; CPLC, *mi-hsin,* pp. 79, 89, etc.

53. Yuan, *Chung-kuo li-tai pu-jen chuan* 9:20–21. See also Hsu Ti-shan, pp. 32–60, passim; CPLC *fang-chi,* pp. 15–19, 21–22, 26, etc.; and n. 52, above.

54. On the importance of *chan-hou* to the K'ang-hsi emperor, see *Ta-Ch'ing shih-ch'ao sheng-hsun,* K'ang-hsi, *ching-t'ien* 10:3a. For some representative works, consult TSCCHP 25:5ff. On the analysis of seals, see Chang Yao-wen, pp. 356ff.; cf. CPLC, *fang-chi,* p. 118.

55. The literature on *feng-shui* in the TSCC, TSCCHP, SKCSTM, and other compendia is vast. For a convenient overview, which includes an excellent analysis of the *lo-p'an,* consult Stephen Feuchtwang, *An Anthropological Analysis of Chinese Geomancy* (Vithagna, 1974). On the relationship of doctors and diviners, see my "Divination, Science and Medicine in Qing Dynasty China" (Paper delivered at the Sixth International Conference on the History of Science in China, Cambridge University, Cambridge, England, August 2–7, 1990).

56. See, e.g., Yuan, *Chung-kuo li-tai pu-jen chuan* 1:22; 2:2; 2:22; 4:16–17; 13:17; 14:11; 15:8–9; 15:38; 16:4–5; 16:7; 18:16; 18:13–14; 18:34; 19:32–33;

19:38; 20:2; 21:10–11; 22:11; 26:6; 27:15–16; 29:29; 33:22–23; 34:26; 35:6–7; 35:16; 36:15; 37:2–3; 37:16; 37:7–8; 38:40; 38:42; 38:43.

57. See ibid. 1:18–19; 13:23; 18:14; 33:23; etc.

58. See Hsu Ti-shan, *Fu-chi mi-hsin ti yen-chiu* (Research on the superstition of spirit-writing) (Chungking, 1940); also David K. Jordan and Daniel L. Overmyer, *The Flying Phoenix: Aspects of Chinese Sectarianism in Taiwan* (Princeton, N.J., 1986).

59. Hsu Ti-shan, *Fu-chi mi-hsin*, p. 32; see also CPLC, *fang-chi*, p. 28.

60. Hsu Ti-shan, *Fu-chi mi-hsin*, pp. 32ff.; CPLC, *fang-chi*, pp. 19, 22. Jordan and Overmyer, pp. 45–63, discuss *fu-chi* and morality books.

61. Hsu Ti-shan, *Fu-chi mi-hsin*, p. 44; CPLC, *fang-chi*, pp. 15, 17, 19; Jordan and Overmyer, *The Flying Phoenix*, pp. 41–44. Yeh Ming-ch'en is one of very few officials acknowledged in Arthur Hummel, ed., *Eminent Chinese of the Ch'ing Period 1644–1912* (Washington, D.C., 1943–1944), as having a belief in popular divination practices. See ibid., p. 905.

62. On shamanism, consult in particular Donald Sutton, "Pilot Surveys of Chinese Shamans, 1875–1945: A Spatial Approach to Social History," *Journal of Social History* 15, no. 1 (1981): 39–50; also the articles by Jack Potter in Arthur Wolf, ed., *Religion and Ritual in Chinese Society* (Stanford, Calif., 1974); and Yih-Yuan Li in *Culture-Bound Syndromes, Ethnopsychiatry, and Alternative Therapies,* ed. William Lebra, (Honolulu, 1976). Significantly, Yuan Shu-shan's *Chung-kuo li-tai pu-jen chuan* ignores spirit writing entirely as a category of divination, and the TSCC devotes a mere fifteen pages to shamans (48:8453–8468), as against 2,172 pages on divination.

63. Hsu Ti-shan, *Fu-chi mi-hsin*, p. 36; see also CPLC, *fang-chi*, p. 16; Sutton, "Chinese Shamans," p. 43; HCCSWP 68:1aff., esp. 8b–10a.

64. CPLC, *mi-hsin*, p. 9. Western accounts of *chiao* and *ch'ien* divination abound, both for the Ch'ing period and for contemporary Taiwan and Hong Kong. See, e.g., David Jordan, *Gods, Ghosts and Ancestors: The Folk Religion of a Chinese Village* (Berkeley, Los Angeles, and London, 1972); also the sources cited in n. 23 above.

65. Jung Chao-tsu, "Chan-pu ti yuan-liu" (Origin of divination) in his *Mi-hsin yü ch'uan-shuo* (Superstitions and legends) (reprint; Taipei, 1969), pp. 43–44; see also CPLC, *mi-hsin*, pp. 10–13.

66. See Frederic Wakeman, Jr., *The Great Enterprise* (Berkeley, Calif., 1986) 1:245, 258, 262, 2811 289, 312n, 504n. Significantly, the ascension of the Shun-chih emperor in 1644 was delayed until the first day *(chia-tzu)* of a new sexagenary cycle, to assure an auspicious start for the Ch'ing dynasty. Ibid. 2:857.

67. CPLC, *shih-ling lei*, p. 6. The warnings on the covers of Ming and Ch'ing calendars—like most other elements of such works—were remarkably consistent over time. See Smith, "A Note on Chinese Calendars," appendix 3. A.3 and A.6. This appendix provides a chronological list (by collection) of about a hundred state

calendars and approximately seventy local almanacs in the Library of Congress, Harvard University, the British Library, and the Bibliothèque Nationale.

68. *Ta-Ch'ing hui-tien,* (Collected statutes of the great Ch'ing) (Peking, 1899), vols. 77–80; HCPFS, pp. 1a–33b. For a discussion of basic calendrical terms and concepts, consult Carole Morgan, *Le Tableau du boeuf du printemps: Étude d'une page de l'almanach chinois* (Paris, 1980), esp. pp. 158–244.

69. Morgan, *Le Tableau du boeuf du printemps,* pp. 92–113.

70. These generalizations are based on a survey of the materials mentioned in n. 67, above, plus an additional twenty or so almanacs in the collection of the University of London's School of Oriental and African Studies. For additional information, see Smith, *Chinese Almanacs.*

71. *Ta-Ch'ing hui-tien* 80:2bff.

72. Smith, "A Note on Qing Calendars," p. 131.

73. On the popularity of almanacs and calendars, see the essays by Evelyn Rawski and James Hayes in *Popular Culture in Late Imperial China,* ed. David Johnson, et al. (Berkeley, Los Angeles, and London, 1985), esp. pp. 23–24, 82–83; also Smith, *Chinese Almanacs.*

74. *Chinese Repository* 7, no. 8 (December 1838): 399; Parker, "The Chinese Almanac," p. 66. See also Smith, "Knowing Fate," pp. 161, 178; Smith, "A Note on Qing Calendars," pp. 132–133; and the observations of S. W. Williams, *Middle Kingdom* 2:80; Douglas, *China,* pp. 277–278; Gray, *China: A History* 2:15–16; Dennys, *Folk-Lore of China,* pp. 27–32; and esp. W. A. P. Martin, *A Cycle of Cathay* (Edinburgh and London, 1897), p. 310.

75. Smith, "A Note on Qing Calendars," appendix 2.A. 1, 37–39; J. J. M. de Groot, *Sectarianism and Religious Persecution in China* (Amsterdam, 1903), pp. 458–459. The new calendars *(hsin-li)* of the Taipings are especially interesting for their imperial-looking exterior (yellow, with double dragons and double phoenixes), their abandonment of most of the inherited cosmology, their propaganda effort—which included information about their social and economic programs as well as a vigorous denunciation of the Manchus and the "heterodoxy" of the old Ch'ing calendar—their refusal to designate auspicious and inauspicious activities, and their deliberate use of Ch'ing taboo characters (such as *li* [calendar], part of the personal name of the Ch'ien-lung emperor).

76. See my "Ritual in Ch'ing Culture" in *Orthodoxy in Late Imperial China,* ed. Kwang-Ching Liu (Berkeley, 1990), p. 304.

77. HCPFS, preface, p. 1a.

78. See Susan Naquin, *Millenarian Rebellion in China* (New Haven, Conn. and London, 1976), pp. 12–18; Daniel Overmyer, *Folk Buddhist Religion* (Cambridge, Mass., 1976), pp. 146–150, 172; C. K. Yang, *Religion in Chinese Society* (Berkeley, Calif., 1961), pp. 230–243. The quotation is from HCPFS, preface, p. 1a.

79. See HCCSWP 69:15b–25a; HCCSWPHP, 74:1a–8b; also n. 19, above. For Jesuit critiques, see in particular Nan Huai-jen (Ferdinand Verbiest), *Wang-t'ui chi-*

hsiung pien (The error of [fate] extrapolation to determine good and bad fortune) (Peking, 1699), *Wang-chan pien* (The error of divination) (Peking, n.d.); also n. 73, above.

80. HCCSWP 69:14b–16a, 23a–b, 24a–25a, 23b–24a; ibid. 63:la–b, 8b–9b, 10b–11a; WHL 9:10a; 19:3a–7b. See also Wang Fu-chih's *Chou-i nei-chuan fa-li* in ICCC, 141:2a–b; and Li Fu-yao's brief essay, titled simply "Divination" *(Pu-shih),* in *Tu-li ts'ung-ch'ao* (Notes on reading about ritual) (1891), *Tu-li hsiao-shih chi,* pp. 21b–22a.

81. See Smith, "Ritual in Ch'ing Culture," pp. 307–308.

82. Wang Wei-te, *Tseng-pu pu-shih cheng-tsung* (Amplified orthodox milfoil divination) (reprint, Taipei, 1961), *ke-yen.* Cf. Nevius, *China and the Chinese,* p. 181. On the self-confirming character of popular beliefs generally, see Keith Thomas, *Religion and the Decline of Magic* (New York, 1971), pp. 642–643.

83. Wang, *Zengbu pu-shih cheng-tsung, ke-yen.*

84. See Smith, "Ritual in Ch'ing Culture," pp. 307–308; also n. 56, above.

85. I have elaborated this argument (and several susequent remarks) in *Fortune-Tellers and Philosophers, passim.*

86. Evan Zuesse, "Divination," in *The Encyclopedia of Religion,* ed. Mircea Eliade (New York and London, 1987) 4:375.

87. Nathan Sivin, "Science and Medicine," pp. 169–170.

88. On medicine, see Paul Unschuld, *Medicine in China: A History of Ideas* (Berkeley, Los Angeles, and London, 1985), esp. p. 197.

89. On Tseng, see Yuan, *Shu pu-shih hsing-hsiang hsueh* 5:14a; on Kuo, see Yuan, *Chung-kuo li-tai pu-jen chuan* 18:11. For relevant proverbs on fate, consult Clifford Plopper, *Chinese Religion Seen through the Proverb* (Shanghai, 1926), pp. 291–315, esp. 294.

90. See Sivin "Science and Medicine," pp. 169–170; cf. Thomas, *Decline of Magic,* p. 657.

91. Sivin "Science and Medicine," p. 170, slightly modified.

92. Patricia Konings, "Astronomical Reports Offered by Ferdinand Verbiest S.J. to the Chinese Emperor" (Paper delivered at the Sixth International Conference on the History of Science in China), Cambridge University, Cambridge, England, August 2–7, 1990.

93. See Henry Veatch in Thomas and Grace Leahey, *Psychology's Occult Doubles: Psychology and the Problem of Pseudoscience* (Chicago, 1983), p. 240. I have discussed the "scientific" dimension of divination in "Divination, Science, and Medicine."

94. See George Park, "Divination and Its Social Contexts," *Journal of the Royal Anthropological Institute* 93, no. 2 (1963): 195–197, 207–208.

95. On the therapeutic effects of divination, see Smith, *Fortune-tellers,* pp. 245, 268–269.

96. Zuesse, "Divination," p. 380.

97. On the role of diviners as mediators, see Richard J. Smith, "Divination in Qing Ritual and Law" (Paper delivered at the Annual Meeting of the Southwest Conference of the Association for Asian Studies), New Orleans, November 4, 1989.

98. See Jordan, *Gods, Ghosts, and Ancestors,* pp. 85-86.

99. Yuan, *Chung-kuo li-tai pu-jen chuan,* 28: 2; cf. CC 2: 363 and 370.

100. See, e.g., Yuan, *Chung-kuo li-tai pu-jen chuan* 1:24; 3:8–9; 5:13; 5:22; 7: 17–18; 7:22–23; 10:9; 12:13; 14:12–13; 15:8–9; 18:13–14; 18:19–20; 18:24–25; 20:18; 20:27; 21:19–20; 23:16–17; 26:5, etc.

101. See Jordan and Overmyer, *The Flying Phoenix,* passim.

102. See Smith, "Divination in Qing Ritual and Law."

103. These activities included *I-ching* divination, physiognomy, geomancy, and especially *ch'ien* divination.

104. On cosmological kingship, see Hao Chang, *Chinese Intellectuals in Crisis: Search for Order and Meaning (1890–1911),* (Berkeley, Calif., 1987), pp. 5–7, 99–100, 181ff., esp. 184–187.

105. Ibid.

106. See Smith, "A Note on Qing Calendars."

107. See Hsia's review of *Archetype and Allegory in the Dream of the Red Chamber,* by Andrew Plaks, *Harvard Journal of Asiatic Studies,* 29 (1979): 197–198, cited in Henderson.

108. San-lien shu-tien, ed., *Ch'en Tu-hsiu wen-chang hsuan-pien* (Selections from Ch'en Tu-hsiu's essays) (Peking, 1984) 1:275, 297. See also Chen's "Resistence," *Hsin-nien tsa-chih* (New youth miscellany) 1, no. 3 (November 15, 1915): 1–5; and Chen Ta-ch'i's "Happy New Year," *Hsin ch'ing-nien* (New youth) 6, no. 1 (January 15, 1918): 5–9. Lu Hsun's essay appears in *The Selected Works of Lu Xun* ed. Gladys Yang and Yang Xianyi, (Beijing, 1980) 4:135–137.

109. I have discussed Chinese divination in modern times at some length in *Fortune-Tellers and Philosophers.* See also Smith, *Chinese Almanacs;* Hung and Chiang, *Chung-kuo ku-tai suan-ming shu,* pp. 276–277.

110. For an illuminating discussion of these distinctions, consult Stanley Tambiah, *Magic, Science, Religion, and the Scope of Rationality* (Cambridge, England, 1990).

8

Purist Hermeneutics and Ritualist Ethics in Mid-Ch'ing Thought

KAI-WING CHOW

Recent studies of the ascendancy of evidential scholarship *(k'ao-cheng hsueh)* in the Ch'ien-lung (1736–1795) and Chia-ch'ing (1796–1820) periods have reached ever-higher levels of sophistication. The dominant view, however, still stresses the empirical or intellectual aspect of the movement as its major point of departure from previous developments in Confucian thought.[1] In this perspective, the quest for verifiable knowledge of classical antiquity had a higher claim than any commitment to Confucian ideology per se.[2] Scholars of this period, engaging in exacting research on the classics, employed ingenious philological and critical methods, and, as a result, the frontiers of ancient philology and history advanced significantly.[3] A corollary to the improvement of academic skills was an apparent erosion of the commitment to Confucian ethics—at least as espoused by Sung dynasty philosophers—for the textual basis of neo-Confucianism received a severe critical challenge from the findings of philological and historical studies.[4]

The subversive potential of the evidential scholarship of the Ch'ien-Chia period is clear enough, but the *k'ao-cheng* commitment to objectivity has been overstated, obscuring the profound faith of these well-intentioned classicists in some specific tenets of Confucianism. In other words, the prejudices of the evidential scholars have been overlooked. As I will demonstrate, classical scholars in eighteenth-century China began their search for authentic Confucianism from the common belief that Confucianism had been pervasively corrupted by heterodox ideas since the Sung. Attempts to recover pure Confucianism involved, first, the purge of non-Confucian elements and, second, the reconstruction of "original" teachings through philogical and textual studies. But the scholars who attempted to do this reconstruction did not approach the classics without preconceptions.

Eighteenth-century classicists not only shared a strong aversion to hetero-doxy; they also endorsed a similar notion of human nature and a ritualist approach to moral cultivation. For our purposes, conventional terms such as *k'ao-cheng* and Han learning *(Han-hsueh)* do not adequately characterize the relation of methodology to the antiheterodoxy and ethical thought of this period. I propose, therefore, to study this period of classical scholarship in terms of "purist hermeneutics."

By hermeneutics, I mean the principles and methods of interpreting texts so as to uphold a religion or an ideology. Its usage in this essay bears resem-blance to the manner in which hermeneutics had been used in the history of biblical studies before Schleiermacher.[5] However, I shall use it in a slightly different sense to denote the methodology of interpreting the Confucian Five Classics. I make no attempt here to treat hermeneutics as a philosophy or a general theory of interpretation as it has been developed in contempo-rary philosophy.[6] My purpose is to show that the critical edge of evidential scholarship in the Ch'ing was guided by a purist impulse. The methodology of evidential scholarship did not imply a kind of intellectual license. It aimed at cleansing heterodox ideas on the one hand and, on the other, at rein-terpreting Confucian ethics from a ritualist perspective by means of a *selec-tive* application of philological evidence. To bring to light the purism of eighteenth-century scholars and the strong ritualism in their ethics, I exam-ine the ideas of three major figures, Tai Chen (1723–1777), Ling T'ing-k'an (1757–1809) and Juan Yuan (1764–1849). They, in varying ways, exerted a profound influence on classical scholarship of the period under study.

Antiheterodoxy in Early Ch'ing Thought

In order to understand the purist nature of eighteenth-century classical scholarship, it is necessary to explain briefly the major intellectual trend in the K'ang-hsi period. The demise of the Ming regime added fuel to the anti-heterodox movement championed by Ku Hsien-cheng (1550–1612) and Kao P'an-lung (1562–1626), both leaders of the Tung-lin Academy.[7] In the wake of the Manchu conquest in 1644, antiheterodoxy emerged as a powerful current. Scholars vigorously attacked or distanced themselves from Buddhism and any forms of syncretism. Wang Yang-ming and his fol-lowers, epitomizing late Ming syncretic tendencies, were increasingly repu-diated as having taught Ch'an Buddhism. But, whereas adherents of the Ch'eng-Chu learning made anti-heterodoxy a major issue in their polemic against Wang Yang-ming, the defenders of Wang retaliated by accusing

Sung neo-Confucianism of infusing Buddhist and Taoist elements into their interpretation of the Confucian texts.

Regardless of intellectual partisanship, scholars stressing the purge of heterodox elements came to focus on exposing noncanonical texts. Huang Tsung-hsi (1610–1695) and Mao Ch'i-ling (1623–1716), for example, criticized Sung neo-Confucians for infusing heterodox elements into the I-ching (Book of changes).[8] On the basis of the pioneering works by Huang and Mao, Hu Wei (1633–1714) completed in 1700 a comprehensive and definitive study titled I-t'u ming-pien (A clarifying critique of the diagrams appended to the Book of changes), revealing the heterodox origin of Chou Tun-i's (1017–1073) T'ai-chi t'u (Diagram of the great ultimate).[9] Later, in 1708, after tracing the origin of the T'ai-chi t'u, the Ho-t'u (Yellow River chart), and the Lo-shu (Lo River diagram), Li Kung (1659–1733), a friend of Hu Wei and a student of Yen Yuan (1635–1704), came to a similar conclusion. Both rejected the idea that these illustrations belonged to the original text of the Book of Changes.[10] Yen Jo-chü's (1636–1704) systematic exposure of the fabrication of the Old Text Shu-ching (Book of history) was but one of several purist attempts to weed out noncanonical textual elements.[11]

However, it should be noted that in the K'ang-hsi period critical scholarship did not wage war on the entire spectrum of neo-Confucian beliefs—partly because there was a strong revival of the Ch'eng-Chu orthodoxy, and partly because Ch'eng I and Chu Hsi were strident in their polemics against Buddhism. In contrast, the strong syncretism informing the teachings of many disciples of Wang Yang-ming became the easy target of purist attacks. The accusation that Wang's defenders brought against the Sung Confucians did not create powerful resonance until the mid-eighteenth century. With the adherents of Ch'eng-Chu learning on the offensive, the notion that all persuasions of Sung learning had to be forsaken before authentic Confucianism could be restored had yet to gain currency.[12]

Confucian purism had a dialectic of its own. A few scholars—notably Ch'en Ch'üeh (1604–1677), Yen Yuan, and Li Kung—quickly came to terms with the radical implications of the view that the process of incorporating heterodox elements had actually begun long ago, in the Sung period. In their opinion, heterodox ideas not only had entered the Confucian classics but also had infiltrated through the exegesis of Sung neo-Confucians, who had unwittingly read heterodox ideas into the classics.[13] In short, Sung scholars had employed terms of Buddhist or Taoist origin to explain the classics. Their corrupted teachings had come down as exegeses, and, as a result, the meaning of the classical language had been drastically altered. However, this more radical critique of neo-Confucianism did not become a major trend until the mid-eighteenth century.

A major factor contributing to the suppression of this more radical anti-heterodoxy was the strong revival of the Ch'eng-Chu learning both inside and outside the Manchu court in the K'ang-hsi period.[14] Another factor that helped protect the Ch'eng-Chu school temporarily from this accusation was its anti-Buddhist rhetoric. But the debunking efforts in the K'ang-hsi period ultimately had the inadvertent effect of undermining the credibility of Sung scholarship. As the purist impulse continued to demand some sort of textual and exegetical decontamination, Ch'ing scholars increasingly came to accept the view that Sung neo-Confucian commentaries were simply unreliable, that they had been hopelessly corrupted by heterodox ideas. This had become the common view of purist classicists from the mid-eighteenth century on.

At issue was the question of how the classics should be read and how to develop a methodology that could help avoid the perverted teachings put forth by Sung and Ming neo-Confucians. The battle against heterodoxy had to be fought largely in the field of philology because the study of language was the principal weapon whereby Han-learning scholars strove to purge heterodox elements from the Confucian classics. It was not philology that led them to discover heterodoxy; rather, it was their understanding of what heterodoxy was that guided their philological efforts.

To the Ch'ing purists, a central feature of neo-Confucian teachings was a Buddhist dualistic ontology, which served as the underpinning of the Sung view of human nature and ethics. Buddhist dualism, which had been subjected to severe attack since the Late Ming period, was regarded as particularly pervasive in the Ch'eng-Chu school of neo-Confucian philosophy.[15] Leading classicists such as Tai Chen, Ling T'ing-k'an, and Juan Yuan, took pains to replace it with a monistic notion of human nature, which was to provide, by means of philological arguments, an ontological foundation for a ritualist theory of self-cultivation.

Tai Chen: Mencius and the Learning of Ritual-Propriety

Tai Chen, the towering classicist of the mid-Ch'ing period, offered a historical explanation for the infusion of Buddhist modes of thinking into Confucianism. Great neo-Confucians such as Ch'eng I and Chu Hsi did not, he believed, deliberately appropriate Buddhism. They were merely the victims of their own intellectual habits, having immersed themselves in Buddhist teachings for a long period of time before returning to Confucianism in the quest for truth.[16] The deeply entrenched modes of thinking and Buddhist terminology had, without their knowledge, found their way into their teachings. With such a historical explanation, Tai Chen exonerated Ch'eng I and Chu Hsi from voluntary subversion of Confucianism. He nonetheless felt obliged to demolish their defiled teachings as a necessary step toward the recovery of pure Confucianism.

In Tai Chen's view, neo-Confucians and Buddhists alike spoke of a realm of absolute reality, *li* (principle), or *t'ien-li* (heavenly principle), that was metaphysical *(hsing-erh-shang)* and independent of the physical world of tangible forms *(hsing-erh-hsia)*. Tai saw in this dichotomized notion of principle and material force *(ch'i)* the basis of a neo-Confucian view of human nature that stressed the preservation of principle ingrained in the human mind and the suppression of human desires *(jen-yü)*.[17] According to Tai Chen, both the Buddhists and Taoists were troubled by ordinary people's indulgence in the gratification of desires. They considered human desires detrimental to the mind-intellect *(hsin-chih)*. Such a negative attitude toward human appetites, Tai Chen argued, was a logical extension of the Buddhist bifurcation of physical constitution *(hsueh-ch'i)* and mind-intellect.[18] This dualism had made its way into neo-Confucian teachings, which accordingly exalted principle as man's "real" nature and condemned his physical makeup for impulsive outbursts of desire. When translated into a theory of government, the demand for a renunciation of desires inevitably slighted the basic needs of the subject.[19]

Tai Chen was certainly not the first to criticize the dualistic ontology implicit in the Ch'eng-Chu school. In fact, adherents of the Ch'eng-Chu school, including individuals such as Ts'ao Tuan (1376–1434), Hsüeh Hsüan (1389–1464), and Lo Ch'in-shun (1465–1547), had been critical of the dualism implicit in Chu Hsi's view of human nature.[20] What was unique, however, was the philological argument Ch'ing classicists employed in rejecting it. For Tai Chen, classical Confucianism never conceived of principle and material force as distinct entities. In the writings of Mencius, Tai found textual evidence for a monistic notion of human nature. Mencius clearly stated that human nature was constituted of nothing but material force and mind-intellect.[21] Mencius never spoke of a distinction between a nature of principle *(i-li chih hsing)* and man's physical nature *(ch'i-chih chih hsing)*.[22] Hence, the corporeal aspects of human existence should not be degraded as an obstacle to moral perfection. The virtues of humanity, duty, ritual-propriety, and wisdom could not be sought independently of desires.[23] In fact, human ability to improve morally and intellectually hinged on the mind, which comprised nothing but material force.

By endorsing a monistic view of human nature, Tai Chen took exception to the neo-Confucians' condemnation of human desire as a source of evil. In his view, there was nothing inherently evil about appetites. Only when man went to excess in seeking fulfillment of them would there be evil consequences. But it was man's ignorance rather than his physical needs that were to blame.[24] Tai agreed that ordinary people out of selfishness (ssu) tended to give free rein to their desires,[25] but selfishness itself stemmed from the lack of knowledge of principle-propriety (li-i). In Tai's view, this ignorance of propriety (pi) was the gravest problem of mankind.[26] His maxim, "morals depend on learning" (te-hsing tzu yü hsüeh-wen) encapsulated the inextricable relation between ethical behavior and learning. As Ying-shih Yü has pointed out, Tai Chen's approach to morals was intellectualistic.[27]

When kept within proper limits, human desires were themselves reflections of heavenly principle, according to Tai. Hence, he argued that self-cultivation consisted of not so much the eradication as the control of desires. He wrote, "To temper one's desires so that they will be fulfilled neither excessively nor inadequately—can we not then call these desires heavenly principles?"[28] But what exactly were heavenly principles, and how were they to be known? According to Tai, moral principles were not to be found within the human mind, contrary to the standard neo-Confucian view. He criticized in particular Chu Hsi's attempt to equate moral principles with the essence of human nature.[29] Tai argued instead that the ancients never conceived of human nature as identical with principle.[30] Rather, the term "principle" (li) in the classical language meant differentiation, or the distinctive patterns (fen-li) found in things. The philological evidence seems to lend substance to Tai's indictment against Chu Hsi and to his own interpretation of the Confucian canon of human nature. But the matter was not quite so simple. In fact, Tai was either a bad historian or a prejudiced scholar, who chose to criticize only his Sung predecessors and spare the Han scholars.

As Chiao Hsun (1763–1820) pointed out, it was the Han commentator Cheng Hsuan who first explained principle in terms of human nature in the "Yüeh-chi" chapter of his Li-chi cheng-i (Correct interpretation of the Record of Rites). The Sung neo-Confucians did not, then, owe their conception of principle to the Buddhists.[31] In fact, the passage containing the terms t'ien-li (heavenly principle) and jen-yü (human desires) can be understood as suggesting some dualistic notion of human nature. At least this potential exposition was adopted by the T'ang exegete K'ung Ying-ta, who explained that human beings at birth had no desire, which was man's original nature. He said, "What is bestowed *(tzu-jan)* is nature *(hsing)*; avarice and desires are feelings *(ch'ing)*."[32] K'ung's comments strongly suggest the possibility of a dualistic interpretation, treating nature and feelings as two components of human beings. Furthermore, to consider feelings as evil and one's essential nature as good was one common trend in Han thought since the time of Tung Chung-shu (c. 179–c. 104 B.C.).[33] Viewed in this light, Sung neo-Confucians simply continued a long-standing tradition of Han thought. If Sung neo-Confucians were criticized for espousing a dualistic view of human nature, they deserved no greater blame than Cheng Hsuan and others. By the same token, if Buddhism was held responsible, it did no more than reinforce the dualistic strain of Han Confucianism that the Sung Neo-Confucians inherited from their T'ang predecessors.

Fang Tung-shu (1772–1851), a critic of Han learning, made a similar charge against Tai Chen's ignorance of the Han origins of this usage.[34] In rejecting Sung exegeses, Tai also violated his own methodical principle of philology by insisting in this instance on accepting only one sense of the word *li* as its meaning. This example clearly shows that Tai Chen formulated his ethics not primarily by means of a thoroughly empirical study of philological evidence, but rather from an ideological rejection of Sung ethical theory and a belief in a monistic concept of human nature. His use of philological evidence was guided by a antiheterodox revulsion against Sung neo-Confucianism.

Tai's interpretation of the classical idea of human nature is closely related to his particular approach to ethics, which stressed the learning of ritual-propriety *(li)*. This strong ritualism is revealed in his own definition of moral principle. For him, moral principles were the absolute *(pu-i)* "differentiated rules" of things, accessible to human beings through intellect. They were universally acknowledged truths. Without common consent, principles could be nothing but a matter of personal opinion.[35] Of all the principles, the most important and relevant to mankind were those of ritual-propriety. The rules of ritual-propriety were important because they served as the absolute standard by which the behavior of ordinary people could be measured and aligned. Tai said: "*Li* are the most proper and absolute rules. . . . Except for the sages, it is extremely difficult to attain perfect balance in one's opinion and purity in one's moral conduct. If these things could be achieved, one's conduct would be in accordance with *li*."[36]

Tai Chen went on to explain the source of ritual-propriety, writing: "*Li* are the rules and the laws of heaven and earth; they are perfect rules, and only those who understand heaven will know them. Etiquette, ceremony, measures and regulations are the rules that the sages perceived in heaven and earth, and instituted as the standard for the myriad generations to come. *Li* are established to govern the feelings of all the people, either in sanction against excess, or in encouragement of those who fall short of the standard."[37] The ancient sages were thus the spokesmen of these sacred rules. Aside from these worthies, all individuals had to learn to expand their intellect and acquire ritual knowledge. All could become enlightened if they would only persist in seeking moral knowledge *(wen-hsüeh).*[38]

Tai Chen's ideas of the source of moral truths are very complex and involve rather contradictory positions. On the one hand, he regards the ancient sages as extraordinary persons who "understood heaven" and who were therefore so perfect in their judgment and moral conduct that they were able to determine the propriety of rituals for the common people. On the other hand, he makes a point of refuting Hsun-tzu's idea that only the sages had access to ritual-propriety. All men, he claims, possess the intellectual ability to ponder and learn ritual-propriety. The only reason the common people found it necessary to learn from the sages was because of the latter's extraordinary wisdom. The sages were simply better endowed intellectually and thus able to perceive and learn much faster and better than common men.[39] Although the education of common men might take longer and require much more effort, Tai suggested that by virtue of their inborn intellect they could eventually perceive ritual-propriety without assistance from the sages. Implicit in this position is an autonomous approach to morality, denying the monopoly of moral truths by the sages.

Yet, presumably in reaction to Sung learning, Tai held that moral truths could not be grasped independently of the classics. When any conflict of interpretation arose between the ancients and ordinary people such as the neo-Confucians, there could be no doubt who should have the final word. "The classics," he wrote, "are the main sources of the way and proper behavior *(tao-i).*"[40] In this passage he rejects the idea that moral truths are directly accessible to everyone and argues that they can be learned only from the ancient sages. He denies common scholars, including the neo-Confucians, the legitimacy of any claim to having comprehended ultimate moral truths directly by means of their intellect.

Tai's belief in the classics as the repository of moral truths presupposes an authoritarian perspective, which enshrined the classics as the ultimate source of morals and put the sages on a pedestal as the only true guardians of ethical behavior. As mentioned earlier, Tai conceived of principle in terms of universally accepted truth. But how was it possible to secure universal agreement on the propriety of principle? It was possible only if instituted as ritual-propriety by the sage-kings and made readily available for verification by subsequent generations. Tai's elitist and authoritarian predilection is unmistakable here. We must conclude, then, that despite his criticism of Hsun-tzu, Tai was ultimately unwilling to grant that all men shared an intrinsic ability to perceive moral truths independently. All he would concede is that everyone had the ability to learn and understand moral truths.

In his authoritarian approach to moral cultivation and his emphasis on eliminating erroneous ideas (ch'u-pi), Tai Chen shared more of Hsun-tzu's outlook than he might have been willing to admit. Tai's fellow student, Ch'eng Yao-t'ien (1725–1814) acutely pointed out the parallel positions of the two men in this regard.[41] In fact, Ch'eng had misgivings about Tai's stress on eliminating erroneous ideas and eradicating selfishness (ch'u-ssu), and felt that the latter's ethical thinking underscored the extirpation of bad conduct and ideas rather than the development of the good inherent in man.[42] Like a latter-day Hsun-tzu, Tai believed that the most effective way to discourage bad deeds and thoughts was through education and the practice of proper rituals.

Ling T'ing-k'an: Hsun Tzu and the Book of Rites and Decorum

Antiheterodoxy and ritualism continued to inform the thinking of another classicist, Ling T'ing-k'an, an admirer of Tai Chen. Ling was not only critical of neo-Confucian teachings for the Buddhist elements they embodied, but he also felt that attempts to purify Confucian teachings by scholars such as Ku Yen-wu, Mao Ch'i-ling, and Tai Chen were not thorough enough.[43] In Ling's view, even Tai could not completely wean himself from Buddhist influence. Although he was certainly worthy of his reputation as a staunch opponent of neo-Confucianism, Ling found in Tai's major critique of neo-Confucianism, the Meng-tzu tzu-i shu-cheng, vestiges of Buddhist ideas. For example, Tai began his treatise with an exposition of the term "principle" and even discussed elementary learning (hsiao-hsüeh) in terms of substance and function (t'i-yung). According to Ling, this dyad offered unequivocal evidence for Buddhism's dualistic mode of thinking, which had been profusely employed in Sung neo-Confucian exegeses of the Confucian classics.

Ling traced the t'i-yung concept to Ch'an Buddhism, pointing out that in the *Analects* the character *yung* (function) was used by itself, not in conjunction with the character *t'i* (substance).[44] But in neo-Confucian writings the two characters came to be used as a dualistic term that was applied liberally in explaining Confucian ideas. What the neo-Confucians had been expounding, Ling maintained, was nothing but Ch'an Buddhism, which had gained a hold on Chinese scholars since the T'ang dynasty.[45] Ling further disputed the inherited notion that the Sung neo-Confucians excelled in their articulation of the moral truths of the classics; scholars of the Han period knew no peer in their knowledge of ancient institutions and regulations *(chih-shu)*. Tai Chen, for one, entertained this view even after he had turned thirty years old.[46] From Ling's perspective, however, any attempt to approach moral truths as abstract principles, as by the neo-Confucians, was nothing but Ch'an Buddhism.[47]

Discontent with Tai Chen's incomplete purge of Buddhism as Ling might be, he still held Tai in high regard and continued to ponder the issues of human nature and desires along the lines set forth in Tai's philosophical writings. Unlike the latter, however, Ling did not go to great length in refuting neo-Confucian dualism. In fact, he wrote sparingly on philosophical issues for he, like most purist classicists, dismissed theoretical formulations as nothing more than personal speculation. Nonetheless, he did put forward his monistic conception of human nature in a famous treatise titled "On Returning to Ritual-Propriety" *(Fu-li lun)*.

Along with Tai Chen, Ling argued that human beings were constituted of material force and the so-called five elements *(wu-hsing)*.[48] Contrary to the neo-Confucian notion, however, Ling maintained that human nature was anything but principle. Rather, it comprised senses and faculties of the body that were in perfect balance *(chih-chung)* before feelings, emotions, and desires arose. In Tai Chen's favored term, they were a part of one's blood forces or physical constitution *(hsueh-ch'i)*. The perfect balance was easily upset in either direction when feelings and desires emanated.[49] But human desires were not to be denigrated as essentially evil, nor conceived as the opposite of true nature. They were necessary for the nourishment of the human body and needed only to be controlled, not extirpated. Ling even reduced the complex nature of desires into likes and dislikes *(hao-wu)*.[50] When the external world was presented to the senses, feelings of liking and disliking arose. As these feelings developed out of physiological and psychological reactions, they were unreasoned and tended either to run to excess or to emanate insufficiently. The balance of nature was disturbed as a result.[51]

Ling developed, as did Tai Chen, a ritualist ethics in conjunction with his monistic notion of human nature. Ritual-propriety provided a means by which to restore *(fu)* the proper balance in people and keep the expression of feelings and desires at an appropriate level. Ling did not employ the term "restoring nature" in the neo-Confucian sense of retrieving something that was lost or blurred by human desires. Because nature was not principles embedded in the mind, it could not be "discovered" by introspection. But the balance in individuals was frequently disrupted, and constant effort was therefore needed to restore equilibrium. In theory, the balance prior to the emergence of feelings and desires was irrelevant because the latter constantly arose in response to internal impulses as well as external stimuli. What mattered was the achievement of a balance during their expression. When feelings and desires were expressed and satisfied in accordance with ritual-propriety, one's nature was restored to its harmonious state.

Although Tai Chen still spoke of ritual-propriety in terms of principle, Ling simply jettisoned the term altogether, applying the rules of purist hermeneutics to criticize both the neo-Confucians and Tai himself. Ling pointed out, for example, that the *Analects,* which faithfully preserve Confucius' sayings, never use the word *li* (principle), but make numerous references to ritual propriety.[52] However, Confucianism was certainly more than the utterances of the master, as important as they were. The classics such as the *I-ching* (Book of changes) and the *Li-chi* (Record of rites) used the term "principle" on a number of occasions.[53] But as pointed out in the section on Tai Chen, Fang Tung-shu criticized Tai for ignoring the fact that Ch'eng I simply followed Cheng Hsuan's comment on the "Record of Music" chapter of the *Li-chi* when he equated principles with human nature. Chu Hsi, Fang went on to say, merely adopted the usage from Ch'eng I.[54] In short, the disgust Ling felt for the neo-Confucian term "principle," and his preoccupation with the concept of ritual-propriety, prompted him to disregard philological evidence that he claimed to be the terra firma for evaluating the purity of Sung exegesis. In spite of his commitment to empirical evidence, Ling's interpretation of classical ideas sometimes was based more on ideological than on philological grounds.

In ritual-propriety Ling perceived the essence of Confucianism, and on its foundation he presented his own interpretation of the classics. Unlike Tai Chen, who regarded Mencius as the most faithful student of Confucius, Ling gave pride of place to Hsun-tzu. As the foregoing discussion has shown, Tai Chen in many ways came closer to Hsun-tzu than Mencius in his approach to moral cultivation—not least in his stress on eliminating erroneous ideas and learning ritual-propriety as a means of expanding one's initial sense of the good. Whether calling for an expansion of innate moral capabilities or a suppression of natural impulses, both teachings underline the exteriority of the knowledge of ritual-propriety and the need for human exertion. Ling, in a preface to a eulogy for Hsun-tzu, said that his writings "record nothing but the lost texts of ritual-propriety, expounding their profound meanings. . . . Mencius always explained *jen* in terms of duty *(i),* whereas Hsun-tzu spoke of *jen* in conjunction with ritual-propriety. . . . [Without ritual-propriety] *jen* is as elusive as it is incomprehensible."[55]

Hsun-tzu's teachings had, of course, long been discredited by neo-Confucians because of his theory of man's evil nature *(hsing-o),* which stood in such sharp contrast to the dominant Mencian conception of man's originally good nature.[56] But in the eyes of Ling T'ing-k'an, Hsun-tzu actually surpassed Mencius—at least in his knowledge of ancient ritual-propriety.[57] Ling's unprecedented perspective on Hsun-tzu may be viewed not only as a deliberate effort to undermine neo-Confucian exaltation of Mencius but also as an earnest attempt to appraise anew the overall doctrine of Confucianism.[58] This appraisal, based on a ritualist interpretation of Confucianism, focused on several critical passages and concepts in the Four Books, particularly the *Doctrine of the Mean* and the *Great Learning.* These two works, both taken from the *Li-chi,* had been important sources of neo-Confucian ethics and metaphysics, but to Ling they were no more than expository writings on ritual-propriety.[59]

Since the rise of neo-Confucianism, the doctrine of *shen-tu* (vigilance in solitude) had been understood as a method of spiritual cultivation associated with the practice of quiet-sitting *(ching-tso).* Neo-Confucians who practiced quiet-sitting and introspection had appropriated these ideas from the Buddhists and Taoists, but *shen-tu,* like the virtually identical concept of *hsiu-shen* (self-cultivation), came straight from the *Chung-yung* and *Ta-hsueh.* Ling agreed that *shen-tu* involved introspection, but he contended that it referred to ritual-propriety as used in the *Doctrine of the Mean* and the *Great Learning.* In solitude, he asserted, one should be vigilant about whether one's conduct was properly cultivated according to ritual-propriety.[60]

Another pivotal expression from the Four Books, *ko-wu* (the investigation of things) occasioned much debate in neo-Confucian circles between scholars of the Ch'eng-Chu tradition, who saw *ko-wu* as involving primarily classical book learning, and of the Wang Yang-ming school, who viewed it in terms of meditative introspection. To Ling, the explanations of both schools were mere speculations, if not outright distortions of the original meaning. In any case, as he explained in a letter to Ch'ien Ta-hsin (1728–1804), the term *wu* (things) could not mean things in general, for if so, an entire lifetime would be insufficient for studying them. He concluded, therefore, that *wu* must mean ritual-propriety and that *ko-wu* was then *ko-li* (the investigation of ritual-propriety). Following the chain-syllogistic logic of the *Ta-hsueh*, he deduced that sincerity in intention *(ch'eng-i)*, rectification of the mind *(cheng-hsin)*, and self-cultivation *(hsiu-shen)*, all required ritual-propriety.[61] In Ling's opinion, to speak of the Way *(tao)* apart from ritual-propriety was both elusive and unreliable. He wrote: "The way of sages is based on ritual-propriety, which is what they saw as real. The way of heterodoxy renounces ritual-propriety and consists of teachings that are mere speculations without substance."[62]

Like Tai Chen, Ling regarded the knowledge of ritual-propriety as external to ordinary humans, except for sages whose nature was so balanced that no external rules were required. Ordinary people and scholars alike had to learn ritual-propriety so that their feelings and desires could be kept in balance, and their nature restrained *(chieh-hsing)*.[63] Like all purist classicists, Ling considered the classics as the repository of absolute ritual-propriety. He regarded the *Book of Rites and Decorum (I-li)* in particular as paramount among the classics. He spent thirty years trying to exhaust the rules he believed to be the absolute moral truths according to which the sage-kings designed the ritual and institutions in high antiquity. The greatness of the duke of Chou was unmatched for, without him, there would be no institutionalization of human ethical relations *(jen-lun)*.[64]

Although both Tai Chen and Ling T'ing-k'an stressed learning ritual-propriety in order to develop good character, their ideas differed subtly. Tai's concern was with principles and the need to come to grips with the meaning of propriety through the exercise of intellect. Ling, by contrast, put a premium on practice and the molding of behavior through habitual action. As Ling envisioned it, the perfect society of the Three Dynasties was made possible because everyone from ruler to subject was bound by ritual-propriety. Nothing went against it, and everyone gradually returned to their balanced nature without being conscious of the process.[65] The advantage of ritual-propriety as a means for cultivating good conduct lay in its exteriority as well as its demand for uniform compliance.

Tai Chen was optimistic enough to believe that universal agreement on the rules of propriety could be attained through the use of human intellect. But Ling had little faith in the possibility that a consensus could be reached on the universal principles of propriety. Lurking behind Ling's thinking was a strong distrust of the ability of common people to understand propriety. What they could offer were mostly personal opinions. If scholars sought principles of moral cultivation through their intellect, the most worthy would go to extremes; the obtuse would fall short of the proper standard.[66] At one point, Ling went so far as to say that, if sages set out to seek principle, they might possibly mistake their own personal opinions (ssu-hsin) for principle. Hence they chose to depend on ritual-propriety as a guide to the restoration of nature.[67] Like many purist classicists, Ling practiced rites in accordance with what he understood of the I-li.[68]

Juan Yuan: Tseng-tzu and Philology

Purist classicism reached its peak in the thinking of Juan Yuan, whose reinterpretation of Confucianism was increasingly couched in terms of k'ao-cheng-style scholarship. Juan shared with Tai Chen and Ling T'ing-k'an a monistic view of human nature as well as a philological approach to the classics; but he arrived at a Confucian ethics that had an even narrower scope. Feeling a strong aversion toward Buddhism and Taoism, Juan carried the methodology of purist hermeneutics even further than did his predecessors. Persistently critical of the enormity and ubiquity of the effect of Buddhist and Taoist ideas on neo-Confucianism, he vowed to discard commentaries and exegeses of the classics written after the Han period. As he put the matter,

> The classical scholarship of the Han dynasty should receive priority because of its temporal closeness to the sages and worthies, and [because] Taoism and Buddhism had not yet gained ascendency. Taoism did not become current until the Chin dynasty [265–420]. . . . The language and characters of Buddhist texts cannot be understood without translation. Erudites of the Northern dynasties and the wise literati of Sung and Ch'i [Southern dynasties] projected their arbitrary opinions into the Buddhist writings. . . . It is not that Confucianism was perverted by Buddhism, but rather the reverse is true. . . . Therefore, I state that the reason why the Han exegeses are superior lies in their anteriority to the rise of Taoism and Buddhism.[69]

Juan Yuan's claim that the Confucians of the Northern dynasties had corrupted Buddhism was not meant to defend the foreign faith. It merely underscored the practice of using a Confucian vocabulary to render Buddhist scriptures. These translated Buddhist texts, tampered with and subtly distorted by Confucian language, became the evidence for Sung neo-Confucians that Buddhism and Confucianism had many parallels and thus paved the way for the neo-Confucian appropriation of Buddhism and the subsequent development of various forms of syncretism. Instead of putting the blame exclusively on the Sung neo-Confucians, Juan went a step further than Tai Chen in demonstrating that their inclusion of unorthodox elements was a historical development with a long tradition that preceded by centuries the actual emergence of neo-Confucianism.

Juan Yuan's purist approach to Confucian ethics was conspicuous in his writings. He advanced a rigorous orthodox stance by means of philological arguments. Despite Juan's high regard for Ling T'ing-k'an, he felt that Ling's theory of moral cultivation was still influenced too much by Taoism. Juan admired Ling for his work "On Returning to Ritual-Propriety," but he had misgivings about the term *fu-hsing* (restoring nature) favored by Ling. In applying philological methods to identify character with meaning, he argued that the phrase *fu-hsing* did not appear in the Confucian classics. It was a term employed by the Taoist, Chuang-tzu, who denounced culture and learning as an erosion of human nature. Juan here echoed Tai Chen's criticism of Chuang-tzu's disparagement of learning.[70] This sort of anti-intellectualist attitude also came to inform the influential work titled "On Retrieving Nature," written by the T'ang scholar Li Ao (772–841), whose thinking in this regard presaged the neo-Confucian concept of human nature.[71] By means of philological deduction, Juan discovered that the ancients spoke of regulating nature *(chieh-hsing)* rather than restoring nature.[72] Confucius taught Yen Hui only returning to ritual-propriety *(fu-li)*, not restoring nature.[73] In fairness to Ling T'ing-k'an, it should be noted that he sometimes opted for the term *chieh-hsing* himself.[74]

Juan Yuan's theory of human nature owed much to Tai Chen. But he tended to be more consistent in articulating his ideas by appealing to philological evidence. He found that the word, *hsing* (nature) was seldom used in the writings of the early Chou dynasty.[75] It first appeared in the *Book of History* and was made up of the character, life *(sheng)* and mind *(hsin)*, hence it connoted blood-forces *(hsueh-ch'i)* and mind-intellect *(hsin-chih)*.[76] Because human desires grew out of feelings and were inalienable elements of human nature, it was a mistake to exclude them from human nature. Besides, desires themselves were not evil, for men were born with a physical being, and they had to satisfy their basic bodily appetites.[77] To corroborate his argument Juan gathered many passages and commentaries by Han scholars such as Cheng Hsuan and Hsu Shen. He wrote: "The *Shuo-wen*

(On Writing) says, 'nature is the *yang* force of man, hence human nature is good. Feelings are the *yin* force with desires. Hsu's explanation provides the ancient meaning. . . . Feelings are part of nature, they are not something independent of or in contrast to nature. Cheng [Hsuan] explained the words, *wu* [things] and *tse* [rules] in terms of nature, which includes feelings. Cheng's view is the old meaning before the Han period."[78]

The meanings that Hsu gave, however, could easily be interpreted as a dualistic concept of human nature. The Han notion of human nature was clearly infused with the *yin* and *yang* idea, and in fact, Hsu Shen was undoubtedly influenced by Tung Chung-shu, who perceived a bifurcation between nature on the one hand and feelings and desires on the other.[79] Juan Yuan knew that by equating life with nature he might be accused of endorsing the teaching of Kao-tzu, so he argued that Kao-tzu's mistake lay not so much in identifying life with nature, as in confusing human nature with animal nature.[80]

From Juan's perspective, the very physical constitution of man demands the satisfaction of various appetites of the senses as well as the desire for leisure *(an-i)*. Like Tai Chen and Ling T'ing-k'an, he was inclined to see desire as a natural impulse that had a life of its own. If unchecked, man's desires would run to extremes and result in immoral practices for the individual and social chaos. Bodily appetites needed restraint or else men would be overwhelmed by desires.[81] In the Duke of Chou's "Chao-Kao," Juan found the first occurrence of such a notion in the term *chieh-hsing*.[82]

Unfortunately, most people were not "intelligent" enough to regulate their desires voluntarily. As explained in the *Doctrine of the Mean,* those who were perfectly intelligent would simply let their nature run its course and they would keep their bodily appetites within limits without the aid of learning *(tzu ch'eng ming wei chih hsing)*. On the other hand, the obtuse needed to be taught the proper way to control their desires *(tzu ming ch'eng wei chih chiao)*.[83] He echoed Ling T'ing-k'an's view in remarking that everyone had to learn ritual-propriety before they could restrain their nature." Teaching *(chiao)* thus meant the ancient Six Rituals *(liu-li)* that the official of education used to instruct subjects in the control of their nature.[84] In Juan's view, the need to restrain nature was what the *Chung-yung* referred to as cultivating the way *(hsiu-tao)* and the *Ta-hsueh* called self-cultivation *(hsiu-shen)*.[85]

Juan Yuan's ritualist notion of self-cultivation was best spelled out in his philological treatise on the meaning of *k'o-chi fu-li* (restraining oneself in order to return to ritual-propriety). In the writings of Ch'eng I, *k'o-chi* had been interpreted as the suppression of selfish desires *(ssu-yü)*. Juan argued that this exposition was philologically unsound. The meaning of *chi* in the phrase *wei jen yu chi* (the realization of *jen* depends on oneself) could not possibly be translated as selfish desires, he maintained. *Chi* simply meant oneself as opposed to other persons. Specifically, *k'o-chi* involved bringing oneself in line with ritual-propriety in matters of seeing, hearing, speaking, and movement. When one so conducts oneself, one is in the state of *jen* (humanity) with others.[86] By stressing the condition of realizing *jen* in relation to others, Juan took aim at the neo-Confucian rendition of *jen* as the essence of mind. For Juan, the mind and *jen* were not identical. If the mind itself were *jen,* one need not learn or practice ritual-propriety, nor would it be necessary to realize *jen* in relation to other human beings.[87] Such an interpretation would certainly deny *jen* to neo-Confucians who contemplated *jen* only in their minds.[88] Hence, the sense of sympathy that Mencius believed to be the essence of *jen* was no more than a beginning *(tuan)*. This frail beginning required realization in concrete human action *(jen chih shih-shih)*.[89] To Juan, in other words, there could be no *jen* without human endeavor.[90] *K'o-chi* thus meant the cultivation of conduct.[91]

In order to provide philological proof for this view, Juan cited Cheng Hsüan's commentary on a passage from the *Doctrine of the Mean*. According to Cheng, the structure of the character *jen* symbolized two people together. This was clear evidence to Juan that the ancients understood *jen* as something to be realized in human relationships.[92] Of course this philological treatment of *jen* ran the risk of reductionism, for the *Analects* contain many passages in which *jen* is used to connote moral qualities that do not relate to human interactions. For instance, Confucius said, "A man of *jen* finds pleasure in hills," and "a man of *jen* is tranquil."[93] Nonetheless, Juan Yuan refused to accept Tai Chen's assertion that *jen* was the quality *(te)* of the cosmos and of the human mind. Whereas Tai still spoke of *jen* as an interior attribute, Juan tended to stress its exterior relational dimension. To Juan, *jen* epitomized nature's endless reproduction of life, as well as the human virtue of helping others to complete their lives and to continue reproducing lives.[94] Moral development, he believed, could not be sought in seclusion.

Juan Yuan's view of self-cultivation bore a closer resemblance to Ling T'ing-k'an's than to Tai Chen's. By stressing concrete actions, things, and events *(shih-shih)*, as well as conduct *(hsing)*, Juan obviously valued practice over intellect. His predilection was particularly apparent in his reappraisal of the relative importance of the Confucian classics. Juan was not always consistent in his writings. Sometimes, he regarded the *Ch'un-ch'iu* (Spring and autumn annals) and the *Hsiao-ching* (Classic of filial piety) as the most important texts.[95] At other times, he considered the *Analects* and the *Hsiao-ching* to be paramount.[96] But the exceptional status he accorded the *Classic of Filial Piety* was unmistakable. He did not dispute the fact that the teachings of Tzu-ssu and Mencius were in tune with those of Confucius. But unlike Tseng-tzu, they received no personal instructions from the sage himself. The ten essays by Tseng-tzu preserved in the *Book of Rites* by Senior Tai were, together with the *Analects,* among the only extant writings by Confucius' direct disciples. For Juan Yuan, then, Tseng-tzu's teachings on filial piety even surpassed those of Mencius in purity and reliability.[97] He went so far as to say that "the way of Confucius lies nowhere other than the *Classic of Filial Piety.*"[98] Hence, to Juan those who committed themselves to the teachings of Confucius had to begin with the writings of Tseng-tzu.[99] His purist impulse and his somewhat naive belief in the methodical logic of chronological proximity led him to a highly restricted understanding of Confucianism.

Ritual-propriety and filial piety thus became the twin pillars of Juan Yuan's ethical thinking, representing for him the proper blend of the doctrines of the duke of Chou and those of Confucius. The former sage stressed restraining nature by means of ritual-propriety, the latter's teachings on filial piety epitomized the essence of the human Way. Juan professed this belief in his preface to the collected exercises by his students in the Hsüeh-hai t'ang (Sea of Learning Academy).[100] He delighted in the term *chieh-hsing,* which seemed to exemplify his idea of self-cultivation. He thus named his study the *Chieh-hsing chai* (Study of restraining the nature) and adopting for himself the name Chieh-hsing chai lao-jen (Old Man of the Study of Restraining the Nature).[101] Juan's notion of human nature and self-cultivation had a great effect not only on his students in the Hsüeh-hai t'ang but also in the Ku-ching ching-she (Academy for the Exposition of the Classics), a school he administered in Hangchow.[102]

Conclusion

From the viewpoint of purist hermeneutics, the history of Confucian ethics since the Han period was one of noble ideas deplorably tainted by unorthodox teachings. What they aimed for was an accurate reconstruction of the archaic rules of human conduct through meticulous philological investigation. These ritual rules would provide a path to the cultivation of true Confucian virtues. From Tai Chen through Ling T'ing-k'an and Juan Yuan, we can see a continuous intellectual movement employing philological arguments designed to purge Confucianism of its Buddhist and Taoist influences. Sung neo-Confucianism was subject to severe attack because it had infused heterodox ideas into classical exegeses. Philology served the purists' cause of decontamination. By selective application of philological evidence, Ch'ing classicists sought to reinstate and promote a monistic notion of human nature embracing feelings and desires. In addition to this Confucian purism, they displayed a tendency in their ethical thinking to emphasize conformity to external authority as well as a profound distrust of both intellectual autonomy and theoretical formulations.

Perhaps the early nineteenth-century neo-Confucian Fang Tung-shu best summarized the nature of the ethical theories of the purist classicists: "In the present, the Han-learning scholars prohibit the quest for principles, and instead depend exclusively on ritual-propriety as their instrument of teaching. What they call ritual-propriety is nothing but the names of things— institutions that are recorded in the commentaries and annotations written by scholars of later times."[103] Despite his disparaging tone, Fang's remark provides an essentially accurate description of the purists' ethical concerns, which were, as I have indicated, deeply enmeshed in their philology. This strong ritualism in ethics was equally reflected in their attempts at redefining Confucianism. The growing appeal of Hsün-tzu's teachings among the purist classicists bears witness to such a ritualist orientation. Tai Chen's criticism of Hsun-tzu notwithstanding, his position on the dynamic nature of moral development and his emphasis on ritual propriety were reminiscent of the latter's views. Ling T'ing-k'an, for his part, exalted Hsun-tzu more than Mencius. Another Ch'ing classicist, Wang Chung (1745–1794), traced all the Han exegetical traditions back to Hsun-tzu.[104] The relative status of Mencius in the thinking of purist hermeneutics could not but decline under the circumstances.[105]

It is important to emphasize, however, that the scholarship of these classicists was influenced by certain ideological biases. Because they regarded ancient Confucian ethics as absolute truths, they tended to promote an anachronistic social ethics. In terms of the relationship of the individual to society, the ethics of purist hermeneutics strongly favored the subjection of the individual to uniformly instituted rules of conduct. Instead of stressing individuality in moral development, they extolled conformity. They began their critique of neo-Confucianism by condemning the latter's indulgence in speculation and introspection. But paradoxically, the intellectualism that characterized their methodology yielded an ethical position that underscored the elite's importance in rendering comprehensible the teachings of ancient sages. This intellectualism was not meant to question the elite's social and intellectual superiority; it rather sought to reverse the populist tendency so prominent in Late Ming Confucianism.

Notes

Abbreviations:

CLTWC   Ling T'ing-k'an, *Chiao-li t'ang wen-chi* (Collected writings from the Studio for Collating Rituals). *Ling Chung-tzu i-shu* (Bequeathed writings of Mr. Ling T'ing-k'an). Anhwei Ts'ung-shu, ser. 4. (Anhwei, 1935).

CHSS   Ch'ien Mu, *Chung-kuo chin san-pai-nien hsueh-shu shih* (History of Chinese thought during the last three centuries) (Taipei, 1957).

ECCP   *Eminent Chinese of the Ch'ing Period,* ed. Arthur W. Hummel (Taipei, 1972).

HSS   Liang Ch'i-ch'ao, *Chung-kuo chin san-pai-nien hsueh-shu shih* (History of Chinese thought during the last three centuries) (Shanghai, 1937).

KHCPTS   *Kuo-hsueh chi-pen ts'ung-shu* (Collected works on the fundamentals of sinology) (Taipei, 1968).

LCTIS   Ling T'ing-k'an, *Ling Chung-tzu i-shu* (Bequeathed writings of Mr. Ling T'ing-k'an). Anhwei Ts'ung-shu, ser. 4. (Anhwei, 1935).

SKTY   *Ssu-k'u ch'üan-shu tsung-mu ti-yao* (Abstracts of the comprehensive catalogue of the Library of Four Treasuries), ed. Yung Jung (Taipei, 1968).

SSCCS   Juan Yuan et al., eds., *Shih-san ching chu-shu* (Commentaries and annotations on the Thirteen Classics) (Beijing, 1980).

TSCCHP   *Ts'ung-shu chi-ch'eng hsin-pien* (New edition of the complete collectania) (Taipei, 1985).

YCSC   Juan Yuan, *Yen-ching shih chi* (Collected writings from the study for the investigation of classics). *I-chi, erh-chi, san-chi,* and *ssu-chi.* Ssu-pu ts'ung-k'an ed.

YCSHC   Juan Yuan, *Yen-ching shih hsu-chi* (Collected writings from the studio for the investigation of classics, continued). Ts'ung-shu chi-ch'eng chien-pien ed. (Taipei, 1966).

1. Ying-shih Yü, "Some Preliminary Observations on the Rise of Ch'ing Confucian Intellectualism," *Ch'ing-hua hsueh-pao* 11, nos. 1–2 (December 1975): 105–129. Benjamin A. Elman, "The Unravelling of Neo-Confucianism: From Philosophy

to Philology in Late Imperial China," *Ch'ing-hua hsueh-pao* 15, nos. 1–2 (December 1983): 67–88.

2. Elman, "The Unravelling," pp. 74–76; and *From Philosophy to Philology: Intellectual and Social Aspects of Change in Late Imperial China* (Cambridge, Mass., 1984), p. 32, 54–55. John Henderson, in explaining the critique of cosmology, makes a similar argument in *The Development and Decline of Chinese Cosmology* (Columbia, 1984), pp. 153–160.

3. HSS, chaps. 13 and 14. Elman, *From Philosophy to Philology,* pp. 54–76, chap. 5.

4. Elman, "The Unravelling," pp. 71–73; and *From Philosophy to Philology,* pp. xix–xxi, 6, 32, 54–55.

5. Hermeneutics, according to Gadamer, did not become a methodological approach to texts independent of biblical study until Schleiermacher. In the hands of Schleiermacher, hermeneutics became a universal approach to the understanding and interpretation of texts, both biblical and secular, without concern for "dogmatic interest." Gadamer, *Truth and Method* (New York, 1975), pp. 162–173. See also Josef Bleicher, *Contemporary Hermeneutics: Hermeneutics as Method, Philosophy and Critique* (London, 1982), pp. 14–16; and Richard E. Palmer, *Hermeneutics* (Evanston, Ill., 1969), pp. 38–40.

6. The term *Hermeneutik* reemerged within the post-Bultmannian German theology when Ernst Fuchs published *Hermeneutik* in 1954. By 1959, the term had gained currency. See James M. Robinson, "Hermeneutic since Barth," in *The New Hermeneutics,* ed. J. M. Robinson and J. B. Cobb, Jr. (New York, 1964), p. 39. Renewed interest in hermeneutics began with Gadamer's monumental *Truth and Method,* which was published in 1960 in German. Since then, hermeneutics has received growing interest in many fields, including philosophy and the social sciences. For a useful discussion, see Susan Hekman, "From Epistemology to Ontology: Gadamer's Hermeneutics and Wittgensteinian Social Science," *Human Studies* 6, no. 3 (1983): 205–206. For a good introduction to various theories of hermeneutics, consult Josef Bleicher's *Contemporary Hermeneutics* (n. 5, above).

7. For discussions of the antiheterodox trend in the Tung-lin scholars, see Heinrich Busch, "The Tung-lin shu-yuan and Its Political and Philosophical Significance," *Monumenta Serica* 14 (1949–1955): 76–86; also Charles O. Hucker, "The Tung-lin Movement of the Late Ming Period," in *Chinese Thought and Institutions,* ed. John K. Fairbank (Chicago, 1957), pp. 143–147. The precise effect of the demise of the Ming dynasty on the rise of antiheterodoxy in Early Ch'ing thought has hitherto remained largely unexplored. This development is treated in chaps. 2 and 6 of my book, *The Rise of Confucian Ritualism in Late Imperial China: Ethics, Classics, and Lineage Discourse* (Stanford, Calif., forthcoming).

8. In 1661 Huang Tsung-hsi fired the first shot at the basic text of neo-Confucian cosmology when he wrote *I-hsueh hsiang-shu lun* (A discussion of the images and numbers associated with the study of the *Book of Changes*). His effort concen-

trated on exposing the heterodox origin of the texts that had been incorporated into the *I-ching*. Huang Tsung-hsi took exception to Chu Hsi's acceptance of certain numerological interpretations advanced by the Sung neo-Confucian Shao Yung. Later, in a similar vein, Mao Ch'i-ling chastised Sung neo-Confucians for corrupting the Confucian classics by infusing them with a heterodox cosmology based on Taoist scripture. ECCP, p. 336. Huang Tsung-hsi, *Nan-lei wen-yueh* (Selected writings of Nan-lei); in *Li-chou i-chu hui-k'an* (Composite edition of Huang Tsung-hsi's bequeathed writings) 4:5b–6b; Pi Hsi-jui, *Ching-hsueh t'ung-lun* (A general account of classical learning), pp. 27–28.

9. See the preface by Wan Ssu-t'ung in Hu Wei, *I-t'u ming pien,* TSCCHP, vol. 16; SKTY 6:35–36, 43–45; Pi Hsi-jui, *Ching-hsueh t'ung-lun,* pp. 27–28, 30–31; Liang Ch'i-ch'ao, HHS, p. 71; John Henderson, *The Development and Decline of Chinese Cosmology,* p. 158; ECCP, p. 336.

10. Li Kung's view was shared by another friend, Wang Fu-li, a descendant of Wang Yang-ming. All concurred that these "Diagrams" were Taoist in origin. Li Kung, *Ta-hsueh pien-yeh* (Exercises in defending the *Great Learning*) 3:5b; *Chou-i chuan-chu* (Commentaries on the *Book of Changes*), p. 1a, in *Yen-Li ts'ung-shu. Shu-ku hsien-sheng nien-p'u* (A chronological biography of Li Kung) 4:13a–b. *Yen-Li hsueh-p'ai yen-chiu lun-ts'ung* (Essays on the school of Yen Yuan and Li Kung). CHSS, p. 216.

11. CHSS, pp. 241–245. Questions regarding the credibility of this classic had long been raised by Wu Yü (fl. c. 1124), Chu Hsi and Wu Cheng. But as Benjamin Elman aptly points out, Sung and Yuan Confucians, with only one exception, did not allow their philological skepticism to override their philosophical belief in the *jen-hsin tao-hsin* passage. Benjamin A. Elman, "Philosophy *(I-Li)* versus Philology *(K'ao-cheng):* The *Jen-hsin Tao-hsin* Debate," *T'oung Pao* 69, nos. 4–5 (1983): 182–189, 192–198.

12. Those who engaged in such purgative exercises did not conceive of themselves as promoting a form of Confucianism that was diametrically opposed to the ethical teachings of the Sung neo-Confucians. They did not mean to dislodge the authority of the Ch'eng-Chu school as a matter of principle. In fact, many sought to prove the spurious origins of the texts attributed to Chu Hsi in order to exonerate the latter from the crime of corrupting Confucianism. Hu Wei was a good example of such an attempt. Ch'ien Mu has pointed out that Yen Jo-chü only took exception to Chu Hsi's understanding of concrete things and place names. His regard for Chu's expositions on ethical principles remained unshaken. CHSS, pp. 232–233. Another scholar who took on himself the same task out of deference for Chu Hsi was Wang Mou-hung (1668–1741). In order to defend Chu Hsi against the accusation of attaching heterodox writings to the *Book of Changes,* Wang argued that a comparison between the personal writings of Chu Hsi and the "nine diagrams" placed at the beginning of the *Book of Changes* clearly showed that the diagrams had been falsely

attributed to Chu Hsi. Wang Mou-hung, *Pai-t'ien tsao-t'ang ts'un-kao* (Preserved writings from the White Field Hut) 1:1a–8b.

13. Yen Yuan, *Ssu-shu cheng-wu* (Correction of errors in the Four Books) 4:5a–b. *Yen-Li ts'ung-shu,* vol. 1. Li Kung, *Shu-ku hou-chi* (Later writings of Li Kung) 13:162.

14. William T. de Bary, ed., *The Message of the Mind in Neo-Confucianism* (New York, 1990), chaps. 4 and 5.

15. Chung-ying Cheng, "Reason, Substance, and Human Desires in Seventeenth-Century Neo-Confucianism," in *The Unfolding of Neo-Confucianism,* ed. William T. de Bary (New York, 1975), pp. 469–503.

16. Tai Chen, *Tai Chen chi* (Collected writings of Tai Chen) (Shanghai, 1980), p. 290.

17. Ibid., pp. 267–268, 273–278, 282–286.

18. Ibid., p. 285.

19. Ibid., p. 328.

20. T'ang Chün-i, *Chung-kuo che-hsueh yuan-lun* (Studies of the foundations of Chinese philosophy) (Hong Kong, 1968), p. 473. See also Irene Bloom, Introduction, to *Knowledge Painfully Acquired: The K'un-chih chi by Lo Ch'in-shun* (New York, 1987).

21. Tai Chen, *Tai Chen chi,* pp. 296–297.

22. Ibid., p. 271.

23. Ibid., pp. 272–273.

24. Ibid., pp. 274–276.

25. Ibid., p. 285.

26. Ibid., p. 296.

27. Ying-shih Yü, *Lun Tai Chen yü Chang Hsueh-ch'eng: Ch'ing-tai chung-chi ssu-hsiang shih yen-chiu* (On Tai Chen and Chang Hsueh-ch'eng: A study of mid-Ch'ing thought) (Taipei, 1980), pp. 15–28.

28. Tai Chen, *Tai Chen chi,* p. 276.

29. Ibid., pp. 267–268.

30. Ibid., pp. 270–271; also p. 467.

31. Hsu Fu-kuan, "Han-hsueh lun-heng" (A discussion of Han learning), *Ta-lu tsa-chih* 54, no. 4 (1977): 7. Cheng Hsuan's comment can be found in *Li-chi cheng-i,* SSCCS, p. 1529.

32. K'ung Ying-ta, *Li-chi cheng-i,* SSCCS, p. 1529.

33. Hsu, "Han-hsueh lun-heng," p. 14. See also his *Liang Han ssu-hsiang shih* (A history of Han dynasty thought) 2:401–402.

34. Fang Tung-shu, *Han-hsueh shang-tui,* in KHCPTS ed., pp. 46–47.

35. Tai Chen, p. 267.

36. Ibid., p. 326.

37. Ibid., p. 318.

38. Ibid., pp. 272–273.

39. Ibid., pp. 298–304.

40. Ibid., pp. 191–192, 213–215.

41. CHSS, p. 358.

42. Ch'eng Yao-t'ien, *Lun hsueh hsiao-chi* (Minor account of discourses on learning), in *Tung-i lu* (Records of general arts), *Anhwei ts'ung-shu*, ser. 2, p. 26b.

43. CLTWC 16:4a–6b.

44. Ibid. 16:4a–6b.

45. Ibid. 16:4a–5a.

46. Hu Shih, *Tai Tung-yuan ti che-hsueh* (The philosophy of Tai Chen) (Taipei, 1971), p. 24.

47. CLTWC 16:6b.

48. Ibid. 16:2b; Tai Chen, *Tai Chen chi,* p. 272.

49. CLTWC 4:1b.

50. Ibid. 16:1a–2b.

51. Ibid. 16:1a.

52. Ibid. 4:7a.

53. Tai Chen, *Tai Chen chi,* p. 265. See *Li-chi cheng-i,* pp. 1529, 1535, 1536–1537, 1544.

54. Fang Tung-shu, *Han-hsueh shang-tui,* pp. 46–47.

55. CLTWC 10:2a.

56. Tai Chün-jen, "Hsun-hsueh yü Sung-ju" (The learning of Hsun-tzu and Sung scholars), *Ta-lu tsa-chih* 39, no. 4:23–24. The criticism of Hsun-tzu by Ch'eng I and Chu Hsi was included in Tai Chen's *Meng-tzu tzu-i shu cheng* (Verification of the literal meanings of *Mencius*).

57. CLTWC 10:1b.

58. Many Ch'ing scholars had reevaluated the role of Hsun-tzu. Some understood Hsun-tzu's notion of human nature as uncivilized rather than evil. Others regarded his stress on ritualism in molding behavior commendable. See Ch'ien Ta-hsin, *Ch'ien-yen t'ang chi* (Collected essays from the Hall of Devotion to Studies) 27:21b. Lu Wen-ch'ao, *Pao-ching t'ang chi* (Collected writings from the Studio of Embracing the Classics) 10:141–142. Chang Hui-yen, *Ming-k'o wen-pien* (Writings from the Tree Plant Handle), *ch'u-pien,* pp. 20a–21b.

59. CLTWC 16:3b, 7a–9b.

60. Ibid. 16:7a.

61. Ibid. 24:16a. Ling's view in this respect was not entirely original. Ku Yen-wu had suggested that *wu* referred to basic human virtues as well as ritual-propriety. See *Jih-chih lu chih-shih* 6:18b–19a. *Ssu-pu pei-yao* ed.

62. CLTWC 4:8a.

63. Ibid. 4:1b. "Li-ching shih-li hsu" (Preface to a study of the rules of the *I-li*), pp. 3a–4a, in LCTIS. See also CLTWC 4:7a; 16:11a–b.

64. CLTWC 5:7a.

65. Ibid. 4:3a.

66. Ibid. 24:16a.

67. Ibid. 4:8b–9a.

68. LCTIS 1:3a–4a.

69. Juan Yüan, preface to Chiang Fan's *Kuo-ch'ao Han-hsueh ssu-ch'eng chi* (An account of the lineage of Han learning of the present dynasty) in the *Ssu-pu pei-yao* (Taipei, 1962), p. 1a.

70. Tai Chen, *Tai Chen chi,* p. 279.

71. YCSC, in the *Ssu-pu ts'ung-k'an, I-chi* 3:123–124.

72. Ibid. 10:1b–3a.

73. Ibid. 10:15a.

74. See the section on Ling.

75. YCSC, *I-chi* 10:6a–b.

76. Ibid. 10:23b–24a.

77. Ibid. 10:21b.

78. Ibid. 10:12b–13b.

79. Hsu Fu-kuan, *Liang Han ssu-hsiang shih* (History of the thought of the former and later Han dynasty) (Taipei, 1976) 2:399–402.

80. YCSC, *I-chi* 10:23b–24a.

81. Ibid. 10:1b–3a.

82. Ibid. 10:5a; see also 4:14b.

83. Ibid. 10:19b–20a.

84. Ibid. 10:23b.

85. Ibid. 10:3a, 23b.

86. Ibid. 8:6b–8b.

87. Ibid. 8:21a.

88. Ibid. 8:6b–8b.

89. Ibid. 9:1a–2a.

90. Ibid. 9:9a.

91. Ibid. 8:9b–11b.

92. Ibid. 8:1a–b.

93. James Legge, The *Analects,* in *The Four Books* (reprint; Taipei, 1966), p. 192 (modified). Other examples can be found on pp. 191, 225, 274, 341. Wing-tsit Chan points out that the term *jen* became a central concept of Confucius' philosophy and acquired new meanings. "The Evolution of the Confucian Concept of Jen," *Philosophy East and West* 4, no. 4 (January 1955) 296–299. See also Lin Yü-sheng, who argues that the term *jen* changed from its pre-Confucian sense of manliness to goodness in the *Analects.* "The Evolution of the Pre-Confucian Meaning of *Jen* and the Confucian Concept of Moral Autonomy," *Monumenta Serica* 31 (1974–1975): 172–188.

94. Tai Chen, *Tai Chen chi,* pp. 316–317.

95. YCSC *I-chi* 2:15a; 11:1a–b.

96. Ibid. 2:18a–19b; 11:1b–2a.

97. Ibid. 11:14b.

98. Ibid. 2:18a.

99. Ibid. 2:12b–13b.

100. Ibid. 4:4a–5b.

101. Ibid. *Hsu-chi,* p. 1.

102. See "On Nature and Feelings" *(Hsing-ching shuo)* by Hsu Yang-yuan and Hu Chin in "Ku-ching ching-she wen-chi" (A collection of essays from the Refined Studio for Explicating the Classics), *Ts'ung-shu chi-ch'eng chien-pien* (Taipei, 1966), pp. 257–263.

103. Fang Tung-shu, *Han-hsueh shang-tui* in KHCPTS ed. p. 62.

104. Kai-wing Chow, "Scholar and Society: The Textual Scholarship and Social Concerns of Wang Chung (1745–1794)," *Chinese Studies* 4, no. 1 (June 1986): 303–306.

105. Chiao Hsun (1763–1820) was unique, despite his agreement on the main methodological premises of historical hermeneutics. Mencius still occupied a very important position in his thinking. Chiao did not think that moral truths had been exhaustively enumerated in the classics, which he considered no more than the rules and institutions of the past. The classics were therefore not to be taken as absolute truths. Moreover, Chiao insisted that personal insight or subjective understanding *(hsing-ling)* was essential to classical studies. *T'iao-ku chi* (Collected writings from the [Studio of] Engraved Bamboo), in *Ts'ung-shu chi-ch'eng chien-pien* 10:144–145; 13:212–214.

9

The "Turn of Fortune" *(Yun-hui):* Inherited Concepts and China's Response to the West

ERH-MIN WANG

China's "response to the West" is a major theme in modern Chinese history. Yet we know that this response was not a simple one, and that Chinese knowledge of the West was often filtered through traditional concepts. Despite vigorous cosmological critiques by *k'ao-cheng* scholars in the preceding centuries, the major elements of an ancient worldview still prevailed in many circles—even as the Chinese began to assimilate new knowledge regarding the West. It is the purpose of this essay to discuss some of the ways the old worldview affected China's nineteenth-century perception of the Western challenge.

The authors of the two major Chinese works on world geography published within a decade of the Opium War seem to have been able to reconcile knowledge of the West with a belief in the so-called five elements or five operating phases *(wu-hsing)* and in the spirits of heaven and of earth. Hsu Chi-yü (1795–1873), author of a "Gazetteer of the Global Seas"—the manuscript edition of which was dated 1844—ascribed the technological skills of the Europeans to the fact that Europe was situated in the northwest —the *ch'ien-hsu* position on the Chinese compass. This gave the Europeans the quality of the element metal—which in turn enabled them to control and manipulate the other elements: wood, water, fire, and earth. He wrote: "[Europe] alone is endowed with the spirit of metal. . . . The people are by nature circumspect, thoughtful and skillful in the making of instruments. Their metal and wood work is so superb that it surpasses belief. They are outstanding in their use of water and fire. . . . In shipbuilding they are even more expert. They are skilled in the making of every single thing connected with ships. They survey the seas and mark every variation in the depth of the water, attaining a high degree of accuracy. It is not an accident that Europeans have succeeded in traversing myriad miles to reach China."[1] The ancient cosmology of the five elements thus explained for Hsu the West's special skills.

Wei Yuan (1794–1856), another prominent intellectual of the mid-nineteenth century, wrote in 1847 that the coming of the Westerners to China was mainly due to the fact that "the spirit of the earth moves from the south to the north." This, he remarked, "is known to those who have noticed the movement of migrant birds." On the other hand, he noted that "the spirit of heaven moves from the west to the east—this is known to those who have crossed the sea."[2] It was, of course, parochial for Wei Yuan to regard birds flying south or water flowing eastward as manifestations of the spirits of heaven and earth, but his conclusion reflects one way he and other Chinese intellectuals of the Late Ch'ing period responded to the West. Although Hsu and Wei drew from different sources of cosmological authority in their interpretation of the Western challenge, their responses illustrate two ways in which traditional knowledge could be applied to new situations.

The Heaven-Man Correlation

Since the ancient Shang and Chou periods, the Chinese had believed in the idea of an interaction between heaven and man, a notion firmly imbedded in the Han cosmology of Tung Chung-shu. All the ups and downs and twists and turns of human affairs were regarded as closely related to the revolving patterns of heaven and earth. These movements, together with the regular sequential changes of the four seasons, were considered to have a direct bearing on people's fortunes.[3] It is not surprising to find that Late Ch'ing thinkers applied these notions to China's nineteenth-century needs— at first only in the realm of foreign relations, but later in domestic affairs as well.

Chinese intellectuals of the 1800s used examples from the revolving movement of the heavenly bodies to draw people's attention to the political vicissitudes in China's external relations. Among Chinese gentry and officials, whether high or low, in office or out of office, there were many who were very much concerned about the heaven-man relationship and discussed it with great enthusiasm. Their concept of this relationship was based on the Confucian classics. Wei Yuan quoted from the *Shih-ching* (Book of poetry) and the *I-ching* (Book of changes) in order to arouse concern regarding the dangerous situation China was in. He read certain passages of the *Book of Poetry* as describing the firm resolve of the poets, and certain passages of the *Changes* as indicating the sages' worries about their times. To have such worries and such resolve, Wei suggested, was the beginning of understanding how, according to the heavenly way, one could move away from *P'i* (hexagram 12, symbolizing stagnation) and back to *T'ai* (hexagram 11, symbolizing peace), thus completing a cycle. In this way, "the slumbering mind would be awakened and human talents that are hollow would be made more solid."[4]

In a letter dated 1859, Tseng Kuo-fan confided to Li Hung-chang his adherence to the teaching of the *Book of Changes,* which regarded fortune, including the timeliness of one's service to the state and one's exact official position, as controlled by heaven. "The way of the *Book of Changes,*" he wrote, "emphasizes timeliness [*shih*] and position [*wei*]. Both are controlled by powerful, unseen forces, leaving no role at all for human effort. I spoke of this when we parted ways yesterday, for your advantage and mine. Such is what I have learned from my experiences in the last few years, not that I myself have always been able to control my own expectations."[5]

Tseng probably wrote this in order to lower Li's ambitions as an official. The letter nonetheless indicates Tseng's belief in the preponderance of heaven's will over human efficacy. It was not, of course, that he would ever argue that one should refrain from making one's best effort. But Tseng believed that such human effort had only a thirty-percent chance of success at a time when heaven allowed it to succeed. In a letter dated 1864, before the capture of Nanking from the Taipings, Tseng admonished his brother Kuo-ch'üan regarding expectations of success as well as of personal benefit from it:

> Since ancient times, the outcomes of great wars and grand undertakings were determined three times out of ten by human endeavor, and seven times out of ten by the will of heaven. Those who worked the hardest may not be those who became famous, and those who became famous may not be those who enjoyed good fortune. In the present military venture, regarding the capture of Wuhan, Kiukiang, and Anking, those who worked hard have become famous. This, in heaven's view, is already fair enough. However, one cannot long count on this. You and I should concentrate on working hard. Don't ask whether you will become famous, even less whether you will enjoy good fortune.[6]

Drawing at random from Chinese writers in the last four decades of the nineteenth century, I intend to show here that such a belief in heaven's will was widely held among enlightened officials, as well as literati who pioneered in the advocacy of reform. The efficacy of human effort was never completely denied. Yet the general belief was that human endeavor would be successful only when heaven ordained it. Nonetheless, as was emphasized by Cheng Tsao-ju (d. 1894), the Tientsin customs *taotai* who served as the Chinese envoy to the United States from 1882 to 1885, human effort had to be made because actual events were determined by the interactions between heaven and man. There was, in other words, an element of unpredictability in the heaven-man correlation. At times, human will could even defy the will of heaven. Cheng wrote: "The alternation of ups and downs [in human affairs] is due to the correlation between heaven and man. The cowardly and mediocre are usually oblivious to basic causes and merely tend to the appearance of things, actually accepting whatever comes. That human will cannot effectively defy heaven's will is only because one fails to grasp the opportunity at the early stage of change."[7]

Cheng included these remarks in his preface to the 1892 edition of Cheng Kuan-ying's *Sheng-shih wei-yen* (Words of warning to a prosperous age). Another preface to the book was written by Ch'en Chih, a secretary of the Board of Rites in Peking, who privately distributed essays championing reform. Ch'en saw in Western trade with China not just an encroachment on the latter but also a heaven-ordained opportunity for the Chinese. "Trade with myriad countries has now existed for more than fifty years," he observed. "People are more knowledgeable and more enlightened. Those countries that follow the will of heaven survive; those that do not will perish. If one does not take what heaven has offered, one will be punished. This is known to those who are virtuous, not to those who are mean; to those who are young and energetic, not to those who are old and weak; to those who are farsighted, not those who are narrow-minded."[8]

Significantly, Ch'en saw Western-inspired reform not as a negation of China's heritage but as restoration of the glories of the Three Dynasties of antiquity. This was the pattern of heaven's will, not a matter of the intrinsic value of Western culture. He opined: "I personally dislike the Westerners and long for the ancient ways. When the rites are lost, they may have to be found in uncultured areas, and we have to follow what is good for us in order to regain the good policies we followed in the Hsia, Shang, and Chou periods. My reading of the situation is that all this can be accomplished very speedily. Therefore I say: the coming of the Westerners to China was actually arranged by heaven. Heaven has given us the chance to restore our ancient age, to renew good government, and to see the beginnings of the great era of unity."[9]

At the core of such views was a long-standing Chinese belief in a correlation between heaven and humanity, which still affected the thinking of numerous writers of the Late Ch'ing period. What was new, however, was perhaps the emphasis on heaven's being disposed toward unprecedented change in human affairs. To Wang T'ao (1828–1897), the famous writer and journalist, heaven was behind the new, drastic change of situation *(pien-chü)* that China was experiencing. Never before had all the countries of the world congregated in China in such a fashion: "Now the four directions of the earth comprise a distance of myriad miles, yet all the countries converge in China. This is unprecedented, a new situation for heaven and earth. It is beyond what human beings anticipated, for it is an act of heaven's mind [*t'ien-hsin*]."[10]

Wang went on to write of a benign intention on the part of heaven: "The purpose of heaven's mind in bringing together numerous Western countries in China is not to weaken China, but to strengthen her; not to harm China, but to bless her. Therefore those who are good at making the best of the situation can turn harm into blessing, making the weak strong. We should not worry about the coming of the Westerners, but should worry at the way China confines herself in seclusion. The way out is to make an effort to change."[11]

Even Yen Fu (1853–1921), who knew a great deal about Western political and economic thought, invoked heaven's will in an effort to justify reform. Yen saw heaven as nature and believed that inherent in nature is the opportunity for change and survival in a pattern verifiable through science and through historical facts. Yen thus reconciled the ancient Chinese concept of heaven with the modern theory of evolution:

There is one thing we do know, namely, those who follow the will of heaven survive, those who do not will perish. What is heaven? Heaven comprises the opportunity provided by nature and the propensity inherent in every situation. It is for the sake of knowing this that we study the present situation and examine the past, "investigate things and extend knowledge" [*ko-wu erh chih-chih*] and do not stop until the truth is known. There is nothing mysterious about this, neither auspicious nor inauspicious. All those who are determined to seek China's survival would want to know more about what is called heaven.[12]

Wang Shu-nan (1851–1936), a scholar connected with an academy in Chihli, whose collected essays were published in 1915, was undoubtedly aware of the Darwinian message that Yen had introduced. Yet Wang regarded modern change as necessary because it is the result of the interaction between heaven and humanity—that which cannot but be so *(pu te pu jan).* "Heaven has enlightened all people under heaven with [the message of] change," he wrote. "Humanity, for its part, must find the institutions [*fa*] that stand for change. Change begins with one or two innovative voices, but the chorus will be joined by millions of people. Change began in one or two countries, but it will be followed by people of all the countries in the five continents."[13] Starting with the ancient concept of heaven, Wang ended up by moving away from a Sinocentric worldview of culture and institutions.

The Turn of Fortune: New Implications for an Inherited Belief

Yun-hui (lit., "turn of fortune or juncture of fate") was a term commonly used in China since at least the third century A.D. As employed in the *Wen-hsuan* (Refined literature; compiled in the sixth century), it refers to a person's luck at a certain point in time.[14] That the term was to take on the implications of a conjunction of cosmological forces was undoubtedly owing to the influence of the Sung philosopher Shao Yung (1017–1077). In Shao's famous cosmological chronology, length of time is divided by the revolving patterns of the heavenly bodies. "The course of the sun constitutes heaven's great cycle *(yuan);* that of the moon constitutes the great conjunction *(hui),* that of the stars constitutes the great revolving movement *(yun),* and that of zodiacal spaces constitutes the great generation *(shih).*" In Shao's numerology, twelve "generations" equal one "revolving movement" *(yun);* thirty "revolving movements" equal one "great conjunction" *(hui);* twelve "great conjunctions" equal one "cycle" *(yun-yuan).*[15] The exact way in which Shao's numerology affected the usage of the term *yun-hui* in the period between the Sung philosophers and the Ch'ing scholars remains to be researched. In any case, the term was applied by many writers of the nineteenth century to the opportunity as well as the crisis resulting from increased contact with the West.

We have already seen how Hsu Chi-yü identified Europe's geographical position with the properties of metal among the five elements. Hsu also believed that the arrival of large numbers of Europeans in China was a result of a cosmic cyclical process that represented to the Chinese the turn of fortune *(yun-hui).* Hsu wrote:

> In coming eastward, the peoples of Europe went from the Great Western Ocean [*Ta-hsi yang,* i.e., Portugal] to the Small Western Ocean [*Hsiao-hsi yang,* i.e.,

the Persian area], building ports on the way. Then they went further and reached the Islands of the South Sea [i.e., the East Indies], and finally turned toward land and assembled in Kwangtung. This movement commenced in a small way in early Ming and really began only towards the end of that dynasty. Today making a journey of myriad miles is to them no more than floating a reed in a pool. The spirit [*ch'i*] of heaven and earth has shifted from the northwest to southeast. This is perhaps brought about by the conjunction of fate [*yun-hui*].[16]

Similarly, Wei Yuan believed that China's encounter with foreigners on the east coast was due to heaven's spirit moving from west to east.[17] Both Hsu and Wei thus believed in cyclical change of a cosmic nature that called for extraordinary measures on the part of China in order to be in step with change.

It is perhaps not surprising that Hsu and Wei, who flourished in the first half of the nineteenth century should have been influenced by an inherited belief in cosmic forces. It is somewhat more surprising that the reformist writers in the last two decades of the Ch'ing dynasty should also have tried to justify radical reformist ideas by referring to cyclic concepts of change. The term *yun-hui* was used not only by such enlightened officials as Cheng Tsao-ju and Sheng Hsuan-huai (1849–1916) but also by advocates of reform including the great translator Yen Fu and the reform activist T'ang Ts'ai-ch'ang (1867–1900).[18]

As is well known, the defeat by Japan in the war of 1894–1895 awakened many Chinese intellectuals to the need for reform. Yet even the most ardent resorted to the concept of *yun-hui* to advance the view that both China's defeat and the postwar reforms had been determined by cosmic forces. In his famous essay "On the Crisis in China's Situation" *(Lun shih-pien chih-chi),* Yen Fu ascribed the problem ultimately to cosmic patterns. "The situation changes, yet none of us knows what is the source of change. If we must name it, we call it 'turn of fortune' [*yun-hui*]. If there is to be such a change, even sages cannot prevent it."[19] In Yen's view, the quality of sagehood— whether Confucian or Taoist, he did not make clear—calls for following the will of heaven. For in the cosmic scheme of things, sagehood is part of nature in the stream of life. The sage cannot possibly divert the course determined by cosmic rhythms. On the other hand, as the "Wen-yen" commentary to the *I-ching* indicates, the character of the sage ("the great man") must naturally be in accord with heaven: "When he acts in advance of heaven, heaven does not contradict him. When he follows heaven, he adapts himself to the time of heaven."[20] Yen gives this crucial classical passage an interpretation that means simply that the sage follows heaven's wishes: "A sage is one who knows which way the conjunction of fate tends to move and can, moreover, trace it back to the beginnings. Because he knows which way the conjunction of fate tends to move, when he follows heaven he therefore adapts himself to its time. Because he can trace fate back to its origins, therefore when he acts in advance of heaven, it does not contradict him."[21]

To Ch'en Chih, the middle-grade official in Peking who wrote essays championing reform in 1896, the fortune awaiting China indeed turned on her adaptability to change—for change was the way of heaven itself: "The way of heaven is to change constantly; the way of the earth is to remain unchanged; while the way of man should be to respond to change. This is why across many thousand miles of land, and after many thousand years of time, for people of many races, the situation is such that by the same turn of fortune [yun-hui], the East and the West would share so many things in common."[22] Once again we see that Chinese reformist thought could abandon Sinocentric parochialism for the more universal view. Yet even a broad-minded person like Ch'en Chih adhered to the traditional cyclic view of history. Ch'en wondered why the East and West had so many things in common. "Has heaven really exhausted all possible changes?" he asked. "Indeed heaven follows the cyclic process (yun) of beginning and end and beginning again; earth follows the cyclic process of growth and withering and growing again; nations follow the cyclic process of unity and division and unifying again. Thus heaven, earth, and man each follows fortune."[23]

There were some keen minds of the late nineteenth century who began to see that the crisis that China was experiencing was something radically new —and that the change they and their contemporaries were witnessing was what we may describe as linear progression. In his postface to Huang-ch'ao ching-shih wen hsu-pien (Supplementary collection of Ch'ing dynasty writings on statecraft, 1897), Sheng Hsuan-huai, or his amanuensis, seemed to suggest as much. On the one hand, he called upon the I-ching to affirm the principle of reversal—of things always coming back to the original orientation. "No plain is not followed by a slope; no going not followed by a return." Yet he acknowledged that heaven's purposes are sometimes unfathomable. "Regarding the principles of heaven and man, some are known and others not known. Therefore, although order and disorder [in government] seem to be circular, yet the changes in [human] affairs have no end or limit."

Sheng praised the greatness of the Ch'ing dynasty but stressed that as a result of the continuous interaction between heaven's will and human effort, the incipient opportunities (chi) were expanded and a situation unknown in all the ages was being created. It was within this new turn of fortune that the dynasty faced difficulties, beginning with the White Lotus Rebellion in the late eighteenth century. Added to the turmoil created by rebellions were the problems in foreign affairs since the early Tao-kuang reign (1821–1850). From 1860 on, especially, "shipping was well developed and technology grew; Christianity spread and complaints multiplied." All such difficulties were "sent down by heaven, and despite the worries of and efforts made by the court, nothing can be done about it." The situation eventually collapsed as a result of the Sino-Japanese War of 1894, leading to dangerous rivalry among the powers. Was this all "caused by heaven or by man? Indeed, this cannot be known."[24]

Implied in Sheng's essay is the acknowledgment that new situations could be created as a result of unpredictable combinations between heaven's will and human effort. This same line of thinking was developed by more utopian reformers—those who visualized a world of happiness, equality, and abundance in the future. T'ang Ts'ai-ch'ang, who during the Boxer crisis in 1900 was to lead a rebellion in Hankow against the Empress Dowager Tz'u-hsi and in favor of the young, reform-minded emperor, discussed the subject of *yun-hui* in 1898. There were many people, he pointed out, who were frightened and wearied by the precipitous change in China's situation. People would ask: "Where is the end of the turn of fortune?" T'ang answered: "People do not realize that in creating such turmoil and turbulence, heaven is aiming at starting the motion *(yun)* toward the Grand Unity. At this time, we should try to enhance our intellectual power and broaden our outlook so that we can act in obedience to heaven. We should deal with the change in the situation with common sense and realism. As the *Book of Changes* says, 'When he acts in advance of heaven, heaven does not contradict him. When he follows heaven, he adapts himself to the time of heaven.' "[25]

That an ardent reformer of T'ang Ts'ai-ch'ang's caliber should have cited the *I-ching* to justify action for the purpose of realizing a utopian future no doubt indicates the wide range of possible interpretations of the *I-ching*'s statement of faith. It may also be concluded, however, that the intellectual changes in modern China had to be legitimated by inherited concepts, and that there was, moreover, a gap between the acceptance of Western technical knowledge and even Western values, on the one hand, and the acceptance of scientific cosmology, on the other. It may be suggested further that Late Ch'ing writings even of the reformist persuasion still had to be put in familiar literary idioms in order to be persuasive. The worldview was in some way inseparable from the prose style.

Notes

This essay was originally translated by Professor Kwang-Ching Liu for the panel titled "Ontology and Human Efficacy in Chinese Thought of the Ch'ing Period" at the annual meeting of the Pacific Coast Branch of the American Historical Association in Honolulu, Hawaii, in August 1986.

1. Hsu Chi-yü, *Ying-huan k'ao-lueh* (A brief survey of the maritime circuit) (manuscript by Hsu Chi-yü, 1844, reproduced in facsimile; Taipei, 1968), p. 109.

2. Wei Yuan, *Hai-kuo t'u-chih* (Illustrated gazetteer of maritime countries) (reprint; Taipei, 1967) 24:1.

3. See, inter alia, Kuo Mo-jo, *Ch'ing-t'ung shih-tai* (The age of bronze) 5th ed. (Beijing, 1962), pp. 18–31.

4. Wei Yuan, *Hai-kuo t'u-chih,* preface.

5. Tseng Kuo-fan, *Tseng Wen-cheng kung shu-cha* (Letters of Tseng Kuo-fan) (1867 ed.) 8:25.

6. Tseng Kuo-fan, *Tseng Wen-cheng kung chia-shu* (Family letters of Tseng Kuo-fan) (reproduced in facsimile, Taipei, 1957), pp. 210–211.

7. Cheng Kuan-ying, *Sheng-shih wei-yen hsu-pien* (Warnings to a prosperous age) (supplement, 1893 ed.), preface by Cheng Tsao-ju.

8. Ibid., preface by Ch'en Chih.

9. Ibid.; see also Wang Erh-min, *Chin-tai Chung-kuo ssu-hsiang shih-lun* (Studies on the history of modern Chinese thought) (Taipei, 1977), pp. 381–439.

10. Wang T'ao, *T'ao-yuan wen-lu wai-pien* (Supplement to Wang T'ao's collected essays) (Shanghai, 1897 ed.) 7:15.

11. Ibid.

12. Yen Fu, trans., *Yuan-fu* ([Adam Smith's] Wealth of nations) (Shanghai, 1931), p. 644.

13. Wang Shu-nan, *T'ao-lu wen-chi* (Collected writings of T'ao-lu) (1915 ed.) 2:15.

14. Hsiao T'ung, comp., *Wen-hsuan* (Refined literature) (reprint; Taipei, 1955) 25:8; 37:10.

15. Cf. Fung Yu-lan, *A History of Chinese Philosophy,* trans. Derk Bodde (Princeton, N.J., 1952–1953) 2:469–470. See also Ch'üan Tsu-wang, *Sung-Yuan hsueh-an* (Record of Sung and Yuan scholarship) (Taipei, 1975) 9:107–109.

16. Hsu Chi-yü, *Ying-huan chih-lueh,* p. 110.

17. See Wang Chia-chien, *Wei Yuan nien-p'u* (Biographical chronicle of Wei Yuan) (Taipei, 1967), p. 135.

18. See above, n. 7; below, n. 24.

19. Yen Fu, *Yen Chi-tao shih-wen ch'ao* (A collection of poetry and prose by Yen Fu) (Shanghai, 1922) 1:1.

20. Translation based on Richard Wilhelm and Cary F. Baynes, *The I-ching or Book of Changes* (Princeton, N.J., 1950), pp. 382–383.

21. See n. 19, above.

22. Ch'en Chih's essay in Mai Chung-hua, comp., *Huang-ch'ao ching-shih-wen hsin-pien* (A new collection of Ch'ing dynasty writings on statecraft) (1897) 16:19.

23. Ibid.

24. Sheng Hsuan-huai, postface, in Sheng K'ang, comp., *Huang-ch'ao ching-shih-wen hsu-pien* (Supplementary collection of Ch'ing dynasty writings on statecraft) (1897).

25. *Hsiang-pao lei-tsuan* (Topically arranged articles from the Hunan News) (Shanghai, 1902) 1:1:10.

10

Escape from Disillusionment: Personality and Value Change in the Case of Sung Chiao-jen

DON C. PRICE

The image of the hero appealed to many early Chinese revolutionaries. One classic description was provided in 1903 by Chiang Pai-li, who wrote: "A hero's ability to accomplish a great undertaking lies in walking a straight path, not a crooked one. He walks a single path, not deviating to another one. He is forthright about his purposes, so that those who will can join him, and those who will not, may leave. If he succeeds, myriads will burn incense in his honor. If not, his grave will be overgrown with brush, and the autumn crickets will chirp there."[1] Aside from its romanticism the image embodies other significant and distinctive components: an exaltation of the active, physical, and military over the ruminative, cerebral, and civil. It is easy to see how they enhance the appeal of the image at a time of widespread, growing appreciation of military power and military culture as a prerequisite to national survival in the modern world. And, for revolutionaries in particular, the moral strength and unhesitating purity of the hero might also commend themselves as the answer to the vainglorious squabblings, opportunistic compromises, and cowardly defections that were identified in a number of revolutionary publications as mortal threats to their cause.

That the heroic persona appealed to the youthful Sung Chiao-jen might seem surprising in the light of his later career. Sung is best remembered either as an unwilling martyr for the cause of parliamentary democracy or a victim of his own miscalculations. Among all the revolutionaries perhaps the most realistic political strategist, he had, in the immediate aftermath of the 1911 revolution, outmaneuvered or persuaded senior leaders of the revolutionary movement to abandon armed struggle and collaborate with former constitutionalists, converting the Revolutionary League into the Kuomintang, a more broadly based and less militantly progressive political party. Its success at the polls had made Sung, at age thirty, a major contender for the prime ministership, when Yuan Shih-k'ai managed to have him assassinated. Some admired him as a farsighted, judicious strategist. Others found his maneuvers too opportunistic, or simply denounced him for unprincipled ambition. Nobody would have thought of him as a reckless, uncompromising hero. But as a youth he was stirred by knight-errant novels, admired Japanese militarism, and praised rebels who disdained to worry about success or failure. Not above striking a romantic pose, he also genuinely sought to perfect in himself the inner virtues of the hero.[2]

Although the bold hero, at least as conceived by those who insisted on purity, and the cautious, calculating politician seem to represent alternative personality types, they also involved a broader range of social and political values at the end of the Ch'ing dynasty. On the one hand, the hero embodied the principle of elitist personalistic authority as well as the supreme civic virtue: subordination of the self to the collective, which together with the personalistic elitism, meant virtuous leadership evoking a loyal following. The statesman, on the other hand, could not disdain compromise. He had to be sensitive to historical trends and the historical moment and to practical questions of political power and the uses for which it could be mobilized, in both the short term and the long term. Such sensitivity is by no means inherently incompatible with elitist and personalistic conceptions of power. But in Sung's case the statesman's imperatives directed his concerns beyond the immediate question of who was morally qualified to wield power and command allegiance, to the question of how power should be distributed within a new institutional order. Convinced that China was on the threshold of an entirely new stage in world history, Sung ultimately arrived at something like Western liberalism's insistence on constitutional guarantees that power must be accountable to a broad constituency.

Reflection on the ostensible changes in Sung's personality and values might at first glance appear to suggest that personality change may have dictated value change, or vice versa. What is the relation between the two, after all? Here I shall propose that in Sung's case the personality types of hero and statesman were both expressions of a bold, ambitious, and rebellious personality in need of moral justification within a convincing system of values. Sung's values stood at the juncture of his inner person and outer world, at least as he knew it. Until his mid-twenties, the world as he knew it was one of crises and opportunities that called on him to act as a hero. Then almost simultaneously, two things happened: his effort to answer this call backfired, and at the same time he was increasingly exposed to a world quite different in both its cosmological and political dimensions from the one he had imagined. In this new world, the kind of heroism to which he had aspired lacked any ontological basis, and in any case the real crises and opportunities called less for the leadership of a hero than for the guidance of a statesman.

A closer examination of Sung's experience should lend these generalizations more concrete meaning and prepare us to address two major questions of broader significance: One is the extent to which this shift in persona can explain the abandonment of his early revolutionary elitism for liberal alternatives. The other is the extent to which his case is representative or atypical of wider trends in modern Chinese political culture, and why.

Sung was born in 1882 into a thoroughly traditional environment in rural T'ao-yuan county, in western Hunan. To say that his background was traditional does not mean that it conformed to any easy stereotype, however. To be sure, there is no reason to doubt that he was brought up to honor at least four of the Confucian Five Relationships,[3] and filial piety, if nothing else, would have motivated him to win a *sheng-yuan* degree and recover for his family the gentry status that his grandfather had attained.[4] His scholarly orientation reflects a certain Late Ch'ing eclecticism, for he particularly admired Wang Yang-ming's thought without granting any incompatibility between his teachings and those of the Ch'eng-Chu orthodoxy, and he appears to have been schooled in *k'ao-cheng* methods as well.[5] On the other hand, unlike his more conventionally minded schoolmates at the nearby Chang-chiang Academy, he showed very little interest in preparation for the examinations but paid a great deal of attention to the study of geography, traditional law enforcement (*hsing*, punishments), and institutional and military history. According to one of his teachers, he was an avid bibliophile and traveled far and wide buying books; another companion of his youth recalled that he kept travel journals or diaries and checked his own observations against the written geographies that he studied.[6] But his intellectual passions, some of them mildly unconventional, were not incompatible with the dominant traditional values in which he had been indoctrinated.

Even his attraction to revolution might at first glance seem to conform to a pattern of idealistic and bookish young scholars diverted from conventional careers to radicalism by the various disorientations of the Late Ch'ing crisis, but this pattern does not do justice to the formation of Sung's revolutionary personality. The anti-Manchuism that burgeoned in Hunan after the traumatic defeat by Japan in 1895 and grew with the commotion of the reform movement and its suppression in the wake of the Empress Dowager's coup d'état of 1898, remained far from dominant in that province even then, but Sung's anti-Manchuism seems to have blossomed earlier, in elements of popular culture and memory to which he was exposed as a child. From an early age he had begun to show a hostility to the reigning dynasty, which both implied a serious challenge to the cardinal Confucian virtue of loyalty and seemed to feed, or feed on, a personality that was assertive to the point of rebellious defiance.

The cultural matrix within which Sung's heroic anti-Manchuism took shape is still poorly understood, and the extant materials on his case, in particular, offer little more than tantalizing hints. He was nicknamed Kung-ming, after one of the heroes of the widely popular traditional Robin Hood novel, *Shui-hu chuan* (The water margin), in which defiance of state authority and social hierarchy were romanticized, although not explicitly endorsed.[7] What made the defiance possible was, of course, a physical capability of self-defense. The heroes of the novel are testimony to a tradition of private cultivation of the martial arts that survived to Sung's day and, according to one account, in Sung's clan. Sung's elder brother was a close associate of local secret society members who soon proved to be ready recruits for anti-Manchu uprisings, and their friendship was based partly on a common interest in the martial arts.[8] Sung Chiao-jen himself (like some other early gentry radicals—e.g., Huang Hsing, T'an Ssu-t'ung) is said to have practiced some skills in the martial arts repertoire and to have been fond of daredevil feats from boyhood. Several boyhood vignettes remind us of *Water Margin* heroes—Sung's tolerance of local ragamuffins' pilfering of the harvest gleanings and his own bold baiting of the arrogant rich. According to one story, a powerful local landlord permitted his goats to destroy the vegetation on a nearby hillside, to the distress of neighbors afraid to complain. The nine-year-old Sung killed the goats with a knife and, presumably as a warning to the world, stashed their heads beneath the teacher's desk at his school. (A *Water Margin* hero would, of course, have decapitated the landlord.)[9]

Where memories of the bloody Manchu conquest lingered, and one of the province's most outstanding scholars (Wang Fu-chih) was famous for his discussion of Han and barbarian differences, Sung's Robin Hood attitudes could easily, and naturally, extend to defiance of the Manchu dynasty. There are anecdotes which have the ten-year-old boy talking of "killing the

Tartars" and organizing his playmates into competing armies of "Ch'ing aristocrats" and "commoners."[10] By age seventeen (1899), his bold defiance of authority and hostility to the reigning dynasty had hardened. He outraged senior guests at a lavish and festive banquet for himself and his new bride at her father's house by denouncing formalistic references to the "emperor's benevolence" with a tirade against misgovernment and a proposal that the emperor be overthrown.[11] The accuracy of such anecdotes is, of course, open to question, but they are too many to be ignored, and they suggest a kind of strong-willed assertiveness that found an outlet in the defiance of corrupt authority, and particularly (although not only) that of the Manchus.

His elder brother, with his circle of friends among secret society fighters, may also have represented for Sung Chiao-jen a polar opposite to their father and an alternative role model. When Sung Chiao-jen was ten, the father, then forty-one, died, reportedly of exhaustion from studying for the examinations. He must have spent over two decades in a demoralizing effort to pass them.[12] One might speculate, although there is no way to prove it, that his father's tragic fate came to symbolize for Sung the evils of China's debilitating examination system and effete literati culture, the bankruptcy of which had been exposed in the Sino-Japanese War and the Boxer uprising. His brother, not a scholar, symbolized a bolder, more vigorous and assertive martial tradition. If this general interpretation is correct, then anti-Manchuism functioned primarily to lend filial legitimacy and conceptual focus not only to his own rebelliousness but also to the emotions prompted by his father's death and his keen frustrations over China's plight and the government's failures.

In any case, Sung was not your typical scholar or examination system careerist. Shunned by most of his schoolmates, who thought him mad, he divulged to a few admiring friends at the Chang-chiang Academy a grand military strategy whereby a hero (*ying-hsiung*) might conquer China and drive out the Manchus.[13] In 1904, as his first effort along this line failed and he sailed down the Hsiang and the Yangtze, fleeing the constabulary, he perused a knight-errant novel set in the Ming dynasty, and composed a heroic song about himself:

> A son of the Han from the valley of the Yuan, Ah!
> I lament my clumsiness.
> Seeking freedom, independence in my corner of Hunan, Ah!
> I've failed on the point of success.

> The mounted Tartar agents swarm the roads, Ah!
> A thousand silver taels the price on my head.
> Like the ancients I would die for virtue's sake, Ah!
> But to what avail, I fear: who'd replace me when I'm dead?[14]

Such are the roots, political, cultural, and personal, of Sung's self-image as a rebellious hero. And yet, Sung did not formulate a systematic challenge to traditional values, despite the apparent conflict between his anti-Man-chuism and the Confucian principle of loyalty. In fact, rather than rejecting that principle, he more likely lamented the absence of a worthy object of his loyalty, seeing that the Manchus had no legitimate claim on it. Substantial evidence of his emerging vision of an ideal order dates from the first year of his exile in Japan, when Sung was twenty-three. This was the year of Japan's stunning victory over Russia. Dissuaded by his friends from entering military school, he nevertheless evinced a keen interest in military power and martial spirit, which he regarded as essential to the restoration of Chi-na's fortunes.[15] On the other hand, he was perhaps even more profoundly impressed by the basis of Japan's national power: a patriotism assiduously cultivated by the state and by the emperor himself.[16] And as he continued to reflect on this patriotism, he found its root in civic virtue and responsibil-ity.[17] Reading a book of Western wisdom, he dwelt on passages that attrib-uted the fortunes of nations to the qualities of their citizens. And in his diary he recorded the report of an interview with a Japanese jail warden, who said, "The quality of the prisons depends not on the systems or regulations, but simply on the rectitude and sincerity of the personnel." "Ah," Sung reflected, "Shouldn't everything under the sun be dealt with this way! No wonder Japan is so strong, if even their jailers understand this principle."[18]

What is the relation of Sung's "hero" to his ideal nation? Clearly, he did not need to become its titular leader, who might be a worthy like the Meiji emperor or King Victor Emmanuel of Italy. But these leaders owed their positions to heroes. The point is that personal virtue was the key both to the restoration of a good order and to its strength, once established. The hero's loyalty to such an order, like that of Confucius's superior man, held firm through hard times; that of the citizen at large had to be fostered by the good ruler. In either case, the interests of the community were placed above one's own. Even the Manchus were disqualified less on purely racial grounds than on the grounds that they did not, nor could they be expected to, place China's interests above their own.[19] And, although it is true that

Sung, as a founding member of the Revolutionary League, was nominally committed to people's rights, he did not object to monarchy in Japan or Britain, much less dwell on the generic problem of devising guarantees against the abuse of state power. In short, Sung's heroic self-image naturally complemented his traditional understanding of the role of government as primarily a fostering one, to use Munro's term.[20] By the same token, doubts about the role of heroes, or about their very existence as Sung imagined them, could in turn cast doubts on the fostering conception of government, with wide repercussions on its concomitant values.

One more point remains to be made about the hero. The hero's romantic, swashbuckling unconventionality may have been his most eye-catching feature, but Sung, drawing on a rich store of Confucian tradition, invested him with weightier moral substance. As Sung's heroic lament made clear, the hero was dedicated, to the point of martyrdom, if need be, to higher purposes. He abandoned conventionality and took up arms not merely to strike a pose, but because he had the moral fortitude that others of smaller minds and hearts did not have to confront the needs of the times and act on them. The implication of this stance is that he must be worthy of the role to which he aspires and must examine himself when criticized.

For Sung, this point was initially driven home a year after his arrival in Japan by the suicide of his comrade in arms Ch'en T'ien-hua. Keenly concerned for China's fate, and disposed to look to the cream of her younger generation for her salvation, Ch'en was bitterly disappointed by the character defects among Chinese students and exiles in Japan, and in particular by their irresponsible reaction to Japanese government measures to supervise them. His farewell letter, published by Sung in the Min-pao, explained his suicide as an appeal to the students to rectify themselves, to purify their motives and conduct.[21] At this point, Sung's Confucian training became directly relevant. He took Ch'en's admonitions to heart, and through the first half of 1906 engaged in a rigorous effort at self-cultivation in the mode of Wang Yang-ming. The constant self-scrutiny and self-reproach that this demanded backfired disastrously. Sung finally entered a sanatorium with a nervous breakdown and abandoned the study of Wang Yang-ming. By this time, he had been disturbed by reports of his elder brother's opium addiction and gambling.[22] Having failed in his own effort to satisfy the requirements for a hero by moral self-perfection, Sung was prepared to cast a critical eye on his comrades and became particularly dissatisfied with the head of the Revolutionary League, Sun Yat-sen.[23] But a serious predicament now confronted him, for Sung had linked China's survival to her moral revival, which must in turn be launched by morally perfected heroes. If her potential elite was so ill qualified, what hope could there be for China?

Fortunately for Sung, his voracious reading in Japan had by now acquainted him with several branches of modern learning and prepared for him an alternative understanding of the world and of himself and thus enabled him to redefine a moral imperative that had developed into an unbearable, discouraging burden. His self-cultivation effort had rested squarely on an inherited neo-Confucian cosmological consensus. According to its premises, outstanding efforts enable outstanding men to realize their latent, heaven-endowed perfection and put into play the transformative powers of heaven itself. But this cosmology had lost its hold on his thinking. Modern psychology and evolutionary theory now enabled him to view mankind against a geological, not merely historical time scale, as a species endowed both with slowly and naturally evolving moral and social capacities and with physical and spiritual limitations. Such a context left no room for the timeless Confucian concept of moral perfection, and reduced the hero as rebel to a figure capable of performing certain tasks, but not necessarily the most important.[24] At the same time, Sung's growing acquaintance with world history led him to conceive of China's situation in terms not of cycles of decadence and regeneration but of universal social and political progress. Within such a context it now became necessary to understand the dynamics of progress in order to maximize its benefits and minimize its dangers for China. Knowledge was now prior to action.[25]

Sung did not immediately abandon revolutionary action. Indeed, his next effort found him addressing a florid appeal to bandit heroes in Manchuria in the spring of 1907, in an effort to establish a northern revolutionary base. But as this undertaking ran aground, Sung discovered in the process a Japanese plot to appropriate Manchurian territory adjacent to Korea by falsification of the border markers and the historical record. His long-standing interest in historical geography now thoroughly aroused, Sung spent several months on intensive research and writing. The fruits of the research he first made available to the Ch'ing government, which reportedly found them invaluable in countering the Japanese claims.[26] Perhaps this accomplishment confirmed Sung's growing appreciation of the learning necessary, and in some cases sufficient, to cope with China's problems. For the next three years, 1908–1910, the revolutionary movement was in a slump. Sung's comrades recalled this as a period of depression for him, but also as one of study. During these years he completed the translation of Kobayashi Ushisaburo's massive two-volume treatise on comparative finance, but it is clear that this is only one of the fields in which he was reading. When in early 1911 Sung returned to Shanghai he began to publish substantial articles on the history of East Asian international relations, British, Japanese, and Chinese domestic politics, financial policy, and constitutional systems.

These wide-ranging articles reflect not only an attention to the learning required of a statesman but also a new revolutionary vision. Nationalism had not disappeared from it, for in Sung's view, imperialism not only continued to nibble away at Chinese territory, but also threatened now to gain a stranglehold on her economy.[27] But what was new was a keen concern for political structures, and a sense that China was now faced with an opportunity to move to a higher stage of political evolution. Even as early as 1906 Sung had earned a bit of money translating Japanese accounts of the constitutional systems of various countries, and he took close note of the special privileges reserved for monarchs.[28] There is no detailed account of his readings after 1907, but he learned a great deal from Kobayashi's *Comparative Finance*. For all the book's forbiddingly dry title, its historical sections reviewed the bitter struggles between kings, cabinets, parliaments, and people over the power to tax and spend. Not only did it consider the implications of various constitutional systems for a major component of national strength; it also provided an excellent survey of the arena in which rulers and ruled struggled over concrete matters of justice and tyranny, welfare and oppression.[29]

Sung's interest in these matters is reflected in his articles on Japanese and British parliamentary politics. The replacement of the Katsura cabinet by the Saionji cabinet in mid-1911 prompted Sung to comment on the way in which the Japanese system allowed cliques of militarists to subvert the whole purpose of party politics and representative government, a situation from which Japan's political life could hardly be rescued except by some great upheaval.[30] If this article made clear Sung's preference for a political system whose responsiveness to the will of the people would be guaranteed by open competition, his enthusiastic article on the parliamentary reform in England expressed his confidence that such systems were the alternative to the oppressions of the past, and the wave of the future. This parliamentary revolution, as he called it, was a "symptom of the universal spread of democratic government" and "proof that the trend of social welfare policies is sweeping over the whole world."[31]

Somehow, over the five years since Sung endorsed the Japanese jailer's stress on personal responsibility as opposed to structures, his priorities had changed radically. It was not so much that he had only now become a democrat, although it is true that the problems of establishing a democratic order were not burning issues for him at the outset. His earlier views were in fact similar to those of many revolutionaries, who felt in principle that the state should serve the people and both should serve the nation and that hereditary rule smacked of selfish interest and the arbitrary exercise of power. In fact, that quasi-democratic premise was probably essential to the shift that did occur in Sung's priorities. But neither the younger Sung nor many others looked much beyond the elimination of the alien monarchy to the larger problem of systematically guaranteeing the accountability of power.[32] Sung Chiao-jen's articles on Britain and Japan focused on precisely this issue. In Japan, despite elections, the people had no real choice, and despite its monarchy, they were oppressed not by the emperor but by cliques of militarists. The prospects for improvement within that system, he concluded, were dim. In England, another monarchy, the electorate had real choices and made its wishes known and, despite strong traditions of hereditary privilege, had managed to eliminate the last major obstacle to representation through elections—the veto power of the lords. The establishment of sound democratic structures had now become an urgent and concrete problem for Sung. Thus, if Sung had become more of a democrat than he was before, it was because he had drawn such important lessons from the way power was distributed within different systems.

I would argue that Sung's disillusionment with heroes and rule by virtue was decisive in his shift in priorities. Others could blame Manchu misrule on the Manchus' alienness, or on their alleged racial inferiority, and look to a vaguely defined democracy as a means of selecting the best men to rule—in other words, as a means for restoring virtuous government. And recognizing, as most did, that China was not ready for instant democracy, they could endorse Sun Yat-sen's formula for transition through temporary military dictatorship.[33] Presumably that dictatorship would be in the right hands. Sun Yat-sen would later call for his party of "foreknowers" *(hsien-chueh-che)* to wield power, assuming implicitly that they would be not only prescient but virtuous.[34] Hu Shih and others would later appeal for a "good government" however constituted, and the activism of "good men" in a "Good Government Party."[35] Sung, for his part, had undergone a decisive reorientation, away from the very idea that revolution should restore virtuous leadership, to the idea that political progress would enable the governed to monitor the government and to determine its policies, through the institutionalization of open political competition.

In this interpretation, Sung's political activity in the aftermath of the Wuchang uprising can be seen as flowing from a coherent and consistent political strategy. Like most revolutionaries and constitutionalists, he recognized the necessity for a period of transition to democracy. But, unlike the revolutionaries who had proposed a delay in the establishment of a representative system, he expected this to be accomplished by continued limitations on the franchise. This formula was reflected in the provisional constitution that he drafted for Hupei's revolutionary government, with the strict limits it imposed on executive power. Full democracy would come in due course. The provincial assembly was hardly the embodiment of virtue, especially from the point of view of a seasoned revolutionary, but it certainly was representative of an important constituency. Against this background, it is also clear that when Sung argued for government by a responsible cabinet, as opposed to the presidential system, he was not seeking merely to block the ambitions of Yuan Shih-k'ai.

Sun Yat-sen's position in this debate is interesting, for he argued that the new constitution should not tie the hands of the man in whom the people had reposed their trust. And, against Sun and a great many of his comrades, Sung led a long struggle to deradicalize the T'ung-meng hui and merge it into a larger coalition, the Kuomintang, which could consolidate the limited gains of the revolution against the threat of a tyranny. A hero might not so readily have jettisoned women's suffrage or the equalization of land rights, but a statesman had to have his priorities straight and could not afford to disregard the prospects of success or failure.[36] The contrast between the roles of hero and statesman provides a useful entreé into the changes in Sung's personality and values. To be sure, our data on the formation of his personality remain sketchy, but, taken together with cameo portraits of other early revolutionaries or veterans of the 1900 Tzu-li chün uprising in Hunan, they suggest a pattern of unconventionality and assertiveness, sometimes to the point of defiance, and sometimes allied with an appreciation of the physical strength and skills associated in popular culture with such independence of character.[37] If this pattern was a well-established minor strain in Chinese popular culture and society, it provided a natural resource for anti-Manchu sentiment and activism in the early stages.[38]

If Sung was first driven to play the role of rebel hero as the only appropriate one for a man determined to rise above his peers' apathy, it was not simply a rational choice in response to the problems of the outer world, reinforced by a keen sense of Confucian responsibility, but an expression of unusually defiant and turbulent elements in his personality that made the choice of revolution possible in the first place. After all, opting for revolution in up-country Hunan at the turn of the century was different from attending prorevolutionary rallies with hundreds of other radicals in Tokyo in 1905. When Sung embraced revolution in T'ao-yuan, it meant offending his peers and his elders, abandoning time-honored and secure career patterns, and endangering his family and the prospects for its perpetuation. It required an unusual measure of assertiveness, complemented by a view of oneself as something like a hero to legitimize such conflict and risk.[39]

As the revolutionary movement grew, and Sung was forced not only to cope with its internal conflicts but also to contemplate the fate of nations and political causes in a more cosmopolitan environment, his personality surely developed, but there were important underlying continuities. His namesake, the heroic Sung Kung-ming of *The Water Margin* led less by force of arms than by virtue and intelligence, and Sung Chiao-jen was a Confucian scholar and student of statecraft. As he perused the biographies of great men in modern world history, contemplated Japan's patriotism and civic virtue, and pondered the lessons of Ch'en T'ien-hua's suicide, it was natural for him to shift his attention to the cultivation of his virtue and the study of modern statecraft. Driven initially to pursue virtue within his nation, then within himself, he finally came to see this pursuit as chimerical, unrelated either to his or his comrades' capacities, or to the real alternatives that confronted China. Her brightest prospect he saw in what he took to be a natural, although not inevitably smooth, advance in political development, but, as he understood it surveying the modern world, such an advance had to do not with virtue, but the prevention of oppression through the progressively broader and carefully institutionalized and guaranteed distribution of power. This became the primary goal of his revolution. And, where the hero had been driven to pursue virtue, the statesman had now to try to understand and facilitate the impersonal trends of such a progress. But in many ways, Sung remained the same man, scholar, strategist, activist. Even as a hero, Sung had been too calculating, or cautious, to throw away his life in a futile gesture, and, as a statesman, he remained courageous enough to risk (and lose) it in the midst of a political campaign, shrugging off his friends' warnings of danger.[40] It is important, then, to distinguish between Sung's more basic traits and drives, the culturally constructed roles of hero and statesman available to him, and the political lessons that he drew from his unique personal experiences.

What does Sung's case tell us about personality and value change in China at large during this period? We might look for a parallel between his experience and broad trends in an earlier period of dynastic collapse. In some sense, the failure of introspective self-cultivation to save China in the Ming, and the subsequent shift to evidential scholarship and statecraft in the Ch'ing find their counterpart in Sung's abandonment of Wang Yang-ming and his pursuit of objective and practical knowledge. In both cases purity of motive yielded to understanding and management as the major preoccupations.[41] And this shift is reminiscent of a phenomenon to which Joseph Levenson drew our attention, as he wrote of the drain of the Chinese *t'i* into the Western *yung*—that is, the supplanting of virtue by expertise as the sine qua non of successful government.[42] The parallel with the Late Ming and High Ch'ing is somewhat strained, however. Sung did not reenact the excesses of the T'ai-chou school, and he found all the old learning inadequate because its horizons were simply too narrow. Levenson is no doubt nearer the mark in seeing a qualitative difference between the empirical explorations of the Early and High Ch'ing and the displacement of the entire Chinese tradition by the inexorable intrusion of modern learning. Sung's acquaintance with Ch'ing scholarship no doubt prepared him to recognize the importance of a wide range of modern learning to cope with China's problems, but its effect on him was surely without parallel in the earlier Ch'ing.

On the other hand, Levenson's pattern does not really capture the interaction of Sung's moral imperative with his new understanding of the world either. Sung did not simply drift toward expertise and technocracy. Instead, he embraced a new cosmology and repudiated a traditional conception of government. He did so in part to escape from a predicament delineated by Thomas Metzger—the predicament of men schooled to believe that the perfection of the superior man was the only real path to the well-being of society, and who yet found it impossible to perfect themselves. Despite the rise of statecraft and of visions of institutional reform, the instinctive response of many Late Ch'ing patriots to China's crisis still was to call for moral regeneration. The stress on the vanguard's personal virtue may have been disproportionately high among revolutionaries, but it does suggest the continued vigor—and at a time when traditional institutions had lost their virtue, the particular appeal—of the idea that the fate of the realm depended on the virtue of superior men. In times of distress, this idea meant personal failure and frustration for those who took their responsibilities seriously. The alternative vision of progress, Western style, could lift a heavy burden from such men, and promise a different approach to the realization of their goals.[43]

Although Sung seems to fit this pattern, nevertheless his particular personal experience casts that of his comrades in a different light. This is not to say that only those, like Sung, who failed at self-cultivation suffered from the predicament Metzger speaks of, for it was not just a matter of personal failure, but the persistent failure of the neo-Confucian consensus and of neo-Confucian self-cultivation to provide an intelligible and practical solution to the terrible ills of the world. Those who never rigorously pursued the chimera of sagely perfection likewise found an escape in Western visions of progress, but it was different from Sung's escape. Ultimately, I think we learn the most from Sung's case by considering the ways in which his value changes were *not* representative of his era. Sung's new vision and values were rooted in an escape not just from predicament but from disillusionment and a keen sense of the perils of relying on virtue. By contrast, many modern Chinese may have found tremendous relief and encouragement in the expectation that technological advances and organizational devices, rather than prior moral perfection, would solve the ills of the world, but they did not necessarily abandon a deep-rooted Confucian conception of government as essentially moral and personalistic.

Since the mid-nineteenth century, Western models had often been admired for political virtues readily comprehensible within the Chinese tradition: George Washington was compared to Yao and Shun, and parliaments were recommended as a means of promoting solidarity and harmony.[44] Revolutionaries denounced monarchy as selfish tyranny and proposed democracy as the alternative. As long as the purpose of the state was to foster a moral community, that would seem logically to require that the leaders be morally qualified and, if morally qualified, then trusted to wield extensive authority. Yuan Shih-k'ai, Chiang Kai-shek, and Mao Tse-tung all encouraged such claims on their behalf. Of course, rule by virtue was not the only form of rule recognized in the Chinese tradition, but it defined the alternatives, the most important of which were minimally acceptable competent rule by force and terminally vicious government. Such categories were more or less applied in the twentieth century, dictatorships being variously tolerated for the duration of the current crisis or condemned as irredeemably inhumane and corrupt. Given the prevalence of such claims and judgments, there was little room for attention to the ways in which political systems could manage and minimize the perennial threat that power would be abused.

Accordingly, most of Sung's contemporaries hoped that the end of the monarch's mandate would usher in a moral community characterized by the kind of civic virtue, patriotic devotion, and conscientious rule that Sung had first so admired in Japan.[45] Failing that, they could accept harsh rule, if it served the purposes of national survival. As for Sung, he had abandoned such moralistic alternatives. His scrutiny of himself, his comrades, and an authoritarian Japan that had at first seemed such a paragon of political virtue inoculated him against the idea that anyone or any small group could simply be trusted with decisive power. Hence his conclusion, implicit in his writings on England and Japan, and in his political strategy during and after the revolution, that the supreme virtue of government lay in distributing power among those subject to it in such a way that it would be used not against them, but on their behalf, and in accordance with their wishes.

We might be tempted at this point to leap to the generalization that Sung, unlike other progressives, was concerned not with morality but with power or that Sung divorced politics and morality. The matter is more complex than that. It was precisely a powerful moral imperative that had driven Sung into politics, and through politics he pursued what were for him supremely moral ends. But he pursued them in collaboration with men whom he did not regard as paragons of virtue, through agencies that were in themselves largely morally neutral and designed to limit abuses by men who were morally unreliable. It was thus through rather subtle calculations that he embraced the responsible cabinet system, limited franchise, and a careful delineation of central and provincial powers as ways to promote the strength and cohesion that China needed and at the same time launch her on a course that would lead to universal suffrage and full democracy.

Sung's political thought thus diverged significantly from the major ideological currents in twentieth-century China and in ways that tend both to highlight the survival of traditional moralistic elements in the modern political mentality and reveal the connections between such elements and the weakness of commitments to representative democracy. It was only to be expected that the politically dominant ideologues should justify authoritarian rule on the basis of their superior leadership, but even the weak group generally regarded as liberals in the republican period have been criticized for focusing their primary attention on protests against violations of civil liberties and for mounting a "half-hearted and uninspired" defense of democracy.[46] One critic of Chinese liberalism has deplored its focus on toleration and the struggle against tyranny, and relative neglect of the only means for guaranteeing toleration and preventing tyranny: the rule of law (fa-chih), especially constitutional law.[47]

By 1911 Sung had taken a keen interest in constitutional systems, and he was profoundly concerned with the kind of constitution that would be adopted under the new republic. If the foregoing analysis is correct, Sung's distinctiveness lay precisely in seeing certain constitutional arrangements as indispensable means to minimize the constant threat of the abuse of power. The threat was constant because of intractable human imperfections (and their implications) to which Sung was more sensitive than most. Perhaps it was not to be expected that early revolutionaries should distrust themselves or the leaders whom they hoped to install, but the repeated betrayal of the hopes that twentieth-century China has placed in revolutionary leaders and reigns of virtue has lately inspired renewed interest in Sung. He has not yet been praised as a prophet of the two-party system, but it is not surprising, in the post-Cultural Revolution era, that Sung has been rehabilitated not only as a dedicated revolutionary, but also as a martyr to constitutional government and an advocate of the rule of law.[48]

Notes

1. Fei-sheng (pseudonym), "Chin-shih erh ta hsueh-shuo chih p'ing-lun" (The two major current doctrines), *Che-chiang ch'ao* 9 (November 8, 1903): 19.

2. Kubota Bunji, "Shingai kakumei to Son Bun/So Kyo-jin—Chugoku kakumei domeikai no kaitai katei" (Sun Yat-sen and Sung Chiao-jen in the Revolution of 1911—The disintegration of the the Chinese Revolutionary League) *Rekishi kenkyu* (Historical research) 408 (May 1974): 1–17. D. C. Price, "Sung Chiao-jen's Political Strategy in 1912," *Chung-hua min-kuo ch'u-ch'i li-shih yen-t'ao hui lun-wen chi* (Papers from the conference on China's early republican history) (Taipei, 1984) 1:33–51.

3. I.e., the proper, hierarchical obligations between parents and children, spouses, siblings, and friends. The relation between monarch and subject was more problematical for him. See below.

4. Sung Chen-lü and Huang Chen-ya, "Sung Chiao-jen hsien-sheng chia-shih chi an-tsang ti-chih k'ao" (Mr. Sung Chiao-jen's family background and burial place), *Ko-ming wen-hsien* (Documents on the revolution) ed. Chung-kuo kuo-min-tang chung-yang wei-yuan-hui tang-shih shih-liao pien-tsuan wei-yuan-hui (Taipei, 1968), 42/43:313.

5. Hu-hsi ai-shih-k'o (pseudonym of Feng Wei-ying), "Yü-fu t'ung-shih" (The tragic history of Yü-fu), *Ko-ming wen-hsien* 42/43:11. Imamura Yoshio, "Sō Kyōjin noto" (Note on Sung Chiao-jen), *Rishi to jōkan* (Reason and emotion) (Tokyo, 1976), p. 137.

6. Hu-hsi ai-shih-k'o, "Yü-fu t'ung-shih;" Lo Chi, Preface to Sung Chiao-jen, *Wo chih li-shih* (My history) (photographic reprint of T'ao-yuan lithographic ed., Taiwan, 1920), p. 17. Ch'ü Fang-mei, "K'u Sung hsien-sheng chih ai-sheng" (Lament for Mr. Sung), *Min-li pao,* April 28, 1913.

7. Wen Szu, "Sung Chiao-jen hsien-sheng erh-san shih" (A few stories about Sung Chiao-jen), *T'ao-yuan wen-shih tzu-liao* (Literary and historical materials on T'ao-yuan); ed. T'ao-yuan Branch, CPPCC (T'ao-yuan, Hunan, 1985), p. 8.

8. Sung Chung-hsiung, personal communication, July 4, 1984. "Sung hsien-sheng Shih-ch'ing shih-lueh" (A brief account of Mr. Sung Shih-ch'ing), *Min-li pao,* April 7, 1913.

9. Sam C. Y. Sung to author, May 26, 1970, with notes on *Wo-chih li-shih* and *Ko-ming wen-hsien,* pp. 7–8; Sung Chung-hsiung, "Wu shu-tsu-fu Chiao-jen shao-nien i-shih" (Anecdotes from the boyhood of my fifth younger paternal great-uncle Chiao-jen), *Sung Chiao-jen chi-nien chuan-chi* (Commemorative vol. on Sung Chiao-jen); ed. T'ao-yuan Branch CPPCC (T'ao-yuan, Hunan, 1987), pp. 63–67.

10. Ibid.; also Ch'eng T'u, *Sung Chiao-jen* (Nanking, 1936), pp. 12–13.

11. Chao Tao-mo, "Sung Chiao-jen i-shih erh-tse," *Sung Chiao-jen chi-nien chuan-chi,* pp. 78–79.

12. Lo Jun-chang, "Sung mu Wan t'ai-fu-jen ch'i chih shou hsu" (On the seventieth birthday of Sung's mother Madam Wan), *Min-li pao,* April 21, 1913.

13. Feng Wei-ying, "Chuan" (Biography), in *Wo chih li-shih,* p. 33.

14. *Wo chih li-shih,* 1904/11/9.

15. *Wo chih li-shih,* 1905/1/14; 1906/1/16. See also the articles that he published himself in his revolutionary journal under the pseudonym Chieh, "Han-tsu ch'in-lueh shih" (History of aggression by the Han), *Erh-shih shih-chi chih Chin-na* (Twentieth century China) 1 (May 1, 1905): 31; and the article by a pseudony-mous contributor (Shang-wu sheng), titled "Kuo-min yü chan-cheng chih kuan-hsi" (The citizenry and war), ibid. 1:43–50.

16. *Wo chih li-shih,* 1905/1/1; 1905/5/3.

17. Sung's linking of the military ethos with civic virtue and personal self-culti-vation very much parallels the thought of Liang Ch'i-ch'ao in his discussion of the "new citizen." See Hao Chang, *Liang Ch'i-ch'ao and Intellectual Transition in China, 1890–1907* (Cambridge, Mass., 1971), chap. 9.

18. *Wo chih li-shih,* 1906/8/30.

19. "Ch'ing t'ai-hou chih hsien-cheng t'an" (The Ch'ing Empress Dowager's dis-cussion of constitutional government), *Sung Chiao-jen chi* (Writings of Sung Chiao-jen), ed. Ch'en Hsu-lu (Beijing, 1984), p. 17.

20. Donald J. Munro, *The Concept of Man in Contemporary China* (Ann Arbor, Mich., 1977), chap. 4.

21. Ernest P. Young, "Problems of a Late Ch'ing Revolutionary: Ch'en T'ien-hua," in *Revolutionary Leaders of Modern China,* ed. Chün-tu Hsueh (New York, 1971), pp. 240–244. "Ch'en Hsing-t'ai hsien-sheng chueh-ming shu" (Mr. Ch'en Hsing-t'ai [T'ien-hua]'s suicide letter), with colophon by Sung, *Min-pao* 2 (May 6, 1906): 1–10 (separate pagination).

22. *Wo-chih li-shih,* 1906/4/8; 1906/10/5; 1907/2/7.

23. Ibid., 1906/11/25; 1907/2/28.

24. On the diminished role of the sage in the newly revealed world see Thomas

A. Metzger, *Escape from Predicament: Neo-Confucianism and China's Evolving Political Culture* (New York, 1977), pp. 217–219. Charlotte Furth expands on this point in "Intellectual Change: from the Reform Movement to the May Fourth Movement," in *Cambridge History of China,* ed. John K. Fairbank (Cambridge, 1984) 12, pt. 1:331–334, 404–405.

25. D. C. Price, "Ko-ming yü hsien-fa: Sung Chiao-jen cheng-chih ts'e-lueh ti fa-chan" (Revolution and constitution: The development of Sung Chiao-jen's political strategy), *Chi-nien hsin-hai ko-ming ch'i-shih chou nien hsueh-shu t'ao-lun hui wen-chi* (Papers from the conference commemorating the seventieth anniversary of the 1911 Revolution) (Beijing, 1983), pp. 2623–2625.

26. Matsumoto Hideki, "Sung Chiao-jen ho Chien-tao wen-t'i" (Sung Chiao-jen and the Chien-tao question), ibid., pp. 2538–2559. Sung later published this research as a book, the text of which has been reprinted in *Sung Chiao-jen chi,* pp. 57–136.

27. Yü-fu (Sung Chiao-jen), "Cheng-fu chieh Jih-pen chai-k'uan shih chao yuan lun" (On the government's contracting a million yen loan from Japan), *Min-li pao,* March 30–31, 1911.

28. *Wo chih li-shih,* 1906/11/11, 24.

29. *Pi-chiao ts'ai-cheng-hsueh* (Tokyo, 1911). For further analysis of the place of this work in Sung's political thought, see my "Constitutional Alternatives and Democracy in the Revolution of 1911," *Ideas across Cultures: Essays in Honor of Benjamin I. Schwartz,* ed. Paul A. Cohen and Merle Goldman (Cambridge, Mass., 1990).

30. Yü-fu, "Jih-pen nei-ko keng-tieh kan-yen" (Thoughts on the change of the Japanese cabinet], *Min-li pao,* September 5, 1911.

31. Yü-fu, "Ying-kuo chih kuo-hui ko-ming" (England's parliamentary revolution), *Min-li pao,* August 30–31, 1911.

32. This is a bit oversimplified, for a few revolutionaries, most notably Wang Ching-wei, dealt with the threat of the abuse and concentration of power in response to Liang Ch'i-chao's attacks; but the debate was carried on at a rather abstract level and yielded no concrete proposals either to guard against the abuse of power by revolutionaries or to prevent the seizure of power by nonrevolutionary militarists. See Michael Gasster, *Chinese Intellectuals and the Revolution of 1911: The Birth of Modern Chinese Radicalism* (Seattle, 1969), chap. 4.

33. "Ko-ming fang-lueh" (Design for the revolution), in *Kuo-fu ch'üan-chi* (Complete works of Sun Yat-sen) (Taipei, 1965) 1:3:1–3.

34. Cf. *Kuo-fu ch'üan-chi,* 2:8:3–4.

35. Jerome Grieder, *Hu Shih and the Chinese Renaissance: Liberalism in the Chinese Revolution, 1917–1937* (Cambridge, Mass., 1970), pp. 191–199.

36. Price, "Sung Chiao-jen's Political Strategy."

37. See, e.g., the notices on Lin Kuei, Ch'en Ying-chen, Yao Hsiao-ch'in and T'ien Pang-hsuan in Tu Mai-chih, Liu Yang-yang, Li Lung-ju comp., *Tzu-li hui*

shih-liao chi (Materials on the history of the Tzu-li hui) (Changsha, 1983), pp. 40, 231, 234, 278, 282.

38. For a discussion of this kind of hero as portrayed in official histories as well as popular literature from earliest times down to the Ch'ing, see James J. Y. Liu, *The Chinese Knight Errant* (Chicago, 1967). Pages 4–9 provide a valuable analysis of the ideals of the knight-errant and their relation to Confucian values. Although the scope of the terms *hsia* (knight-errant) and *ying-hsiung* or *hao-chieh* (hero) is not identical, the models can be conflated for the purposes of this discussion. See, e.g., pp. 124–5, 135.

39. Commenting on self-assertion in strong literary characters, Joseph S. M. Lau observes, "It is through affirmation of a cause, be it altruistic, self-serving, or even absurd, that these characters in traditional narratives define and sustain their concept of self. 'What sort of man am I?'—anticipating a unique answer—is a question foreign to the bulk of old China's heroes and heroines." See his "Duty, Reputation and Selfhood in Traditional Chinese Narratives," in *Expressions of Self in Chinese Literature,* ed. Robert E. Hegel and Richard C. Hessney (New York, 1985), p. 383.

40. [Hsu] Hsueh-erh, "T'ung-yen" (Words of grief), in *Sung Yü-fu* (Shanghai, 1913; photographic reprint, Taiwan, 1963) 2:2 (discontinuous pagination).

41. Benjamin A. Elman, *From Philosophy to Philology* (Cambridge, Mass., 1984), pp. 53–56.

42. Joseph R. Levenson, *Confucian China and Its Modern Fate* (Berkeley, Calif., 1958), chap. 4.

43. Metzger, *Escape from Predicament,* pp. 81, 158–161, 214–220.

44. Fred W. Drake, "A Nineteenth Century View of the United States of America from Hsu Chi-yü's *Ying-huan chih-lueh,*" *Papers on China* 19:39–42. Lloyd E. Eastman, "Political Reformism in China before the Sino-Japanese War," *Journal of Asian Studies* 27, no. 4 (August 1968): 695–710.

45. On the persistence of these very traditional values and goals in new institutional settings, see Metzger, *Escape from Predicament,* pp. 210–211, 231–233.

46. Eugene Lubot, *Liberalism in an Illiberal Age: New Culture Liberals in Republican China, 1919–1937* (Westport, Conn., 1982), pp. 108, chaps. 5, 6, passim. Democracy was defended on the grounds that it was more "effective" than dictatorship (T'ao Meng-ho, Chuan-hua Lowe), or more "advanced." Hu Shih did, to be sure, argue at one point that the Kuomintang monopoly of power was responsible for its corruption and proposed that opposition parties should be allowed to check the abuses; there were a few other outstanding spokesmen for constitutionally guaranteed political pluralism, like Lo Lung-chi, Carsun Chang, Ch'en Ch'i-t'ien, and Ch'u An-p'ing, recently discussed at the conference on "Oppositional Politics in Twentieth Century China, September 20–22, 1990, at Washington and Lee University.

47. Lin Yü-sheng, "Kuan-yü cheng-chih chih-hsu ti liang chung kuan-nien: chien

lun jung-jen yü tzu-yu" (On two concepts of political order: With a discussion of toleration and liberty), *Chih-shih fen-tzu* (The Chinese intellectual) 7 (1985): 90–105.

48. [Ch'en Hsu-lu], Hsu-yen (Preface) to *Sung Chiao-jen chi,* pp. 12–13; Lin
Tseng-p'ing, "Sung Chiao-jen, wei min-chu hsien-cheng erh hsien-shen te chieh-ch'u
ke-ming-chia" (Sung Chiao-jen, an outstanding revolutionary who dedicated his life
to constitutional democracy), *Sung Chiao-jen chi-nien chüan-chi,* pp. 122–141.

Contributors

Hao Chang is professor of history at Ohio State University. A specialist in Chinese intellectual history, he has published numerous articles and several books on the subject in both Chinese and English. His most recent book is *Chinese Intellectuals in Crisis: Search for Order and Meaning, 1890–1911.*

Kai-wing Chow is assistant professor of history and Asian studies at the University of Illinois at Champaign-Urbana. A specialist in the intellectual and cultural history of late Imperial China, his forthcoming publications are *The Rise of Confucian Ritualism in Late Imperial China: Ethics, Classics, and Lineage Discourse* and "Ritual, Cosmology, and Ontology: Chang Tsai's (1020–1077) Moral Philosophy and Neo-Confucian Ethics," *Philosophy East and West.*

Benjamin A. Elman received his Ph.D. in oriental studies from the University of Pennsylvania in 1980 and is currently professor of history at UCLA, where he specializes in late Imperial Chinese cultural history. His first book was titled *From Philosophy to Philology: Social and Intellectual Aspects of Change in Late Imperial China.* His recent work *Classicism, Politics, and Kinship: The Ch'ang-chou School of New Text Confucianism in Late Imperial China* received the Berkeley Prize from University of California Press in 1991. He is presently researching the cultural aspects of the Ming-Ch'ing civil service examinations from 1370 to 1905.

D. W. Y. Kwok is professor of history at the University of Hawaii. His major work, *Scientism in Chinese Thought 1900–1950,* remains the standard treatment of the doctrinal effect of science on Chinese thought. He has authored numerous essays on Chinese tradition, anarchism and anarchists, populism, and the New Culture Movement, which have appeared in several languages. Kwok has recently completed translations of Lu Jia's *Xinyu* and Jia Yi's *Xinshu,* and his edited translation of a history of the Cultural Revolution is in progress.

San-pao Li is professor of Asian and Asian-American studies at California State University, Long Beach. An intellectual historian who focuses his research on nineteenth-century China, he is the author of several important studies on K'ang Yu-wei. His forthcoming works include *Moral Imperatives Redefined: Early Intellectual Radicalism of K'ang Yu-wei, 1858–1927.* He recently served as visiting professor and chair of the Department of Political Science, Tunghai University, Taiwan.

On-cho Ng received both his B.A. (hons.) and M.Phil. at the University of Hong Kong. His doctorate in Chinese history was awarded by the University of Hawaii in 1986. He taught at the University of California, Riverside, and is currently assistant professor of history at Pennsylvania State University. He is engaged in a book-length study on Ch'eng-Chu Confucianism in the Early Ch'ing and has a forthcoming article on the subject in *Philosophy East and West*.

Don C. Price is professor of history at the University of California, Davis. A specialist in modern Chinese intellectual history, he is the author of *Russia and the Roots of the Chinese Revolution, 1896–1911,* as well as several articles on early revolutionary thought. He is currently writing an intellectual biography of Sung Chiao-jen.

Richard Shek is professor of humanities at California State University, Sacramento. His current research focuses on traditional Chinese religion and culture, with a particular emphasis on Buddhism and Taoism in the Six Dynasties period. He is presently coediting a volume with Kwang-Ching Liu titled *Heterodoxy in Late Imperial China*.

Richard J. Smith is professor of history and chair of Asian studies at Rice University, Houston. He is the author of a number of articles and several books on China, the most recent of which are *Fortune-tellers and Philosophers: Divination in Traditional Chinese Society* and *Chinese Almanacs*.

Erh-min Wang has been a research fellow in the Institute of Modern History, Academia Sinica, from 1955 to 1977 and from 1989 to the present. From 1977 to 1989 he taught as a senior lecturer and reader in the Department of History, Chinese University of Hong Kong. He has written seven books on China's modern history and has compiled Chinese research materials on maritime defense, the Sino-French War, missionary affairs, modern industry, commercial treaties, diplomatic affairs, and the correspondence of prominent figures. He has also written about one hundred articles on various topics in modern Chinese history.

Glossary

an-i 安逸
an-ming 安命

ch'ai-tzu 拆字
chan-hou 占候
chan-yun 占雲
Ch'an 禪
Chang Chih-tung 張之洞
Chang Hsueh-ch'eng 章學誠
Chang Tsai 張載
Chang Ying 張英
chang-yu tsun-pei 長幼尊卑
Chao Chih-hsin 趙執信
"Chao-kao" 召誥
Chao Shu-ch'iao 趙舒翹
Chen-k'o 真可
chen-shun 貞順
Chen Te-hsiu 真德秀
Ch'en Chih 陳熾
Ch'en Ch'ueh 陳確
Ch'en Hung-mou 陳宏謀
Ch'en Ta-ch'i 陳大齊
Ch'en T'ien-hua 陳天華
ch'en wei chün ssu ch'i wei fu wang
        臣為君死妻為夫亡
cheng 證
Cheng-ch'i ko 正氣歌
Cheng-chia lun 正家論
cheng-hsin 正心
Cheng Hsuan 鄭玄
cheng jen-hsin 正人心
Cheng Kuan-ying 鄭觀應
cheng-lun 正論
Cheng-meng 正蒙
cheng-ming 正名

cheng-tao 正道
Cheng Tsao-ju 鄭藻如
"Cheng Yü" 鄭語
ch'eng 誠
Ch'eng-Chu 程朱
ch'eng-ch'uan tu-shui 乘船渡水
Ch'eng Hao 程灝
ch'eng-i 誠意
Ch'eng I 程頤
Ch'eng Yao-tien 程瑤田
chi 機
chi-hsiung 吉凶
chi-hsiung chih chao 吉凶之兆
Chi Huang 嵇璜
chi-t'an 乩壇
Chi Yun 紀昀
ch'i (concrete things; implements) 器
        (vital force, material force, etc.)
        氣
ch'i-cheng 七政
ch'i-chih 氣質
ch'i-chih chih hsing 氣質之性
ch'i-hsiang 氣象
ch'i-lin 麒麟
ch'i-men tun-chia 奇門遁甲
ch'i-meng 祈夢
ch'i-ping 氣秉
chia-hsun 家訓
Chia I 賈誼
Chia-jen 家人
Chia-li 家禮
chia-p'in ssu hsien-ch'i 家貧思賢妻
Chiang Chien 蔣堅
chiang-hsueh 講學
Chiang I 蔣彝

Chiang Kai-shek 蔣介石
Chiang Pai-li 蔣百里
chiao 玦
Chiao Hsün 焦循
chieh 節
Chieh-hsiao tz'u 節孝祠
chieh-hsing 節性
Chieh-hsing chai 節性齋
Chieh-hsing chai lao-jen 節性齋老人
ch'ieh yü chi 切於己
chien-ai 兼愛
chien-hsing 見性
chien-t'i 賤體
ch'ien 籤 or 簽
Ch'ien-ching wan-tien hsiao i wei
    hsien 千經萬典孝義為先
ch'ien-hsu 乾戌
Ch'ien Mu 錢穆
ch'ien-pu 錢卜
ch'ien-sheng fen-ting 前生分定
Ch'ien Ta-hsin 錢大昕
ch'ien-ts'ai ju fen-t'u, jen-i chih ch'ien-
    chin 錢財如糞土仁義值千金
Ch'ien-tzu wen 千字文
ch'ien wei fu k'un wei mu
    乾為父坤為母
Ch'ien Wen-yuan 錢文源
chih (order) 治
    (matter) 質
    (wisdom) 智
chih-chiao pei-chiao 擲玦杯玦
chih-chih 致知
chih-chung 至中
Chih-hsu 智旭
Chih-kuei tzu 知歸子
chih-li 治曆
chih-ming 知命
chih-shan 至善
chih-shu 制數
Chih-yen 直言
ch'ih 恥
Chin 晉

chin-hsing 盡性
chin-shih 進士
Chin-ssu lu 近思錄
Chin Yao-chi 金耀基
Chin Yueh-lin 金岳霖
ch'in-min 親民
Ch'in-t'ien chien 欽天監
ching 敬
ching-chung pao-kuo 精忠報國
ching-shih chih hsueh 經世之學
ching-tien 敬天
ching-tso 靜坐
Ch'ing 清
ch'ing 情
Ch'ing-pai lei-ch'ao 清稗類鈔
chiu-kung 九宮
Ch'iu Chün 邱濬
ch'iu chung-ch'en pi yü hsiao-tzu chih
    men 求忠臣必於孝子之門
ch'iu fang-hsin 求放心
ch'iung-li 窮理
Chou 周
Chou An-shih 周安士
Chou-kung chieh-meng 周公解夢
Chou Tun-i 周敦頤
chu-ching 主敬
Chu Hsi 朱熹
Chu-hung 株宏
Chu-tzu chih-chia ko-yen 朱子治家
    格言
Chu Yung-ch'un 朱用純
Chuang-tzu 莊子
chueh 覺
chueh-yü 絕欲
ch'u-pi 去蔽
ch'u-ssu 去私
ch'uan-hsin 傳心
Ch'un-ch'iu 春秋
ch'un-niu 春牛
chü 局
chü-jen 舉人
Chü-shih chuan 居士傳

chüan 卷

chün-chün ch'en-ch'en fu-fu tzu-tzu
　　君君臣臣父父子子

chün tse ching, ch'en tse chung 君則敬
　　臣則忠

chün-tzu 君子

chün-tzu ho erh pu-t'ung 君子和
　　而不同

Ch'ü T'ung-tsu 瞿同祖

Ch'üan Tsu-wang 全祖望

chung (middle) 中
　　　 (loyalty) 忠

chung-lieh 忠烈

chung tse chin ming 忠則盡命

chung-tuan 忠端

Chung-yung 中庸

En-ming 恩銘

erh 二

erh-i 二儀

Erh-lin-chü chi 二林居記

erh-shih-pa hsiu 二十八宿

erh-shih-ssu ch'i 二十四氣

Erh-shih-ssu hsiao 二十四孝

Erh-ya 爾雅

fa 發

fa-chia 法家

fa-su tz'u-yen 法肅辭嚴

fa-t'ien 法天

fan-yü 泛喻

fang-chi 方技

Fang Hsiao-ju 方孝孺

fang-shih 方士

Fang Tung-shu 方東樹

fang-wai chih lu-huo 方外之爐火

fei-sheng 飛昇

fen 分

fen-li 分理

feng-chiao 風角

Feng Ching 馮景

feng-shui 風水

feng-shui hsien-sheng 風水先生

fu (return) 復
　　(putrid) 腐

fu-chi 扶乩

Fu Hsi 伏羲

fu-hsing 復性

Fu-hsing shu 復性書

fu-jui 符瑞

Fu-li lun 復禮論

fu-mu en-shen 父母恩深

fu-na yü hsieh 弗納於邪

Fung Yu-lan 馮友蘭

Han 漢

Han-ch'ing ko 含清閣

Han-hsueh 漢學

Han T'an 韓菼

Han Yü 韓愈

Hanlin 翰林

hao-jan chih ch'i 浩然之氣

hao-sheng ai-wu 好生愛物

hao-wu 好惡

ho 和

Ho Hsin-yin 何心隱

Ho-t'u 河圖

Hou-ch'eng chi tsa chieh 侯城集雜識

hsi 習

Hsi-ming 西銘

Hsi-shih hsien-wen 昔時賢文

hsi-tz'u 繫辭

Hsi-tz'u chuan 繫辭傳

Hsia 夏

Hsiang 湘

hsiang 象

hsiang-jen 相人

hsiang-jen ou 向人偶

hsiang-jui 祥瑞

hsiang-mien 相面

hsiang-yü 相雨

hsiao 孝

Hsiao-ching 孝經

Hsiao-ching chu 孝經注

Hsiao-ching yen-i 孝經演義
Hsiao hsi-yang 小西洋
Hsiao-hsueh 小學
Hsiao-hsueh chi-chieh 小學集解
hsiao-jen 小人
hsiao-jen t'ung erh pu-ho 小人同
    而不和
hsiao-tao 小道
hsiao-t'i 小體
hsiao-tz'u 孝慈
Hsiao-tz'u lu 孝慈錄
hsieh 邪
Hsieh-chi pien-fang shu 協紀辨方書
hsieh-chiao 邪教
hsieh-shen 邪神
hsieh-shu 邪術
hsieh-yen 邪言
hsien-chueh-che 先覺者
hsin (heart-mind) 心
    (faithfulness) 信
hsin-chih 心智
hsin-hsueh 心學
hsin-t'i 心體
hsing (star) 星
    (actions) 行
    (punishment) 刑
    (nature) 性
hsing chi li 性即理
hsing-ch'i 形氣
hsing erh hsia 形而下
hsing erh shang 形而上
Hsing-ming ku-hsun 性命古訓
hsing-o 性惡
hsing-se 形色
hsing-shan 性善
hsiu 宿
hsiu-hsing 修行
hsiu-shen 修身
Hsu Chen-chi 徐貞吉
Hsu Chi-yü 徐繼畬
Hsu Pen 徐本
Hsu Shen 許慎

Hsu Ti-shan 許地山
Hsu Tzu-p'ing 徐子平
Hsu-yun 盧雲
hsuan-hsueh 玄學
hsuan-tse 選擇
hsueh 學
hsueh-ch'i 血氣
Hsueh Chia-san 薛家三
Hsueh-erh 學而
Hsueh-hai t'ang 學海堂
Hsueh Hsuan 薛瑄
hsun-ku 訓詁
Hsun-meng chiao-erh ching
    訓蒙教兒經
Hsun-tzu 荀子
Hu Shih 胡適
Hu Wei 胡渭
Hua-yen 華嚴
Hua-yen nien-fo san-mei lun 華嚴念佛
    三昧論
Huang-ch'ao ching-shih wen hsu-pien
    皇朝經世文續編
Huang-ch'ao ching-shih wen-pien
    皇朝經世文編
Huang Hsiang 黃香
Huang Hsing 黃興
huang-lien 黃蓮
Huang Tao-chou 黃道周
Huang Tsung-hsi 黃宗羲
hui 會
Hui-chou 徽州
Hui-t'u nü-erh ching 繪圖兒女經
Hui Tung 惠棟
Hui-yuan 慧遠
huo 禍
huo-fu 禍福
huo-jen tso-luan 惑人作亂
Huo Yen-lo tuan-an 活閻羅斷案

i (duty, right behavior, etc.) 義
    (intention, will) 意
I-ch'eng chüeh-i lun 一乘決疑論

i-chia chih chi tsai-yü ho 一家之計
    在於和
I-ching 易經
i-fa 已發
i hsiao shih chün 以孝事君
i hsiao tso chung 移孝作忠
I-hsing chü 一行居
I-hsing-chü chi 一行居集
i-jih wei chün chung-sheng wei chu
    一日為君終身為主
I-ko yuan-kuo 一個圓果
i-li (moral principles) 義理
    (morality and profit) 義利
i-li chih hsing 義理之性
i-li chih-hsueh 義理之學
i-pen 一本
I-shu tien 藝術典
I-t'u ming-pien 易圖明辨
I wei chün-tzu mou pu-wei hsiao-jen
    mou 易為君子謀不為小人謀

jen 仁
Jen-ch'en ching hsin lu 人臣警心錄
jen-chi 人極
jen-chih hsing-chih 人之性質
jen chih lun 人之倫
jen chih shih-shih 仁之實事
jen-ch'ing 人情
jen-chueh 人爵
jen-hsing 人性
jen-i 仁義
jen-je tzu-hui yao-shan 人熱自會搖扇
jen jen-hsin yeh 仁人心也
jen-lun 人倫
Jen-p'u 人譜
jen-sheng lun-chi 人生倫記
Jen-sheng pi-tu 人生必讀
jen-tao 人道
jen yeh che jen yeh 人也者人也
jen-yü 人欲
jih-yung ch'ang-hsing 日用常行
jou-te 柔德

Juan Chi 阮籍
Juan Yuan 阮元
Jui-chin 瑞金

kan-ying 感應
k'an-hsiang 看相
k'an-yü 堪輿
kang 綱
kang-ch'ang wan-ku chung-i ch'ien-
        ch'iu 綱常萬古忠義千秋
K'ang Yu-wei 康有為
Kao P'an-lung 高攀龍
Kao T'ao 皋陶
Kao-tzu 告子
Kao Yu 高誘
k'ao-cheng 考證
k'ao-cheng hsueh 考證學
ko-li 格義
ko-wu 格物
ko-wu erh chih-chih 格物而致知
k'o-chi 克己
k'o-chi fu-li 克己復禮
k'o-chi fu-li wei-jen 克己復禮為仁
k'o-i ch'ien-chih 可以前知
k'o-tao chih tao 可道之道
Ku-chin t'u-shu chi-ch'eng
        古今圖書集成
Ku-ching ching-she 詁經精舍
Ku Hsien-ch'eng 顧憲成
Ku yao-yen 古謠諺
Ku Yen-wu 顧炎武
kuan 關
kuei-shen 鬼神
kuei-tao 貴道
kuei-t'i 貴體
kung-kuo 功過
kung-li 公理
Kung-po Liao 公伯寮
Kung Tzu-chen 龔自珍
kung-yü 公欲
K'ung-ming 孔明
K'ung Ying-ta 孔穎達

Kuo Chü-ching 郭居敬
kuo-luan ssu liang-chiang 國亂思良將
Kuo Sung-t'ao 郭嵩燾
Kuo-yü 國語
Kuomintang 國民黨

Lao-tzu 老子
li (principle) 理
   (ritual, propriety) 禮
Li Ao 李翱
Li-chi 禮記
Li-chi cheng-i 禮記正義
li-ch'i 理氣
Li Chih 李贄
li-chih 吏治
li-i chih hsing 禮義之行
"Li-jen" 里仁
li-kuan (officials in charge of criminal
      law) 理官
         (officials in charge of ritual)
      禮官
Li Kuang-ti 李光地
Li Kung 李塨
li-ming 立命
Li-pu 禮部
li-shu 曆書
Li Wen-t'ien 李文田
"Li-yun" 理運
Li Yung 李顒
li-yü 理慾
Liang Ch'i-ch'ao 梁啟超
liang-chih pen-t'i 良知本體
liang-neng 良能
Ling T'ing-k'an 凌廷堪
liu-ho 六和
Liu I-min 劉遺民
liu-jen 六壬
liu-li 六禮
Liu Ming-ch'uan 劉銘傳
liu-shu 六書
Liu Tsung-chou 劉宗周
Lo Ch'in-shun 羅欽順

lo-p'an 羅盤
Lo-shu 洛書
Lo Yu-kao 羅有高
Lu Chi 陸績
Lu Hsiang-shan 陸象山
Lu Hsün 魯迅
Lu Lung-ch'i 陸隴其
Lu Shih-i 陸世儀
Lu-Wang 陸王
Lü-shih Ch'un-ch'iu 呂氏春秋
Lü Ts'ai 呂才
luan 亂
lun-ch'ang kuai-ch'uan li-chien hsiao-
      wang 倫常乖舛立見消亡
Lun shih-pien chih-chi 論世變之亟
Lun-yü 論語

Ma Jung 馬融
Man-chiang-hung 滿江紅
mang-shen 芒神
Mao Ch'i-ling 毛奇齡
Mao Tse-tung 毛澤東
meng-chan 夢占
Meng Tsung 孟宗
Meng-tzu cheng-i 孟子正義
Meng-tzu tzu-i shu-cheng 孟子字義
      疏證
mi-hsin 迷信
min-k'o 憫客
Min pao 民報
min-yung 民用
ming (name) 名
      (bright) 明
      (fate, external necessity) 命
ming-chia 名家
Ming-i tai-fang lu 明夷待訪錄
ming ming-te 明明德
ming-shan 明善
ming-te 明德
ming-yun 命運
Mou-tzu 牟子
mu 畝

na-ts'ai 納采
na-yin 納音
nan hsiao ts'ai-liang 男效才良
nei 內
Nei-tse yen-i 內則演義
niao-chiao 鳥叫
nien-Fo 念佛
nien-kuo I-ching hui suan-kua
　　念過易經會算卦
nien-shen fang-wei t'u 年神方位圖
nü-chen 女貞
nü-mu chen-lieh 女慕貞烈

pa-kua 八卦
pa-tzu 八字
Pai-chia hsing 百家姓
pan-i 搬移
pao 報
pao-ying 報應
p'ei-t'ien 配天
pen-hsin chih ch'üan-te 本心之全德
pen-jan chih hsing 本然之性
pen-mo 本末
pen-t'i 本體
P'eng Lung 彭瓏
P'eng Shao-chi 彭紹繼
P'eng Shao-chieh 彭紹節
P'eng Shao-hsien 彭紹賢
P'eng Shao-kuan 彭紹觀
P'eng Shao-sheng 彭紹昇
P'eng T'ien-lun 彭天綸
P'eng Ting-ch'iu 彭定求
pi-jan 必然
Pi Kan 比干
Pi Tzu-feng 畢紫風
Pi Yuan 畢沅
pien 變
pien-chü 變局
Po-niu 伯牛
Po yin-yang chia yen 駁陰陽家言
pu 部
pu-cheng 不正

Pu-fei-ch'ien kung-te li 不費錢功
　　德例
pu hsiao fu-mu ching shen wu-i
　　不孝父母敬神無益
pu-hsin shu hsin ch'i-yun
　　不信書信氣運
pu-i 不易
pu jung wen 不容紊
pu-k'o fang-wu 不可方物
pu-ling 不靈
pu-shih 卜筮
Pu-shih cheng-tsung 卜筮正宗
pu te pu jan 不得不然

San-Fo ying-chieh t'ung-kuan t'ung-
　　shu 三佛應劫統觀通書
san-kang 三綱
san-tai 三代
san-ts'ai 三才
san-ts'ung 三從
San-tzu ching 三字經
sha 煞
Shan nü-jen chuan 善女人傳
shan-shu 善書
Shang-shu 尚書
Shao Yung 邵雍
shen 神
shen chih ssu-yü 身之私欲
Shen Kua 沈括
shen-tu 慎獨
shen-t'ung 神童
shen-yuan 申冤
sheng (victory, overcome) 勝
　　　　(produce, life) 生
sheng chih li 生之理
Sheng Hsuan-huai 盛宣懷
sheng-sheng 生生
Sheng-shih wei-yen 盛世危言
Sheng-yü kuang-hsun 聖諭廣訓
sheng-yuan 生員
shih (time, timeliness) 時
　　　(world, generation) 世

(affair, event) 事
(situation, strength) 勢
shih-chieh 世界
Shih-ching 詩經
shih-hsien li 時憲曆
Shih-hsien shu 時憲書
shih-ling 時令
Shih-po 史伯
Shih-san-ching chiao-k'an-chi
　　十三經校勘記
Shih-san-ching chu-shu 十三經注疏
shih-shih 實事
Shih-t'iao shou-chin hsiu chü-huang
　　十條手巾繡菊黃
Shih-ting 實定
shou-fen an-ming 守分安命
shou-hsiao-ti tz'u chien-wen
　　首孝弟次見聞
shou-ming 受命
Shou-p'ai fang-men hsi-ch'i ch'ang
　　手拍房門喜氣昌
shou-shih 授時
shu 數
Shu-ching 書經
shu-ming 術命
Shui-hu chuan 水滸傳
Shun 舜
shun-t'ien-che ts'un ni-t'ien-che wang
　　順天者存逆天者亡
Shuo-kua 說卦
Shuo-wen 說文
Shuo-wen chieh-tzu 說文解字
ssu-chu 四柱
ssu-hsin 私心
Ssu-k'u ch'üan-shu 四庫全書
Ssu-k'u ch'üan-shu tsung-mu
　　四庫全書總目
Ssu-pien lu 思辨錄
Ssu-shu shih-ti 四書釋地
ssu-tuan 四端
ssu-yü 私欲
su 俗

suan 酸
suan-ming 算命
sui 歲
sui-ming 隨命
Sun Yat-sen 孫逸仙
Sung Chiao-jen 宋教仁
Sung-hsueh 宋學
Sung Kung-ming 宋公明
Sung Wen-sen 宋文森

ta ch'i hsin 達其心
Ta-Ch'ing hui-tien 大清會典
Ta Ch'ing shih-ch'ao sheng-hsun
　　大清十朝聖訓
Ta-chuan 大傳
Ta-hsi yang 大西洋
Ta-hsueh 大學
Ta-hsueh yen-i 大學衍義
ta-t'i 大體
ta-t'ung 大同
T'a huo-yen shih 踏火焰詩
Tai Chen 戴震
Tai Tung-yuan 戴東原
t'ai 胎
T'ai-chi t'u 太極圖
T'ai-chou 泰州
t'ai-hsu 太虛
t'ai-i 太一
T'ai-shang kan-ying p'ien 太上感應篇
T'an Ssu-t'ung 譚嗣同
T'ang 唐
T'ang Chien 唐鑑
T'ang Ts'ai-ch'ang 唐才常
tao 道
tao-ch'i 道器
tao-hsin 道心
tao-hsueh 道學
tao-i 道義
Tao-te ching 道德經
Tao-tsang chi-yao 道藏輯要
tao wen-hsueh 道問學
T'ao Chu 陶澍

T'ao-yuan 桃源
te-chih-pen 德之本
Te-ch'ing 德清
te-hsing liang-chih 德性良知
te-hsing tzu yü hsüeh-wen 德性資於
　　　學問
teng-hua 燈花
ti-i 地義
ti-wei lai-i-ning 地緯賴以寧
t'i 體
t'i-yung 體用
t'iao-li 條理
t'ien 天
t'ien-ching 天經
t'ien-ching lai-i-ch'ing 天經賴以清
t'ien-chüeh 天爵
t'ien-hsia chih ta-tao 天下之達道
t'ien-hsin 天心
t'ien-hsing 天性
t'ien-jen ho-i 天人合一
t'ien-li 天理
t'ien-li liang hsin 天理良心
t'ien-li liu-hsing 天理流行
t'ien-ming 天命
t'ien-ming chih wei-hsing 天命之謂性
t'ien-ti ch'ang-ching 天地常經
t'ien-ti chih hsing 天地之性
t'ien-tsun ti-pei 天尊地卑
T'ien wu erh jih min wu erh wang
　　　天無二日民無二王
t'ien-yun 天運
Ting Jih-ch'ang 丁日昌
Ting Lan 丁蘭
t'ing-t'ien yu-ming 聽天由命
Tou-fu hui 豆腐會
tsa-tzu 雜字
tsai-i 災異
Ts'ao Tuan 曹端
tse 則
ts'e-tzu 測字
Tseng Kuo-ch'üan 曾國荃
Tseng Kuo-fan 曾國藩

Tseng Shen 曾參
Tso-chuan 左傳
Tso-jen ching 做人鏡
tsun te-hsing 尊德性
ts'un t'ien-li 存天理
T'u-shu chi-ch'eng 圖書集成
Tu Wei-ming 杜維明
tuan 端
Tuan Yü-ts'ai 段玉裁
t'uan 象
tui-tui 對對
t'ui-ming 推命
Tung Chung-shu 董仲舒
Tung-lin 東林
Tung Yung 董永
t'ung 同
t'ung-ch'ing 同情
T'ung-chih 同治
t'ung-hsin t'ung-te 同心同德
t'ung-jen 同仁
t'ung-kan kung-k'u 同甘共苦
T'ung-meng hui 同盟會
t'ung-shu 通書
t'ung-shu hsuan-tse 通書選擇
t'ung-tao 同道
tzu 滋
Tzu-cheng yao-lan 資政要覽
tzu ch'eng ming wei chih hsing
　　　自誠明謂之性
Tzu-hsia 子夏
tzu-jan 自然
Tzu-li chün 自立軍
Tzu-lu 子路
tzu ming ch'eng wei chih chiao
　　　自明誠謂之教
Tzu-ssu 子思
Tz'u-hsi 慈禧

wai 外
wan-wu sang-chih 玩物喪志
Wang Chi 王畿
wang-ch'i 望氣

Wang Chin 汪縉
Wang Chung 汪中
Wang Ch'ung 王充
Wang Erh-min 王爾敏
Wang Fu-chih 王夫之
wang-hou 望候
Wang Hsiang 王祥
Wang Ken 王艮
Wang Ming-sheng 王鳴盛
Wang Nien-sun 王念孫
Wang Shih-chen 王士禎
Wang Shu-nan 王樹枬
wang-tao 王道
Wang T'ao 王韜
Wang Wei-te 王維德
Wang Yang-ming 王陽明
wang-yen 妄言
wei 位
Wei-cheng 為政
wei-fa 未發
wei jen yu chi 為仁由己
Wei Yuan 魏源
wen 文
Wen-ch'ang 文昌
wen-chien chih chih 聞見之知
wen-chih 文質
wen-feng 文風
Wen-hsing ko 文星閣
Wen-hsuan 文選
wen-hsueh 問學
wen-ku erh chih-hsin 溫故知新
wen-ming 問名
wen-wu 文物
Wen-yen 文言
wu 物
wu-ch'ang 五常
wu-hsing 五行
wu-lun 五倫
Wu-lun shu 五倫書
wu-pi 無蔽
wu-sheng 無生

wu-ssu 無私
wu-wo 無我
Wu Yü 吳虞
wu-yü 無欲

ya yu fan-pu chih i 鴉有反哺之義
yang 陽
Yang-meng san-tzu ching 養蒙三字經
Yang-ming shih-hui lu 陽明釋毀錄
Yang Wen-hui 楊文會
yang yu kuei-ju chih en 羊有跪乳之恩
Yao 堯
yao-shu 妖書
Yeh Ming-ch'en 葉名琛
Yen Fu 嚴復
Yen Hui 顏回
Yen Jo-chü 閻若璩
Yen-lo 閻羅
Yen-tzu 晏子
Yen Yuan 顏元
yin 陰
yin-hsiang 印相
yin jen-ch'ing 因人情
yin-Shih yang-Ju 陰釋陽儒
yin-yang shu-hsing nan-nü i-hsing
        陰陽殊性男女異行
yin-yang shu-shih 陰陽術士
ying-erh ch'ung-fu 盈耳充腹
ying-hsiung 英雄
Yu Jo 有若
yu-tao chih shih 有道之士
yü 欲
yü ch'in-shou wu-i 與禽獸無異
Yü-t'an 玉壇
Yü Ying-shih 余英時
yü-yung 御用
yuan (round) 圓
     (cycle) 元
Yuan-Ming 元明
Yuan-ming 原命
Yuan-shan 原善

Yuan Shih-k'ai 袁世凱
yuan yü t'ien-ti chih hua 源於天地
　　之化
yueh 樂
"Yueh-chi" 樂記
Yueh Fei 岳飛
Yueh-lun 樂論
yueh-shen 約身

yun 運
Yun-ch'i 運氣
yun-hui 運會
yun-yuan 運元
yung (commonality) 庸
　　(utility, application) 用
yung-shen 用神
"Yung-yeh" 雍也

Index